R. Gupta's®

Objective Environmental Sciences

A Comprehensive Book for
UGC-NET, FCI, SSC, RRB, UPSC, PCS, Banking, CTET and Other Recruitment and Entrance Examinations

by

Dr. B.B. Singh

RAMESH PUBLISHING HOUSE, NEW DELHI

Published by
O.P. Gupta *for* Ramesh Publishing House

Admin. Office
12-H, New Daryaganj Road, Opp. Officers' Mess,
New Delhi-110002 ✆ 23275224, 23245124

E-mail: info@rameshpublishinghouse.com
For Online Shopping: www.rameshpublishinghouse.com

Showroom
• Balaji Market, Nai Sarak, Delhi-6 ✆ 23253720,23282525
• 4457, Nai Sarak, Delhi-6, ✆ 23918938

Book Code: R-1203

ISBN: 978-81-7812-908-2

17th Edition: November, 2023

Price: ₹ 280

Printed at: B.K.Offset, Delhi

CONTENTS

OBJECTIVE ENVIRONMENTAL SCIENCES

1

GENERAL : ENVIRONMENTAL SCIENCES

1. Environmental Studies are very important for :
(*a*) getting clean drinking water
(*b*) hygienic living conditions
(*c*) clean and fresh air
(*d*) All of the above

2. Which of the following is telling us what we should and should not do–what is right and wrong, good and bad–within the context of a certain ethical system?
(*a*) Philosophical ethics
(*b*) Normative ethics
(*c*) Descriptive ethics
(*d*) None of the above

3. The different levels of environmental and conservation awareness are :
(*a*) Pollution and Environmental degradation
(*b*) Consumption overpopulation
(*c*) Sustainable earth
(*d*) All of the above

4. Which is not correctly matched regarding the use of total energy?
(*a*) Transportation → 31.2%
(*b*) Domestic works → 13.7%
(*c*) Agriculture → 62.3%
(*d*) All of the above

5. Which of the following is still a very important source of energy for millions of Indians living in villages?
(*a*) Oil (*b*) Coal
(*c*) Fossil fuels (*d*) Fuel wood

6. The characteristic/s of a community is/are :
(*a*) diversity (*b*) periodicity
(*c*) dominance (*d*) All of these

7. National Biodiversity Strategy and Action Plan (NBSAP) was established in :
(*a*) 1986 (*b*) 1988
(*c*) 1999 (*d*) 2004

8. The criteria for the selection of species under *ex-situ* conservation is/are :
(*a*) vulnerability of the species of extinction
(*b*) ecological importance of the species
(*c*) economic and aesthetic importance of the species
(*d*) All of the above

9. The establishment of national parks and sanctuaries came under :
(*a*) *in-situ* conservation of biodiversity
(*b*) *ex-situ* conservation of biodiversity
(*c*) Natural development Plan of Biodiversity
(*d*) All of the above

10. Which is **NOT** a controlling method of Eutrophication?
(*a*) The wastewater must be treated before its discharge into water streams
(*b*) It can be minimised by removing nitrogen and phosphorus at the source
(*c*) Physico-chemical methods can be adopted
(*d*) Algal bloom release toxic chemicals during eutrophication

11. Major pollutants of motor vehicular emission in India are :
(*a*) Oxides of nitrogen and lead
(*b*) Diesel particulates and carbon monoxide
(*c*) Ozone and carbon dioxide, other toxics
(*d*) All of the above

12. Environmental GIS describes the use of :
(*a*) data on atmospheric absorption of radiation

(*b*) locations based data management tools to assist in the decision making processes
(*c*) electromagnetic waves in specific regions
(*d*) None of the above

13. MIC and Chemobyl tragedies occurred at :
(*a*) Bhopal 1984, Ukraine 1990
(*b*) Bhopal 1984, Ukraine 1988
(*c*) Bhopal 1984, Ukraine 1986
(*d*) Bhopal 1986, Russia 1988

14. Exposure to UV radiations cause :
(*a*) damage to eye sight
(*b*) sun burn
(*c*) cancer of skin
(*d*) All of the above.

15. Sewage water treatment that involves bacteria is called :
(*a*) Primary treatment
(*b*) Activated sludge treatment
(*c*) Tertiary treatment
(*d*) Cyclic treatment

16. Indoor Pollution is due to :
(*a*) Lead from newspaper and ceramic crockery
(*b*) Formaldehyde from furniture
(*c*) Ozone and acid aerosols in smog
(*d*) All of the above

17. Sewage water is purified for recycling by the action of :
(*a*) Light
(*b*) Micro-organisms
(*c*) *Eichhornia* aquatic plants
(*d*) Fishes

18. Disappearance of fish from water bodies indicate excess of......... in water.
(*a*) Zn (*b*) Hg
(*c*) Fluoride (*d*) P

19. The most common indicator organism that represents polluted water is :
(*a*) *Escherichia coli*
(*b*) *Vibrio cholerae*
(*c*) *Entamoeba coli*
(*d*) *Entamoeba histolytica*

20. Positive pollution of soil is due to :
(*a*) reduction in soil productivity
(*b*) addition of wastes in soil
(*c*) excessive use of fertilizers
(*d*) All of the above

21. Air pollution effects are mostly found on :
(*a*) leaves (*b*) flowers
(*c*) stems (*d*) roots

22. Which one among the following chemicals is used for causing defoliation of forest trees?
(*a*) Amo 1618
(*b*) Phosphon D
(*c*) Malic Hydrazide
(*d*) 2, 4 Dichlorophenoxy acetic acid

23. Which chemicals are washed out in large amounts by fertilizers in water supply?
(*a*) Nitrites (*b*) Nitrates
(*c*) Sulphates (*d*) Phosphates

24. Most important causative pollutant in soil is :
(*a*) Plastic (*b*) Glass junk
(*c*) Iron Junk (*d*) Detergents

25. Use of lichens and *Nerium* in case of pollution is :
(*a*) Treatment of polluted water
(*b*) Promote Pollution due to SO_2
(*c*) Bioindicators of SO_2 Pollution
(*d*) Green muffler

26. In leaded petrol, antinocking agent is tetramethyl/tetraethyl lead. In unleaded petrol, this agent is :
(*a*) Methyl-ethyl ether
(*b*) Propane
(*c*) Methyl tertiary butyl ether
(*d*) Dibromomethane

27. Lead in petroleum is present in the form of tetraethyl and tetramethyl lead in automobile exhausts, it is released as
(*a*) nitrates of lead
(*b*) oxides of lead
(*c*) pure lead
(*d*) chlorides of lead

28. Green Petrol is :
(*a*) Leaded petrol
(*b*) Unleaded petrol
(*c*) Gasohol
(*d*) Low sulphur Diesel

29. Photochemical smog related to air pollution is related to :
(*a*) oxides of sulphur
(*b*) oxides of nitrogen
(*c*) oxides of oxygen
(*d*) oxides of carbon

30. Ecofriendly detergents do not contain :
(*a*) PO_4 and bleaches
(*b*) alcohols
(*c*) water softners
(*d*) Fluorescers

31. Choose the correct pair :
(*a*) CNG : Ecofriend
(*b*) Land scape pollution by throwing garbage and rubbish over land: Third pollution
(*c*) Ground water pollution due to seepage of sewage and toxic chemicals. Third poison
(*d*) All of these

32. Ganga Action Plan to restore the quality of the river Ganga was launched in :
(*a*) 1988 (*b*) 1992
(*c*) 1985 (*d*) 1981

33. When was NEPA (National Environmental Policy Act) enforced in India?
(*a*) 1968 (*b*) 1969
(*c*) 1985 (*d*) 1959

34. The newspaper contains one of the following toxic materials :
(*a*) Cd (*b*) Pb
(*c*) Mg (*d*) Hg

35. The first indoor pollutant from furniture of which the masses became aware?
(*a*) CO_2 (*b*) Formaldehyde
(*c*) Radon (*d*) Ozone

36. Which is the major source of harmful radiations in the house?
(*a*) Tubelight (*b*) Colour TV
(*c*) Oven (*d*) Heater

37. Ceramic crockery of substandard quality could become a source of pollutant if food taken in it. This pollutant is :
(*a*) Cd (*b*) Pb
(*c*) Cr (*d*) Hg

38. Some times secondary pollutants like Ozone, PAN (Peroxy acyl nitrate), HNO_3, H_2SO_4 formed from primary pollutants are more toxic than primary pollutants. This phenomenon of increased toxicity in pollutants is called :
(*a*) Biomagnification
(*b*) Eutrophication
(*c*) Synergism
(*d*) Green house effect

39. Which one is not produced as exhaust of vehicle?
(*a*) SO_2 (*b*) CO_2
(*c*) CO (*d*) flyash

40. In air pollution, industries are :
(*a*) line sources (*b*) point sources
(*c*) area sources (*d*) diffuse sources

41. Carbon monoxide is a pollutant as it :
(*a*) Inactivates nerves and cause numbness
(*b*) Inhibits Glycolysis
(*c*) Combine with oxygen and shift oxygen dissociation curve
(*d*) Combines with Haemoglobin and cause haemolysis

42. Which of the following pollutant forms a toxic and stable substance in blood by combining with haemoglobin?
(*a*) CO_2 (*b*) CO
(*c*) CH_4 (*d*) O_2

43. Carbon monoxide is harmful for man because :
(*a*) it is carcinogenic
(*b*) it damages kidney
(*c*) it competes with oxygen in blood
(*d*) it changes *p*H of body

44. CO_2 contents in air is about :
(*a*) 0.34% (*b*) 4%
(*c*) 3.34% (*d*) 0.034%

45. Level of CO_2 in atmosphere has increased from :
(*a*) 270 to 340 ppm (*b*) 250 to 300 ppm
(*c*) 300 to 350 ppm (*d*) 330 to 350 ppm

46. One of the important effects of SO_2 and its transformation products on plants is :
(*a*) Plasmolysis
(*b*) Destruction of chlorophyll
(*c*) Destruction of Golgi bodies
(*d*) Destruction of cell wall

47. Taj Mahal is threatened due to the effect of :
(*a*) chlorine (*b*) sulphur dioxide
(*c*) oxygen (*d*) hydrogen

48. Lichen deserts indicate :
(*a*) Air pollution due to CO
(*b*) Air pollution due to SO_2
(*c*) Pollution due to smoke
(*d*) Noise pollution

49. Lichens are best ecological indicator of :
(*a*) air pollution (*b*) water pollution
(*c*) noise pollution (*d*) All of these

50. Lichens have disappeared from cities because they are highly susceptible to :
(*a*) CO_2 (*b*) O_3
(*c*) NO_2 (*d*) SO_2

51. Rao and Le Balance found that SO_2 destroy lichens and moss completely. It lowers *p*H and causes loss of Mg^{++} from chlorophyll. This forms a compound which results in chlorosis. This compound formed after loss of Mg^{++} is called :
(*a*) Etiolin (*b*) Protochlorophyll
(*c*) Phaeophytin (*d*) Leucoplast

52. Nowadays, the buses of Delhi are running on :
(*a*) Liquefied Petroleum Gas (LPG)
(*b*) Compressed Natural Gas (CNG)
(*c*) Compressed Lead Gas (CLG)
(*d*) High Speed Diesel (HSD)

53. The composition of Compressed Natural Gas (CNG) is :
(*a*) CH_4, C_2H_6 and C_4H_8 and other gases
(*b*) CH_4, $(CO + H_2)$
(*c*) $CO + N_2$
(*d*) $LPG + H_2$

54. The favourable points of CNG over LPG is/are :
(*a*) CNG is stored at high pressure whereas LPG is stored at very low temperatures
(*b*) Liquefication of LPG makes this fuel more complex to store whereas storage and distribution of CNG is easy
(*c*) CNG is less expensive than LPG
(*d*) All of the above

55. Which of the following is promoting natural disasters over 70%?
(*a*) Pollution
(*b*) Urbanisation
(*c*) Delhi Metro
(*d*) Rivers overflowing

56. The most efficient cause/s of wastage and degeneration of fresh water resources is/are :
(*a*) Reckless over-consumption and misuse
(*b*) Pollution and Natural water and its Eutrophication
(*c*) Pollution and depletion of underground water table
(*d*) All of the above

57. Match the following :

Column A	**Column B**
A. Biological digestion	1. Process of conversion of cellulosic materials to useful byproduct
B. Pyrolysis	2. Destructive dissolution
C. Composting	3. Biological decomposition

Codes :

	A	B	C
(*a*)	1	2	3
(*b*)	2	3	1
(*c*)	2	1	3
(*d*)	3	2	1

58. The important steps which are to be followed in Rainwater harvesting from roof :
(*a*) Collection of rain water
(*b*) Separation of first rain flush
(*c*) Filtration and storage of rain water and then distribution
(*d*) All of the above

59. Human activities that are responsible for polluting the stratospheric ozone :
(*a*) Combustion of fossil fuels and organic matter
(*b*) Excessive use of nitrogen fertilisers
(*c*) Excessive use of chlorofluorocarbons
(*d*) All of the above

60. Land use planning must aim at :
(*a*) minimal loss
(*b*) acceptable income
(*c*) both of the above
(*d*) None of the above

61. The Ministry of Environment and Forests classified how many categories of biomedical waste?
(*a*) 12 (*b*) 14
(*c*) 16 (*d*) 51

62. A synergistic chemical is :
(*a*) that pose a major danger in combustion
(*b*) that do not major danger
(*c*) that pose dangers in combination with water
(*d*) a highly combustible chemical

63. The most important cause for the loss of biodiversity is :
(*a*) global warming (*b*) climate change
(*c*) ozone depletion (*d*) None of these

64. A nation's natural resources often determine its wealth and status in world economic system by determining its :
(*a*) industrial development
(*b*) wealth
(*c*) air pollution
(*d*) political influence

65. Critical information for land use planning is :
(*a*) depth of the soil (*b*) materials used
(*c*) slope of the land (*d*) drainage features

66. The important tool for controlling soil erosion :
(*a*) cropping system
(*b*) vegetation
(*c*) water fall in year
(*d*) underground soil

67. Sewage infection of water can be demonstrated by presence of cysts of :
(*a*) *Entamoeba histolytica*
(*b*) *Escherichia coli*
(*c*) *Entomoeba coli*
(*d*) *Plasmodium vivax*

68. Which pigment protects plants from UV radiation damage?
(*a*) chlorophyll (*b*) xanthophyll
(*c*) carotenoids (*d*) phycocyanin

69. Ecofriendly method is :
(*a*) Energy plantation (*b*) Use of CNG
(*c*) Van Mahotsava (*d*) All of the above

70. Which one of the following is not a random sampling method?
(*a*) Stratified Sampling
(*b*) Cluster Sampling
(*c*) Systematic Sampling
(*d*) Judgement Sampling

71. Ozone Day, World Environment Day and National Pollution Prevention Day are celebrated respectively :
(*a*) June 5, Sept. 16, Oct. 21
(*b*) June 5, Sept. 16, Dec. 2
(*c*) Sept. 16, June. 5, Dec. 28
(*d*) Sept. 16, June. Dec. 2

72. Chlorofluorocarbons are major depleter of ozone layer in stratosphere. They split to release chlorine. One atom of chlorine converts how many molecules of ozone into oxygen?
(*a*) 1 lakh (*b*) 2 lakh
(*c*) 40 lakh (*d*) 1 million

73. Green Muffler is planting of trees and shrubs to reduce noise pollution. It is done :
(*a*) on wastelands
(*b*) along roads
(*c*) along canals
(*d*) on the slopes of hills

74. Concentration of CO_2 in present day atmosphere is
(*a*) ~ 220 ppm (*b*) ~ 280 ppm
(*c*) ~ 360 ppm (*d*) ~ 390 ppm

75. The acidity of normal rain water is due to
(*a*) Co_2
(*b*) Cl_2
(*c*) No_2
(*d*) So_2

76. Reasons of lung cancer is :
(*a*) Asbestos (*b*) Calcium fluoride
(*c*) Cement factory (*d*) Bauxite mining

77. Melanin protects from :
(*a*) UV rays (*b*) visible rays
(*c*) Infra red rays (*d*) X-rays

78. Which of the following is absent in polluted water :
(*a*) hydrilla (*b*) water hyacinth
(*c*) larva of stone fly (*d*) blue green algae

79. *Escherichia coli* is used as an indicator organism to determine pollution of water with :
(*a*) industrial effluents
(*b*) pollen of aquatic plants
(*c*) heavy metals
(*d*) faecal matter

80. Fluoride pollution mainly affects :
(*a*) teeth (*b*) kidney
(*c*) brain (*d*) heart

81. Cyclone collector is used to minimise :
(*a*) radioactive pollution
(*b*) air pollution
(*c*) noise pollution
(*d*) water pollution

82. Water pollution can be controlled by :
(*a*) having septic tanks for each house
(*b*) checking mixing of industrial waste with water bodies
(*c*) use of degradable pesticides
(*d*) All of the above

83. Green *muffler* is specific for :
(*a*) reducing smog
(*b*) sound insulation
(*c*) preventing haze formation
(*d*) reducing ground frost

84. *Plantation of rows* of trees along roads sides, rails, residential complexes, hospitals and institutes is known as :
(*a*) shelter belt (*b*) green muffler
(*c*) wind break (*d*) both (*a*) and (*c*)

85. Good *urban land management* consists in :
(*a*) leaving large land depressions unfilled
(*b*) creation of gardens and parks
(*c*) growing broad green belts
(*d*) All of the above

86. Bregoil is a product similar to saw dust prepared from waste of paper industry is used to control :
(*a*) marine pollution (*b*) air pollution
(*c*) land pollution (*d*) noise pollution

87. Good *water management* consists in :
(*a*) Identification of aquifers and their judicious exploitation
(*b*) Recycling sewage water
(*c*) Prevention of flow of effluents into nearby water streams
(*d*) All of the above

88. A crop helpful in *Dryland reclamation* is :
(*a*) sunflower (*b*) paddy
(*c*) sugarcane (*d*) cotton

89. Catalytic converter brought down air pollution by automobiles by :
(*a*) converting CO to CO_2
(*b*) N_2O to N_2
(*c*) Complete oxidation of hydrocarbons
(*d*) All of the above

90. Pollutants originate from sources like :
1. Automobile exhausts
2. Fuel
3. Combustion of coal
4. Smog

Tick out the source of emission of carbon monoxide
(*a*) 1 and 2 (*b*) 2 and 3
(*c*) 3 and 4 (*d*) All of these

91. Due to attack of fumes of SO_2 and H_2SO_4, the marble $(CaCO_3)$ of Taj Mahal and Red stone of Red Fort changed into calcium sulphate which is bulky and cause :

(*a*) stone leprosy (*b*) stone mosaic
(*c*) corrosion (*d*) None of these

92. At petrol filling stations, workers feel headache, giddiness and sleeplessness. It is due to a chemical that emitted from petrol. It is :
(*a*) Benzene (*b*) Ozone
(*c*) Aldehydes (*d*) Chlorides

93. An ozone depleting agent being used in fire extinguishers is
(*a*) Nitrogen oxide
(*b*) Halon
(*c*) Chlorofluoro carbon
(*d*) Methyl bromide

94. Which of the following is pollutant as well as protectant
(*a*) CO_2 (*b*) Ozone
(*c*) CFC (*d*) PAN

95. Oxides of sulphur and nitrogen are important pollutants of :
(*a*) air
(*b*) water
(*c*) both (*a*) and (*b*)
(*d*) soil

96. Some of the chemicals commonly used these days are :
1. DDT 2. Dieldrin
3. DDE 4. Endrin
Those which pass from mother to the foetus through placenta are :
(*a*) 1 and 2 (*b*) 2 and 3
(*c*) 3 and 4 (*d*) 4 and 1

97. Plants like *Allium cepa. Zea mays, Saccharum officinarum, Triticum aestivm* and *Medicago sativa* absorb the natural pollutants. Which of the following pollutant(s) is absorbed by these :
(*a*) CO_2 (*b*) CO
(*c*) NO_2 (*d*) SO_2

98. The types of gully erosion that create problems on agricultural lands are :
(*a*) U-and V-gullies (*b*) X-and Y-gullies
(*c*) runoff diversions (*d*) All of these

99. The effective planning of soil erosion control is :
(*a*) developing the best source of action to reduce the movement of soil from crop fields
(*b*) selecting the middle course of action
(*c*) performing the complementary course of action
(*d*) All of the above

100. In biological systems sulphur is largely bound in
(*a*) Lipids
(*b*) Proteins
(*c*) Nucleic acids
(*d*) Proteins and nucleic acids

101. The Sardar Sarovar Dam Project is located at :
(*a*) Bhagirathi river (*b*) Narmada river
(*c*) Bhramaputra river (*d*) Kaveri river

102. Planning for erosion control must have :
(*a*) extent of erosion
(*b*) runoff diversions
(*c*) location of waterways and drainage
(*d*) All of these

103. Who amongst the following formed Narmada *Bachow Andolan*?
(*a*) S.L. Bahuguna (*b*) Medha Patkar
(*c*) Arundhati Roy (*d*) Javed Ali

104. Which is a correct food chain in the Antarctic ecosystem ?
(*a*) Phytoplankton – Krill – Carnivorous Plankton – Emperor Penguin
(*b*) Phytoplankton – Krill – Carnivorous Plankton – Squid – Elephant Seal – Leopard Seal
(*c*) Phytoplankton – Herbivorous Zoo Plankton – Carnivorous Plankton – Adelic Penguin – Emperor Penguin
(*d*) Herbivorous Zoo Plankton - Phytoplankton – Carnivorous Plankton – Elephant Seal – Leopard Seal

105. Pyramid of trophic levels is always upright in case of
(*a*) Biomass (*b*) Energy
(*c*) Number (*d*) All of the above

106. Which is a ozone depleting?
(*a*) N_2O (*b*) CFC-12
(*c*) CFC-11 (*d*) All of these

107. Which of the following is a correct match ?
(*a*) Periyar – Kerala
(*b*) Ranthambore – M.P.
(*c*) Panna – U.P.
(*d*) Bandhvgarh – Bihar

108. High concentration of pollution in India is due to :
(*a*) absence for sound environmental legal regime
(*b*) lack of environmental enforcement at local level
(*c*) generation of high biomedical wastes
(*d*) All of the above

109. The highest premature deaths in India is mainly due to :
(*a*) Outdoor air pollution
(*b*) Indoor air pollution
(*c*) Both of the above
(*d*) None of the above

110. The Environmental Protection Act was enacted in :
(*a*) 1986 (*b*) 1985
(*c*) 1987 (*d*) 1972

111. Fresh water achieves its greatest density at :
(*a*) 4°C (*b*) 0°C
(*c*) – 4°C (*d*) 100°C

112. The regional environmental problem is :
(*a*) desertification (*b*) ozone depletion
(*c*) climatic changes (*d*) All of these

113. The major stratospheric ozone layer over Antarctica was discovered in :
(*a*) 1983 (*b*) 1985
(*c*) 1987 (*d*) 1980

114. The most rigorous global environmental issues are :
(*a*) acid rain and air pollution
(*b*) global warming and ozone depletion
(*c*) noise and water pollution
(*d*) All of the above

115. Biological treatment of water pollution is done by :
(*a*) lichens (*b*) fungi
(*c*) phytoplanktons (*d*) reforestation

116. Sewage water can be made fit for drinkable/recycling with the help of :
(*a*) hydrophytes
(*b*) microorganisms
(*c*) fishes
(*d*) alum and sodium hypochlorite

117. In the treatment of waste water before discharge, which treatment stage involves biological treatment?
(*a*) Primary stage
(*b*) Secondary treatment stage
(*c*) Reverse osmosis
(*d*) Tertiary treatment stage

118. The best method to dispose night soil is :
(*a*) incineration
(*b*) compositing
(*c*) sewage system]
(*d*) pitting and trenching

119. In activated sludge method of sewage treatment, the BOD of the sewage after biological treatment is reduced by about :
(*a*) 50% (*b*) 60%
(*c*) 75% (*d*) 90%

120. For effective chlorination of water, free residual chlorine should be :
(*a*) 0.1-0.2 ppm (*b*) 0.3-0.4 ppm
(*c*) 0.5-0.6 ppm (*d*) 0.7-0.8 ppm

121. Of the following types of microbes, which one has been genetically altered to protect crops from frost, marine pollution, organic wastes etc?
(*a*) *Pseudomonas* (*b*) *Escherichia*
(*c*) *Thiobacillus* (*d*) *Klebsiella*

122. The ways to control pollution :
(*a*) cyclones
(*b*) electrostatic precipitators and scrubbers
(*c*) dilution and treatment before disposal and plantation of trees
(*d*) All of these

123. One of the best method to reduce air pollution is growing of plants capable of fixing oxides of nitrogen, C and S and radioactivity. Which plant has maximum power of absorbing CO_2 and oxide of nitrogen in a polluted area?

(a) *Robinia pseudoacacia*
(b) *Phaseolus vulgaris*
(c) *Daucos carota*
(d) *Coleus indica*

124. Nitrogen oxide can be absorbed by plants like :
(a) Pinus (b) Quercus
(c) Junipers (d) All of these

125. Carbon monoxide can be absorbed by plants like :
(a) Bean (b) Coleus
(c) Carrot (d) All of these

126. Which aquatic animal has been released on a large scale in the Ganga to rid it of waste flesh?
(a) Gharial (b) Turtle
(c) Dolphin (d) Fishes

127. Activated sludge process is concerned with waste management. It is a :
(a) chemical treatment
(b) biological treatment
(c) mechanical means
(d) nuclear means

128. Sewage is broken down in :
(a) Primary treatment
(b) Secondary treatment
(c) Tertiary treatment
(d) None of these

129. A sewage treatment process in which a portion of the decomposer bacteria present in the waste is recycled into the beginning of the process, is called :
(a) Cyclic treatment
(b) Primary treatment
(c) Activated sludge treatment
(d) Tertiary treatment

130. Superbug claimed to clean up oil slicks in ocean is :
(a) *Escherichia coli*
(b) *Bacillus thuringenesis*
(c) *Pastueralla pestis*
(d) *Pseudomonas putida*

131. NEERI is :
(a) National Environmental Engineering Research Institute
(b) National Ecological and Environmental Research Institute
(c) National Eugenics and Ecological Research Institute
(d) National Ethological and Ecological Research Institute

132. Most inhabitants of Kolkata suffer from bronchitis/asthma. It is due to excess of SO_2 pollutants in :
(a) air (b) water
(c) soil (d) adulterated food

133. Death while sleeping in closed room with burning coal furnace is due to :
(a) CO_2 (b) CO
(c) CCl_4 (d) SO_2

134. Pollution indicators plants are :
(a) resistant to pollution
(b) purifier of air pollutants
(c) sensitive to pollutants
(d) can indicate onset of disaster

135. Air pollution is not caused by :
(a) pollen grains
(b) automobiles
(c) industries
(d) hydro-electric power

136. The effect of pollution is first and most marked on :
(a) flora of a place
(b) biogeochemical cycles
(c) natural balance of our environment
(d) fauna of an area

137. The major source of pollution upto 80% of total air pollution in metropolitan cities is :
(a) automobiles (Traffic)/Transportation
(b) coal based industries
(c) pesticides
(d) radioactivity and noise

138. Major air pollutant is :
(a) CO_2 (b) N_2
(c) SO_2 (d) CO

139. Most polluted city of India and world are :
(a) Kolkata in India and Tokyo in world
(b) Delhi in India and New York in world
(c) Mumbai in India and Paris in world
(d) None of these

140. Highest level of oxides of Nitrogen (NO, NO_2) in air is recorded in :
(*a*) Bengluru (*b*) Chennai
(*c*) Mumbai (*d*) Kolkata

141. Of the following four metropolitan Indian cities, where polluted air hangs above like a cloud?
(*a*) Mumbai (*b*) Delhi
(*c*) Kolkata (*d*) Chennai

142. Which one of the following is usually not considered a pollutant?
(*a*) SO_2 (*b*) CO_2
(*c*) Hydrocarbons (*d*) CO

143. Taj Mahal is being damaged by :
(*a*) air pollution from Mathura refinery
(*b*) Yamuna flood
(*c*) nuclear pollution and railway yard
(*d*) Both (*a*) and (*B*)

144. Particulates in air cause :
(*a*) permanent opening of stomata
(*b*) closure of stomata
(*c*) coiling of leaves
(*d*) yellowing of leaves

145. Lead is considered mainly :
(*a*) air pollutant
(*b*) water pollutant
(*c*) land pollutant
(*d*) radioactive pollutant

146. What is it that smoking produces in the largest amount?
(*a*) NO_2 (*b*) CO_2
(*c*) CO (*d*) Particulates

147. Coal burning hearths or stoves produce a hazardous gas which suffocates living beings even to death :
(*a*) SO_2 (*b*) CO_2
(*c*) CO (*d*) H_2S

148. The SO_2 mainly affects :
(*a*) nucleus (*b*) cell membranes
(*c*) cell wall (*d*) ribosomes

149. Which city in the world has the highest SO_2 pollution?
(*a*) Milan (*b*) Seoul
(*c*) New Delhi (*d*) New York

150. Removal of desirable substances/plants is called :
(*a*) negative pollution
(*b*) positive pollution
(*c*) erosion
(*d*) conservation

151. Safe limit of water fluoride level is :
(*a*) 0.1 × 0.4 mg/litre
(*b*) 0.5 × 0.8 mg/litre
(*c*) 0.9 × 1.2 mg/litre
(*d*) 1.3 × 1.6 mg/litre

152. Stress reaction is caused by :
(*a*) Noise Pollution
(*b*) Nuclear Pollution
(*c*) Air Pollution
(*d*) Thermal Pollution

153. Anxiety and stress are *first symptoms* caused by :
(*a*) noise pollution
(*b*) air pollution
(*c*) water pollution
(*d*) radiation pollution

154. *Knock knee* disease is :
(*a*) Caused by hormonal imbalance and excess of Hg
(*b*) Due to deficiency of tyrosine
(*c*) Due to excess fluoride concentration in water
(*d*) Due to high BOD and high temperature of water by thermal pollution

155. A person has impaired nervous system and signs of madness due to intake of a metal contaminated water. This metal is :
(*a*) Hg (*b*) Ca
(*c*) pb (*d*) Fluoride

156. Leukemia may be due to :
(*a*) radiations
(*b*) effluents of industries
(*c*) pesticides in crop fields
(*d*) Aflatoxins

157. The target tissue of the carcinogenous mustard gas is :
(*a*) liver (*b*) lungs
(*c*) skin (*d*) colon

158. Dizziness, palpitation and flickering before eyes and finally death is caused by :
(*a*) Heavy metal salts (*b*) radiations
(*c*) Carbon monoxide (*d*) Sulphur dioxide

159. Bronchitis/Asthma is caused by :
(*a*) exposure to asbestos
(*b*) exposure to cotton dust
(*c*) exposure to coal dust and silica
(*d*) exposure to SO_2

160. Mottling of teeth (fluorosis) and skeletal deformities due to an element in drinking water :
(*a*) Zinc (*b*) Fluoride
(*c*) Boron (*d*) Chlorine

161. Which of the following symptoms indicate radiation sickness?
(*a*) red and ulcerated skin
(*b*) nausea and anaemia
(*c*) nausea and loss of hair
(*d*) ulcerated skin, nausea and loss of hair

162. Photochemical smog bring about :
(*a*) Floral bud shedding
(*b*) Defoliation
(*c*) Discolouration and curling of petals
(*d*) Bleaching and blazing of foliage

163. The toxic effect of carbon monoxide is due to its greater affinity for haemoglobin as compared to oxygen by (approx) :
(*a*) 200 times (*b*) 2 times
(*c*) 1000 times (*d*) 20 times

164. Green audit is :
(*a*) Estimation of crop yield and crop area
(*b*) Estimation of forest area and pasture land
(*c*) Effect of environment over vegetation of an area
(*d*) Checking of impact of an establishment over environment

165. Pollution can be controlled by :
(*a*) sewage treatment
(*b*) by checking atomic blasts
(*c*) manufacturing electrically opened vehicles
(*d*) All of the above

166. Where is NEERI previously known as PHERI located?
(*a*) Nagpur (*b*) Shimla
(*c*) Bengluru (*d*) Cochin

167. Electrostatic scrubbers meant to absorb pollutants also produce :
(*a*) SO_2 (*b*) CO
(*c*) Dust (*d*) Ozone

168. A mutagenic pollutant is :
(*a*) chlorinated hydrocarbons
(*b*) organophosphates
(*c*) nitrogen oxides
(*d*) resins

169. Which will not cause air pollution?
(*a*) CO_2 (*b*) CO
(*c*) H_2 (*d*) SO_2

170. The example of natural pollution is :
(*a*) Volcanoes (*b*) SO_2
(*c*) DDT (*d*) Smoke

171. It is advised not to have brick kiln near fruit orchard to
(*a*) save trees from soil erosion and depletion layer
(*b*) safeguard trees from large labour population
(*c*) protect the orchard from operation of Trucks and Carts used for transporting fruits
(*d*) save trees from poisonous fumes (H_2F_2) of smoke from brick kiln chimneys

172. Which of the following is not produced by motor vehicle?
(*a*) SO_2
(*b*) Hydrocarbon gases
(*c*) Flyash
(*d*) CO

173. The congres grass/carrot grass that causes allergy arrived in India in 1956. It is :
(*a*) *Parthenium hysterophorous*

(*b*) *Eichhornia crassipes*
(*c*) *Opuntia dilleni*
(*d*) *Sorghum halepens*

174. Which pollutant gas is released by cud-chewing cattles/ruminants?
(*a*) CH_4 (*b*) CO_2
(*c*) CO (*d*) NO_2

175. When did the **Bhopal** disaster occur?
(*a*) Dec. 3, 1982 (*b*) Dec. 3, 1984
(*c*) Dec. 3, 1986 (*d*) Dec. 3, 1980

176. Leakage of Methyl isocyanate (MIC) caused the biggest industrial disaster of the recent times in 1984 (Bhopal Tragedy). What did the industrial plant manufacture where the leakage occurred?
(*a*) Fertilizer (*b*) Explosives
(*c*) Pesticides (*d*) Cement

177. The pollutant common in plants most hazardous pollutants of automobile exhaust is :
(*a*) Cd (*b*) Pb
(*c*) Hg (*d*) Cr

178. 60% of SO_2 pollution is due to :
(*a*) burning of coal (*b*) burning of oil
(*c*) automobile (*d*) industries

179. Which gas was liberated in Bhopal gas tragedy?
(*a*) Ethyl isothiocyanate
(*b*) Sodium isothiocyanate
(*c*) Methyl isocyanate
(*d*) Phenyl isocyanate and phosgene

180. Atmosphere at a place has been loaded with :
1. Sulphuric acid mists
2. Ammonium sulphate mists
3. Vapoursen

The aerosoles that influce temperature status of atmosphere are those noted at :
(*a*) 1 alone (*b*) 2 alone
(*c*) 2 and 3 (*d*) All of these

181. Following aerosoles were noticed in the atmosphere of a place :
1. Acid fumes
2. Ammonia
3. Sulphur-dioxide

Aerosols responsible for change of pH of rain water are noted at :
(*a*) 1 alone (*b*) 1 and 2
(*c*) 2 and 3 (*d*) All of these

182. Persistent exposures to even low levels of environmental chemicals, sometimes induce mutagenic, teratogenic or carcinogenetic effects on various organisms; such mutagens may :
(*a*) cause cell death
(*b*) induce chromosomal abnormalities
(*c*) induce gene mutation
(*d*) All of the above

183. Which is the gas that produces the most damaging acid rains?
(*a*) SO_2 (*b*) NO_2
(*c*) CO_2 (*d*) H_2

184. Cadmium damages :
(*a*) heart
(*b*) liver and kidneys
(*c*) stomach
(*d*) lungs

185. Forests are destroyed mainly by :
(*a*) acid rains due to SO_2 and NO_2 pollution
(*b*) air pollutants like ozone, SO_2, N_2O
(*c*) soil pollutants
(*d*) waterborne pollutants

186. Which one of the following diseases is due to an allergic reaction by inhalation of certain air borne pollens :
(*a*) Enteric fever
(*b*) Hay fever/Asthma
(*c*) Skin cancer
(*d*) Goitre

187. Air pollutant causing leaf curling is :
(*a*) SO_2 (*b*) O_3
(*c*) H_2S (*d*) CO

188. Environmental acid depositions cause :
(*a*) lake and forests to die
(*b*) green house effect to lessen
(*c*) acid indication in human
(*d*) All of these

189. Tropical rain forest destruction is very serious because :

(*a*) if will lead to a severe reduction in biodiversity
(*b*) tropical soils can not support agriculture for long
(*c*) large tracts of forests absorb CO_2, reducing the threat of global warming
(*d*) All of the above

190. In Ganganagar district a farmer has following crops and plantation :
1. Cotton
2. Grapes
3. Apple

Pollution by sulphur and oxides of sulphur will affect :
(*a*) 1 alone (*b*) 1 and 2
(*c*) 2 and 3 (*d*) All of these

191. Pollution related diseases are :
(*a*) Siderosis due to iron dust
(*b*) Phossy Jaw by excessive phosphates
(*c*) Plumbism due to lead
(*d*) All of the above

192. Tobacco crop is highly sensitive to :
(*a*) Ozone (*b*) Sulphur dioxide
(*c*) Nitric Oxide (*d*) None of the above

193. Leafy vegetables, field crops, fruits and forest trees are mostly harmed by :
(*a*) Ozone (*b*) NO_2
(*c*) SO_2 (*d*) CO_2

194. In crop-fields situated in vicinity of a cement factory studies carried out on plants had shown :
1. blocking of stomatal pores
2. affecting gaseous exchange and water relations
3. changes in other physiological processes

The setting down of pollutant particles has been the cause of :
(*a*) 1 alone (*b*) 1 and 2
(*c*) 1 and 2 (*d*) All of these

195. Symptoms like necrosis of leaves, defoliation of young terminal branches, hardening of floral buds, necrosis for fruit tips, stigmatic surfaces and reduction in fruit size have been observed in aerial parts of mango orchards in areas around a town in Uttar Pradesh. The area has around it :
(*a*) brick kilns
(*b*) thermal power station
(*c*) smelters and steel factories
(*d*) All of the above

196. Which of the following disease has been declared as killer disease under factory act?
(*a*) TB (*b*) Shigellosis
(*c*) Silicosis (*d*) Asbestosis

197. Aerosols reduce GPP by :
(*a*) Competing with CO_2
(*b*) reducing photosynthesis
(*c*) decreasing O_2 concentration
(*d*) being toxic to chloroplast

198. Chlorosis in plants is caused by air pollution due to :
(*a*) CO (*b*) NO_2
(*c*) SO_2 (*d*) hydrocarbons

199. In coming years ulcerated skin, nausea, loss of hair and anaemia will be common due to :
(*a*) pollutants in air
(*b*) use of detergents
(*c*) water pollution
(*d*) depletion of ozone layer

200. In coming years skin cancer diseases, mutations will be common due to :
(*a*) air pollution
(*b*) use of detergents
(*c*) depletion of ozone layer
(*d*) water pollution

201. Recent reports of acid rains (reported first by Robert Augus 1872) in big industrial cities are due to the effect of atmospheric pollution by :
(*a*) more release of SO_2 and NO_2 by burning of fossil fuels
(*b*) more release of CO_2 by burning of coal/wood, cutting of forests and increasing population
(*c*) excessive release of NH_3 by coal gas/industries
(*d*) excessive release of CO by incomplete combustion of carbonaceous fuels

202. In India, acid rains are not common due to :
(*a*) less SO_2 in air
(*b*) factories with long chimneys
(*c*) dust in air
(*d*) rural areas

203. The lowest pH due to acid rain is :
(*a*) 2.1 (*b*) 2.4
(*c*) 3 (*d*) 4.5

204. A rain is called *acid rain* when its *p*H is :
(*a*) Less than 7
(*b*) Less than 5.6 (generally between 3-5)
(*c*) Less than 4.6 (generally between 2-4)
(*d*) Less than 2

205. Acid rains in some industrial cities are due to :
(*a*) excessive release of CO_2 by burning of fossil fuels
(*b*) excessive concentration of SO_2 and NO_2 in air by deforestation
(*c*) excessive release of SO_2 by industries and coal gas
(*d*) deforestation, population explosion and release of CO_2 by automobile exhausts

206. Acid rain is caused by sulphur oxides, nitrogen oxides and hydrochloric acid which are produced by industries, automobiles and thermal power plants using fossil fuels. It causes :
(*a*) defoliation, chlorosis, necrosis of plant foliage
(*b*) leaching of mineral salts in soil and decolourisation of red stone of Red fort
(*c*) death of fishes due to clogging of their gills by exudation of large amount of mucus caused by solubility and availability of toxic metal like Aluminium
(*d*) All of the above

207. Smog is a combination of :
(*a*) air and water vapour
(*b*) water and smoke
(*c*) smoke and fog
(*d*) fire and water

208. Term *smog* was given in 1905 by :
(*a*) des Voeux (*b*) Hult
(*c*) Canon (*d*) Le Chatelier

209. A smog that occurs due to low temperature and has reducing environment is
(*a*) Los Angeles smog
(*b*) Photochemical smog
(*c*) London smog
(*d*) All of the above

210. Smog that occurs mainly by automobile exhausts at high temperature over cities due to still air is called :
(*a*) London smog
(*b*) Classical smog
(*c*) Both (*a*) and (*b*)
(*d*) Photochemical smog

211. London smog of 1952 was that killed about 400 lives persons, was :
(*a*) Photochemical and rich in NO_2
(*b*) Coal induced and rich in SO_2
(*c*) Effect of nuclear accident
(*d*) Due to atomic explosion

212. Some pollutants are :
1. Carbon monoxide
2. Nitrogen dioxide
3. Ethylene
4. Lead tetraethyl
5. Sulphur-dioxide
6. Unburnt hydrocarbons
7. Partially oxidised products formaldehyde and acetaldehyde

The photochemical SMOG formation takes place by :
(*a*) 1 and 6 (*b*) 6 and 7
(*c*) 1 and 7 (*d*) All of these

213. In the above question, toxic pollutants of automobile exhaust in these are :
(*a*) (1) and (2) (*b*) (2) and (3)
(*c*) (3) and (2) (*d*) All of these

214. Photochemical smog always contain :
(*a*) ozone (*b*) methane
(*c*) CO (*d*) PAN

215. Classical smog is :
(*a*) Dark brown
(*b*) Yellow brown
(*c*) Los.Angeles smog
(d) Smog with sec. pollutants

216. Term *over kill* is concerned with :
(*a*) nuclear holocaust
(*b*) global warming
(*c*) pesticide poisoning
(*d*) soil erosion

217. The pollutant that directly affects the nervous system is :
(*a*) DDT
(*b*) Aldrin
(*c*) Lindane
(*d*) Organic phosphate

218. Following are the water borne diseases except :
(*a*) Cholera (*b*) Pertusis
(*c*) Typhoid (*d*) Hepatitis

219. Which industry workers suffer from Byssinosis?
(*a*) Cardboard (*b*) Coal miners
(*c*) Textile (*d*) Paper

220. A disease caused by eating fish contaminated by industrial waste water containing mercury compounds is known as :
(*a*) Hiroshima disease (*b*) Minamata disease
(*c*) Bright's disease (*d*) Osteoschlerosis

221. Which pollutant gas has adversely affected the flower growing industry in Los Angeles?
(*a*) SO_2 (*b*) CO_2
(*c*) Ozone (*d*) N_2O

222. Cotton dust produced in industry during ginning process cause :
(*a*) siderosis (*b*) asbestosis
(*c*) pneumoconiosis (*d*) asthma

223. Which disease in children is caused by the body through intensive use of nitrate fertilizers which enter into food chains/water?
(*a*) Cyanosis (Blue baby)
(*b*) Methaemoglobianaemia
(*c*) Mumps
(*d*) Both (*a*) and (*b*)

224. Itai-Itai, (Ouch-ouch) a bone softening disease is due to :
(*a*) cadmium (*b*) mercury
(*c*) zinc (*d*) lead

225. Deficiency of fluorine in drinking water caused :
(*a*) dental caries (*b*) dental fluorosis
(*c*) skeletal fluorosis (*d*) goitre

226. What was the cause of '**Yusho**' disease which occurred in Japan in 1968 from a leak in a canning factory?
(*a*) PCBs (*b*) HCHO
(*c*) Hg (*d*) Pb

227. Harmful ultraviolet radiations cause :
(*a*) liver cancer (*b*) skin cancer
(*c*) mouth cancer (*d*) lung cancer

228. UV radiation cause :
(*a*) snow blindness on watching snow at hills
(*b*) sun burn
(*c*) mutations
(*d*) All of the above

229. Bone cancer and Leukemia is caused by :
(*a*) Strontium^{90}
(*b*) Iodine^{131}
(*c*) Mercury compounds
(*d*) Lead

230. Occupational diseases are due to :
(*a*) radiations (*b*) bacteria
(*c*) chemical hazards (*d*) viruses

231. An isotope that causes damage to RBC, bone marrow, spleen; lymph nodes and causes skin cancer is :
(*a*) Sr^{90} (*b*) I^{131}
(*c*) Cs^{137} (*d*) I^{127}

232. Xeroderma pigmentosum is :
(*a*) sensitivity of skin to UV rays
(*b*) spots formed by UV rays
(*c*) tanning of skin due to light
(*d*) both (*a*) and (*b*)

233. Exposure of plants to high fluoride concentrations results in necrosis or chlorosis characteristically in :
(*a*) petiole but not in lamina
(*b*) only midrib of lamina
(*c*) stem tip leaf margins
(*d*) stem tips only

234. Mango necrosis (Black Tip) is due to :
(*a*) SO_2 (*b*) CO
(*c*) CO_2 (*d*) PAN

235. The depletion of O_3 layer in coming years leads to :
(*a*) Epiloma (*b*) Myoloma
(*c*) Papiloma (*d*) Metastasis

236. Which causes fibrosis in lungs?
(*a*) Lead (*b*) Asbestos
(*c*) CFC (*d*) DDT

237. Sulphurous smog is :
(*a*) photochemical smog
(*b*) oxidising smog
(*c*) classical smog
(*d*) Los Angeles smog

238. In a photochemical smog, which gas causes eye and mucous membrane irritant?
(*a*) SO_2 (*b*) O_3
(*c*) CO (*d*) N_2O

239. The main component of photochemical smog is/are :
(*a*) PAN (*b*) O_3
(*c*) Both (*a*) and (b) (*d*) SO_2

240. PAN (Peroxyacylnitrate) is a secondary pollutant and is found in :
(*a*) smog (*b*) fertilizer
(*c*) herbicide (*d*) pesticide

241. Which organism's case of colour change after the industrial revolution is quoted as the most striking example of **Industrial melanism** and natural selection as a result of environmental change?
(*a*) Spotted Lady bird (*b*) Speckled wood
(*c*) Peppered moth (*d*) Dot moth

242. **Industrial melanism** [occurrence of melanic (black) forms in an industrial area] was studied in Britain in an isecct (Peppered moth) which is :
(*a*) *Betula* (*b*) *Biston*
(*c*) *Aphids* (*d*) *Papilio*

243. Population of Peppered Moth (*Biston betularia*) in England changed from 1% dark and 99% of light moths to 99% dark and 1% light between 1848 to 1898. The selective agent causing the change was :
(*a*) agricultural revolution
(*b*) smoke from coal base factories
(*c*) birds
(*d*) tree bark

244. Most abundant pollutant in the atmosphere among hydrocarbons is :
(*a*) methane (*b*) propane
(*c*) butane (*d*) benzpyrene

245. Which pollutant gas is released by cudchewing cattles ruminants?
(*a*) CH_4 (*b*) CO_2
(*c*) CO (*d*) NO_2

246. Which of the following gases can deplete the ozone layer in the stratosphere (upper atmosphere)?
(*a*) Methane
(*b*) Carbon monoxide
(*c*) Ammonia
(*d*) Sulphur dioxide

247. The gas which is produced in flooded rice paddy fields, marshes and cud chewing cattles (ruminants, Biomass burning. coal mines Tundras and is associated with global warming and depletion of ozone layer is :
(*a*) CH_4 (*b*) Cl
(*c*) CO_2 (*d*) H_2S

248. Which pollutant gas does a landfill produce?
(*a*) Methane (*b*) Ammonia
(*c*) H_2S (*d*) SO_2

249. The source of *methane pollution* :
(*a*) Paddy fields
(*b*) Marshes
(*c*) Cattles and other herbivores
(*d*) All of the above

250. The source of aerosol in upper atmosphere is :
(*a*) sea currents
(*b*) petroleum based industries
(*c*) jet planes
(*d*) ruminants

251. Aerosols having carbon and fluorine compounds, are chiefly released by :
(*a*) Automobiles
(*b*) Refineries
(*c*) All of the above
(*d*) Jets

252. As innocous activity as a hair spraying can, on a large scale, drastically affect :
(*a*) ozone layer (*b*) ionosphere
(*c*) troposphere (*d*) magnetosphere

253. DDT concentration recorded in man's body has been :
(*a*) 13-31 ppm (*b*) 30-70 ppm
(*c*) 1.3-3.1 ppm (*d*) 0.3-7 ppm

254. DDT is banned because it :
(*a*) affects the reproduction in birds
(*b*) has short half life
(*c*) is uneconomical in use
(*d*) is dangerous to animals and man

255. Phosphate pollution is caused by :
(*a*) phosphate rocks
(*b*) agricultural fertilizers
(*c*) sewage and phosphate cycle
(*d*) sewage and agricultural fertilizers

256. Agent orange as weed killer/defoliant was used by USA in Vietnam. It was named so because of :
(*a*) orange in colour
(*b*) orange stripe on packing
(*c*) producing orange clouds
(*d*) killing greenary

257. *Agent orange* contains
(*a*) 2, 4-D
(*b*) 2, 4, 5-T
(*c*) Dioxin as contaminant/carcinogen
(*d*) All of the above

258. The recent source of pollution of underground water is :
(*a*) sewers (*b*) biogas plants
(*c*) thermal powers (*d*) landfills

259. Third pollution is :
(*a*) landscape pollution
(*b*) noise pollution
(*c*) pollution due to radiations
(*d*) Gulf war pollution

260. A most harmful environmental pollutant/soil pollutant :
(*a*) Human waste
(*b*) Fossil fuel and iron junks
(*c*) Polythene sheet
(*d*) Excessive nutrients in soil

261. Main cause of increase in salinity of arid land due to irrigation is :
(*a*) Contribution of solutes through irrigation
(*b*) Dissolution of solutes due to irrigation
(*c*) Solutes being brought up from lower soil horizon with the evaporation of water
(*d*) Contribution of solutes by plants grown with irrigation

262. Jhuming (shifting cultivation) requires :
(*a*) Huge amount of fertilizers
(*b*) Long time for the regeneration of soil
(*c*) Excessive soil erosion for crop production
(*d*) Alternate crop pattern

263. Jhuming occurs in India in :
(*a*) Hilly area (*b*) Madhya Pradesh
(*c*) North east (*d*) Malabar areas

264. Which one of the following is likely to have the highest levels of DDT deposition in its body?
(*a*) Phytoplanktons (*b*) Sea crab
(*c*) Sea gull (*d*) Eel

265. Fish eating birds like sea gulls are endangered because :
(*a*) chlorinated hydrocarbons interfere with their reproductive ability
(*b*) chlorinated hydrocarbons (like DDT) cause mutations
(*c*) DDT in them is carcinogenic
(*d*) All of the above

266. Which harmful item was discussed in Rachel Carson's **'Silent Spring'** book on damage of wildlife?
(*a*) PCB (*b*) CFC
(*c*) CO_2 (*d*) DDT

267. The concentration of DDT is maximum in breast muscles of birds/sea gulls that eat :
(*a*) flesh (*b*) sea fish
(*c*) sea plants (*d*) All of these

268. The main effect of DDT on birds pelicans is :
(*a*) fewer feathers (*b*) stunted growth
(*c*) blindness (*d*) thinner eggshells

269. The amplification of DDT in the various trophic levels is known as :
(*a*) green house effect (*b*) biomagnification
(*c*) eutrophication (*d*) pollution

270. The first biocide used on a large scale to kill mosquitoes was :
(*a*) DDT (*b*) 2,4-D
(*c*) Hg (*d*) CFC

271. DDT and other chlorinated hydrocarbons are toxic because these are :
(*a*) quantitative pollutants and kill few insects only
(*b*) biodegradable pollutants and pollute the atmosphere
(*c*) non-biodegradable pollutants and accumulated in the organisms through food chain
(*d*) None of these

272. The get propulsion liberates an aerosol in outer atmosphere which causes air pollution. It is
(*a*) Fluorocarbons (*b*) CO_2
(*c*) SO_2 (*d*) Ozone

273. Green house gases are/is :
(*a*) CO_2
(*b*) Chlorofluorocarbons (CFCs) and Halons (Bromine)
(*c*) CH_4 and N_2O
(*d*) All of these

274. If the greenhouse effect becomes real and melts polar ice, which one of the following regions will first disappear under water?
(*a*) Hawaii Island (*b*) Maldives
(*c*) Mauritius (*d*) Islands of Kiribati

275. The most serious pollutant to rubber tyres is :
(*a*) CO_2 (*b*) CO
(*c*) O_3 (*d*) NO_2

276. Which satellite recorded the presence of an ozone hole?
(*a*) TIROS-N (*b*) GOES
(*c*) NIMBUS-7 (*d*) LANDSAT-3

277. Peeling of ozone umbrella (which protects us from harmful UV rays) is made by :
(*a*) CFMs/CFCs (*b*) CO_2
(*c*) Coal burning (*d*) PAN

278. Photocopying and other electrical equipment produce :
(*a*) methane
(*b*) ozone
(*c*) hydrogen sulphide
(*d*) nitrogen dioxide

279. Ozone depletion in stratosphere ozone hole would result in :
(*a*) forest fires and acid rains
(*b*) global warming
(*c*) increased incidence of skin cancer due to reaching of UV radiations on earth
(*d*) green house effect

280. Ozone increases :
(*a*) photosynthesis (*b*) transpiration
(*c*) respiration (*d*) both (*b*) and (*c*)

281. Today concentration of green house gases is high because of :
(*a*) use of refrigerators
(*b*) deforestation
(*c*) increased combustion of fossil fuel
(*d*) All of the above

282. Maximum threat to the world is from :
(*a*) Global warming (*b*) Ozone hole
(*c*) Water pollution (*d*) Soil erosion

283. Natural sink of stratospheric ozone layer is :
(*a*) SO_2
(*b*) HCF
(*c*) Freons
(*d*) Sulphur flux of oceans

284. Ozone layer of stratosphere requires protection from indiscriminate use of :
(*a*) Pesticides and medicines
(*b*) Aerosols and high flying jets
(*c*) Atomic explosions and industrial wastes
(*d*) Turbo-propelled aeroplanes

285. The result of ozone hole is :
(*a*) Global warming
(*b*) Acid rain
(*c*) Green House Effect
(*d*) UV radiations reach the earth

286. Which important green house gas other than methane is being produced from the agricultural fields?
(*a*) Ammonia (*b*) Sulphur dioxide
(*c*) Nitrous oxide (*d*) None of these

287. Pick out the one that has the capacity to trap maximum infrared radiation :
(*a*) CH_4 (*b*) CO_2
(*c*) CFC (*d*) SO_2

288. Pollutant helping in early degradation of ozone layer is :
(*a*) Freon
(*b*) SO_2
(*c*) CO_2
(*d*) Chlorinated hydrocarbons

289. Ozone hole is due to mainly two green house gases which are :
(*a*) CO_2, CH_4 (*b*) N_2O and CFCs
(*c*) N_2O and CH_4 (*d*) CFC and CH_4

290. Eutrophication results in the reduction of :
(*a*) minerals (*b*) dissolved oxygen
(*c*) dissolved CO_2 (*d*) algal growth

291. Fluoride content of water that may cause fluorosis is :
(*a*) 8 ppm (*b*) 1 ppm
(*c*) 10 ppm (*d*) 6 ppm

292. Which plant brought from America for controlling water pollution has become a problem in India :
(*a*) *Opuntia* (*b*) *Lantana*
(*c*) *Eichhornia* (*d*) *Kalmath weed*

293. Maximum biomagnification would be in case of aquatic ecosystem in :
(*a*) Fish (*b*) Birds
(*c*) Zooplanktons (*d*) Phytoplanktons

294. Water is often treated with chlorine (sodium hypochlorite) to :
(*a*) kill germs
(*b*) remove hardness of water
(*c*) to remove suspended particles
(*d*) to increase oxygenation

295. Water pollution is due to :
(*a*) agricultural discharges
(*b*) sewage
(*c*) industrial effluents
(*d*) All of the above

296. Warm ocean surge or Peru Current that recourse after 5-8 years so in East Pacific along South America is known as :
(*a*) El Nino (*b*) Aye Aye
(*c*) Gulf stream (*d*) Magnox

297. Thermal pollution is more prevalent near :
(*a*) hot water springs
(*b*) coal based power plants
(*c*) temperate zones
(*d*) tropical zones

298. Pesticides cause mainly the pollution of :
(*a*) air (*b*) soil
(*c*) water (*d*) land

299. Water pollution is caused by :
(*a*) NH_3
(*b*) Plankton
(*c*) Industrial effluents
(*d*) Agriculture

300. Among following pollutants which one has the most lasting effect?
(*a*) CO (*b*) Pesticides
(*c*) Smoke (*d*) SO_2

301. El-nino is related to :
(*a*) Thermal pollution (*b*) Soil pollution
(*c*) Air pollution (*d*) Noise pollution

302. Water blooms are formed by :
(*a*) Algae
(*b*) Planktonic blue green Algae
(*c*) Diatoms
(*d*) Lemna and Hydrilla

303. Which statement is incorrect?
(*a*) CO is major air pollutant
(*b*) all pollutants are not waste products
(*c*) lichens are affected by SO_2
(d) N_2 and Mg can pollute H_2O

304. Silent spring is a :
(*a*) Book on effect of DDT on birds
(*b*) An unpolluted area in Kashmir
(*c*) A biosphere reserve in Garhwal
(*d*) A protected valley in Kerala

305. As it passes into food chain, the concentration of DDT/chlorinated hydrocarbons :
(*a*) remains same (*b*) decreases
(*c*) increases (*d*) unpredictable

306. Which of the following organism is likely to have more concentration of DDT in its body?
(*a*) Herbivores (*b*) Carnivores
(*c*) Top carnivores (*d*) Primary producers

307. Maximum biomagnification of DDT through food web is seen in :
(*a*) algae (*b*) man
(*c*) fish (*d*) higher plants

308. Spraying of DDT on crops produces pollution of :
(*a*) Soil and water (*b*) Air and soil
(*c*) Crops and air (*d*) Air and water

309. The maximum biomagnification would be in which of the following in case of aquatic ecosystem?
(*a*) fishes/eel fish (*b*) birds/sea gulls
(*c*) zooplanktons (*d*) phytoplanktons

310. Country contributing maximum to ozone hole formation is :
(*a*) USA (*b*) Russia
(*c*) Japan (*d*) India

311. Of the following different occupations of women workers, tell which were first to die of cancer from nuclear radiations?
(*a*) Assemblers of colour TV parts
(*b*) Painters of luminous watch dials
(*c*) Nurses handling X-ray machines
(*d*) Air hostesses

312. Of the following radioisotopes, which one is most dangerous to *Homo sapiens*
(*a*) $Cesium^{137}$ (*b*) $Iodine^{131}$
(*c*) $Strontium^{90}$ (*d*) $Phosphorus^{32}$

313. Which part of body is first to be affected by nuclear radiation?
(*a*) Bone marrow (*b*) Liver
(*c*) Lungs (*d*) Brain

314. Protists are least sensitive to nuclear radiations but most sensitive are :
(*a*) mammals (*b*) birds
(*c*) reptiles (*d*) toads

315. The Chernobyl disaster in the then USSR was (now Ukraine) was caused on 26.4. 1986 by a :
(*a*) nuclear test
(*b*) nuclear reactor accident
(*c*) nuclear waste disposal leak
(d) nuclear weapon accident

316. In hospitals sterilization is brought by :
(*a*) spraying DDT (*b*) UV radiation
(*c*) infrared radiation (*d*) alpha radiation

317. Which secondary pollutant is produced by UV rays of sun light?
(*a*) SO_2 (*b*) CO
(*c*) fluorides (*d*) ozone

318. Radiations from outer space are not health hazardous as :
(*a*) they are harmless
(*b*) only 0.1% of them reach the earth
(*c*) these are useful
(*d*) they provide energy

319. Most outstanding danger at present for survival of living being on earth is :
(*a*) radiation hazard (*b*) deforestation
(*c*) desertification (*d*) glaciation

320. Radioactivity is absorbed by plants like :
(*a*) Lichens (*b*) Ginkgo
(*c*) both (*a*) and (*b*) (*d*) Pines

321. Most hazardous radiations to higher animals and plants are :
(*a*) non-ionising
(*b*) ionising
(*c*) radioactive (isotopes)
(*d*) None of these

322. Polonium is a pollutant emitted from :
(*a*) Laboratory
(*b*) Reactors
(*c*) Automobile exhausts
(*d*) Thorium rich sands

323. Which of the following radioactive isotopes is used in the detection of thyroid cancer?
(*a*) $Iodine^{131}$ (*b*) $Carbon^{14}$
(*c*) $Uranium^{238}$ (*d*) $Phosphorus^{32}$

324. Strontium^{90} is most dangerous radioactive isotope. In human body it enters particularly in bones through :
(*a*) breathing of polluted air
(*b*) drinking water
(*c*) soil
(*d*) food chain

325. Above what level of intensity is sound considered hazardous noise pollution?
(*a*) Above 30 dB (*b*) Above 80 dB
(*c*) Above 100 dB (*d*) Above 120 dB

326. Noise above 80 dB is uncomfortable and painful. It is a slow poison and causes :
(*a*) high BP deafness, anxiety stress
(*b*) headache and high cholesterol level
(*c*) dilates cerebral blood vessels and eyes
(*d*) All of these

327. The intensity of noise pollution is measured in :
(*a*) mach (*b*) hertz
(*c*) decibels (*d*) noy

328. What is the intensity of sound in normal conversation :
(*a*) 10 × 20 dB (*b*) 30 × 60 dB
(*c*) 70 × 90 dB (*d*) 0 × 30 dB

329. Range of human hearing is :
(*a*) 20 × 400 Hz (*b*) 100 × 1000 Hz
(*c*) 20 × 15000 Hz (*d*) 1000 × 15000 Hz

330. **Eutrophication** (mineral pollution) is maximum in :
(*a*) utter layers of deep lakes
(*b*) bottom layers of deep lakes
(*c*) upper layers of shallow lakes
(*d*) bottom layers of shallow lakes

331. **Biomagnification** refers to :
(*a*) high production in agroecosystems
(*b*) high production in marine ecosystems
(*c*) increasing concentration of pollutant into higher trophic level through successive food chains
(*d*) increasing concentration of pollutants into organism of lower trophic levels through food chains

332. Sewage and Garbage in H_2O kill fish due to :
(*a*) increase in bacterial activity
(*b*) increase in bacteria and decrease in O_2
(*c*) decrease in bacteria and increase in BOD
(*d*) high BOD

333. Sewage stimulates activity of osmotrophs (decomposer). A high content of which refers to water pollution :
(*a*) Diatoms and *Oscillatoria*
(*b*) Fungi
(*c*) *E. coli* and *Beggotia*
(*d*) All correct

334. In polluted water, index of pollution is :
(*a*) MPN (*b*) BOD
(*c*) Daphnia (*d*) All of these

335. If in a river biochemical or Biological oxygen demand (BOD) percentage is high then :
(*a*) river is dry
(*b*) river is polluted
(*c*) river water is good for drinking
(*d*) river water is good for factory

336. BOD is related to :
(*a*) Microbes
(*b*) Microbes and organic matter
(*c*) Organic matter
(*d*) None of these

337. The most publicised oil spill disaster is :
(*a*) wreck of Torrey Canyon oil Tanker in 1967
(*b*) blow out of an oil well at Santa Barbara
(*c*) release of petrochemicals in Goa by Zuari Chemicals
(*d*) explosion is Brauni oil refinery

338. A sewage is labelled as *strong* if its biological oxygen demand is around :
(*a*) 100 mg/litre (*b*) 200 mg/litre
(*c*) 300 mg/litre (*d*) 500 mg/litre

339. The chief source of water pollution is :
(*a*) smog (*b*) industries
(*c*) detergents (*d*) sewage

340. Match the following :

1. Acid rain	(A) Biological amplification
2. DDT	(B) Mineral pollution
3. BOD	(C) Smog

4. Eutrophication (D) Sewage pollution
5. PAN (E) SO_2

(*a*) 1 – (E), 2 – (A), 3– (D), 4 – (B), 5 – (C)
(*b*) 1 – (E), 2 – (D), 3– (A), 4 – (B), 5 – (C)
(*c*) 1 – (C), 2 – (D), 3– (A), 4 – (B), 5 – (E)
(*d*) 1 – (C), 2 – (B), 3– (D), 4 – (A), 5 – (E)

341. Which does not result in pollution?
(*a*) Automobiles plants
(*b*) Nuclear power plants
(*c*) Hydroelectric power plants
(*d*) Thermal power

342. The water of nuclear power plants may lead to :
(*a*) radioactive pollution
(*b*) water pollution
(*c*) thermal pollution
(*d*) None of these

343. Events that take place in eutrophication are given below :
1. excessive growth of algae
2. depletion of dissolved oxygen
3. bacteria feed on dead algal cells
4. aquatic body becomes rich in phosphates

The correct order of events that occur here is :
(*a*) 1, 4, 3 and 2 (*b*) 4, 1, 3 and 2
(*c*) 1, 2, 4 and 3 (*d*) 4, 3, 2 and 1

344. Mass killing of fishes occur in :
(*a*) oligotrophic lakes (*b*) salt lakes
(*c*) eutrophic lakes (*d*) fast flowing river

345. Eutrophication is a stage of reduced free oxygen in water. It is caused due to :
(*a*) excessive NO_3 and PO_4
(*b*) salts of heavy metals
(*c*) seepage of mineral oils
(*d*) sewage

346. Loss of Biodiversity, coral bleaching and deforestation are global issues as :
(*a*) these result in indespread interest around the world
(*b*) these have global impact
(*c*) these are problems of common man
(*d*) None of the above

347. The most variable component of the atmosphere is :
(*a*) Helium (*b*) Water vapours
(*c*) Oxygen (*d*) Nitrogen

348. Which of the following is **NOT** envisaged in Tehri Dam Project?
(*a*) 400 cusecs of drinking water to UP
(*b*) 300 cusecs of drinking water to Delhi
(*c*) Generating 2,500 MW of electricity
(*d*) All of the above

349. The responsibilities for sharing environmental benefits and losses may be build by :
(*a*) developing appropriate policies
(*b*) building international networks
(*c*) cooperation and co-ordinated participation
(*d*) All of the above

350. Tibilisi Conference, 1977 was known for :
(*a*) forming objectives and principles for environmental education at all levels
(*b*) finding the ozone hole at Antarctica
(*c*) developing and applying rules for reducing air pollution
(*d*) increasing the CNG fuel in New Delhi

351. Which of the following is **NOT** an objective of Environmental education in India?
(*a*) Awareness
(*b*) Knowledge
(*c*) Skills
(*d*) Increasing air pollution

352. The developer of three-fold classification of environmental education is :
(*a*) Ernest Hackel (1970)
(*b*) Newman (1981)
(*c*) Salim Ali (1982)
(*d*) Pitter (1985)

353. Major health effects due to depletion of ozone layer is/are :
(*a*) increase in eye cataracts and mutation
(*b*) increase in skin cancer and melonema
(*c*) decrease in growth of ocean flora and fauna
(*d*) All of the above

354. Fluorosis can lead to :
(*a*) severe skeleted problems
(*b*) prevent dental caries
(*c*) stiffiness and pain in joints
(*d*) (*a*) and (*c*) only

355. Goitre is an enlargement of :
(*a*) Pancreas (*b*) Thyroid gland
(*c*) Testes (*d*) Spleen

356. Disposal of fly ash is carried out in :
(*a*) ash ponds (*b*) air tumbler
(*c*) thermal plants (*d*) none of these

357. The symptoms of goitre include :
(*a*) enlargement of the throat
(*b*) swelling problems in oesophagus also
(*c*) breathing problems
(*d*) All of the above

358. Which of **NOT** correctly matched?
(*a*) CNG → Compressed Natural Gas
(*b*) GDP → Gross Domestic Product
(*c*) GNP → Gross National Product
(*d*) LPG → Local Petroleum Gas

359. The typical composition of management of solid wastes do **not** depend on :
(*a*) land use (*b*) locality
(*c*) season of year (*d*) None of these

360. Which of the following cause damage to blood?
(*a*) Iron (*b*) Lead
(*c*) Calcium (*d*) Arsenic

361. Most poisonous pollutant in water is :
(*a*) Lead (*b*) Zinc
(*c*) Phosphate (*d*) Arsenic

362. Pigeons are highly alert as they can detect a sound frequency of :
(*a*) 0.1 Hz (*b*) 10 Hz
(*c*) 1.0 Hz (*d*) 4 Hz

363. Sound limit in industry is :
(*a*) 75 dB (*b*) 55 dB
(*c*) 30 dB (*d*) 45 dB

364. Water Pollution increases :
(*a*) MPN
(*b*) BOD
(*c*) Turbidity and deoxygenation
(*d*) All of these

365. MPN (Most probable number) indicates :
(*a*) Thermal pollution
(*b*) Air pollution
(*c*) Faecal pollution
(*d*) Industrial pollution

366. *Tubifex* in water indicates its :
(*a*) Purity
(*b*) Organic loading
(*c*) Toxic Metals
(*d*) High salt contents

367. The absence of caddis fly, mayfly and Dragonfly around a water body indicates that it is :
(*a*) highly polluted (*b*) mildly polluted
(*c*) tolerably polluted (*d*) not polluted

368. Presence of mosquito larva, *E.coli* and 20 different algae in water indicates that this water is :
(*a*) fit for drinking
(*b*) unfit for human use
(*c*) can be used after physical treatment
(*d*) indicative of radioactive pollution

369. Highly polluted waters have :
(*a*) High Algal Genus index
(*b*) Low Algal Genus index
(*c*) No Algal at all
(*d*) A few algal genera and a few bacteria

370. Which oil tanker accident (occurred in March 1967) first alerted the public of the grave problem of oil spills in oceans?
(*a*) Agro Merchant
(*b*) Ocean Eagle
(*c*) Beagle
(*d*) Torrey Canyon

371. Which regions of seas/oceans are the most polluted?
(*a*) Estuarine (*b*) Coastal
(*c*) Sea depths (*d*) Coral reefs

372. Often in the water bodies subjected to sewage pollution, fishes die because of the :
(*a*) foul smell
(*b*) pathogens in the sewage
(*c*) clogging of their gills by solid particles
(*d*) reduction in dissolved oxygen caused by microbial activity

373. Which of the following is not a water pollutant but present in ordinary tap water?
(*a*) Barium (*b*) Fluorine
(*c*) Chlorine (*d*) Chromium

374. BOD is :
(*a*) amount of O_2 altered by organisms in water
(*b*) amount of O_2 altered by microbes for decomposition of organic matter
(*c*) amount of O_2 present in water at 37°C
(*d*) All of the above

375. Domestic waste constitutes :
(*a*) biodegradable pollutants
(*b*) non-biodegradable pollutants
(*c*) effluents
(*d*) air pollutants

376. Which is not a non-degradable pollutant?
(*a*) DDT (*b*) Sewage
(*c*) Plastics (*d*) Heavy metals

377. The name *Amoco Cadiz* is related with :
(*a*) nuclear waste site
(*b*) oil slick
(*c*) toxic cloud
(*d*) forest fire

378. Which type of waste is produced in the maximum amount in a household
(*a*) Plastics (*b*) Metal
(*c*) Paper (*d*) Organic matter

379. Safe limit of water fluoride level is :
(*a*) 0.1 × 0.4 mg/litre
(*b*) 0.5 × 0.8 mg/litre
(*c*) 0.9 × 1.2 mg/litre
(*d*) 1.3 × 1.6 mg/litre

380. The first rate pollution monitor are :
(*a*) molluscs
(*b*) butterflies
(*c*) honey bee
(*d*) plants

381. The increased productivity of lakes and streams brought about by nutrient enrichment particularly by phosphate and nitrate of detergents and fertilizers is known as :
(*a*) green house effect
(*b*) eutrophication
(*c*) biomagnification
(*d*) biochemical oxygen demand

382. Which of the following household activities pour maximum pollutant in water?
(*a*) Toilet cleaning
(*b*) Washing and bathing
(*c*) Dish washing
(*d*) Drinking and cooking

ANSWERS

1	2	3	4	5	6	7	8	9	10
(*d*)	(*b*)	(*d*)	(*c*)	(*d*)	(*d*)	(*c*)	(*d*)	(*a*)	(*d*)
11	**12**	**13**	**14**	**15**	**16**	**17**	**18**	**19**	**20**
(*d*)	(*b*)	(*c*)	(*d*)	(*b*)	(*d*)	(*b*)	(*a*)	(*a*)	(*d*)
21	**22**	**23**	**24**	**25**	**26**	**27**	**28**	**29**	**30**
(*a*)	(*d*)	(*b*)	(*d*)	(*c*)	(*c*)	(*d*)	(*b*)	(*b*)	(*a*)
31	**32**	**33**	**34**	**35**	**36**	**37**	**38**	**39**	**40**
(*d*)	(*c*)	(*b*)	(*b*)	(*c*)	(*a*)	(*a*)	(*c*)	(*d*)	(*b*)
41	**42**	**43**	**44**	**45**	**46**	**47**	**48**	**49**	**50**
(*d*)	(*b*)	(*c*)	(*d*)	(*a*)	(*b*)	(*b*)	(*b*)	(*a*)	(*d*)
51	**52**	**53**	**54**	**55**	**56**	**57**	**58**	**59**	**60**
(*c*)	(*b*)	(*a*)	(*d*)	(*b*)	(*d*)	(*a*)	(*d*)	(*d*)	(*c*)
61	**62**	**63**	**64**	**65**	**66**	**67**	**68**	**69**	**70**
(*a*)	(*a*)	(*c*)	(*d*)	(*d*)	(*b*)	(*a*)	(*c*)	(*d*)	(*d*)

71	**72**	**73**	**74**	**75**	**76**	**77**	**78**	**79**	**80**
(*d*)	(*a*)	(*b*)	(*a*)	(*b*)	(*a*)	(*a*)	(*c*)	(*d*)	(*a*)
81	**82**	**83**	**84**	**85**	**86**	**87**	**88**	**89**	**90**
(*b*)	(*d*)	(*b*)	(*b*)	(*d*)	(*a*)	(*d*)	(*a*)	(*d*)	(*d*)
91	**92**	**93**	**94**	**95**	**96**	**97**	**98**	**99**	**100**
(*a*)	(*a*)	(*b*)	(*b*)	(*a*)	(*d*)	(*b*)	(*a*)	(*a*)	(*a*)
101	**102**	**103**	**104**	**105**	**106**	**107**	**108**	**109**	**110**
(*b*)	(*d*)	(*b*)	(*d*)	(*a*)	(*d*)	(*a*)	(*b*)	(*c*)	(*a*)
111	**112**	**113**	**114**	**115**	**116**	**117**	**118**	**119**	**120**
(*a*)	(*a*)	(*b*)	(*b*)	(*c*)	(*b*)	(*b*)	(*c*)	(*d*)	(*a*)
121	**122**	**123**	**124**	**125**	**126**	**127**	**128**	**129**	**130**
(*a*)	(*d*)	(*a*)	(*d*)	(*d*)	(*b*)	(*b*)	(*b*)	(*c*)	(*d*)
131	**132**	**133**	**134**	**135**	**136**	**137**	**138**	**139**	**140**
(*a*)	(*a*)	(*b*)	(*c*)	(*a*)	(*c*)	(*a*)	(*d*)	(*a*)	(*d*)
141	**142**	**143**	**144**	**145**	**146**	**147**	**148**	**149**	**150**
(*b*)	(*b*)	(*a*)	(*b*)	(*a*)	(*d*)	(*c*)	(*b*)	(*a*)	(*a*)
151	**152**	**153**	**154**	**155**	**156**	**157**	**158**	**159**	**160**
(*b*)	(*a*)	(*a*)	(*c*)	(*c*)	(*a*)	(*b*)	(*c*)	(*d*)	(*b*)
161	**162**	**163**	**164**	**165**	**166**	**167**	**168**	**169**	**170**
(*d*)	(*d*)	(*a*)	(*d*)	(*d*)	(*a*)	(*d*)	(*a*)	(*c*)	(*a*)
171	**172**	**173**	**174**	**175**	**176**	**177**	**178**	**179**	**180**
(*d*)	(*c*)	(*a*)	(*a*)	(*b*)	(*c*)	(*b*)	(*a*)	(*c*)	(*d*)
181	**182**	**183**	**184**	**185**	**186**	**187**	**188**	**189**	**190**
(*d*)	(*d*)	(*a*)	(*b*)	(*b*)	(*b*)	(*a*)	(*a*)	(*d*)	(*a*)
191	**192**	**193**	**194**	**195**	**196**	**197**	**198**	**199**	**200**
(*d*)	(*b*)	(*c*)	(*d*)	(*a*)	(*d*)	(*b*)	(*c*)	(*d*)	(*c*)
201	**202**	**203**	**204**	**205**	**206**	**207**	**208**	**209**	**210**
(*a*)	(*c*)	(*b*)	(*b*)	(*c*)	(*d*)	(*c*)	(*a*)	(*c*)	(*d*)
211	**212**	**213**	**214**	**215**	**216**	**217**	**218**	**219**	**220**
(*b*)	(*d*)	(*d*)	(*a*)	(*a*)	(*a*)	(*d*)	(*b*)	(*c*)	(*b*)
221	**222**	**223**	**224**	**225**	**226**	**227**	**228**	**229**	**230**
(*c*)	(*c*)	(*d*)	(*a*)	(*a*)	(*a*)	(*b*)	(*d*)	(*a*)	(*c*)
231	**232**	**233**	**234**	**235**	**236**	**237**	**238**	**239**	**240**
(*b*)	(*a*)	(*c*)	(*a*)	(*d*)	(*b*)	(*c*)	(*b*)	(*c*)	(*a*)
241	**242**	**243**	**244**	**245**	**246**	**247**	**248**	**249**	**250**
(*c*)	(*b*)	(*c*)	(*a*)	(*a*)	(*a*)	(*a*)	(*a*)	(*b*)	(*c*)
251	**252**	**253**	**254**	**255**	**256**	**257**	**258**	**259**	**260**
(*d*)	(*a*)	(*a*)	(*c*)	(*a*)	(*d*)	(*b*)	(*a*)	(*c*)	(*c*)
261	**262**	**263**	**264**	**265**	**266**	**267**	**268**	**269**	**270**
(*c*)	(*b*)	(*c*)	(*c*)	(*a*)	(*d*)	(*b*)	(*d*)	(*b*)	(*a*)

271	272	273	274	275	276	277	278	279	280
(*c*)	(*a*)	(*d*)	(*d*)	(*c*)	(*c*)	(*a*)	(*b*)	(*c*)	(*d*)
281	**282**	**283**	**284**	**285**	**286**	**287**	**288**	**289**	**290**
(*d*)	(*b*)	(*c*)	(*b*)	(*d*)	(*c*)	(*c*)	(*a*)	(*b*)	(*b*)
291	**292**	**293**	**294**	**295**	**296**	**297**	**298**	**299**	**300**
(*c*)	(*c*)	(*a*)	(*a*)	(*d*)	(*a*)	(*b*)	(*c*)	(*c*)	(*b*)
301	**302**	**303**	**304**	**305**	**306**	**307**	**308**	**309**	**310**
(*a*)	(*b*)	(*d*)	(*a*)	(*c*)	(*c*)	(*b*)	(*a*)	(*b*)	(*a*)
311	**312**	**313**	**314**	**315**	**316**	**317**	**318**	**319**	**320**
(*b*)	(*c*)	(*a*)	(*a*)	(*b*)	(*b*)	(*d*)	(*b*)	(*a*)	(*c*)
321	**322**	**323**	**324**	**325**	**326**	**327**	**328**	**329**	**330**
(*b*)	(*c*)	(*a*)	(*d*)	(*b*)	(*d*)	(*c*)	(*b*)	(*c*)	(*b*)
331	**332**	**333**	**334**	**335**	**336**	**337**	**338**	**339**	**340**
(*c*)	(*b*)	(*d*)	(*d*)	(*b*)	(*b*)	(*a*)	(*c*)	(*b*)	(*a*)
341	**342**	**343**	**344**	**345**	**346**	**347**	**348**	**349**	**350**
(*c*)	(*c*)	(*b*)	(*c*)	(*a*)	(*a*)	(*b*)	(*a*)	(*d*)	(*a*)
351	**352**	**353**	**354**	**355**	**356**	**357**	**358**	**359**	**360**
(*d*)	(*b*)	(*d*)	(*d*)	(*b*)	(*a*)	(*d*)	(*d*)	(*d*)	(*b*)
361	**362**	**363**	**364**	**365**	**366**	**367**	**368**	**369**	**370**
(*d*)	(*a*)	(*a*)	(*d*)	(*c*)	(*b*)	(*b*)	(*b*)	(*a*)	(*d*)
371	**372**	**373**	**374**	**375**	**376**	**377**	**378**	**379**	**380**
(*b*)	(*d*)	(*c*)	(*b*)	(*a*)	(*b*)	(*b*)	(*d*)	(*b*)	(*a*)
381	**382**								
(*b*)	(*b*)								

2

Population and Biotic Community

1. Population means :
   (a) All the animals of a place
   (b) All the animals and plants found in an area
   (c) Human beings living in an area
   (d) Animals/plants of a species living in a specific area

2. Species ecology is :
   (a) Autecology
   (b) Synecology
   (c) Community ecology
   (d) Palaeoecology

3. Population whose members reproduce asexually is :
   (a) Panmictic (b) Species
   (c) Amphimictic (d) Apomictic

4. Population whose members reproduce sexually is :
   (a) Panmictic (b) Apomictic
   (c) Amphimictic (d) Species

5. Ecotype is :
   (a) Genetically different but phenotypically similar
   (b) Genetically similar but ecologically different individuals
   (c) Genetically adapted ecological race
   (d) Genetically and phenotypically dissimilar members of different species ecologically adapted to an area

6. Family herd and tribe are units :
   (a) Higher in rank than a population
   (b) Higher in rank than a species
   (c) Intermediate between local population and species
   (d) Subordinate in rank to local population

7. Average height of Watusi tribesman is :
   (a) 1.4 m (b) 2.2 m
   (c) 1.2 m (d) 1.6 m

8. Liger is a :
   (a) Natural hybrid between lion and tigeress
   (b) Natural hybrid between tiger and lioness
   (c) Fertile hybrid between captive lion and tigers
   (d) Fertile hybrid between captive tiger and lioness

9. The factors involved in formation of new species are :
   (a) Competition and variations
   (b) Isolation and competition
   (c) Competition and mutations
   (d) Isolation and mutations

10. An animal leading a solitary life is :
   (a) Deer (b) Seal
   (c) Fox (d) Hamster

11. An animal which lives in flocks is :
   (a) Deer (b) Monkey
   (c) Elephant (d) Parrot

12. An animal found in herds is :
   (a) Deer (b) Swan
   (c) Parrot (d) Monkey

13. A monogamous animal is :
   (a) Seal (b) Deer
   (c) Swan (d) Hamster

14. A polygamous animal is :
(*a*) Rat (*b*) Deer
(*c*) Fox (*d*) Wolf

15. The occurrence of two forms of individuals in the same species is known as :
(*a*) Differentiation (*b*) Dimorphism
(*c*) Monoecious (*d*) Polymorphism

16. *Physalia* shows :
(*a*) Polymorphism (*b*) Dimorphism
(*c*) Trimorphism (*d*) Metamerism

17. Family formation is common feature in :
(*a*) All animals
(*b*) Majority of animals
(*c*) Almost all animals
(*d*) A few animals

18. Rats have :
(*a*) Monogamy (*b*) Polygamy
(*c*) Polyandry (*d*) No fixed partners

19. Presence of different types of flowers in male and female mulberry/palm papaya is :
(*a*) Dichogamy
(*b*) Dimorphism
(*c*) Bisexuality
(*d*) Monoecious nature

20. The dominant individual/leader of a herd is :
(*a*) Always a male (*b*) Always a female
(*c*) Generally a male (*d*) Generally a female

21. Altruistic behaviour occurs in :
(*a*) Spotted Deer (*b*) Termite
(*c*) Honey Bee (*d*) All of the above

22. Cooperative interaction is essential for perpetuation of :
(*a*) Micro-organisms (*b*) Plants
(*c*) Animals (*d*) Both (*b*) and (*c*)

23. Demography is the study of statistics that affect :
(*a*) geography
(*b*) population growth
(*c*) local concentration of individuals
(*d*) family pedigrees

24. Ecologically fixed and genetically irreversed species are called :
(*a*) Ecotone
(*b*) Ecological equivalents
(*c*) Ecotype
(*d*) None of the above

25. Exponential growth occurs when there is :
(*a*) asexual reproduction only
(*b*) sexual reproduction only
(*c*) no inhibition from crowding
(*d*) a fixed carrying capacity

26. A bacterium can divide every 20 minutes. Beginning with a single individual, how many bacteria will there be in the population if there is exponential growth for three hours?
(*a*) 18 (*b*) 440
(*c*) 512 (*d*) 1024

27. Organisms with very high intrinsic growth rates have :
(*a*) long generation times
(*b*) short generation times
(*c*) no courtship behaviours
(*d*) no carrying capacities

28. Logistic growth occurs when there is :
(*a*) asexual reproduction only
(*b*) sexual reproduction only
(*c*) no inhibition from crowding
(*d*) a fixed carrying capacity

29. Beginning with a single bacterium, how large will be the population if there is logistic growth, with a carrying capacity of 18, for a period of 3 hours?
(*a*) 18 (*b*) 440
(*c*) 512 (*d*) 1024

30. The world's average annual rate of population growth for all humans is now about :
(*a*) 0.5% (*b*) 1.0%
(*c*) 1.7% (*d*) 5.6%

31. If an animal population becomes too large for its feeding source or its habitat, its members starve and die but humans escape this disaster by :
(*a*) immigration only
(*b*) emmigration only
(*c*) transportation of food only
(*d*) both (*b*) (*c*)

32. The Netherlands is a small country still it has a high population. Reason you conclude, can be :
(*a*) high birth rate
(*b*) low death rate
(*c*) all places are equally inhabitable
(*d*) environmental conditions are very favourable

33. The assemblage of individuals of same kind inhabiting a particular area is called :
(*a*) community (*b*) biome
(*c*) population (*d*) organism

34. The carrying capacity of a population is determined by its :
(*a*) population growth rate
(*b*) birth rate
(*c*) death rate
(*d*) limiting resource

35. The growth of human population is most rapid in :
(*a*) temperate regions
(*b*) Asia
(*c*) tropical and subtropical regions
(*d*) North America

36. Community is :
(*a*) A particular species
(*b*) A particular group of animals
(*c*) All the organisms in a given area
(*d*) None of the above

37. Mutualism and proto-cooperation are :
(*a*) Positive interactions
(*b*) Negative interactions
(*c*) Both of these
(*d*) None of these

38. Association of nitrogen fixing bacteria with the leguminous roots is :
(*a*) Mutualism (*b*) Commensalism
(*c*) Neutralism (*d*) Parasitism

39. Many of the bacteria living in the human large intestine feeding on undigested food without harming the host are :
(*a*) Predators (*b*) Commensals
(*c*) Symbionts (*d*) Parasites

40. Mycorrhiza an association of fungus and angiospermic root is referred as :
(*a*) Amensalism (*b*) Mutualism
(*c*) Parasitism (*d*) Commensalism

41. Competition between two species :
(*a*) Results in dying of one species
(*b*) Forces one of the species to live elsewhere
(*c*) Switch over to another kind of food
(*d*) All of the above

42. A group of several species living together with mutual tolerance or adjustment and beneficial interactions in a natural area is known as :
(*a*) Species (*b*) Population
(*c*) Biotic community (*d*) Family

43. Interaction between the two organisms in which one organism kills and feeds on the second organism is known as :
(*a*) Scavenging (*b*) Predation
(*c*) Parasitism (*d*) None of these

44. The relationship between the two organisms where one receives benefit at the cost of the other is known as :
(*a*) Parasitism (*b*) Predation
(*c*) Scavenging (*d*) Symbiosis

45. The relationship between the two organisms or species in which both the partners derive benefit from each other is known as :
(*a*) Parasitism (*b*) Symbiosis
(*c*) Commensalism (*d*) None of these

46. Competition among the plants in a community is for :
(*a*) Water (*b*) Nutrients
(*c*) Sunlight (*d*) For all these

47. Which is a protective device in animals?
(*a*) Competition (*b*) Commensalism
(*c*) Mimicry (*d*) Symbiosis

48. Female mosquitoes sucking human blood at intervals are :
(*a*) Permanent parasites
(*b*) Endoparasites
(*c*) Semiparasites
(*d*) Intermittent parasites

49. Mimicry is a device for :
(*a*) Concealment from predator
(*b*) Concealment from prey
(*c*) Both (*a*) and (*b*)
(*d*) Becoming conspicuous

50. Population of ferocious Red Ant is kept under check by :
(*a*) Rufus Wood Pecker
(*b*) Red-billed Ox Pecker
(*c*) Yellow-billed Ox Pecker
(*d*) Sparrow

51. Climax community is :
(*a*) First stable community
(*b*) Unstable
(*c*) Unstable that develops in the beginning of succession
(*d*) The last stable community

52. Succession is
(*a*) Series of physical changes that occur in an area
(*b*) Development of biotic communities on a bare area
(*c*) Series of biotic communities that appear in a previously bare area
(*d*) Both (*a*) and (*b*)

53. Dominant species represents most abundant :
(*a*) Herb that binds the soil and provides organic matter to it
(*b*) Shrub that appears for the first time
(*c*) First tree
(*d*) Species having major effect on physical environment

54. For better survival of human population, which is the most important step?
(*a*) Reduction n the use of various resources
(*b*) Afforestation
(*c*) Conservation of wildlife
(*d*) Ban on mining activity

55. Large gap between birth and death rates in Haryana will result in :
(*a*) more old persons
(*b*) low rate of fertility
(*c*) more school going children
(*d*) low dependency ratio

56. Which of the following factors is not a determinant of population size?
(*a*) Natality (*b*) Immigration
(*c*) Emigration (*d*) Migration

57. Emigration term is used for :
(*a*) outward movement of individuals from a given population
(*b*) movement of individuals from outside into a given population
(*c*) movement involving return to an area
(*d*) none of the above

58. Emigration affects population in :
(*a*) animals
(*b*) land plants
(*c*) animals and land plants
(*d*) land plants and aquatic plants.

59. The population of an area tends to decrease by :
(*a*) migration (*b*) mortality
(*c*) immigration (*d*) None of these

60. The population of an area tends to increase by :
(*a*) mortality (*b*) emigration
(*c*) natality (*d*) All of the above

61. A population with more than 50% in post reproductive are group would be :
(*a*) declining (*b*) increasing
(*c*) expanding (*d*) stable

62. Population dispersion is the :
(*a*) spatial distribution of individuals
(*b*) movement away from a natal site
(*c*) movement from one fixed point to another and back again
(*d*) mixing of two populations

63. Population density is the :
(*a*) number of species per community
(*b*) number of communities per ecosystem
(*c*) number of individuals per species
(*d*) number of individuals per species per unit area or volume

64. Parameter for describing a population is :
(*a*) Time (*b*) Number and kind
(*c*) Space or area (*d*) All of these

65. Replacement of existing communities by any external condition is termed
(*a*) Primary succession
(*b*) Secondary succession
(*c*) Autogenic succession
(*d*) None of the above

66. The area where two major communities meet and blend together is termed as
(*a*) Ecotype (*b*) Biotype
(*c*) Ecotone (*d*) Meeting place

67. Indian wolf has become an important animal because
(*a*) It's name appears in Red Data Book.
(*b*) It is only an important member of food chain of almost all Indian forests.
(*c*) Wild dogs disappeared due to their presence.
(*d*) It has been chosen as a State animal.

68. Walkley and Black rapid titration method is used for the determination of
(*a*) Organic carbon content of soil
(*b*) Nitrate content of soil
(*c*) Phosphate content of soil
(*d*) Fluoride content of soil

69. The aggregate of processes that determine the size and composition of any population is called :
(*a*) Population explosion
(*b*) Population density
(*c*) Population dispersal
(*d*) Population dynamics

70. Environmental resistance refers to :
(*a*) The difference between biotic potential and actual number in a population
(*b*) Hazards in a population of a species
(*c*) Interaction between environment and population
(*d*) Sustainance of a population

71. When a tiger attacks cheetals, the stag with best antlers is surrounded by other individuals to protect it. It is an example of :
(*a*) Cooperation (*b*) Group formation
(*c*) Altruism (*d*) Herding

72. Which of the following leads a solitary life?
(*a*) Swan (*b*) Man
(*c*) Spider (*d*) Monkey

73. Which among the following does not lead a monogamous life?
(*a*) Seal (*b*) Fox
(*c*) Swan (*d*) Wolf

74. Rats are :
(*a*) Monogamous
(*b*) Bigamous
(*c*) Polygamous
(*d*) Do not have fixed partners

75. Ants communicate through :
(*a*) sound (*b*) pheromones
(*c*) contact (*d*) both (*a*) and (*b*)

76. The factor which does not affect the population size is :
(*a*) Immigration (*b*) Emigration
(*c*) Migration (*d*) Birth rate

77. Rapid decline in a population due to high mortality rate is :
(*a*) Population density
(*b*) Population crash
(*c*) Population explosion
(*d*) All of the above

78. Which one of the following is an endoenzyme in soil ?
(*a*) Cellulase (*b*) Invertase
(*c*) Protease (*d*) Dehydrogenase

79. Genetically adapted population to a particular habit is :
(*a*) Mule (*b*) Ecotype
(*c*) Ecosphere (*d*) Ecology

80. A fertile hybrid between captive tiger and lioness is :
(*a*) Mule (*b*) Liger
(*c*) Tigress (*d*) Tigon

81. Which of the following chemical compounds help in transmitting the message to other members of same species?
(*a*) Hormone (*b*) Ptyalin
(*c*) Pheromones (*d*) None of the above

82. The population tends to increase as individuals are added by :
(*a*) Natality (*b*) Immigration
(*c*) None of these (*d*) Both of these

83. The most distinct and easily observation unit is :
(*a*) Cell (*b*) Tissue
(*c*) Organs (*d*) Individual organism

84. The occurrence of two forms among the organism same kind is known as :
(*a*) Dimorphism
(*b*) Trimorphism
(*c*) Polymorphism
(*d*) None of the above

85. A green alga Volvox, a colonial from consists of over :
(*a*) 100 cells (*b*) 1000 cells
(*c*) 10,000 cells (*d*) 60,000 cells

86. The chemicals of intraspecific communication are :
(*a*) Allochemics (*b*) Kairomones
(*c*) Auxins (*d*) Pheromones

87. Match the terms in Column A with suitable term in Column B :

	Column A		Column B
A.	Decline in death rate	1.	Polymorphism
B.	Complete count of individuals in area an	2.	Ant
C.	Honey bee	3.	Population explosion
D.	Polygamous	4.	Census
E.	Pheromone	5.	Peacock
		6.	Population crash

Codes :

	A	B	C	D	E
(*a*)	3	4	1	6	2
(*b*)	3	4	2	5	2
(*c*)	3	4	1	5	2
(*d*)	6	3	1	5	2

88. Which of the following morphological forms is also known as ecophenes?
(*a*) Ecospecies (*b*) Ecad
(*c*) Ecotype (*d*) None of the above

89. The relationship between one species and another within a community that has evolved through interactions is based upon :
(*a*) requirement and mode of obtaining food only
(*b*) requirement and mode of obtaining shelter only
(*c*) on the habits of the species only
(*d*) All of these

90. The interaction among organisms in a community called as biotic factors influence :
(*a*) the structure of a community only
(*b*) composition of a community only
(*c*) function of a community only
(*d*) All of these

91. Population growth curve is :
(*a*) Hyperbolic (*b*) Parabolic
(*c*) Linear (*d*) Logistic

92. Number of immigration is more than emigration and death is lower than natality, growth curve of population will show :
(*a*) exponential phase
(*b*) lag phase
(*c*) declining phase
(*d*) steady phase

93. In the given graphic representation of age groups of a population shows :

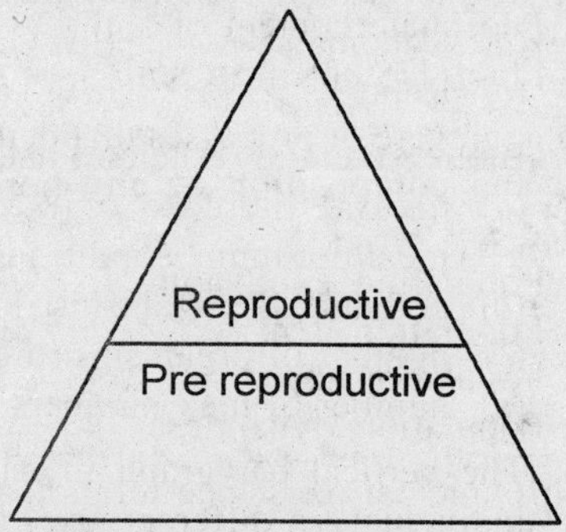

(*a*) declining population
(*b*) increasing population
(*c*) stable population
(*d*) fluctuating population

94. Indian population is characterised by more :
(*a*) old persons
(*b*) reproductive persons
(*c*) prereproductive individuals
(*d*) both (*a*) and (*b*)

95. After exponential increase, population becomes stagnant. The growth curve of this population is :

(*a*) J-shaped (*b*) S-shaped
(*c*) Fluctuating (*d*) Circular

96. Human population shows :
(*a*) J-shaped growth curve
(*b*) S-shaped growth curve
(*c*) Z-shaped growth curve
(*d*) All of the above

97. Proportion of young individuals is highest in :
(*a*) declining population
(*b*) stable population
(*c*) both (*a*) and (*b*)
(*d*) expanding population

98. Which of the following factor controls the human population density?
(*a*) Industry (*b*) Communication
(*c*) Climate (*d*) Natural resources

99. Density of population is (S = size, W = weight, N = number)
(*a*) D = S/W (*b*) D = S/N
(*c*) D = N/S (*d*) None of these

100. The term biotic potential was used by :
(*a*) Chapman (*b*) Gause
(*c*) Reiter (*d*) Tansley

101. Biotic Potential (Potential natality) refers to :
(*a*) natural increase of population under ideal/optimum conditions
(*b*) potential of organisms in a biome
(*c*) number of organisms in a biome
(*d*) number of max numbers in a population

102. The vertical bar graph in which number of individuals in different age groups at a given time is shown from youngest at bottom to oldest at top is like a :
(*a*) Pyramid (*b*) Bell
(*c*) Parabolic (*d*) Flat

103. Of the following humic groups which is not soluble in both acid and alkali ?
(*a*) Fulvic acid
(*b*) Humic acid
(*c*) Humin
(*d*) All of the above

104. The sources of thermal pollution are
(*a*) Power plants
(*b*) Cooling forests
(*c*) Industrial effluents
(*d*) All of the above

105. Which can counteract biotic potential :
(*a*) competition among organisms
(*b*) predation
(*c*) limitation of food
(*d*) All of the above

106. Environment resistance is :
(*a*) resistance towards disease
(*b*) resistance towards maximum reproductive rate
(*c*) resistance towards growth rate
(*d*) All of the above

107. The force operating in an ecosystem which opposes the unchecked growth of population is :
(*a*) mortality
(*b*) biotic control
(*c*) environmental resistance
(*d*) fecundity

108. On being attacked by predator, the cheetals surround a stag with best antlers for its protection. It is :
(*a*) Dominance-subordination
(*b*) Altruism
(*c*) Competitive interaction
(*d*) Group formation

109. Emigration influences population of :
(*a*) Land plants
(*b*) Land and aquatic plants
(*c*) Animals
(*d*) Animals and plants

110. In terrestrial organisms, population density is expressed in space units :
(*a*) Cubic metre (*b*) Cubic centimetre
(*c*) Metre (*d*) Square metre

111. In aquatic organisms, population density is expressed in space units :
(*a*) Cubic metre/cubic centimetre
(*b*) Metre
(*c*) Kilometre
(*d*) Square metre/square centimetre

112. Migration is :
(*a*) Outward movement of individuals
(*b*) Inward movement of individuals
(*c*) Two-way departure and return of all the individuals
(*d*) Starvation based mortality

113. Insect society is product of :
(*a*) Instinctive behaviour
(*b*) Biological evolution
(*c*) Learnt behaviour
(*d*) Both (*a*) and (*b*)

114. Human society is product of :
(*a*) Learnt behaviour
(*b*) Biological evolution
(*c*) Instinctive behaviour
(*d*) Both (*a*) and (*b*)

115. A permanent loss from population can be due to :
(*a*) Immigration (*b*) Emigration
(*c*) Migration (*d*) All of the above

116. Emigration is :
(*a*) Going out of some individuals to return after some time
(*b*) Temporary inward movement of some individuals
(*c*) Permanent outward movement of some individuals from a population
(*d*) Permanent inward movement of some individuals into a population

117. The most thinly populated country of the world is :
(*a*) Australia (*b*) Austria
(*c*) Maldives (*d*) Canada

118. The most thickly populated country of the world is :
(*a*) Japan (*b*) Indonesia
(*c*) India (*d*) China

119. Which one is larger?
(*a*) Territory
(*b*) Defended area
(*c*) Home range
(*d*) Nesting and nursing area

120. Boundary of a territory is marked by :
(*a*) Defaecation
(*b*) Pheromones present in excreta
(*c*) Excreta
(*d*) Urination

121. An animal would defend :
(*a*) Territory (*b*) Home range
(*c*) Feeding area (*d*) Both (*a*) and (*b*)

122. Territory is defended against :
(*a*) Any intruder
(*b*) Predator
(*c*) Intruder of same species
(*d*) Intruder of species having same feeding habits

123. Chemicals used for transmitting messages to members of same species are :
(*a*) Allochemics (*b*) Kairomones
(*c*) Auxins (*d*) Pheromones

124. Lemmings reduce their number by committing suicide every :
(*a*) Eight years
(*b*) Alternate year
(*c*) Four years
(*d*) Two years

125. Which factor maintains the distinctive traits of species?
(*a*) Specific niche
(*b*) Reproductive isolation
(*c*) Cooperative interaction
(*d*) Continuous intercommunication

126. A force acting against maximum population growth is :
(*a*) Population pressure
(*b*) Carrying capacity
(*c*) Saturation point
(*d*) Environment resistance

127. When population reaches carrying capacity?
(*a*) Mortality rate = Birth rate
(*b*) Mortality rate > Birth rate
(*c*) Mortality rate < Birth rate
(*d*) None of the above

128. The carrying capacity of a population is determined by its :
(*a*) birth rate (*b*) death rate
(*c*) limiting resource (*d*) All of these

129. The population generally stabalizes :
(*a*) Around the carrying capacity
(*b*) Below the carrying capacity
(*c*) Above the carrying capacity
(*d*) Irrespective of carrying capacity

130. Actual birth rate occurring per unit time is :
(*a*) Realised natality (*b*) Biotic potential
(*c*) Vital index (*d*) Potential mortality

131. Which one has the correct sequence of organisational complexity?
(*a*) Population → Species Community → Ecosystem
(*b*) Population → Community → Species → Ecosystem
(*c*) Population → Variety → Community → Ecosystem
(*d*) Species → Variety → Ecosystem → Population

132. The most favourable habitat of a plant is called :
(*a*) Ecotype (*b*) Ecoline
(*c*) Microhabitat (*d*) Niche

133. Which of the following is not responsible for the increase in population in India?
(*a*) better sanitary conditions
(*b*) education
(*c*) decline in child mortality
(*d*) traditional belief

134. Which are necessary condition for the *Hardy Weinberg law* for applying to genetic population?
(*a*) a high mutation rate and random mating
(*b*) selective mating and a small population
(*c*) a low mutation rate and a small population
(*d*) no migration and a large population

135. Gene pool of a population tends to remain stable if cartain conditions are met. These conditions are large populations, no migration, no mutation, no genetic drift and :
(*a*) random mating
(*b*) netural selection
(*c*) reduction of predators
(*d*) moderate environmental changes

136. Gene flow is :
(*a*) Transfer of genes between interbreeding population
(*b*) Transfer of genes from females to males of an organism
(*c*) Transfer of genes from outside to chromosome/DNA
(*d*) Transfer of genes through transgenic animals/plants

137. What is the importance of the 42nd Amendment to the Constitution brought in the year 1976 ?
(*a*) Insertion of Article 48-A
(*b*) Insertion of Article 51-A (g)
(*c*) Insertion of Article 48-A and
(*d*) None of the above

138. Who issues the Ecomark notification ?
(*a*) Ministry of Environment and Forest, Govt. of India
(*b*) Ministry of Human Health and Family Welfare, Govt. of India
(*c*) Department of Science and Technology, Govt. of India
(*d*) Bureau of Indian Standards

139. The annual growth rate for developing countries is :
(*a*) 5% (*b*) 2%
(*c*) 2.5% (*d*) 0.8%

140. Which one of the following is a waste recycling method of solid waste management?
(*a*) Pelletisation (*b*) Composting
(*c*) Incineration (*d*) Sanitary Landfill

141. Environment consists of :
(*a*) living objects of the surroundings
(*b*) non-living objects of the surroundings
(*c*) non-living objects events and influences of the surroundings
(*d*) living and non-living objects, events and Influences of the surroundings

142. Man must conserve environment because :
(*a*) it supports food yielding plants
(*b*) it supports useful plants and animals
(*c*) man is constituent of environment
(*d*) environment provides all the necessities of living beings

143. Interaction of two different organisms in which one receives benefit without the cost of the other is :
(*a*) Parasitism (*b*) Scavenging
(*c*) Symbiosis (*d*) Commensalism

144. Series of changes on previously barren area is :
(*a*) Sere
(*b*) Climatic climax
(*c*) Primary succession
(*d*) Secondary succession

145. What is relationship between Egret and Cattle?
(*a*) Commensalism (*b*) Protocooperation
(*c*) Mutualism (*d*) Parasitism

146. What is true of commensalism?
(*a*) One organism is harmed while the other is unaffected
(*b*) One organism is benefitted while the other is unaffected
(*c*) One is benefitted while the other is harmed
(*d*) Both are benefitted

147 A climax community is recognised by
(*a*) Grasses, herbs and shrubs
(*b*) Trees
(*c*) High biomass
(*d*) Uniform composition

148. Lichens and mossess occur in :
(*a*) Psammosere (*b*) Hydrosere
(*c*) Xerosere (*d*) Hydrarch

149 Plants and animals living in a particular area constitute :
(*a*) Flora and fauna
(*b*) Community
(*c*) Ecosystem
(*d*) Ecology

150. Community is :
(*a*) Species structure and diversity index of an area
(*b*) Biomass
(*c*) Autotrophic and heterotrophic components
(*d*) All of the above

151. The phenomenon of one organism being benefitted without affecting the other is :
(*a*) Scavenging (*b*) Amensalism
(*c*) Commensalism (*d*) Symbiosis

152. Plankton is :
(*a*) Sea scum
(*b*) Floating microscopic plants and animals
(*c*) Floating plants
(*d*) Any layer of aquatic organisms

153. The spread of *Opuntia* was controlled by :
(*a*) Allowing cattle to graze over it
(*b*) Allowing sheep and goats to browse over it
(*c*) Introducing insect
(*d*) Spraying herbicide

154. The relation between algae and fungi in a lichen is :
(*a*) Symbiosis (*b*) Parasitism
(*c*) Commensalism (*d*) Protocooperation

155. Association between Sea Anemone and Hermit Crab in gastropod shell is that of :
(*a*) Symbiosis (*b*) Commensalism
(*c*) Parasitism (*d*) Amensalism

156. Association in which one is benefitted without affecting the other is :
(*a*) Symbiosis (*b*) Saprophytism
(*c*) Parasitism (*d*) Commensalism

157. Zoochorellae in *Hydra* produce an association called :
(*a*) Commensalism (*b*) Parasitism
(*c*) Mutualism (*d*) Predation

158 Symbiosis is :
(*a*) Mutually beneficial association
(*b*) Mutually harmful association
(*c*) Harmful to one and beneficial to other
(*d*) Advantageous to one but neutral to other

159 Competition for light, nutrients and space is most severe between :
(*a*) Closely related organisms growing in different niches
(*b*) Closely related organisms growing in the same area/niche
(*c*) Distantly related organisms growing in the same habitat
(*d*) Distantly related organisms growing in different niches

160. Plant succession occurring in a sandy area is :
(*a*) Psammosere (*b*) Halosere
(*c*) Xerosere (*d*) Hydrosere

161. Two factors which are important in the formation of new species are :
(*a*) continuous variations and competition
(*b*) competition and mutations
(*c*) isolation and mutations
(*d*) isolation and competition

162. Territoriality involves :
(*a*) competition (*b*) cooperation
(*c*) predation (*d*) parasitism

163. Area covered by members of a species in search of food and mates is called :
(*a*) Range
(*b*) Home range
(*c*) Geographical distribution
(*d*) Territory

164. Area defended by an individual, for mating, proper food and shelter to be provided to the mate and offspring, is called :
(*a*) Niche (*b*) Habitat
(*c*) Territory (*d*) Range

165. Territory is much smaller than the :
(*a*) home range (*b*) range
(*c*) niche (*d*) habitat

166. Which of the following is not an example of sexual dimorphism?
(*a*) Man (*b*) Peacock
(*c*) Mucor (*d*) Date palm

167. When is a man a part of biotic community?
(*a*) Always
(*b*) Only when lives in big cities
(*c*) Only when he lives in a forest
(*d*) Never

168. Insect societies are products of :
(*a*) biological evolution
(*b*) instinctive behaviour
(*c*) both (*a*) and (*b*)
(*d*) learnt behaviour

169. Insect societies differ from human societies in being based on :
(*a*) learnt behaviour
(*b*) instinctive behaviour
(*c*) pshychological evolution
(*d*) none of the above

170. Origin of human society is based on :
(*a*) instinctive behaviour
(*b*) learnt behaviour
(*c*) political evolution
(*d*) biological evolution

171. Sympatric speciation is caused by :
(*a*) migration/interbreeding
(*b*) geographical isolation
(*c*) reproductive isolation
(*d*) genetic isolation

172. Sibling species illustrate the principle of speciation :
(*a*) through geographic isolation
(*b*) through mechanical isolation
(*c*) through behavioural differences
(*d*) due to their inability for cross fertilization

173. Allopatric speciation is due to :
(*a*) interplay of geographical isolation and reproductive isolation
(*b*) geographical isolation
(*c*) adaptive radiation
(*d*) reproductive isolation

174. Sympatric population is not isolated by :
(*a*) Behavioural barriers
(*b*) Geographical barriers
(*c*) Habitat barriers
(*d*) Seasonal barriers

175. Which of the following chemical compound helps in transmitting the message to other species of members?
(*a*) Alternative (*b*) Ptyalin
(*c*) Pheromones (*d*) None of the above

176. Term species in ecology refesr to :
(*a*) Autecology
(*b*) Synecology
(*c*) Community ecology
(*d*) Palaecology

177. Population surge 230 years ago was due to :
(*a*) Industrial revolution
(*b*) Agricultural revolution
(*c*) Cultural revolution
(*d*) Intellectual revolution

178. The levelling of an S-shaped curve describing population growth is caused by :
(*a*) carrying capacity
(*b*) the competitive exclusion
(*c*) environmental resistance
(*d*) a change in the biotic potential

179. The abundance of a species population within its habitat is called :
(*a*) niche density (*b*) absolute density
(*c*) relative density (*d*) regional density

180. Pheromones secreted by certain exocrine cutaneous gland affect :
(*a*) genitalia
(*b*) skin colour
(*c*) breast
(*d*) mutual behaviour of members of a species

181. Crow also incubates the eggs of :
(*a*) Pigeon (*b*) Dove
(*c*) Cuckoo (*d*) Weaver bird

182. Pheromones of insects are :
(*a*) Growth promoters
(*b*) Growth inhibitors
(*c*) Means of communication
(*d*) Chemicals of unknown utility

183. Population density of terrestrial organisms is measured in terms of individuals per :
(*a*) Metre (*b*) $Metre^2$
(*c*) $Metre^3$ (*d*) $Metre^4$

184. Population density of aquatic organisms is expressed in terms of individuals per :
(*a*) Metre (*b*) $Metre^2$
(*c*) $Metre^3$ (*d*) $Metre^4$

185. The dominant individual in a herd is :
(*a*) always a female (*b*) always a male
(*c*) usually a male (*d*) usually a female

186. Tiger has a :
(*a*) Monogamous fixed partnership
(*b*) Patriarchy group
(*c*) Matriarchal group
(*d*) Solitary life

187. Which of these helps in the survival of a species?
(*a*) Group formation
(*b*) Maintenance of territory
(*c*) Communication
(*d*) All of the above

188. Honey bees perfrorm dancing motion to signal :
(*a*) Distance of food source
(*b*) Direction of food source
(*c*) Availability of food
(*d*) Distance and direction of food source

189. Brown skinned human race :
(*a*) Mongoloid (*b*) Polynesian
(*c*) Red Indian (*d*) Australoid

190. The members or a form of polymorphic species :
(*a*) Interbreed with members of their own form
(*b*) Do not reproduce sexually
(*c*) Interbreed with members of other forms only
(*d*) Interbreed among themselves and with members of other forms also

191. Prevention of interbreeding due to geographical isolation is found in :
(*a*) Allopatric species (*b*) Sympatric species
(*c*) Sibling species (*d*) None of the above

192. Allopatric species are those which :
(*a*) interbreed
(*b*) can not interbreed due to geographical factors
(*c*) do not interbreed at all
(*d*) can not interbreed due to reproductive isolation

193. *Sympatric species* are those which :
(*a*) interbreed freely
(*b*) do not interbreed because of difference in their behaviour
(*c*) do not interbreed because of their different geographical distribution
(*d*) do not interbreed at all

194. Inability of different organisms to interbreed is called :
(*a*) Sterility
(*b*) Reproductive isolation
(*c*) Both (*a*) and (*b*)
(*d*) None of these

195. Which one can live in isolation?
(*a*) A cell (*b*) An organism
(*c*) Neither (*a*) nor (*b*) (*d*) Both (*a*) and (*b*)

196. Average height of Zulu tribesman is :
(*a*) 1 m (*b*) 1.2 m
(*c*) 1.4 m (*d*) 2.2 m

197. Which one of the following have raised check bone oblique eyes and yellowish skin colour?
(*a*) Negroids (*b*) Mongoloids
(*c*) Polynesians (*d*) Caucaroids

198. World's tallest human races is :
(*a*) Zulu (*b*) Watusi
(*c*) Negroid (*d*) Mongoloid

199. Altruistic behaviour is found in :
(*a*) white ants (*b*) honey bees
(*c*) spotted deer (*d*) all of these

200. Worker termites are :
(*a*) adolescent (*b*) adult male
(*c*) adult female (*d*) larva

201. Waggle dance in honey bee is an example of :
(*a*) communication (*b*) cooperation
(*c*) competition (*d*) None of these

202. The faster or waggle dance is completed the :
(*a*) farther away is the food
(*b*) closer is the food
(*c*) greater is the amount of food available
(*d*) higher is the food off the ground

203. If the honey bee is performing *round dance* (rund tanz) it is conveying the information of food source from the hive at a distance of about :
(*a*) 50 mt (*b*) 100 mt
(*c*) 1000 mt (*d*) 2000 mt

204. Tail waggling dance (schwanzeltanz) is performed by a worker bee :
(*a*) when food is near the hive
(*b*) when food source is quite away (250 feet) from the hive
(*c*) when food is near the hive but is heavy and requires assistance of many bees
(*d*) when it attracts is partner

205. When food source, found by a scout bee is located in a direction from the hive exactly opposite to that of the sun, the bee would dance as follows :
(*a*) Round dance in a clockwise direction on the comb
(*b*) Round dance in anticlock wise direction on the comb
(*c*) Tail waggling dance with a straight course vertically upwards
(*d*) Tail waggling dance with straight course vertically downwards

206. A community which starts succession in a habitat is :
(*a*) Pioneer community
(*b*) Seral community
(*c*) Biotic community
(*d*) Ecosere

207. The early settlers on a barren area are :
(*a*) Ferns (*b*) Mosses
(*c*) Lichens (*d*) Diatoms

208. What does the following sequence represent :
Blut-Green Algae → Crustose Lichens → Foliose Lichens → Mosses → Shrubs → Dicotyledonous trees
(*a*) A food pyramid
(*b*) Ecological succession
(*c*) Genetic drift
(*d*) Phylogenetic trend

209. Succession in a 6 metre deep pond exhibits a sequence of :
(*a*) Submerged Plants → Reeds → Herbs → Floating Plants → Shrubs → Trees
(*b*) Floating Plants → Submerged Plants → Reeds → Herbs → Shrubs → Trees
(*c*) Shrubs → Trees → Submerged Plants → Floating Plants → Reeds → Herbs
(*d*) Submerged Plants → Floating Plants → Reeds → Herbs → Shrubs → Trees

210. Last stabilised community in a plant succession is known as :
(*a*) Seral Community
(*b*) Pioneer Community
(*c*) Ecosere
(*d*) Climax Community

211. Intermediate community between pioneer and climax communities is called :
(*a*) Seral Community
(*b*) Biotic Community
(*c*) Temporary Community
(*d*) Ecosere

212. Climax vegetation of a region is generally :
(*a*) Xerophytic
(*b*) Hydrophytic
(*c*) Mesophytic
(*d*) Depends upon the climate

213. The first plants to reappear on a burnt forest area will be :
(*a*) Grasses (*b*) Ferns
(*c*) Mosses (*d*) Liverworts

214. A mutually beneficial association necessary for survival of both partners is :
(*a*) Mutualism/Symbiosis
(*b*) Commensalism
(*c*) Amensalism
(*d*) Both (*a*) and (*b*)

215. Which one is true?
(*a*) Commensalism when none of the interacting populations affect each other
(*b*) Symbiosis when the interaction is useful to both the populations
(*c*) Symbiosis when neither populations affects each other
(*d*) Commensalism when the interaction is useful to both the populations

216. In ecological succession from pioneer to climax community, the biomass shall :
(*a*) Decrease
(*b*) Increase and then decrease
(*c*) No relation
(*d*) Increase continuously

217. Association of animals when both partners are benefitted :
(*a*) Colony (*b*) Mutualism
(*c*) Commensalism (*d*) Amensalism

218. An association of individuals of different species living in the same habitat and having functional interactions is :
(*a*) Population (*b*) Ecological niche
(*c*) Biotic community (*d*) Ecosystem

219. Insectivorous plants are adopted to soils :
(*a*) Rich in water
(*b*) Deficient in water
(*c*) Deficient in nitrogenous compounds
(*d*) Deficient in trace elements

220. Primary succession is development of communities on :
(*a*) Newly exposed habitat
(*b*) Cleared forest area
(*c*) Freshly harvested crop field
(*d*) Pond filled after a dry season

221. A parasite living within tissue of host is :
(*a*) Epiphyte (*b*) Endophyte
(*c*) Ectophyte (*d*) None of the above

222. A scout bee, finding a new food source, communicates its location to other bees and
(*a*) Can communicate, the direction of food source through its round as well as tail waggling dances
(*b*) Can communicate the direction of the food source through its tail waggling dances
(*c*) Can communicate the direction of the food source through its tail waggling dances
(*d*) Cannot communicate the direction of the food source

223. Which of the following statement is correct with respect of honey bees?
(*a*) Communication in honey bee was discovered by Karl von Frisch
(*b*) Bees wax is a waste product of honey bees
(*c*) Honey is predominantly sucrose and a rabinose
(*d*) *Apis indica* is the largest wild honey bee in India

224. Who decoded the language of honey bee :
(*a*) Charles Darwin (*b*) William Harvery
(*c*) Karl Von Frisch (*d*) Carolus Linnaeus

225. What guides the subsequent bees to visit the same food source?
(*a*) Smell earlier bees left upon the flowers
(*b*) Smell of flowers
(*c*) Smell of flowers and earlier bees
(*d*) Shape of flowers

226. Pheromone is :
(*a*) a product of endocrine gland
(*b*) a protein
(*c*) used for communication by animals
(*d*) a gene to identify opposite sex

227. Pheromones are secreted by certain exocrine skin gland of organisms for :
(*a*) courtship (*b*) territory marking
(*c*) agression (*d*) Both (*a*) and (*b*)

228. Periodic departure and return is called phenology. It is :
(*a*) migration (*b*) immigration
(*c*) emigration (*d*) any of these

229. Triggered by the cooler and shorter days of autumn, many birds spend the summer months in southern regiongs. This is called :
(*a*) Hibernation (*b*) Adaptation
(*c*) Migration (*d*) Homing instinct

230. Migration of birds is by nature :
(*a*) a rational act
(*b*) photoperiodic phenomenon
(*c*) an instinctive behaviour
(*d*) all of the above

231. Scent producing glands are :
(*a*) anal glands (*b*) adrenal glands
(*c*) bertholins gland (*d*) prostate gland

232. Salt glands provide a way of getting rid of excess salts in :
(*a*) all marine forms
(*b*) marine fishes and marine birds
(*c*) marine birds
(*d*) sea gulls

233. Diapause is a stage related to :
(*a*) delay in development
(*b*) death
(*c*) differentiation
(*d*) cleavage

234. Similar environments on different continents produce similar ecological communities. Ecologically similar species in such non-adjacent communities are known as :
(*a*) sibling species
(*b*) ecological equivalents
(*c*) parallel species
(*d*) geographic competitors

235. Waggle dance of honey Bee is an example of :
(*a*) Courtship
(*b*) Threatening adversaries
(*c*) Communication for feeding site
(*d*) Communication for imminent danger

236. Competition between individuals of a population is :
(*a*) Intraspecific (*b*) Interspecific
(*c*) Internecine (*d*) Local

237. Study of inter-relationships between organisms and their environment is :
(*a*) Ecology (*b*) Ecosystem
(*c*) Phytogeography (*d*) Ethology

238. Study of inter-relationships between a species/individual and its environment in a forest is :
(*a*) Synecology (*b*) Forest Ecology
(*c*) Autecology (*d*) Ecology

239. Ecology is connected with the study of :
(*a*) Environment factors
(*b*) Plant adaptations
(*c*) Effect of plants on environment
(*d*) All of the above

240. Study of inter-relationships between an entire community and its environment is :
(*a*) Autecology
(*b*) Resource Ecology
(*c*) Species Ecology
(*d*) Synecology

241. Synecology is study of inter-relationship between environment and :
(*a*) Individual plant (*b*) A population
(*c*) A community (*d*) Individual animal

242. Individuals of a species which occur in a particular area constitute :
(*a*) Flora (*b*) Fauna
(*c*) Population (*d*) Both (*a*) and (*b*)

243. Biotic potential is increase in population under :
(*a*) Natural conditions
(*b*) Climatic conditions
(*c*) Optimum conditions
(*d*) Given conditions

244. Proportion of young individuals is highest in case of :
(*a*) Declining population
(*b*) Stable population
(*c*) Both (*a*) and (*b*)
(*d*) Expanding population

245. Large gap between birth and death rates will result in :
(*a*) More old persons
(*b*) Low rate of fertility
(*c*) More school going children
(*d*) Low dependency ratio

246. Competition is the most severe between two :
(*a*) Closely related species growing in different niches
(*b*) Closely related species growing in the same habitat
(*c*) Distantly related species growing in the same habitat
(*d*) Distantly related species growing in different niches

247. A population with equal number of births and deaths will show :
(*a*) Acceleration phase of growth
(*b*) Plateau phase
(*c*) Exponential growth phase
(*d*) Initial phase of growth

248. In case of scarcity of food or limitation of habitat, animal population is sure to starve and die. Human escape this disaster by :
(*a*) Emigration
(*b*) Immigration
(*c*) Transportation of food
(*d*) Both (*a*) and (*c*)

249. Ecology (= oekologie) was coined by :
(*a*) Linnaeus (*b*) Haeckel
(*c*) Harvey (*d*) Odum/Lamarck

250. The term of ecology was actually coined by :
(*a*) Aristotle (*b*) Reiter
(*c*) Linnaeus (*d*) Odum

251. Many angiosperms and ferns synthesize a molecule similar to ecdysone. It causes the insect herbivore that eat it to :
(*a*) become tiny adults and leave few offspring
(*b*) die
(*c*) stop ceding
(*d*) fail to become reproducting adults.

252. No predator can become proficient at acquiring prey because :
(*a*) they are not as intelligent as their prey
(*b*) predators are too large to be fast enough
(*c*) prey population evolve anti-predatory traits
(*d*) all of the above

253. Symbiosis is an association between two species in which :
(*a*) both live together in direct contact
(*b*) both benefit
(*c*) one benefits and other is neither benefitted nor harmed
(*d*) one benefits and other is harmed

254. Which of the following interaction will not promote co-evolution?
(*a*) Interspecific competition
(*b*) Commensalism
(*c*) Mutualism
(*d*) Parasitism

255. The kind of climax community in an area depends mostly on the areas :
(*a*) pool of available colonist
(*b*) soil organisms
(*c*) climate
(*d*) bed rock

256. Mostly agriculture makes use of plants from :
(*a*) early primary succession
(*b*) early secondary succession
(*c*) late primary succession
(*d*) late secondary succession

257. The growth of human population is most rapid in :
(*a*) Tropical and subtropical regions
(*b*) Temperate region
(*c*) Asia
(*d*) North America

258. Floating hydrophytes are characterized by :
1. well developed aerenchyma
2. absence of stomata on the lower side of leaf
3. lamina system poorly developed
4. sunken stomata
5. root system poorly developed

The correct characters are :
(*a*) All are correct (*b*) 1, 2, 3 and 5
(*c*) 2 and 5 (*d*) 2, 4, and 5

259. Xerophytes are characterized by :
(1) well developed cuticle
(2) well developed root system
(3) deciduous leaves with
(4) sunken stomata

The correct characters are :
(*a*) All are correct (*b*) 1 and 2
(*c*) 3 and 4 (*d*) 1, 3 and 4

260. More of the number of species in a community, more will be :
(*a*) competition
(*b*) biotic stability
(*c*) short term adaptation
(*d*) biotic unstability

261. Plant community may be defined as :
(*a*) genetically different individuals having same phenotype
(*b*) genotypically similar individuals of a population
(*c*) genetically adapted ecological races
(*d*) none of the above

262. Occurrence of 200 chlorella in the body wall of Hydra is :
(*a*) predation
(*b*) commensalism
(*c*) a food chain involving a parasite
(*d*) mutualism

263. When an organism is benefitted without affecting the other the relationship is termed?
(*a*) predation (*b*) parasitism
(*c*) commensalism (*d*) symbiosis

264. A flowering plant and the animal that pollinates it are examples of :
(*a*) Parasitism
(*b*) Mutualism
(*c*) Interspecific competition
(*d*) Commensalism

265. Animals which can tolerate only a narrow range of salinity are said to be :
(*a*) Euryhaline (*b*) Stenohaline
(*c*) Catadromous (*d*) Anadromous

266. Antagonistic interaction include :
(*a*) Scavenging (*b*) Competition
(*c*) Amensalism (*d*) Both (*b*) and (*c*)

267. The most successful parasite is the one that :
(*a*) has a life cycle involving only one host
(*b*) is permanently attached to the host
(*c*) is highly specialised
(*d*) makes minimum demands on the host

268. Lichens are described as indicators of :
(*a*) Air pollution
(*b*) Water pollution
(*c*) Xerophytic succession
(*d*) Mesophytic succession

269. In commensalism :
(*a*) One of the partners is benefitted at the cost of the second partner
(*b*) Both the partners are reciprocally benefitted
(*c*) One partner is benefitted and the other one is not at loss
(*d*) No partner is benefitted by the association

270. Which can counteract biotc potential?
(*a*) Limitation of food
(*b*) Competition from other organisms
(*c*) Availability of lower trophic level organisms
(*d*) None of the above

271. The sum total of the populations of the same kind of organisms constitute :
(*a*) Colony (*b*) Genus
(*c*) Community (*d*) Species

272. Ecology is study of relationships of
(*a*) Members of a family
(*b*) Man and environment
(*c*) Organisms and environment
(*d*) Soil and water

273. Competition is severe in a population that has a distribution :
(*a*) Irregular (*b*) Uniform
(*c*) Random (*d*) Non-random

274. Information about birth rate, death rate, sex ratio, age distribution, etc. of a population is obtained from :
(*a*) Mortality table (*b*) Life table
(*c*) Natality table (*d*) Both *(a)* and *(c)*

275. Which is correct about human races?
(*a*) All races can interbreed but most will produce infertile young ones
(*b*) All races can interbreed and produce fertile offspring
(*c*) Different races cannot interbreed
(*d*) Some human races can interbreed

276. Which is correct?
(*a*) Honey Bees communicate among themselves by secreting pheromones
(*b*) Last succession in series of biotic succession is called a sere
(*c*) Number of individuals of particular species present in a unit area at a given time is known as population size
(*d*) Home range of members of a species has larger area than that of territory

277. Sound of Crickets and Cicadas is :
(*a*) Warning call
(*b*) Mating call
(*c*) Circadian rhythm
(*d*) Circannual rhythm

278. The aggregate of processes that determine the size and composition of any population is known as :
(*a*) Population dynamics
(*b*) Population dispersal
(*c*) Population explosion
(*d*) Population density

279. The abundance of a species population within its habitat is called :
(*a*) Absolute density (*b*) Regional density
(*c*) Relative density (*d*) Niche density

280. Synecology is study of :
(*a*) Human environment of a place
(*b*) Biotic environment of a place
(*c*) Abiotic component of a place
(*d*) Biotic community in relation to environment of a place

281. In a population, rate of addition of new members is higher than the rate of individuals lost. It shows :
(*a*) Zero population growth
(*b*) Declined growth
(*c*) Exponential growth
(*d*) None of the above

282. For success of an animal population, the most important factor is ?
(*a*) Adaptability
(*b*) Natality
(*c*) Unlimited food
(*d*) Inter-specific activity

283. What constitutes the most important boundary between different species?
(*a*) Territory
(*b*) Morphology
(*c*) Reproductive isolation
(*d*) Mode of nutrition

284. Offspring of a stallion and janet is called :
(*a*) Stajon (*b*) Hinny
(*c*) Mule (*d*) Mare

285. Population density is expressed by :
(*a*) $D = N + S$ (*b*) $D = N \times S$
(*c*) $D = N \div S$ (*d*) $D = N - S$

286. Fingers and legs are shorter in colder regions. It is :
(*a*) Jorden's rule (*b*) Lindeman's rule
(*c*) Allen's rule (*d*) Gloger's rule

287. The study of interactions of an individual organism or a single species with the living and non-living component of its environment is :
(*a*) autoecology (*b*) autoecious
(*c*) autogamy (*d*) autonomy.

288. Ecological studies of plants were first started by :
(*a*) Warming (*b*) Daubenmire
(*c*) Good (*d*) Raunikiaer.

289. Synecology refers to the ecological study of:
(*a*) a population of species growing together
(*b*) animals
(*c*) plants
(*d*) microbes

290. All the living organisms on earth constitute :
(*a*) Community (*b*) Biosphere
(*c*) Species (*d*) Biome

291. Individuals of the same species in a particular locality constitute :
(*a*) Population (*b*) Hydrosphere
(*c*) Flora (*d*) Fauna

292. Migration refers to :
(*a*) one way outward movement
(*b*) one way inward movement
(*c*) periodic departure and return
(*d*) death of individuals

293. Which of the following is an example of protocooperation?
(*a*) Echiuroid worm and small annelid
(*b*) *Sea anemone* and hermit crab
(*c*) Nitrogen fixing bacteria and leguminous plants
(*d*) Trichophyta in the gut of termite

294. Gametophyte and sporophyte stages of a fern plant should ecologically be considered as :
(*a*) Two distinct species
(*b*) Two stages of a species
(*c*) Two varieties of a species
(*d*) Two organisms of a colony

295. Which of the following is related with synecology?
(*a*) Same species
(*b*) Different species
(*c*) Both (*a*) and (*b*)
(*d*) None of the above

296. Competition is most severe in two :
(*a*) Species (*b*) Families
(*c*) Niche (*d*) Orders

297. Which of the following shows the polymorphism?
(*a*) *Carica papaya* (*b*) *Apis indica*
(*c*) Volvox (*d*) Both (*b*) and (*c*)

298. Cross fertilization in plants is a kind of :
(*a*) Competitive interaction
(*b*) Co-operative interaction
(*c*) Parental care
(*d*) All of the above

299. An interaction between two or more organisms when the resource necessary for them are limited, refers to :
(*a*) Co-operation (*b*) Competition
(*c*) Aggregation (*d*) Family formation

300. Sub groups of a population capable of inter breeding are called as :
(*a*) Sub population (*b*) Dummies
(*c*) Demes, (*d*) Biomes

301. In red deer, the herd is :
(*a*) Matriarchal
(*b*) Patriarchal
(*c*) Both (*a*) and (*b*)
(*d*) Not applicable

302. Biotic potential is counteracted by :
(*a*) Limitation of food supply
(*b*) Competition with other organisms
(*c*) Producer is the largest
(*d*) Both (*a*) and (*b*)

303. A population can grow exponentially :
(*a*) when food is the only limiting resource
(*b*) when first invading a suitable and previouly unoccupied habitat
(*c*) only if there is no predation
(*d*) only in the laboratory

304. Which of the following does not directly affect biotic potential?
(*a*) a female's age of first reproduction
(*b*) carrying capacity of the environment
(*c*) length of time a female is fertile
(*d*) None of these

305. A bird introduced from another country became a serious pest due to :
(*a*) Better adaptation to new area
(*b*) More sexual reproduction
(*c*) Better nesting habitats
(*d*) Absence of natural competition

306. An example of mutualism is :
(*a*) *Riccia* (*b*) *Selaginella*
(*c*) Lichen (*d*) *Spirogyra*

307. Which take part in symbosis of lichen?
(*a*) Alga-Fungus
(*b*) Alga-Alga
(*c*) Fungus-Fungus
(*d*) Fungus-Gymnosperm

308. Nature of climax community depends upon :
(*a*) Water (*b*) Temperature
(*c*) Soil fertility (*d*) Climate

309. Succession showing changes in communities at a place is called :
(*a*) Geographical succession
(*b*) Biotic succession
(*c*) Physiographic succession
(*d*) Climatic succession

310. The association between ants and some members of family rubiaceae is :
(*a*) Ornithophily (*b*) Entomophily
(*c*) Myrmecophily (*d*) Anemophily

311. Plants growing on sandy soils are :
(*a*) Oxylophytes (*b*) Psammophytes
(*c*) Psychrophytes (*d*) Lithophytes

312. Deserts can be converted into green land by :
(*a*) Tropical trees (*b*) Oxylophytes
(*c*) Halophytes (*d*) Psammophytes

313. Which is not a primary coloniser?
(*a*) Viruses (*b*) Lichens
(*c*) Blue-Green Algae (*d*) Mosses

314. Which of the following is wrong?
(*a*) Lichen, an association of fungus and alga, is an example of mutualism
(*b*) Epiphytes, using other plants for support only and not for water or food, show commensalism
(*c*) Sea Anemone and Hermit Crab association is an example of protocooperation
(*d*) Mutualism, protocooperation and commensalism cannot be included under symbiosis

315. If green plants are removed from an aquarium, the fishes will :
(*a*) Die
(*b*) Increase in number
(*c*) Decrease in size
(*d*) Not be affected

316. Plants obtaining nourishment from other plants by haustoria are :
(*a*) Epiphytes (*b*) Parasites
(*c*) Xerophytes (*d*) Halophytes

317. Hyperparasite is parasite which :
(*a*) Kills its host
(*b*) Completes life cycle in one host
(*c*) Uses host machinery for reproduction
(*d*) None of the above

318. Fungal association of roots of higher plants in mycorrhiza is :
(*a*) Parasitism (*b*) Hyperparasitism
(*c*) Mutualism (*d*) Commensalism

319. Which is not characteristic of intestinal symbionts?
(*a*) Feeding one extra food of host
(*b*) Providing vitamins to host
(*c*) Anaerobic respiration
(*d*) Aerobic respiration

320. Ecological succession on sand is :
(*a*) Psammosere (*b*) Xerosere
(*c*) Halosere (*d*) Hydrosere

321. A successful parasite is the one which :
(*a*) Grows rapidly
(*b*) Reproduces fast
(*c*) Sticks to host for long
(*d*) Makes minimum demands from its host

322. Plants growing on sandstone are :
(*a*) Psammophytes (*b*) Oxylophytes
(*c*) Lithophytes (*d*) Phanerophytes

323. Organisms inhabiting a common environment belong to the same :
(*a*) Species (*b*) Genus
(*c*) Population (*d*) Community

324. A biotic community is an assemblage of :
(*a*) food web
(*b*) food chain
(*c*) closely related species
(*d*) interacting populations

325. A community is not able to survive without :
(*a*) predator
(*b*) non-living components
(*c*) parasites
(*d*) decomposers

326. Which of the following term is used for the "study of plant community?
(*a*) Phytology
(*b*) Ecosystem
(*c*) Phytosociology
(*d*) Population ecology

327. When the vegetation of any region reaches climatic climax, it is :
(*a*) Hydrophytic (*b*) Xerophytic
(*c*) Lithophytic (*d*) Mesophytic

328. Primary succession starts with :
(*a*) Lichens (*b*) Trees
(*c*) Herbs (*d*) Animals

329. In a biotic community, the most important factor for survival of an animals is :
(*a*) green food (*b*) day length
(*c*) predator (*d*) soil moisture

330. The basic unit in ecological studies is population. The sum of all the populations of the same kind of organism form:
(*a*) Community (*b*) Species
(*c*) Colony (*d*) Genus

331. Primary succession refers to the development of communities on a :
(*a*) newly exposed habitat with no record of earlier vegetation
(*b*) pond freshly filled with water after a dry phase
(*c*) forest clearing after devastating fire
(*d*) freshly cleared crop field

332. The first plants to appear on a badly burnt forest area will most probably be :
(*a*) Mosses (*b*) Liverworts
(*c*) Ferns (*d*) Grasses

333. The quills of porcupine are an example of :
(*a*) avoiding predation by defence
(*b*) avoiding predation by escape
(*c*) a chemical deterrent to escape
(*d*) mimicry

334. An advantage of being a herbivore that feeds only on one or a few related plant species is :
(*a*) only a few detoxifying enzymes are needed
(*b*) it is easy to obtain a well rounded diet
(*c*) it is easy to find enough food
(*d*) there will be no other herbivore competing for food source

335. A leaf adapted to a warm dry climate is :
(*a*) large and thin (*b*) small and thin
(*c*) large and thick (*d*) small and thick

336. An insect survives the cold of winter in a dormant stage by converting its glycogen to :
(*a*) ATP (*b*) Alcohol
(*c*) Lactic acid (*d*) Brown fat

337. A community with no living green plant is :
(*a*) rocky shore
(*b*) plankton
(*c*) a mud flat
(*d*) the deep ocean floor

338. It is a flock of sheep what is it of lions?
(*a*) Troop (*b*) Flock
(*c*) Flight (*d*) Herd

339. In which type of community, the number of species per unit area will be more :
(*a*) Temperate forest
(*b*) Deciduous forest
(*c*) Tropical rain forest
(*d*) Taiga forest

340. Physical space occupied by an organism (and also, its functional role in a community) is called :
(*a*) Niche (*b*) Microhabitat
(*c*) Macrohabitat (*d*) Habitat

341. Animals– Cockroaches scorpions, ants, lizards, mice–which share their abode are called :
(*a*) Opportunists (*b*) Inquilines
(*c*) Domesticants (*d*) Households

342. Generally succession leads to a climax community composed of :
(*a*) Grasses (*b*) Shrubs
(*c*) Herbaceous flora (*d*) Trees

343. The effect of interspecific competition on niches to make them :
(*a*) smaller (*b*) larger
(*c*) change location (*d*) more triangular

344. The most effective defences of plants against the herbivores are :
(*a*) Morphological (*b*) Temporal
(*c*) Chemical (*d*) Developmental

345. Population of an area tends to increase when :
(*a*) Reproductivity decreases
(*b*) Immigration increases
(*c*) Emigration occurs
(*d*) Predation increases

346. Density of a population (D) is :

(*a*) $D = \frac{S(size)}{W(weight)}$ (*b*) $D = \frac{S(space)}{N(Number)}$

(*c*) $D = \frac{N(number)}{S(space)}$ (*d*) None of the above

347. A force that acts against maximum population growth is :
(*a*) Population pressure
(*b*) Carrying capacity
(*c*) Saturation point
(*d*) Environment resistance

348. Which one is the famous plant ecologist of India?
(*a*) Charles Darwin
(*b*) Ramdeva Misra
(*c*) Birbal Sahani
(*d*) Jagdish Chandra Bose

349. After exponential increase, population becomes stagnant. The growth curve is :
(*a*) J-shaped (*b*) S-shaped
(*c*) Fluctuating (*d*) Circular

350. Allopatric speciation is caused by :
(*a*) Temporal isolation
(*b*) Adaptive radiation
(*c*) Geographic isolation
(*d*) Reproductive isolation

351. Percentage ratio of natality over mortality is :
(*a*) Population dynamics
(*b*) Vital index
(*c*) Population density
(*d*) Total count

352. Lichens are normally grow in cities :
(*a*) Because of absence of the right type of algae and fungi
(*b*) Because of lack of moisture
(*c*) Because of air pollution
(*d*) Because natural habitat is missing

353. Primary productivity of ecosystem refers to :
(*a*) increase in primary consumers
(*b*) net production of primary producers
(*c*) CO_2 fixation of organic carbon
(*d*) increase in mortality of primary producers

354. The individuals in the uppermost ring pyramid represent the one with :
(*a*) maximum number
(*b*) maximum biomass
(*c*) the ultimate consumer in the chain
(*d*) minimum biomass

355. Which of the following is a temporary parasite?
(*a*) Glochidium larva
(*b*) Tapeworm
(*c*) *Entamoeba histolytica*
(*d*) *Entamoeba gingivalis*

356. An association of a small fish (*Fierasfer*) inhabiting in the cloaca of sea cucumber is an example of :
(*a*) amensalism (*b*) parasitism
(*c*) mutualism (*d*) commensalism

357. The animals which preys the other living species is known as :
(*a*) predator
(*b*) canabalistic
(*c*) primary consumer
(*d*) parasite

358. An association of different interrelated populations belonging to different species in common environment which can survive in nature is called :
(*a*) Biotic community (*b*) Population
(*c*) Herd (*d*) Family

359. A direct food relation between two species of animals in which one animal kills and feed on another is referred to as :

(*a*) Predation (*b*) Parasitism
(*c*) Symbiosis (*d*) Scavenging

360. An association of two species where one is benefitted and other remains unaffected or unharmed, it is called :
(*a*) Symbiosis (*b*) Parasitism
(*c*) Predation (*d*) Commensalism

361. An association of two species of organisms where both the partners derive benefit from each other is called :
(*a*) Mutualism (*b*) Commensalism
(*c*) Competition (*d*) Parasitism

362. An association between a sea anemone *Adamsia*, and a hermit crab living in a gastropod shell is :
(*a*) Protocooperation (*b*) Commensalism
(*c*) Mutualism (*d*) Amensalism

363. The ecological niche of an organism denotes :
(*a*) habitat of the organism
(*b*) on whom the organism feeds
(*c*) the status of an organism with in a particular community
(*d*) all of the above

364. The transition zone where who different types of communities meet is called :
(*a*) Ecotype (*b*) Ecoline
(*c*) Ecotone (*d*) ecosystem

365. The conversion of a lake to a terrestrial community is a form of :
(*a*) Primary succession
(*b*) Secondary succession
(*c*) Late secondary succession
(*d*) None of the above

366. An ecological community is an assemblage of :
(*a*) Food webs
(*b*) Food chains
(*c*) Closely related species
(*d*) Interacting population

367. Which of the following is a negative interaction between the populations?
(*a*) Symbiosis (*b*) Mutualism
(*c*) Parasitism (*d*) Commensalism

368. One of the following relationship is useful to one organism and of no significance to other :
(*a*) Commensalism (*b*) Parasitism
(*c*) Mutualism (*d*) Amensalism

369. Plants growing well in hill crevices are :
(*a*) Lithophytes (*b*) Ermophytes
(*c*) Chasmophytes (*d*) Psammophytes

370. A community is :
(*a*) Autotrophs and heterotrophs
(*b*) Collection of plants and animals
(*c*) Organisms living in a habitat
(*d*) Web of life

371. Plants which are attached to stones and rocks :
(*a*) Aerophytes (*b*) Psammophytes
(*c*) Halophytes (*d*) Lithophytes

372. What could be the meeting point of biological and ecological hierarchies?
(*a*) Organisms (*b*) Population
(*c*) Family (*d*) Genus

373. The sum of the population of the same kind constitutes a :
(*a*) Species (*b*) Genus
(*c*) Colony (*d*) Community

374. The philosophy behind the existence of a community is :
(*a*) Interaction
(*b*) Co-existence
(*c*) Helotism
(*d*) Dominance by some

375. Last stage of plant suession is :
(*a*) Ecotype
(*b*) Seral community
(*c*) Climax community
(*d*) Ecotone

376. Types of interaction that occur in predation and parasitism are :
(*a*) +, + (*b*) –, –
(*c*) +, 0 (*d*) +, –

377. Relationship between two organisms in which one obtains some benefit at the cost of other is :
(*a*) Parasitism (*b*) Predation
(*c*) Symbiosis (*d*) Scavenging

378. A protective device in a community is :
(*a*) Commensalism (*b*) Mimicry
(*c*) Parasitism (*d*) Competition

379. Mutualism occurs between :
(*a*) Butterfly and flower
(*b*) *Escherichia coli* and man
(*c*) Zoochlorellae and *Hydra*
(*d*) Hermit Crab and Sea Anemone

380. According to the species equilibrium theory, smaller is islands have fewer species because they have :
(*a*) high rate of extinction
(*b*) lower rate of colonization
(*c*) a smaller species pool to draw from
(*d*) lower birth rates

381. Competition between individuals of the species is called :
(*a*) interspecific (*b*) intraspecific
(*c*) feedback (*d*) all of the above

382. Which of the following levels of organisation emphasizes the structural aspects in terms of relation and requirement of organisms ?
(*a*) Autecological level
(*b*) Synecological level
(*c*) Both (*a*) and (*b*)
(*d*) None of the above

383. Synecology is study of :
(*a*) biosphere
(*b*) individuals
(*c*) environment
(*d*) community in relation to environment

384. The leaves are absent in the xerophyte :
(*a*) *Calotropis procera*
(*b*) *Zizyphus jujuba*
(*c*) *Acaçia nilotica*
(*d*) *Capparis aphylla*

385. Which of the following feature is found in xerophytes?
(*a*) Equally developed palisade and spongy parenchyma
(*b*) Multistratose epidermis
(*c*) Non-functional stomata
(*d*) None of these

386. Halophytes growing on mud are called as :
(*a*) pelophilous (*b*) heliophilous
(*c*) psammophilous (*d*) lithophilous

387. Euhalophytes grow where the concentration of NaCl ranges :4
(*a*) Between 0.1 – 0.5%
(*b*) Between 0.01 – 0.1 %
(*c*) Above 1.0%
(*d*) Between 0.5 – 1.0%

388. The product arising as a result of geographical response of an ecospecies to a particular habitat is the definition of :
(*a*) ecotype (*b*) ecad
(*c*) acclimatisation (*d*) ecospecies

389. Members of a biological species are potentially able to :
(*a*) introgress
(*b*) express all the same genes
(*c*) interbreed
(*d*) All of the above

390. Which of the following niches is concerned with the trophic position of an organism?
(*a*) Multifactor niche
(*b*) Spatiat niche
(*c*) Habitat niche
(*d*) Trophic niche

391. Plants growing on rocks are called as :
(*a*) psychrophytes (*b*) lithophytes
(*c*) halophytes (*d*) sciophytes

392. Plants growing on cold soil are called as :
(*a*) oxylophytes (*b*) sciophytes
(*c*) psammophytes (*d*) psychrophytes

393. Mark the free floating hydrophyte :
(*a*) *Sagittaria* (*b*) *Typha*
(*c*) *Najas* (*d*) *Spirodela*

394. Mark the rooted submerged hydrophyte :
(*a*) *Ranunculus* (*b*) *Najas*
(*c*) *Potamogeton* (*d*) None of these

395. The mesophytes are characterised by :
(*a*) uniform mesophyll
(*b*) absence of cuticle
(*c*) well developed root-shoot systems
(*d*) All of these

396. Mark the true xerophyte :
(*a*) *Capparis aphylla*
(*b*) *Solanum xanthocarpum*
(*c*) *Euphorbia milli*
(*d*) All of the above

397. The species equilibrium theory of R.H. Mac Arthur and E.O. Wilson predicts a dynamic equilibrium of species because :
(*a*) the number of species changes through time
(*b*) the number of species changes from place to place
(*c*) there is regular turnover of species in a community
(*d*) succession is always taking place

398. When two competing species undergo niche shifts, and the shifts are accompanied by changes in morphologies, the morphological changes are called :
(*a*) convergent evolution
(*b*) geographic displacements
(*c*) divergent speciation
(*d*) character displacements

399. The American ecologist R.H. MacArthur observed in 1958, that five species of similar warblers coexist on spruce trees because they :
(*a*) eat different kinds of insects
(*b*) forage in different places
(*c*) are kept below their carrying capacities by predators
(*d*) cooperate in their foraging efforts

400. According to the species equilibrium theory, islands that are farther from a mainland have fewer species because they have :
(*a*) a smaller species pool to draw from
(*b*) higher rates of extinction
(*c*) lower rates of colonization
(*d*) lower carrying capacities

401. Origin of human society is the result of :
(*a*) Biological evolution
(*b*) Psychological evolution
(*c*) Retrogressive evolution
(*d*) More of psychological evolution and less of biological evolution

402. The dominant individual in a herd is :
(*a*) always a female (*b*) always a male
(*c*) usually a male (*d*) usually a female

403. Hinny is derived from :
(*a*) male donkey and mare
(*b*) lion and tigress
(*c*) tiger and lioness
(*d*) stallion and female donkey

404. Which of the following leads a solitary life?
(*a*) Swan
(*b*) Man
(*c*) Spider and Hamster
(*d*) None of these

405. Tigon is produced by :
(*a*) tiger and lioness
(*b*) tigress and lion
(*c*) lion and female leopard
(*d*) None of the above

406. Matriarchy is shown by :
(*a*) Beer (*b*) Zebra
(*c*) Monkey (*d*) African elephant

407. Patriarchy is exhibited by :
(*a*) Red deer (*b*) Zebra
(*c*) Antelope (*d*) Both (*a*) and (*c*)

408. When a tiger attacks cheetals, the stag with best antlers is surrounded by other individuals to protect it. It is an example of :
(*a*) cooperation (*b*) group formation
(*c*) altruism (*d*) herding

409. Study of interrelationship between living organisms and their environment is called :
(*a*) Phytosociology (*b*) Phytogeography
(*c*) Ecology (*d*) Ecosystem

410. Plants and animals living in a given area constitute :
(*a*) population (*b*) ecosystem
(*c*) community (*d*) plankton

411. Carrrying capacity of an environment is :
(*a*) birth rate
(*b*) death rate
(*c*) limiting resources
(*d*) population growth rate

412. It there is a large gap between birth rate and death rate in Haryana we can infer that Haryana would tend to have :
(*a*) more of old men
(*b*) more school-going children
(*c*) low rate of fertility
(*d*) low dependency ratio

413. Demography is the study ofstatics that deals with :
(*a*) geography
(*b*) population growth
(*c*) local concentration of individuals
(*d*) family pedigrees

414. Which of the following is monogamous :
(*a*) Seal
(*b*) Deer
(*c*) Woodpecker
(*d*) Swan

415. Which of the following is polygamous?
(*a*) Rat (*b*) Wolf
(*c*) Deer (*d*) Fox

416. The human population first began to grow exponentially at the time of :
(*a*) tool using revolution
(*b*) agricultural revolution
(*c*) industrial revolution
(*d*) first World War

417. About how many people starve to death each day?
(*a*) 1000 (*b*) 10,000
(*c*) 70,000 (*d*) 600,000

ANSWERS

1	**2**	**3**	**4**	**5**	**6**	**7**	**8**	**9**	**10**
(*d*)	(*a*)	(*d*)	(*c*)	(*c*)	(*d*)	(*b*)	(*c*)	(*d*)	(*d*)
11	**12**	**13**	**14**	**15**	**16**	**17**	**18**	**19**	**20**
(*d*)	(*a*)	(*c*)	(*b*)	(*b*)	(*a*)	(*d*)	(*d*)	(*b*)	(*c*)
21	**22**	**23**	**24**	**25**	**26**	**27**	**28**	**29**	**30**
(*d*)	(*d*)	(*b*)	(*c*)	(*c*)	(*c*)	(*b*)	(*d*)	(*a*)	(*c*)
31	**32**	**33**	**34**	**35**	**36**	**37**	**38**	**39**	**40**
(*d*)	(*d*)	(*c*)	(*d*)	(*c*)	(*c*)	(*a*)	(*b*)	(*b*)	(*b*)
41	**42**	**43**	**44**	**45**	**46**	**47**	**48**	**49**	**50**
(*d*)	(*c*)	(*b*)	(*a*)	(*b*)	(*d*)	(*c*)	(*d*)	(*c*)	(*a*)
51	**52**	**53**	**54**	**55**	**56**	**57**	**58**	**59**	**60**
(*d*)	(*c*)	(*d*)	(*b*)	(*a*)	(*d*)	(*a*)	(*a*)	(*b*)	(*c*)
61	**62**	**63**	**64**	**65**	**66**	**67**	**68**	**69**	**70**
(*a*)	(*a*)	(*d*)	(*d*)	(*b*)	(*c*)	(*a*)	(*a*)	(*d*)	(*a*)
71	**72**	**73**	**74**	**75**	**76**	**77**	**78**	**79**	**80**
(*c*)	(*c*)	(*a*)	(*d*)	(*b*)	(*c*)	(*b*)	(*d*)	(*a*)	(*d*)
81	**82**	**83**	**84**	**85**	**86**	**87**	**88**	**89**	**90**
(*c*)	(*d*)	(*d*)	(*a*)	(*d*)	(*d*)	(*c*)	(*c*)	(*d*)	(*d*)
91	**92**	**93**	**94**	**95**	**96**	**97**	**98**	**99**	**100**
(*d*)	(*a*)	(*b*)	(*c*)	(*b*)	(*b*)	(*d*)	(*c*)	(*c*)	(*a*)
101	**102**	**103**	**104**	**105**	**106**	**107**	**108**	**109**	**110**
(*a*)	(*a*)	(*c*)	(*d*)	(*d*)	(*b*)	(*c*)	(*b*)	(*c*)	(*d*)
111	**112**	**113**	**114**	**115**	**116**	**117**	**118**	**119**	**120**
(*a*)	(*c*)	(*d*)	(*a*)	(*b*)	(*c*)	(*a*)	(*a*)	(*c*)	(*b*)

121	**122**	**123**	**124**	**125**	**126**	**127**	**128**	**129**	**130**
(*a*)	(*c*)	(*d*)	(*c*)	(*b*)	(*d*)	(*a*)	(*c*)	(*a*)	(*a*)
131	**132**	**133**	**134**	**135**	**136**	**137**	**138**	**139**	**140**
(*a*)	(*c*)	(*b*)	(*d*)	(*a*)	(*a*)	(*c*)	(*a*)	(*c*)	(*b*)
141	**142**	**143**	**144**	**145**	**146**	**147**	**148**	**149**	**150**
(*d*)	(*c*)	(*c*)	(*c*)	(*b*)	(*b*)	(*b*)	(*c*)	(*c*)	(*d*)
151	**152**	**153**	**154**	**155**	**156**	**157**	**158**	**159**	**160**
(*c*)	(*b*)	(*c*)	(*a*)	(*b*)	(*d*)	(*c*)	(*a*)	(*b*)	(*a*)
161	**162**	**163**	**164**	**165**	**166**	**167**	**168**	**169**	**170**
(*c*)	(*a*)	(*b*)	(*c*)	(*a*)	(*c*)	(*a*)	(*c*)	(*b*)	(*b*)
171	**172**	**173**	**174**	**175**	**176**	**177**	**178**	**179**	**180**
(*c*)	(*d*)	(*b*)	(*b*)	(*c*)	(*a*)	(*a*)	(*c*)	(*a*)	(*d*)
181	**182**	**183**	**184**	**185**	**186**	**187**	**188**	**189**	**190**
(*c*)	(*c*)	(*b*)	(*c*)	(*c*)	(*d*)	(*d*)	(*a*)	(*d*)	(*d*)
191	**192**	**193**	**194**	**195**	**196**	**197**	**198**	**199**	**200**
(*a*)	(*b*)	(*b*)	(*b*)	(*c*)	(*b*)	(*b*)	(*b*)	(*d*)	(*a*)
201	**202**	**203**	**204**	**205**	**206**	**207**	**208**	**209**	**210**
(*a*)	(*b*)	(*a*)	(*b*)	(*d*)	(*a*)	(*c*)	(*a*)	(*d*)	(*a*)
211	**212**	**213**	**214**	**215**	**216**	**217**	**218**	**219**	**220**
(*c*)	(*b*)	(*b*)	(*a*)	(*b*)	(*d*)	(*b*)	(*c*)	(*c*)	(*a*)
221	**222**	**223**	**224**	**225**	**226**	**227**	**228**	**229**	**230**
(*b*)	(*b*)	(*a*)	(*c*)	(*c*)	(*c*)	(*d*)	(*a*)	(*c*)	(*b*)
231	**232**	**233**	**234**	**235**	**236**	**237**	**238**	**239**	**240**
(*a*)	(*b*)	(*a*)	(*b*)	(*c*)	(*a*)	(*a*)	(*c*)	(*a*)	(*d*)
241	**242**	**243**	**244**	**245**	**246**	**247**	**248**	**249**	**250**
(*c*)	(*c*)	(*c*)	(*d*)	(*a*)	(*b*)	(*b*)	(*b*)	(*b*)	(*b*)
251	**252**	**253**	**254**	**255**	**256**	**257**	**258**	**259**	**260**
(*a*)	(*c*)	(*a*)	(*a*)	(*c*)	(*b*)	(*a*)	(*b*)	(*a*)	(*b*)
261	**262**	**263**	**264**	**265**	**266**	**267**	**268**	**269**	**270**
(*c*)	(*d*)	(*c*)	(*b*)	(*d*)	(*d*)	(*d*)	(*a*)	(*c*)	(*a*)
271	**272**	**273**	**274**	**275**	**276**	**277**	**278**	**279**	**280**
(*d*)	(*c*)	(*a*)	(*b*)	(*b*)	(*d*)	(*b*)	(*a*)	(*d*)	(*d*)
281	**282**	**283**	**284**	**285**	**286**	**287**	**288**	**289**	**290**
(*a*)	(*b*)	(*c*)	(*b*)	(*c*)	(*c*)	(*a*)	(*a*)	(*b*)	(*b*)
291	**292**	**293**	**294**	**295**	**296**	**297**	**298**	**299**	**300**
(*a*)	(*c*)	(*b*)	(*b*)	(*b*)	(*a*)	(*d*)	(*b*)	(*b*)	(*c*)
301	**302**	**303**	**304**	**305**	**306**	**307**	**308**	**309**	**310**
(*a*)	(*a*)	(*b*)	(*b*)	(*d*)	(*c*)	(*a*)	(*d*)	(*b*)	(*c*)
311	**312**	**313**	**314**	**315**	**316**	**317**	**318**	**319**	**320**
(*b*)	(*d*)	(*a*)	(*d*)	(*a*)	(*b*)	(*d*)	(*c*)	(*d*)	(*a*)
321	**322**	**323**	**324**	**325**	**326**	**327**	**328**	**329**	**330**
(*d*)	(*c*)	(*d*)	(*d*)	(*b*)	(*c*)	(*d*)	(*a*)	(*a*)	(*b*)

331	332	333	334	335	336	337	338	339	340
(*a*)	(*d*)	(*a*)	(*a*)	(*d*)	(*b*)	(*d*)	(*d*)	(*c*)	(*a*)
341	**342**	**343**	**344**	**345**	**346**	**347**	**348**	**349**	**350**
(*b*)	(*d*)	(*a*)	(*a*)	(*d*)	(*c*)	(*d*)	(*b*)	(*c*)	(*c*)
351	**352**	**353**	**354**	**355**	**356**	**357**	**358**	**359**	**360**
(*b*)	(*c*)	(*c*)	(*c*)	(*a*)	(*d*)	(*a*)	(*a*)	(*a*)	(*d*)
361	**362**	**363**	**364**	**365**	**366**	**367**	**368**	**369**	**370**
(*a*)	(*b*)	(*c*)	(*c*)	(*a*)	(*d*)	(*c*)	(*a*)	(*c*)	(*c*)
371	**372**	**373**	**374**	**375**	**376**	**377**	**378**	**379**	**380**
(*d*)	(*a*)	(*a*)	(*a*)	(*c*)	(*d*)	(*a*)	(*b*)	(*c*)	(*a*)
381	**382**	**383**	**384**	**385**	**386**	**387**	**388**	**389**	**390**
(*b*)	(*a*)	(*d*)	(*d*)	(*b*)	(*a*)	(*c*)	(*a*)	(*c*)	(*d*)
391	**392**	**393**	**394**	**395**	**396**	**397**	**398**	**399**	**400**
(*b*)	(*d*)	(*d*)	(*c*)	(*c*)	(*a*)	(*c*)	(*d*)	(*b*)	(*c*)
401	**402**	**403**	**404**	**405**	**406**	**407**	**408**	**409**	**410**
(*d*)	(*d*)	(*d*)	(*c*)	(*a*)	(*d*)	(*d*)	(*c*)	(*c*)	(*c*)
411	**412**	**413**	**414**	**415**	**416**	**417**			
(*c*)	(*a*)	(*b*)	(*d*)	(*c*)	(*b*)	(*c*)			

3

BIOSPHERE

1. Concentration of green house gases is increasing due to :
(*a*) deforestation
(*b*) increased use of refrigerators
(*c*) increased combustion of coal and petroleum and increase in CO_2 concentration
(*d*) All of the above

2. Climate of world is threatened by :
(*a*) increasing amount of CO_2
(*b*) increasing amount of O_2
(*c*) increasing amount O_3
(*d*) None of the above

3. Carbon dioxide is called green house gas because :
(*a*) it is transparent to solar radiation and opaque to infrared rays
(*b*) it is strong absorbers of infrared radiations
(*c*) None of the above
(*d*) Both (*a*) and (*b*)

4. Which of the following is being developed as an alternative of CFCs in refrigeration to protect ozone layer of atmosphere?
(*a*) Ethylene (*b*) Isobutane
(*c*) Benzene (*d*) Hydrogen

5. Halons are constituents of :
(*a*) Aerosols
(*b*) Refrigerants
(*c*) Fire extinguishers
(*d*) Pesticides

6. Which one has the least green house effect?
(*a*) CO_2 (*b*) Nitrous oxide
(*c*) Water vapours (*d*) Ozone

7. Which green house gas other than methane is produced from agricultural fields?
(*a*) Nitrous oxide (*b*) Ammonia
(*c*) SO_2 (*d*) None of these

8. UV rays from sunlight causes a reaction that produces :
(*a*) Ozone (*b*) SO_2
(*c*) CO (*d*) CH_4

9. Ozone protect earth :
(*a*) by filtering out incoming UV rays
(*b*) from heat of sun responsible for global warming
(*c*) by killing microbes in exosphere
(*d*) all above stataments are wrong as ozone is pollutant

10. The natural sink of stratospheric ozone layer is :
(*a*) SO_4
(*b*) HCFs
(*c*) freons
(*d*) sulphur flux of oceans

11. Choose the correct discoverers and their discoveries :

A.	Green House effect	1.	Beijerinck
B.	Nitorgen fixation	2.	Winogradsky
C.	*Bacillus radicicola* and Nodule formation	3.	*Tyndall*

Codes :

	A	B	C
(*a*)	3	2	1
(*b*)	2	1	3
(*c*)	1	2	3
(*d*)	2	3	2

12. Ozone layer is disrupted by :
(*a*) Automobile exhausts
(*b*) Factories
(*c*) Supersonic jets
(*d*) All of these

13. The major source of methane that cause global warming is :
(*a*) Wheat fields and marshes
(*b*) Rice/paddy fields, cattles and marshes
(*c*) Sugarcane plantation and buffaloes
(*d*) Fruit orchards

14. 'Ozone hole' refers to :
(*a*) reduction in the thickness of ozone layer in stratosphere
(*b*) reduction in ozone thickness in troposphere
(*c*) hole in the ozone layers in stratosphere
(*d*) increases concentration of ozone in troposphere

15. Which one is not dangerous for life?
(*a*) Bio-pollutants (*b*) Ozone layer
(*c*) Nuclear blast (*d*) Deforestation

16. Ozone hole in antarctic zone can be attributed to :
(*a*) Satellites
(*b*) Hydrofluorocarbons
(*c*) Chlorofluorocarbons
(*d*) Chlorinated hydrocarbons

17. Green House effect is caused by :
(*a*) CO_2 only
(*b*) CO_2, CO_2 vapours and CFC
(*c*) CH_4, N_2O and CO_2
(*d*) any gases which absorb the infrared heat reflected from earth

18. Biosphere is defined as :
(*a*) Part of the earth water and atmosphere which inhabits living organisms
(*b*) Part of the soil where animals and plants are found
(*c*) Atomosphere in which life exists
(*d*) None of the above

19. Biosphere consists of :
(*a*) Lithosphere (*b*) Atmosphere
(*c*) Hydrosphere (*d*) All of the above

20. Component of biosphere related with soil is :
(*a*) Lithosphere (*b*) Hydrosphere
(*c*) Atmosphere (*d*) None of the above

21. Phenomenon of rain, dew, snow *i.e.*, different forms of water coming to earth under force of gravity is called as :
(*a*) Geotropism (*b*) Climatic factors
(*c*) Precipitation (*d*) Calcification

22. Process of evapo-transpiration and precipitation is called :
(*a*) Carbon cycle
(*b*) Nitrogen cycle
(*c*) Hydrological cycle
(*d*) All of the above

23. Agents which make free atmospheric nitrogen available to plants are :
(*a*) Lightning
(*b*) Free living nitrogen fixing bacteria
(*c*) Symbiotic nitrogen fixing bacteria
(*d*) All of the above

24. Maintenance of soil fertility without addition of nutrition is due to :
(*a*) Floods
(*b*) Crop residue
(*c*) Favourable temperature
(*d*) Microbial activity

25. A logical sequence of carbon cycle is :
(*a*) Producer – Consumer – Decomposer
(*b*) Decomposer – Producer – Decomposer
(*c*) Consumer – Producer – Consumer
(*d*) Producer – Decomposer – Consumer

26. Rise of atmospheric temperature because of high concentration of carbon dioxide is known as :
(*a*) Green house effect
(*b*) Biomagnification
(*c*) Pollution
(*d*) Ecotone

27. Non biological nitrogen fixation is :
(*a*) Electrochemical and photochemical
(*b*) Rhizobial
(*c*) Cyanobacterial
(*d*) None of the above

28. Green-house gases are :
(*a*) Absorbers of long-wave radiations from earth

(*b*) Transparent to both solar radiations and long-wave radiations from earth
(*c*) Absorbers of solar radiations for warming the atmosphere of earth
(*d*) Transparent to emissions from earth for passage into outer space

29. Climate of the world is threatened by :
(*a*) Increasing concentration of atmospheric oxygen
(*b*) Decreasing amount of atmospheric oxygen
(*c*) Increasing amount of atmospheric carbon dioxide
(*d*) Decreasing amount of atmospheric carbon dioxide

30. Amount of carbon fixed annually through photosynthesis is :
(*a*) 4.6×10^{10} kg
(*b*) 7×10^{13} kg
(*c*) 7×10^{20} kg
(*d*) 4.6×10^{21} kg

31. In one year, one hectare of forest shall :
(*a*) Consume 10 tonnes of CO_2 and evolve 10 tonnes of O_2
(*b*) Consume 20 tonnes of CO_2 and evolve 10 tonnes of O_2
(*c*) Consume 30 tonnes of CO_2 and evolve 30 tonnes of O_2
(*d*) Consume 30 tonnes of CO_2 and evolve 10 tonnes of O_2

32. Biogeochemical cycles are also known as :
(*a*) Sedimentary cycles
(*b*) Gaseous cycles
(*c*) Material cycling
(*d*) Cycles of water

33. Earth is an :
(*a*) Open system
(*b*) Closed system
(*c*) Both (*a*) and (*b*)
(*d*) Neither (*a*) nor (*b*)

34. Source of energy in the biosphere is :
(*a*) Producer (*b*) Decomposer
(*c*) Sunlight (*d*) Heat of earth

35. *Pseudomonas* is an important component of nitrogen cycle. It is :
(*a*) Fixes elemental nitrogen
(*b*) Produces elemental nitrogen
(*c*) Transfers nitrogen
(*d*) Changes ammonium nitrogen to nitrate state

36. Water cycle is made up of two overlapping cycles :
(*a*) Ground water atmospheric cycles
(*b*) Surface water and atmospheric cycles
(*c*) Global and local cycles
(*d*) Oceanic and fresh water cycles

37. Sedimentary cycle having a small gaseous component is found in :
(*a*) Phosphorus (*b*) Nitrogen
(*c*) Carbon (*d*) Sulphur

38. Earth is protected from ultra-violet radiations by means of :
(*a*) Ozone layer (*b*) Nitrogen
(*c*) Oxygen (*d*) Carbon dioxide

39. Ozone layer occurs in :
(*a*) Ionosphere (*b*) Stratosphere
(*c*) Thermosphere (*d*) Troposphere

40. Maximum control of hydrological cycle is exerted by :
(*a*) Epiphytes (*b*) Forests
(*c*) Plankton (*d*) Grassland

41. Ecological cycle directly driven by sunlight is :
(*a*) Carbon (*b*) Phosphorus
(*c*) Hydrologic (*d*) Nitrogen

42. Biosphere is :
(*a*) Area occupied by living beings
(*b*) Plants of the world
(*c*) Plants of a particular area
(*d*) Special plants

43. Source of carbon to plants is :
(*a*) Carbon dioxide of carbonate rocks
(*b*) Fossil fuels
(*c*) Atmospheric carbon dioxide
(*d*) All of the above

44. Biogeochemical cycling refers to cycling of :
(*a*) Energy in the ecosystem
(*b*) Nutrient in the ecosystem

(*c*) Water
(*d*) Gases between plants and animals

45. Ecosystems obtain nitrogen from outside through the process of :
(*a*) Industrial fixation
(*b*) Electrochemical and photochemical fixation
(*c*) Biological fixation
(*d*) All of the above

46. Earth is an open system for :
(*a*) Minerals (*b*) Energy
(*c*) Gases (*d*) Water

47. Lithosphere is reservoir of :
(*a*) Carbon (*b*) Oxygen
(*c*) Phosphorus (*d*) Nitrogen

48. Amount of nitrogen fixed by nitrogen fixing organisms is :
(*a*) 70% (*b*) 30%
(*c*) 50% (*d*) 90%

49. Carbon is found in lithosphere as :
(*a*) Carbohydrate
(*b*) Carbonic acid
(*c*) Carbon
(*d*) Carbonate

50. Which has a sedimentary cycle :
(*a*) Nitrogen (*b*) Carbon
(*c*) Water (*d*) Sulphur

51. Gas being produced by paddy fields and involved in global warming is :
(*a*) Chlorine (*b*) Methane
(*c*) CO_2 (*d*) H_2S

52. Greem house effect is warming due to :
(*a*) Infra-red rays reaching earth
(*b*) Moisture layer in atmosphere
(*c*) Increase in temperature due to increase in carbon dioxide concentration of atmosphere
(*d*) Ozone layer of atmosphere

53. Green house effect is related to :
(*a*) Increased growth of green algae
(*b*) Global warming
(*c*) Cultivation of vegetable in the houses
(*d*) Development of terrace gardens

54. The inhabited thin part of earth and its atmosphere in which organisms live and interact together is called :
(*a*) Biome (*b*) Biosphere
(*c*) Ecotone (*d*) Biocoenosis

55. The term ecosphere for biosphere was used by :
(*a*) Odum (*b*) Cole
(*c*) Daubenmired (*d*) Raunkiaer

56. Belt on which life exists above and below the surface of earth is :
(*a*) Biome (*b*) Biosphere
(*c*) Ecosystem (*d*) Biotic belt

57. Biosphere is
(*a*) area of living organisms on earth surface
(*b*) area in which organisms intersect
(*c*) zone of living organisms in lithosphere (coil), hydrosphere water and atmosphere (air)
(*d*) All of the above

58. The term biosphere (living crust) was given by :
(*a*) Odum (*b*) Haeckel
(*c*) Vernadsky (*d*) Lingegren

59. Biome is :
(*a*) a part of earth and its atmosphere
(*b*) part of earth inhabited by organisms
(*c*) total fauna on earth
(*d*) communities interacting together

60. Biosphere extends from ocean bottom to mountain tops to a distance of :
(*a*) 7.5 km (*b*) 22.5 km
(*c*) 12 km (*d*) 75 km

61. Biome have :
(*a*) plant communities
(*b*) animal communities
(*c*) trees only
(*d*) (*a*) and (*b*)

62. Biome is a :
(*a*) community of plants
(*b*) community of animals
(*c*) small sized ecosystem
(*d*) large sized ecosystem

63. Source of energy in the biosphere is :
(*a*) producer (*b*) decomposer
(*c*) sun (*d*) heat of earth

64. Biosphere consists of interacting functional units called :
(*a*) Ecosystems (*b*) Populations
(*c*) Communities (*d*) Species

65. Which can occur in isolation without any interaction?
(*a*) Lithosphere
(*b*) Atmosphere
(*c*) Hydrosphere
(*d*) No one can live in isolation

66. What is not true of the biosphere?
(*a*) matter is used again and again
(*b*) energy is received from the sun
(*c*) matter is received from outside
(*d*) enegy dissipates as heat

67. All the ecosystems of world are called
(*a*) biosphere (*b*) ecosphere
(*c*) Both (*a*) and (*b*) (*d*) None of these

68. An environment dominated by man and used by man alone is called :
(*a*) Biosphere
(*b*) Oosphere
(*c*) Noosphere
(*d*) Man and Biosphere (MAB)

69. The strata zone of atmosphere near to earth with maximum density :
(*a*) Thermosphere (*b*) Stratosphere
(*c*) Mesosphere (*d*) Troposphere

70. Ionosphere which protect earth from cosmic rays, is a component of :
(*a*) thermosphere (*b*) mesosphere
(*c*) stratosphere (*d*) troposphere

71. Earth is protected from dangerous UV radiation by/which gas of atmosphere holds up UV rays :
(*a*) oxygen layer
(*b*) CO_2
(*c*) ozone layer
(*d*) photochemical smog layer

72. Composition of air remains unchanged :
(*a*) above height of 80 km
(*b*) below height of 60 km
(*c*) below height of 80 km
(*d*) None of the above

73. The peak concentration ozone above surface of earth is at :
(*a*) 23 km (*b*) 15 km
(*c*) 13 km (*d*) 30 km

74. Layer of ozone is present in :
(*a*) Stratosphere (*b*) Troposphere
(*c*) Thermosphere (*d*) Mesosphere

75. What is true for earth?
(*a*) Earth is an open system for energy as it receives energy
(*b*) Earth is a closed system as it does not take any new matter
(*c*) Both (*a*) and (*b*)
(*d*) Neither (*a*) nor (*b*)

76. Spaceship earth is an open as well as closed system. It is an open system with reference to :
(*a*) material
(*b*) energy
(*c*) gaseous cycles
(*d*) sedimentary cycles

77. Land forms__ __ part of earth surface.
(*a*) 30% (*b*) 36%
(*c*) 50% (*d*) 70%

78. Match of followings :

A.	Matter and energy	1. Environment
B.	Atmospheric vapour	2. Living crust
C.	Annual precipitation	3. 4.46×10^{20}
D.	Biosphere	4. λ 0.15 – 4μ
E	Solar radiation	5. 0.13×10^{20} G

Codes :

	A	B	C	D	E
(*a*)	1	2	3	4	5
(*b*)	1	5	3	2	4
(*c*)	2	1	3	4	5
(*d*)	2	3	5	1	4

79. Environment is controlled by :
(*a*) matter (*b*) energy
(*c*) both (*a*) and (*b*) (*d*) only (*b*) is correct

80. The environmental equilibrium is restored by :
(*a*) producers (*b*) decomposers
(*c*) consumers (*d*) top consumers

81. Biogeochemical cycles are also called :
(*a*) nutrient cycles
(*b*) cycles of matter
(*c*) both are correct
(*d*) only (*b*) is correct

82. Study of **Biogeochemical** cycles is called Biogeochemistry its father is vernadsky (= Winodgsky). It involves :
(*a*) cycling of energy
(*b*) cycling of gases
(*c*) cycling of nutrients
(*d*) cycling of water

83. Biogoechemical cycles are of :
(*a*) Two types (*b*) Three types
(*c*) Four types (*d*) Five types

84. In sedimentary cycles, the reserve pool is :
(*a*) air
(*b*) water
(*c*) lithosphere,
(*d*) lithosphere and atomosphere

85. Sedimentary cycle having a small gaseous component also is found in :
(*a*) 'P'cycle (*b*) 'S'cycle
(*c*) 'N'cycle (*d*) 'C'cycle

86. Which is involved in sedimentary cycle?
(*a*) C (*b*) N
(*c*) H (*d*) S

87. The reservoir pool for gaseous cycles of matter is :
(*a*) atmosphere (*b*) hydrosphere
(*c*) both (*a*) and (*b*) (*d*) lithosphere

88. Maximum oxygen comes from :
(*a*) phytoplanktons (*b*) grassland
(*c*) forests (*d*) herbs and shrubs

89. The reservoir pool of carbon is :
(*a*) air and water (*b*) fossil fuels
(*c*) rocks (*d*) All of these

90. For recycling of materials which one is most necessary?
(*a*) producers (*b*) consumers
(*c*) decomposers (*d*) None of the above

91. CO_2 content of atmosphere has incrèased in the last 150 years from :
(*a*) 25 to 35 ppm
(*b*) 270 to 340 ppm
(*c*) 0.027 to 0.34 ppm
(*d*) 0.2 to 0.3 ppm

92. Role of bacteria in carbon cycle (which predominently depend on sun energy) is :
(*a*) Photosynthesis
(*b*) Chromosynthesis
(*c*) Breakdown of organic compound
(*d*) Assimilation

93. A free living nitrogen fixing Cyanobacteria is :
(*a*) *Anabaena* (*b*) *Aulosira*
(*c*) *Azotobacter* (*d*) All of these

94. Phosphorus is mostly found in rocks in combination with :
(*a*) calcium (*b*) iron
(*c*) aluminium (*d*) All of these

95. Phosphorus cycle is :
(*a*) gaseous cycle
(*b*) perfect cycle
(*c*) imperfect cycle
(*d*) partly gaseous and partly sedimentary

96. In the phosphorus cycle, phosphate becomes available by weathering of rocks frist to :
(*a*) Consumers (*b*) Producers
(*c*) Decomposers (*d*) None of these

97. Which one of the following pairs is a sedimentary type of biogeochemical cycle?
(*a*) Phosphorus and Carbon dioxide
(*b*) Oxygen and Nitrogen
(*c*) Phosphorus and Nitrogen
(*d*) Phosphorus and Sulphur

98. A long term global cycle which is linked by water and in which sea floor rising play an important role is :
(*a*) water cycle
(*b*) carbon cycle
(*c*) phosphorus cycle
(*d*) carbon and nitrogen cycle

99. Phosphorus of ocean becomes available to land plants due to :
(*a*) sea birds
(*b*) deep sea activities
(*c*) ocean spray
(*d*) All of these

100. Volcano eruption disturbs :
(*a*) phosphorus cycle (*b*) nitrogen cycle
(*c*) carbon cycle (*d*) sulphur cycle

101. The largest reservoir of sulphur and phosphorus in biosphere is :
(*a*) atmosphere (*b*) ocean
(*c*) organism (*d*) rocks

102. Phosphorus cycles in the form of :
(*a*) HPO^{-3} (*b*) P_2 (gas)
(*c*) PO^{-3}_4 (*d*) $Al_2(PO_4)_3$

103. Which of the following changes food into usable energy?
(*a*) Phosphorus (*b*) Calcium
(*c*) Magnesium (*d*) Carbon

104. Match the following :

A.	sedimentary cycle	1.	gaseous cycle
B.	water	2.	soil
C.	atmospheric nitrogen fixation	3.	140-700 mg/m^2/year
D.	biological nitrogen fixation	4.	35 mg/m^2/year
E.	biogenetic nutrients	5.	essential exhaustible

Codes :

	A	B	C	D	E
(*a*)	2	1	4	3	5
(*b*)	2	5	3	4	1
(*c*)	2	5	3	4	1
(*d*)	2	1	5	4	3

105. How many *green house gases* exist?
(*a*) 2 (*b*) 4
(*c*) 3 (*d*) 6

106. Which gas contributes most to green house effect on earth?
(*a*) CO_2 (*b*) CH_2
(*c*) CFC (*d*) Freon

107. Heating of earth surface/global warming is due to :
(*a*) Air pollution
(*b*) Thermal pollution
(*c*) Land pollution
(*d*) Noise pollution

108. Green house gases include :
(*a*) CO_2, CFC, CH_4 and NO_2
(*b*) CO_2, O_2, N_2, NO_2 and NH_3
(*c*) CH_4, N_2, CO_2 and N_3
(*d*) CFC, CO_2, NH_3 and N_2

109. The circulation or cycling of elements in an ecosystem is known as :
(*a*) Geological cycling
(*b*) Geo-chemical cycling
(*c*) Bio-geochemical cycling
(*d*) Chemical cycling

110. The sphere of living matter found on the surface of earth comprises :
(*a*) Lithosphere (*b*) Hydrosphere
(*c*) Atmosphere (*d*) Biosphere

111. The term biosphere is used for a zone containing living beings :
(*a*) In lithosphere, hydrosphere and atomosphere
(*b*) In lithosphere and hydrosphere
(*c*) In hydrosphere
(*d*) On lithosphere

112. Biosphere is made of :
(*a*) Living beings and their remains
(*b*) Living beings + Lithosphere + Hydrosphere + Atmosphere
(*c*) Living beings + Lithosphere
(*d*) Living organisms + Lithosphere + Hydrosphere

113. Which is not a green house gas :
(*a*) Chlorofluorocarbon
(*b*) Methane
(*c*) Carbon dioxide
(*d*) Hydrogen

114. Which gas of the atmospheric holds up ultraviolet rays :
(*a*) O_2 (*b*) O_3
(*c*) N_2 (*d*) CO_2

115. Checking of re-radiating heat by atmospheric dust O_3, CO_2 and water vopours is :
(*a*) Ozone layer effect
(*b*) Solar effect
(*c*) Radioactive effect
(*d*) Green house effect

116. Liberation of H_2S/foul smell in water of tanks, pounds, etc. is due to :
(*a*) Anaerobiosis
(*b*) Aerobiosis
(*c*) Psammophytes
(*d*) Biological magnification

117. CO_2 and O_2 balance in atmosphere is due to :
(*a*) Photosynthesis (*b*) Respiration
(*c*) Leaf anatomy (*d*) Photorespiration

118. Biosphere is :
(*a*) A protected area
(*b*) Ecosystem
(*c*) In which individuals interact
(*d*) Earth crust

119. Fertiliser obtained from Sea Birds along the coast of Chile and Peru is :
(*a*) Guano (*b*) Bone meal
(*c*) Dung (*d*) Urea

120. Nitrogen fixation is :
(*a*) Nitrogen → Ammonia
(*b*) Nitrogen → Nitrates
(*c*) Nitrogen → Amino acid
(*d*) Both (*a*) and (*b*)

121. Burning of fossil fuels affects :
(*a*) nitrogen cycle (*b*) carbon cycle
(*c*) phosphorus cycle (*d*) water cycle

122. In carbon cycle, source of carbon to plants is :
(*a*) atmospheric CO_2
(*b*) carbonate rocks
(*c*) fossil fuels
(*d*) All of these

123. Water cycle is made up of 2 overlapping cycles. These are :
(*a*) ground H_2O and atmosphere H_2O cycle
(*b*) Surface H_2O and atmospheric cycle
(*c*) larger global and smaller local H_2O cycles
(*d*) oceanic and fresh H_2O cycles

124. Amount of water vapour present any time in the atmosphere :
(*a*) 0.13×10^{20} G (*b*) 13×10^{20} G
(*c*) 1.3×10^{20} G (*d*) 0.013×10^{20} G

125. The process of evapo-transpiration and precipitation is known as :
(*a*) carbon cycle
(*b*) hydrological cycle
(*c*) nitrogen cycle
(*d*) All of these

126. Which cycle is directly driven by solar radiations?
(*a*) Phosphorus (*b*) Carbon
(*c*) Water (*d*) Nitrogen

127. Hydrological cycle is under the control of :
(*a*) grasslands (*b*) forests
(*c*) planktons (*d*) hydrophytes

128. Global water cycle involves :
(*a*) forest trees
(*b*) algae
(*c*) microoganisms
(*d*) evaporation of water from water bodies

129. Local water cycle involves :
(*a*) living beings (*b*) physical factors
(*c*) atmosphere (*d*) None of these

130. The *Pseudomonas aeruginosa* and *Thiobacillus* are important part of N_2 cycle, as they reduce NO_3 into elemental nitrogen. It is called :
(*a*) nitrification (*b*) denitrification
(*c*) N_2 fixation (*d*) transfer nitrogen

131. The chief architect in nitrogen cycle is
(*a*) producers
(*b*) animals rich in proteins
(*c*) bacteria
(*d*) lightening

132. *Nitrobacter bacterium* convert :
(*a*) nitrites into nitrates
(*b*) NH_3 into nitrites
(*c*) nitrogen into nitrates
(*d*) None of the above

133. *Azotobacter* and *Clostridium* are nitrogen fixing bacteria and found in :
(*a*) nodulated roots
(*b*) leaves of certain plant
(*c*) free in soil
(*d*) None of the above

134. Nitrosomonas changes :
(*a*) NH_3 into nitrites
(*b*) nitrogen into nitrites
(*c*) nitrites into nitrates
(*d*) nitrogens into nitrates

135. Peak concentration of ozone occurs in the atmosphere above a height of :
(*a*) 10 km (*b*) 15 km
(*c*) 20 km (*d*) 25 km

136. Amount of nitrogen fixed electrochemically and photochemically is :
(*a*) 140 $mg/m^2/yr$
(*b*) 78 $mg/m^2/yr$
(*c*) 35 $mg/m^2/yr$
(*d*) 15 $mg/m^2/yr$

137. Crystalline rocks are natural source of biogenetic element :
(*a*) Calcium (*b*) Phosphorus
(*c*) Magnesium (*d*) Calcium

138. All living organisms of earth constitute :
(*a*) Biote (*b*) Biosphere
(*c*) Atmosphere (*d*) Environment

139. Green house effect is due to accumulation of :
(*a*) O_3 and depletion of CO_2
(*b*) O_3 and CO_2
(*c*) CO_2 and depletion of O_3
(*d*) Green plants

140. Biochemical cycle with gaseous phase is :
(*a*) Carbon (*b*) Sodium
(*c*) Phosphorus (*d*) Magnesium

141. A biogeochemical cycle without an atmospheric component is :
(*a*) Carbon cycle
(*b*) Phosphorus cycle
(*c*) Nitrogen cycle
(*d*) Sulphur cycle

142. The most crucial role in H_2O cycle is played by :
(*a*) Evaporation from water sheets
(*b*) Transpiration by plants
(*c*) Absorption of H_2O by plants
(*d*) Percolation of rain water into soil upto water table

143. Which one is sedimentary cycle :
(*a*) Oxygen cycle
(*b*) Nitrogen cycle
(*c*) Hydrogen cycle
(*d*) Phosphorus cycle

144. Under anaerobic conditions, denitrifying bacterium *Pseudomonas* changes :
(*a*) Nitrate to molecular nitrogen
(*b*) Nitrate to ammonia
(*c*) Nitrate to nitrate
(*d*) Nitrite to nitrate

145. Ozone layer is found in :
(*a*) Thermosphere
(*b*) Stratosphere
(*c*) Mesosphere
(*d*) Lithosphere

146. Nitrogen content of biosphere remains constant due to :
(*a*) Nitrogen fixation
(*b*) Nitrogen cycle
(*c*) Industrial pollution
(*d*) Absorption of nitrogen

147. A green house gas is :
(*a*) H_2 (*b*) CO
(*c*) CO_2 (*d*) N_2

148. The reason for green-house effect is :
(*a*) Higher CO_2 concentration causing global warming
(*b*) Absorption of infra-red rays by gases and dust particles
(*c*) Both (*a*) and (*b*)
(*d*) Rarefaction of CO_2

149. Maximum green house gas released by which of the following country?

(*a*) India (*b*) USA
(*c*) France (*d*) Britain

150. Nitrogen is a critical element of the ecosystem because it is :
(*a*) Essential element
(*b*) Abundant in atmosphere
(*c*) Labile
(*d*) Fixed by microbes

151. Carbon dioxide content of atmospheric is about :
(*a*) 6.5% (*b*) 3.334%
(*c*) 0.34% (*d*) 0.034%

152. Zone of atmosphere near the ground is :
(*a*) Troposphere
(*b*) Stratosphere
(*c*) Mesosphere
(*d*) Homosphere

153. Role of bacteria in carbon cycle is :
(*a*) Photosynthesis
(*b*) Chemosynthesis
(*c*) Breakdown of organic compounds
(*d*) Assimilation of nitrogen compounds

154. In case CO_2 of earth's atmosphere disappears, the temperature of earth's surface would :
(*a*) Increase
(*b*) Decrease
(*c*) Depend on oxygen concentration
(*d*) Remain the same

155. Old leguminous roots turn green due to :
(*a*) Conversion of leghaemoglobin to chl *a*
(*b*) Breakdown of leghaemoglobin
(*c*) Conversion of leghaemoglobin to chl *b*
(*d*) Conversion of leghaemoglobin to chl *c*.

156. Most vital process for existence of life on earth is :
(*a*) Reproduction of plants and animals
(*b*) Respiration of animals
(*c*) Photosynthesis by plants
(*d*) Communication in animals

157. Which one depicts nitrogen fixation :
(*a*) $N_2 + 3H_2 \longrightarrow 2NH_3$
(*b*) $2NH_3 \longrightarrow N_2 + 3H_2$
(*c*) $2N_2$ + Glucose $\longrightarrow$ 2 amino acids
(*d*) $2NH_4^+ + 2O_2 + 8e^- \longrightarrow N_2 + 4H_2O$

158. Green house effect is due to :
(*a*) CO_2
(*b*) CH_4, SO_2 and NO_2
(*c*) Combination of many gases
(*d*) Gases which absorb infra-red rays reflected from earth

159. Instrument used for measuring atmospheric humidity is :
(*a*) Potometer (*b*) Hygrometer
(*c*) Porometer (*d*) Auxanometer

160. Which one has the least green house effect?
(*a*) Carbon dioxide (*b*) Nitrogen gas
(*c*) Water vapours (*d*) Ozone

161. Belt on which life exists above and below the surface of earth is :
(*a*) Biotic belt (*b*) Biome
(*c*) Biosphere (*d*) Ecosystem

162. The limiting factor in soil nitrification is :
(*a*) Soil *p*H (*b*) Light
(*c*) Temperature (*d*) Air

163. Green house effect is increasing due to :
(*a*) Increasing CO_2 concentration
(*b*) Increasing SO_2 concentration
(*c*) Increasing concentration of chlorofluorocarbons
(*d*) Hole in ozone layer

164. Atmosphere consists of :
(*a*) Lithosphere + Hydrosphere
(*b*) Lithosphere + Stratosphere + Hydrosphere
(*c*) Troposphere + Stratosphere + Ionosphere
(*d*) None of the above

165. Life in biosphere is abundant between :
(*a*) 6000 mt below sea level to 6000 mt above sea level
(*b*) 6000 mt below sea level to 2000 mt above sea level
(*c*) 200 mt below sea level to 6000 mt above sea level
(*d*) 1100 mt below sea level to 9000 mt below sea level

166. Stratosphere part of atmosphere is characterised by :

(*a*) rise in temp with height
(*b*) rise in ozone level
(*c*) lack of dust and water vapours
(*d*) All of the above

167. Earth is alive and functions as a super organism is the concept of Gaia Hypothesis. It was forwarded by :
(*a*) Richard Dwakins
(*b*) Lovelock
(*c*) Hutton
(*d*) Lewis Thomas

168. Annual world precipitationis :
(*a*) 7×10^{10} g
(*b*) 7×10^{20} g
(*c*) 4.46×10^{10} g
(*d*) 4.46×10^{20} g

169. Which of the following does not contribute directly to the recycling pathways of trophics?
(*a*) Plants
(*b*) Bacteria and fungi
(*c*) Carnivores
(*d*) Herbivores

170. Recycling of material is carried out by :
(*a*) Algae (*b*) Fungi
(*c*) Viruses (*d*) Bacteria

171. Inorganic element that changes food into us ables energy is :
(*a*) S (*b*) P
(*c*) Ca (*d*) Mg

172. Degradation of proteins play a part in :
(*a*) Calvin cycle
(*b*) Water cycle
(*c*) Sulphur cycle
(*d*) Nitrogen cycle

173. The agent/s which make/s free atmospheric nitrogen available to plants is/are:
(*a*) lightening
(*b*) free living nitrogen fixing bacteria
(*c*) symbiotic nitrogen fixing bacteria
(*d*) all of these

174. Which one depicts Nitrogen fixation :
(*a*) $N_2 \rightarrow NH_3$
(*b*) $N_2 \rightarrow NO_3$
(*c*) $N_2 \rightarrow$ Aminoacids
(*d*) Both (*a*) and (*b*)

175. In which of the following cycle an atmospheric cycle is absent :
(*a*) Carbon cycle
(*b*) Phosphorus cycle
(*c*) Nitrogen cycle
(*d*) Sulphur cycle

176. In case CO_2 of earth disapper the temperature will :
(*a*) increase
(*b*) decrease
(*c*) remain uneffected
(*d*) depend on other factors

177. Putrefaction, lightening and thunder help in :
(*a*) N_2 cycle
(*b*) P cycle
(*c*) S cycle
(*d*) Hydrologic cycle

178. In nature, bulk of nitrogen is fixed by :
(*a*) lightening
(*b*) denitrifying bacteria
(*c*) symbiotic bacteria
(*d*) anaerobic bacteria

179. The phosphorus rich fertilizer obtained from sea birds long the coast of chile and Peru, is :
(*a*) Guano (*b*) Bone meal
(*c*) Dung (*d*) Urea

180. Which of the following contribute to the carbon cycle?
(*a*) respiration
(*b*) fossil fuel buring
(*c*) photosynthesis
(*d*) All of the above

181. Which of the following is the major source of phosphorus :
(*a*) Plants
(*b*) Animals
(*c*) Crystalline rocks
(*d*) Deserts

ANSWERS

1	**2**	**3**	**4**	**5**	**6**	**7**	**8**	**9**	**10**
(*d*)	(*a*)	(*d*)	(*b*)	(*c*)	(*a*)	(*a*)	(*a*)	(*a*)	(*c*)
11	**12**	**13**	**14**	**15**	**16**	**17**	**18**	**19**	**20**
(*a*)	(*c*)	(*b*)	(*a*)	(*b*)	(*c*)	(*d*)	(*a*)	(*d*)	(*a*)
21	**22**	**23**	**24**	**25**	**26**	**27**	**28**	**29**	**30**
(*c*)	(*c*)	(*d*)	(*d*)	(*a*)	(*a*)	(*a*)	(*a*)	(*c*)	(*b*)
31	**32**	**33**	**34**	**35**	**36**	**37**	**38**	**39**	**40**
(*d*)	(*c*)	(*c*)	(*c*)	(*b*)	(*c*)	(*d*)	(*a*)	(*b*)	(*b*)
41	**42**	**43**	**44**	**45**	**46**	**47**	**48**	**49**	**50**
(*c*)	(*a*)	(*c*)	(*b*)	(*d*)	(*b*)	(*c*)	(*a*)	(*d*)	(*d*)
51	**52**	**53**	**54**	**55**	**56**	**57**	**58**	**59**	**60**
(*b*)	(*c*)	(*b*)	(*b*)	(*b*)	(*b*)	(*d*)	(*c*)	(*d*)	(*b*)
61	**62**	**63**	**64**	**65**	**66**	**67**	**68**	**69**	**70**
(*d*)	(*d*)	(*c*)	(*a*)	(*d*)	(*c*)	(*c*)	(*c*)	(*d*)	(*a*)
71	**72**	**73**	**74**	**75**	**76**	**77**	**78**	**79**	**80**
(*c*)	(*c*)	(*a*)	(*a*)	(*c*)	(*b*)	(*a*)	(*b*)	(*c*)	(*b*)
81	**82**	**83**	**84**	**85**	**86**	**87**	**88**	**89**	**90**
(*c*)	(*c*)	(*a*)	(*c*)	(*b*)	(*d*)	(*c*)	(*a*)	(*d*)	(*c*)
91	**92**	**93**	**94**	**95**	**96**	**97**	**98**	**99**	**100**
(*b*)	(*c*)	(*b*)	(*d*)	(*c*)	(*b*)	(*d*)	(*c*)	(*a*)	(*a*)
101	**102**	**103**	**104**	**105**	**106**	**107**	**108**	**109**	**110**
(*d*)	(*c*)	(*a*)	(*a*)	(*d*)	(*a*)	(*a*)	(*a*)	(*c*)	(*d*)
111	**112**	**113**	**114**	**115**	**116**	**117**	**118**	**119**	**120**
(*a*)	(*b*)	(*d*)	(*b*)	(*d*)	(*a*)	(*a*)	(*d*)	(*a*)	(*d*)
121	**122**	**123**	**124**	**125**	**126**	**127**	**128**	**129**	**130**
(*b*)	(*a*)	(*c*)	(*a*)	(*b*)	(*c*)	(*b*)	(*d*)	(*a*)	(*b*)
131	**132**	**133**	**134**	**135**	**136**	**137**	**138**	**139**	**140**
(*c*)	(*a*)	(*c*)	(*a*)	(*d*)	(*c*)	(*b*)	(*b*)	(*b*)	(*a*)
141	**142**	**143**	**144**	**145**	**146**	**147**	**148**	**149**	**150**
(*b*)	(*a*)	(*d*)	(*a*)	(*b*)	(*b*)	(*c*)	(*c*)	(*b*)	(*c*)
151	**152**	**153**	**154**	**155**	**156**	**157**	**158**	**159**	**160**
(*d*)	(*a*)	(*c*)	(*b*)	(*b*)	(*c*)	(*a*)	(*d*)	(*b*)	(*b*)
161	**162**	**163**	**164**	**165**	**166**	**167**	**168**	**169**	**170**
(*c*)	(*a*)	(*a*)	(*c*)	(*c*)	(*d*)	(*b*)	(*d*)	(*a*)	(*d*)
171	**172**	**173**	**174**	**175**	**176**	**177**	**178**	**179**	**180**
(*b*)	(*d*)	(*d*)	(*d*)	(*b*)	(*b*)	(*a*)	(*a*)	(*a*)	(*d*)
181									
(*c*)									

4

Ecosystem: Structure and Function

1. An ecosystem is :
(*a*) different communities of plants, animals and microbes together with their physico-chemical environments
(*b*) an interacting system of Biotic communities and their abiotic environment
(*c*) open and closed depending upon community
(*d*) All of the above

2. Ecosystem is a self-sufficient, self-maintaining dynamic system in which there is a :
(*a*) noncyclic, unidirectional (one way passage) flow of energy
(*b*) cyclic exchange of nutrients
(*c*) communities and abiotic components function together
(*d*) All of the above

3. Temperature changes in the environment affect most of the animals which are :
(*a*) Aquatic (*b*) Desert
(*c*) Poikilothermal (*d*) Homoisothermal

4. A pond/lake is :
(*a*) A biome
(*b*) A natural ecosystem
(*c*) An artificial ecosystem
(*d*) A community of plants and animals only

5. Biome is :
(*a*) The fauna of an ocean
(*b*) The flora of land
(*c*) Communities of organisms interacting with one another
(*d*) The part of the earth and its atmosphere which is inhabited by living organisms

6. Ecological niche of an organism denotes :
(*a*) Habitat of the organism
(*b*) On whom the organism feeds
(*c*) The status of an organism within a particular community
(*d*) All of the above

7. The transition zone where two different types of communities meet is called :
(*a*) Ecotype (*b*) Ecocline
(*c*) Ecotone (*d*) Ecosystem

8. Grassland biome for its maintenance requires :
(*a*) Periodic fire (*b*) Intensive grazing
(*c*) Mowing (*d*) All of the above

9. Which of the following is a biome :
(*a*) Wheat field (*b*) Rain water pond
(*c*) Grass field (*d*) Deciduous forest

10. Primary consumers in detritus food chain are :
(*a*) Harbivores
(*b*) Bacteria, fungi etc.
(*c*) Insect larvae, nematodes
(*d*) All of the above

11. Total organic matter present in an ecosystem is called :
(*a*) Biomass (*b*) Biome
(*c*) Litter (*d*) Food

12. Detritus food chain in comparison to grazing food chain is :
(*a*) Generally longer (*b*) Generally equal
(*c*) Generally shorter (*d*) None of these

13. Putrefying organisms are :
(*a*) Producer organisms
(*b*) Reducer organisms

(c) Consumer organisms
(d) Parasitic organisms

14. The most important organisms for an ecosystem are :
(a) Herbivores (b) Carnivores
(c) Green plants (d) Protozoa

15. A peacock eats snakes which eat frogs. These eat hoppers which in turn thrive on leaves of the plants. The peacock is :
(a) Primary consumer
(b) Secondary consumer
(c) Decomposer
(d) Apex of the food pyramid

16. A food chain is :
(a) Group of organisms which eat the same type of food
(b) Animals eating the plants
(c) Series of plants/animals which are interrelated in the form of organism being eaten as food by the other
(d) None of these

17. A food chain consists of :
(a) Producers
(b) Consumers
(c) Decomposers
(d) Both (a) and (b)

18. Trophic levels in a food chain are formed by :
(a) Producers (b) Consumers
(c) Decomposers (d) All of these

19. A food chain always starts with :
(a) Photosynthesis (b) Respiration
(c) Nitrogen fixation (d) Decay

20. Primary consumers are :
(a) Green plants (b) Herbivores
(c) Carnivores (d) All of the above

21. Secondary consumers are :
(a) Green plants (b) Herbivores
(c) Carnivores (d) All of the above

22. Physical and chemical conditions of soil are studied under :
(a) Topographic factors
(b) Edaphic factors
(c) Biotic factors
(d) Climatic factors

23. Given below are assertion and reason. Point out if both are true with reason being correct explanation (A), both are true but reason is not correct explanation (B), assertion is true but reason is wrong (C), and both are wrong (D), **Assertion.** Cold blooded animals have no fat layer. **Reason.** Cold blooded animals use their fat for metabolic process during hibernation :
(a) A (b) B
(c) C (d) D

24. Plains with snow, ice and frozen soil for most of the year are found in :
(a) Chapparal (b) Taiga
(c) Tundra (d) Savannah

25. Animal that survives one third loss of body weight due to water loss is :
(a) Lizard (b) *Necturus*
(c) *Chiton* (d) Camel

26. Bacteria and fungi are :
(a) Scavengers
(b) Primary consumers
(c) Secondary consumers
(d) Decomposers

27. Ultimate source of energy for living beings is :
(a) Carbohydrates (b) Fats
(c) Sunlight (d) ATP

28. Hydrophyte with both hydrophytic and xerophytic traits is :
(a) *Agave* (b) *Nerium*
(c) *Vallisneria* (d) None of the above

29. Relationship between different organisms can best be studied by :
(a) Food webs
(b) Pyramid of mass
(c) Pyramid of energy
(d) Eltonian pyramids

30. Stratification is seen in :
(a) Tundra (b) Temperate forest
(c) Tropical forest (d) Desert

31. Grasslands of Asia are :
(*a*) Savannah (*b*) Pampas
(*c*) Steppes (*d*) Veldt

32. Which one is inverted pyramid :
(*a*) Pyramid of biomass in grassland
(*b*) Pyramid of biomass in pond ecosystem
(*c*) Pyramid of numbers in grassland ecosystem
(*d*) Pyramid of energy in a pond ecosystem

33. The term biocoenosis was coined by :
(*a*) Darwin (*b*) Haeckel
(*c*) Odum (*d*) Mobius

34. Ecological pyramid which is never inverted :
(*a*) Pyramid of energy
(*b*) Pyramid of biomass
(*c*) Pyramid of numbers
(*d*) Pyramid of species richness

35. Estuaries occur in :
(*a*) Orissa and Tamil Nadu
(*b*) Kerala and Tamil Nadu
(*c*) Kerala and Orissa
(*d*) Kerala, Tamil Nadu and Orissa

36. Phytoplankton is component of :
(*a*) Pond ecosystem (*b*) Desert ecosystem
(*c*) Grass ecosystem (*d*) Forest ecosystem

37. Factors connected with form and behaviour of earth's surface are :
(*a*) Edaphic
(*b*) Topographic
(*c*) Tropical rain forests
(*d*) Deciduous forests

38. Of all the species of insects known, nearly 70-80% are found in :
(*a*) Tropical savannah
(*b*) Chapparal
(*c*) Tropical rain forests
(*d*) Deciduous forests

39. Decomposers are :
(*a*) Animalia and Monera
(*b*) Protista and Animalia
(*c*) Fungi and Plantae
(*d*) Bacteria and Fungi

40. Crop ecosystem is man engineered artificial ecosystem because self regulatory mechanism do not operate in it. In such ecosystems **productivity** is high but biomass is not allowed to accumulate. Therefore, in such ecosystems :
(*a*) P/B is high against high B/P of natural ecosystem
(*b*) P/B is low against high B/P of natural ecosystem
(*c*) P/B is high against low B/P in natural ecosystem
(*d*) Data insufficient to predict any result

41. Which of the food chain directly depends on solar radiations :
(*a*) Predator (*b*) Grazing
(*c*) Detritus (*d*) None of these

42. Producers in any grazing food chain :
(*a*) Feed the herbivores
(*b*) Feed the carnivores
(*c*) Clean the atmosphere
(*d*) Capture solar energy

43. Converters or transducer organisms in the food chain are called :
(*a*) Herbivores (*b*) Carnivores
(*c*) Decomposers (*d*) Producers

44. Biological equilibrium is an equilibrium among the :
(*a*) Producers
(*b*) Producers and consumers
(*c*) Decomposers
(*d*) Producers, consumers and decomposers

45. Trophic level in a food chain which cycles the various materials between environment and living organisms is constituted by :
(*a*) Producers (*b*) Consumers
(*c*) Decomposers (*d*) All of the above

46. Food web is constituted by :
(*a*) Various interlinked food chains in a community
(*b*) Relationship between animals and plants
(*c*) Relationship between organisms and their environment
(*d*) Relationship between animals, plants and microbes

47. Root is feebly developed and stem is soft with a large number of air cavities in :
(*a*) Lithophytes (*b*) Halophytes
(*c*) Hydrophytes (*d*) Aerophytes

48. Vegetation of a geographic region with low rainfall, high temperature, loose and sandy soil is of the type called :
(*a*) Grassland
(*b*) Scrub forest
(*c*) Xerophytic
(*d*) Evergreen tropical forest

49. If phytophanktons are destroyed in the sea :
(*a*) It will affect food chain
(*b*) No effect will be seen
(*c*) Algae will get more space to grow
(*d*) Primary consumer will grow more

50. Ecological pyramids were given by :
(*a*) Elton (*b*) Haeckel
(*c*) Odum (*d*) Reiter

51. Competition for food, light and space is most severe between two :
(*a*) closely related species growing in different niche
(*b*) distantly related species growing in same niche
(*c*) closely related species occupying same niche
(*d*) distantly related species growing in different niche

52. In terrestrial ecosystem, maximum energy is present in :
(*a*) T_3 (*b*) T_2
(*c*) T_1 (*d*) T_4

53. In pond ecosystem the shape of pyramid of number is :
(*a*) Linear (*b*) Irregular
(*c*) Upright (*d*) Inverted

54. In parasitic food chain the pyramid of number is :
(*a*) Linear (*b*) Upright
(*c*) Inverted (*d*) Inverted upright

55. In grassland ecosystem the pyramid of biomass is :
(*a*) Linear (*b*) Upright
(*c*) Inverted (*d*) Inverted upright

56. Pyramid of energy in ecosystem is :
(*a*) Inverted
(*b*) Upright
(*c*) Linear
(*d*) Both (*a*) and (*b*)

57. In pyramid of food, the producers occupy :
(*a*) The base
(*b*) Position near the base
(*c*) Apex
(*d*) Position near apex

58. Energy flow in an ecosystem is :
(*a*) Unidirectional
(*b*) Bidirectional
(*c*) Multidirectional
(*d*) All of the above

59. Ascending trophic level in grazing food chain pyramid represents :
(*a*) Gradual decrease in biomass from apex to base
(*b*) Gradual decrease in biomass from producers to the tertiary consumers
(*c*) Gradual increase of the biomass from producers to the tertiary consumers
(*d*) No change in biomass

60. Rate of storage of organic matter not used by heterotrophs is termed as :
(*a*) Net productivity
(*b*) Net primary productivity
(*c*) Gross primary productivity
(*d*) Secondary productivity

61. Graphic representation of biomass relationship between the producers and consumers in an ecosystem is called :
(*a*) Trophic level
(*b*) Ecological system
(*c*) Ecological niche
(*d*) Ecological pyramid

62. This is an inverted pyramid :
(*a*) Pyramid of numbers in a grassland ecosystem

(*b*) Pyramid of energy in a pond ecosystem
(*c*) Pyramid of Biomass in a grassland ecosystem
(*d*) Pyramid of biomass in a lake pond ecosystem

63. When DDT is introduced into a food chain the level in which the greatest concentration is found would be :
(*a*) Producers (*b*) Herbivores
(*c*) Top consumers (*d*) Decomposers

64. What is true?
(*a*) Diaphragm helps in respiration of Frog
(*b*) Pericardial and cerebrospinal fluids are similar
(*c*) Some mammals hibernate
(*d*) Mesorchium connects ovary and kidney of Frog

65. Organisms living at the bottom of a lake are :
(*a*) Nekton (*b*) Benthos
(*c*) Plankton (*d*) Pelagic

66. Maximum biomass of autotrophs in oceans is made of :
(*a*) Benthic brown algae, coastal red algae and daphnids
(*b*) Benthic diatoms and marine viruses
(*c*) Sea grasses and slime moulds
(*d*) Free floating microalgae, cyanobacteria and nanoplankton

67. Frog feeding on herbivorous insect is :
(*a*) Primary consumer
(*b*) Secondary consumer
(*c*) Tertiary consumer
(*d*) Top carnivore

68. A recently discovered ecosystem is :
(*a*) Crater (*b*) Tundra
(*c*) Floating Iceberg (*d*) Vent

69. Controlling factor in ecosystem is :
(*a*) Soil moisture (*b*) Food
(*c*) Predation (*d*) Temperature

70. Vivipary occurs in :
(*a*) *Betula* (*b*) *Rhizophora*
(*c*) Mango (*d*) *Psidium*

71. Factor related to structure of earth's surface is :
(*a*) Edaphic (*b*) Topographic
(*c*) Biotic (*d*) Temperature

72. Which is an example of positive feed back?
(*a*) Seasonal growth
(*b*) Vessel diameter and blood pressure
(*c*) Allosteric inhibition of enzymes
(*d*) Both (*a*) and (*b*)

73. In upright pyramid of biomass, herbivores occupy the position :
(*a*) 1 (*b*) 2
(*c*) 3 (*d*) 4

74. Agriculture and urbanisation are two examples of man's activities to create new :
(*a*) species (*b*) ecosystems
(*c*) biosphere (*d*) lithosphere

75. The minerals in living system are released by the activity of :
(*a*) consumers of first order
(*b*) secondary consumers
(*c*) decomposers
(*d*) producers

76. Which is amphibious?
(*a*) *Casuarina* (*b*) *Wolffia*
(*c*) *Polygonum* (*d*) *Hydrilla*

77. Hibernation occurring in certain animals is :
(*a*) Occasional (*b*) Intermittent
(*c*) Rhythmic (*d*) Periodic

78. No animal can live :
(*a*) Alone
(*b*) Without friend
(*c*) Without foes
(*d*) In area with high temperature

79. Animals have shorter and smaller extremities in colder areas. It is :
(*a*) Allen's law (*b*) Cope's law
(*c*) Dollo's law (*d*) Bergman's law

80. Terai forest is :
(*a*) Tropical
(*b*) Coniferous
(*c*) Deciduous
(*d*) Temperate deciduous

81. Savannah is found commonly in :
(*a*) U.S.A. (*b*) Russia
(*c*) Australia (*d*) Africa

82. Which one has always a steeper vertical gradient?
(*a*) Pyramid of mass
(*b*) Pyramid of energy
(*c*) Pyramid of numbers
(*d*) Pyramid of energy in aquatic ecosystem

83. Which one is exclusive xerophytic adaptation?
(*a*) Absence of stomata
(*b*) Long tap root system
(*c*) Stipular leaves
(*d*) Spines

84. Which one has evergreen vegetation and drought adapted animals?
(*a*) Chaparral (*b*) Savannah
(*c*) Tundra (*d*) Deciduous forest

85. Determining factor for carrying capacity of an ecosystem is :
(*a*) Limitation of resources
(*b*) Birth rate
(*c*) Death rate
(*d*) Air

86. Tree ecosystem show inverted pyramid of numbers. It shows :
(*a*) number of organisms go on increasing
(*b*) size of individuals go on decreasing with each trophic level
(*c*) Both (*a*) and (*b*)
(*d*) None of these

87. If all green plants of earth are destroyed :
(*a*) All plants shall die
(*b*) Only herbivorous animals shall die
(*c*) All animals shall die ultimately
(*d*) Nothing shall happen to animals

88. Animals in cold regions have fur for :
(*a*) Hair is a good insulating material
(*b*) Hairs trap air which acts as insulator
(*c*) They like fur
(*d*) None of the above

89. The increased productivity of lakes and streams brought about by nutrient enrichment is known as :
(*a*) Green house effect
(*b*) Eutrophication
(*c*) Biomagnification
(*d*) Biochemical oxygen demand

90. The typical biome of an area having 50 to 100 cm of rainfall is :
(*a*) Desert (*b*) Grassland
(*c*) Deciduous forest (*d*) Coniferous forest

91. An ecological niche is normally occupied by :
(*a*) A population
(*b*) A small community
(*c*) Competing species
(*d*) Competing genera

92. Grassland of U.S.A. is referred to as :
(*a*) Prairies (*b*) Steppes
(*c*) Pampas (*d*) Veldts

93. Plankton, Nekton and Benthos are not the components of one of ecosystems which is :
(*a*) Oceans (*b*) Fresh water rivers
(*c*) Grassland (*d*) Pond or lake

94. The food chain in which micro-organisms breakdown the energy rich compounds synthesized by producers :
(*a*) Predator food chain
(*b*) Parasitic food chain
(*c*) Detritus food chain
(*d*) None of these

95. When a big fish eats a small fish which eats water fleas supported by phytoplankton, water fleas are :
(*a*) Producers
(*b*) Primary consumers
(*c*) Secondary consumers
(*d*) Top consumers

96. Deciduous plants are those in which leaves fall :
(*a*) Once in a year (*b*) Twice in a year
(*c*) Many times a year (*d*) None of the above

97. Which ecological pyramid can never occur in an inverted form?
(*a*) Pyramid of numbers
(*b*) Pyramid of energy
(*c*) Pyramid of biomass
(*d*) Pyramid of species richness

98. Which forests have maximum diversity?
(*a*) Subtropical rain forests
(*b*) Coniferous forests
(*c*) Tropical forests
(*d*) Deciduous forests

99. Which one is not a factor of the abiotic environment :
(*a*) Sunlight (*b*) Decomposers
(*c*) Water (*d*) Temperature

100. A functional aspect of an ecosystem is :
(*a*) Producers, consumers and abiotic environment
(*b*) Regulation of populations
(*c*) Light, temperature, oxygen and carbon dioxide
(*d*) Both (*a*) and (*c*)

101. Which is true of a food chain :
(*a*) Passage of food from one trophic level to the next higher one
(*b*) Passage of energy from one trophic level to the next higher one
(*c*) Dissipation of energy at successive trophic levels
(*d*) All of the above

102. A food web :
(*a*) Increases variety of food at each trophic level
(*b*) Delicately balances the interrelations amongst organisms
(*c*) Decreases variety of food but increases quantity of food at each trophic level
(*d*) Increases variety as well as quantity of food at each trophic level

103. Which is true :
(*a*) Tigers prey upon herbivores
(*b*) Tigers prey upon all types of land animals
(*c*) Tigers prey upon most of land animals but can also eat aquatic animals
(*d*) Tigers prey upon medium-sized land animals

104. During winter, Polar Bear :
(*a*) Hibernates
(*b*) Aestivates
(*c*) Remains active
(*d*) Migrates to warmer areas

105. How do they protect themselves from wave action :
(*a*) *Nereis* and tube-worms are fast swimmers
(*b*) Sea Anemones and Limpets have burrowing habits
(*c*) *Fucus* and *Laminaria* are firmly attached to rocks
(*d*) All of the above

106. Which of the following occurs in abiotic component of ecosystem?
(*a*) Flow of energy
(*b*) Cycling of materials
(*c*) Consumers
(*d*) Flow of energy and cycling of materials

107. A man-made microecosystem is :
(*a*) Plants grown in a pond
(*b*) Crop field
(*c*) Tank formed naturally in your court yard
(*d*) Lake in a forest

108. A treeless biome is :
(*a*) Tundra (*b*) Grassland
(*c*) Desert (*d*) All of the above

109. Correct sequence in a food chain is :
(*a*) Grass → Insects → Birds → Snake
(*b*) Grass → Snake → Insects → Deer
(*c*) Grass → Wolf → Deer → Buffalo
(*d*) Bacteria → Grass → Rabbit → Wolf

110. In an ecosystem, tropic level of man is :
(*a*) Producer (*b*) Herbivore
(*c*) Omnivore (*d*) Carnivore

111. Secondary producers are :
(*a*) Herbivores (*b*) Heterotrophs
(*c*) Carnivores (*d*) Green plants

112. Drought resistance of succulents is connected with :
(*a*) Higher frequency of stomata
(*b*) Regulation of stomatal movement
(*c*) Fleshy mesophyll
(*d*) Well developed xylem

113. Biome has organisms of various trophic levels :
(*a*) Reacting with abiotic environment
(*b*) Constitute a sociological unit
(*c*) Live a symbiotic life
(*d*) Inhabit a desert

114. A rat feeding on Potato tuber is :
(*a*) Producer (*b*) Primary consumer
(*c*) Carnivore (*d*) Decomposer

115. Lentic ecosystem occurs in :
(*a*) Rain water
(*b*) Running water
(*c*) Standing water
(*d*) Gravitational water

116. Match the items of column I with those of column II :

	Colum – I		Column – II
a	Grass	p	Decomposer
b	Grasshopper	q	Secondary Carnivore
c	Frog	r	Producer
d	Hawk	s	Primary Consumer
–	–	t	Primary Carnivore

(*a*) $a-r, b-p, c-t, d-s$
(*b*) $a-p, b-r, c-s, d-t$
(*c*) $a-r, b-t, c-s, d-q$
(*d*) $a-r, b-s, c-t, d-q$

117. A non-succulent xerophyte with thick leathery leaves having white sticky waxy coating is :
(*a*) *Nerium* (*b*) *Calotropis*
(*c*) *Bryophyllum* (*d*) *Ruscus*

118. An ecosystem contains :
(*a*) Producers (*b*) Consumers
(*c*) Decomposers (*d*) All of the above

119. Climatology is science of :
(*a*) Edaphic factors
(*b*) Topographic factors
(*c*) Climatic factors
(*d*) Biotic factors

120. Ecosystem of a pond is :
(*a*) Lotic (*b*) Lentic
(*c*) Benthic (*d*) Xeric

121. Mangrove of marshy Sunderbans is characterised by :
(*a*) Pneumatophores (*b*) Prop roots
(*c*) Vivipary (*d*) All of the above

122. Humus accumulate in Tundra region because :
(*a*) There is no fibre to destroy dead leaves
(*b*) There is low temperature that inhibit bacterial action
(*c*) Low temperature favours humus formation
(*d*) In Tundra dry conditions prevent bacterial action

123. Which is not true?
(*a*) Jelly Fishes are glassy
(*b*) Lions are brownish in colour
(*c*) Camels are sand coloured
(*d*) Sea Cucumbers are olive-green

124. Niche represents :
(*a*) Habitat
(*b*) Microhabitat
(*c*) Habitat as well as interrelations
(*d*) Habitat as well as climate

125. Alpine tundra is found in :
(*a*) Siberia (*b*) Greenland
(*c*) Both (*a*) and (*b*) (*d*) Himalayas

126. Rainfall is absent but precipitation occurs in:
(*a*) Arctic desert (*b*) Tropical desert
(*c*) Chapparal (*d*) Savannah

127. Taiga refers to :
(*a*) Temperate deciduous forest
(*b*) Subtropical semi-deciduous forest
(*c*) Evergreen forest
(*d*) North temperate coniferous forest

128. Chapparal occurs in area :
(*a*) Africa (*b*) Siberia
(*c*) Mediterranean (*d*) Arabia

129. Rainfall occurs in chapparal during :
(*a*) The whole year (*b*) Summer
(*c*) Winter (*d*) Spring-autumn

130. Deserts occur in areas of :
(*a*) Adverse human disturbance
(*b*) Underground saline water
(*c*) Little underground water
(*d*) Rain shadow

131. All types of latitudinal biomes are found telescoped on high hills found in :
(*a*) Tropical areas (*b*) Subtropical areas
(*c*) Temperate areas (*d*) None of the above

132. Epiphytes are rare in Delhi because it has :
(*a*) Large number of automobiles
(*b*) Large amount of factories
(*c*) Semi-arid climate
(*d*) Moist climate

133. Annual rainfall in the area of a tropical deciduous forest is :
(*a*) Over 300 cm (*b*) 200 – 250 cm
(*c*) 100 – 150 cm (*d*) 50 – 75 cm

134. Water storage tissue has :
(*a*) Large-sized thin walled cells
(*b*) Mucilage
(*c*) Large-sized vacuoles
(*d*) All of the above

135. Which ecosystem does not show variations dependent upon geographic location and rainfall :
(*a*) Marine ecosystem
(*b*) Fresh water ecosystem
(*c*) Desert ecosystem
(*d*) Tropical ecosystem

136. Photic zone is spread upto a depth of :
(*a*) 10 m (*b*) 10 – 100 m
(*c*) 100 – 200 m (*d*) 200 m

137. Plant life is restricted in sea to :
(*a*) Photic zone (*b*) Aphotic zone
(*c*) Abyssal area (*d*) Continental shelf

138. Ox-bow lakes occur in :
(*a*) Areas of previous glaciation
(*b*) Temperate regions
(*c*) Near sea shore
(*d*) Part of a river

139. Free floating plant found below the surface of water is :
(*a*) *Pistia* (*b*) *Lemna*
(*c*) *Ranunculus* (*d*) *Ceratophyllum*

140. Upper reaches of a river does not possess many living beings because of :
(*a*) Low temperature
(*b*) High speed
(*c*) Little depth
(*d*) Both (*a*) and (*b*)

141. Agroecosystem is unstable because of :
(*a*) Lack of variety
(*b*) Lack of biological control
(*c*) Both (*a*) and (*b*)
(*d*) Being man-made

142. Biome represents :
(*a*) All the organisms of earth
(*b*) Flora of a land
(*c*) Flora and fauna of a land
(*d*) A major ecosystem delimited by climate or geography

143. Vegetation of Delhi is predominantly :
(*a*) Halophytic (*b*) Xerophytic
(*c*) Mesophytic (*d*) Hygrophytic

144. Grassland with scattered trees is :
(*a*) Savannah
(*b*) Deciduours forest
(*c*) Evergreen forest
(*d*) Tropical rain forest

145. Biotic factors refer to :
(*a*) Gases produced by industries
(*b*) Nutrient deficient soils
(*c*) Living organisms
(*d*) Fossil fuels

146. Energy enters an ecosystem through :
(*a*) Herbivores (*b*) Producers
(*c*) Carnivores (*d*) Decomposers

147. Decomposers are :
(*a*) Autotrophs
(*b*) Heterotrophs
(*c*) Autoheterotrophys
(*d*) Chemoautotrophs

148. Sun loving plants are :
(*a*) Halophytes (*b*) Sciophytes
(*c*) Heliophytes (*d*) Autotrophs

149. A submerged rooted hydrophyte is :
(*a*) *Vallisneria* (*b*) *Trapa*
(*c*) *Utricularia* (*d*) *Nymphaea*

150. Moderate rain during summer produces :
(*a*) Desert (*b*) Grassland
(*c*) Scrub forest (*d*) Deciduous forest

151. Relationships in an ecosystm can be depicted through :
(*a*) Pyramid of energy
(*b*) Pyramid of biomass
(*c*) Pyramid of numbers
(*d*) All of the above

152. Type of plants having adaptations to check transpiration is :
(*a*) Xerophytes (*b*) Lithophytes
(*c*) Halophytes (*d*) Epiphytes

153. Xerophytes possess :
(*a*) Sunken stomata (*b*) Deep roots
(*c*) Thick cuticle (*d*) All of the above

154. Characteristic of hydrophytes is :
(*a*) Poorly developed roots
(*b*) Well developed roots
(*c*) Well developed xylem
(*d*) Stem with sclerenchyma

155. Viviparity and pneumatophores are features of :
(*a*) Hydrophytes (*b*) Halophytes
(*c*) Mesophytes (*d*) Xerophytes

156. Ecosystem has two components :
(*a*) Animals and humans
(*b*) Plants and animals
(*c*) Biotic and abiotic.
(*d*) Weeds and trees

157. A habitat not suitable for primary productivity is :
(*a*) Cave
(*b*) Pond
(*c*) Meadow
(*d*) Forested river bank

158. Which part of the world has high density of organisms?
(*a*) Grasslands
(*b*) Savannahs
(*c*) Deciduous forest
(*d*) Tropical rain forest

159. The most favoured habitat of a plant is called:
(*a*) Ecological habitat (*b*) Microhabitat
(*c*) Ecotype (*d*) Ecocline

160. Green plants constitute :
(*a*) First trophic level
(*b*) Second trophic level
(*c*) Third trophic level
(*d*) Fourth trophic level

161. Tip of an ecological pyramid is occupied by :
(*a*) Producers (*b*) Herbivores
(*c*) Carnivores (*d*) None of the above

162. Zooplanktonic forms are :
(*a*) Primary producers
(*b*) Carnivores
(*c*) Primary consumers
(*d*) Secondary consumers

163. Food webs are 3-D web of interrelations in which several food chains are interlinked. It helps to provide :
(*a*) shelter
(*b*) more variety and quality of food at each trophic level
(*c*) alternate pathways for flow of energy
(*d*) All of these

164. Alpine plants show :
(*a*) Mesophytism (*b*) Halophytism
(*c*) Xerophytism (*d*) Luxurian growth

165. A habitat with long severe winter and growing season of a few months of summer forms:
(*a*) Grasslands (*b*) Tundra ecosystem
(*c*) Taiga (*d*) Savannah

166. Alpine forests of Himalayas have :
(*a*) Tall evergreen coniferous trees
(*b*) Tall broad-leaved evergreen trees
(*c*) Tall broad-leaved deciduous trees
(*d*) Dwarf shrubby plants

167. *Rhododendron* is characteristic component of vegetation?
(*a*) Tropical forests (*b*) Mangroves
(*c*) Alpine zone (*d*) Gangetic platin

168. Temperate forests occur in India in :
(*a*) Indo-Gangetic plains
(*b*) Himalayas
(*c*) Eastern India
(*d*) Southern Peninsula

169. In India, tropical evergreen forest occur in :
(*a*) Himachal Pradesh
(*b*) Madhya Pradesh
(*c*) Asom
(*d*) Tamil Nadu

170. In India, rain forests are found in :
(*a*) Uttar Pradesh and Bihar
(*b*) Madhya Pradesh and Orissa
(*c*) Tamil Nadu and Andhra Pradesh
(*d*) Western Ghats and Eastern Himalayas

171. In India, temperate evergreen vegetation occurs mostly in :
(*a*) Rajasthan and South Punjab
(*b*) Eastern and Western Himalayas less than 3500 m
(*c*) Western Himalayas above 3500 m
(*d*) Western Ghats and Asom

172. Difference between tropical rain forest and temperate forest is :
(*a*) Tropical forest has more of angiosperms while temperate forests have more of gymnosperms
(*b*) Tropical forest is homogeneous while temperate one is heterogeneous
(*c*) Plants of temperate forests are more mesophytic
(*d*) Trees of temperate forests are taller than those of tropical forests

173. The forest that colours in autumn is :
(*a*) Temperate evergreen forest
(*b*) Temperate deciduous forest
(*c*) Tropical evergreen forest
(*d*) Tropical deciduous forest

174. Ephemerals are a type of xerophytes :
(*a*) Drought escaping (*b*) Drought resisting
(*c*) Drought enduring (*d*) None of the above

175. Succulents occur in :
(*a*) Deserts
(*b*) Tundra
(*c*) Temperate deciduous forests
(*d*) Tropical rain forests

176. Extreme xerophytic condition occurs in :
(*a*) Cactus (*b*) *Nerium*
(*c*) *Capparis* (*d*) *Brassica*

177. *Mesembryanthemum* belongs to the category :
(*a*) Mesophyte
(*b*) Fleshy xerophyte
(*c*) Non-succulent perennial xerophyte
(*d*) Epiphyte

178. Xerophytic plants have :
(*a*) Extensive root system small and thick leaves
(*b*) Extensive shoot system
(*c*) Profuse and large flowers
(*d*) Extensive air spaces

179. Thick cuticle occurs on the leaves of plants belonging to :
(*a*) Cool habitats (*b*) Warm habitats
(*c*) Dry habitats (*d*) Wet habitats

180. Stomata are sunken in :
(*a*) Mesophytes (*b*) Xerophytes
(*c*) Hygrophytes (*d*) Hydrophytes

181. Annual plants lacking perennating buds belong to :
(*a*) Therophytes (*b*) Cryptophytes
(*c*) Phanerophytes (*d*) Chaemophytes

182. Who proposed the concept of ecological pyramids :
(*a*) Odum (*b*) Elements
(*c*) Tansley (*d*) Elton

183. Transfer of energy in different trophic levels of an ecosystem is :
(*a*) Bioenergetics (*b*) Biosystem
(*c*) Geobiocoenosis (*d*) Holocoenosis

184. Which one is nature's cleaner :
(*a*) Consumers
(*b*) Producers
(*c*) Decomposers and scavengers
(*d*) Symbionts

185. Which one has maximum biomass :
(*a*) Pond ecosystem
(*b*) Lake ecosystem
(*c*) Grassland ecosystem
(*d*) Forest ecosystem

186. Submerged hydrophytes exchange gases through :
(*a*) Stomata (*b*) Hydathodes
(*c*) Lenticels (*d*) General surface

187. Biotic community alongwith its interacting physical environment comprises?
(*a*) Phytosociology
(*b*) Phytogeography
(*c*) Ecosystem
(*d*) Ecology

188. Number fo individual of a species in a particular ecosystem at a given time remains constant due to :
(*a*) Predators (*b*) Parasites
(*c*) Man (*d*) Food

189. Total amount of living material at various levels of a food chain is depicted by :
(*a*) Pyramid of energy
(*b*) Pyramid of numbers
(*c*) Pyramid of biomass
(*d*) All of the above

190. Relatively more abundant animals of desert grassland are :
(*a*) Arboreal (*b*) Fossorial
(*c*) Diurnal (*d*) Aquatic

191. Tropical plants *Prosopis, Acacia* and *Capparis* belong to :
(*a*) Evergreen forest (*b*) Deciduous forest
(*c*) Grassland (*d*) Thorn forest

192. Rate of conversion of light energy into chemical energy of organic molecules in an ecosystem is :
(*a*) Gross primary productivity
(*b*) Net primary productivity
(*c*) Net secondary productivity
(*d*) Gross secondary productivity

193. Halophytes grow on physiologically dry soil due to :
(*a*) Excessive salt in water
(*b*) Excessive salt in plants
(*c*) Excessive humidity outside
(*d*) Dry soil

194. Tropical forest are dense due to :
(*a*) Wild animals
(*b*) High temperature and less rain
(*c*) Low temperature and excess rain
(*d*) High temperature and excess rain

195. An ecological niche is a :
(*a*) Habitat of a plant
(*b*) Habitat of a small community
(*c*) Habitat of nocturnal animals
(*d*) Kind of plant-animal association

196. Sal forest *(Shorea robusta)* is a :
(*a*) Deciduous forest (*b*) Evergreen forest
(*c*) Rain forest (*d*) None of the above

197. Relative of roots, the shoots are massive in plants of :
(*a*) Deserts
(*b*) Moist temprerate
(*c*) Tundra
(*d*) Moist tropical forests

198. Tropical rain forests are found in :
(*a*) Andamans
(*b*) Bihar
(*c*) Himachal Pradesh
(*d*) Jammu and Kashmir

199. Submerged hydrophytes have a well developed :
(*a*) Vascular system (*b*) Aerenchyma
(*c*) Root system (*d*) Stomatal system

200. Stem of submerged hydrophytes is soft and weak because of :
(*a*) Absence of phloem
(*b*) Absence of stomata
(*c*) Absence of xylem
(*d*) Feebly developed supporting tisue and xylem

201. Aquatic plants generally have a :
(*a*) Well developed vascular system
(*b*) Reduced vascular system
(*c*) Well developed root system
(*d*) Well developed stomatal system

202. The floating leaves of an aquatic plant has :
(*a*) Stomata on upper surface
(*b*) Stomata on lower surface
(*c*) Stomata on both the surfaces
(*d*) No stomata

203. A plant devoid of roots is :
(*a*) *Wolffia/Ceratophyllum*
(*b*) *Vallisneria*
(*c*) *Hydrilla*
(*d*) *Azolla*

204. *Typha* is a :
(*a*) Submerged hydrophyte
(*b*) Floating hydrophyte
(*c*) Emerged hydrophytes
(*d*) Attached hydrophytes with floating leaves

205. In submerged hydrophytes the stomata occur :
(*a*) On lower surface
(*b*) On upper surface
(*c*) No where
(*d*) On both the surfaces

206. Which is a wrong statement about biomes?
(*a*) Diversity of organisms decreases as we move from high altitude to low altitude
(*b*) Diversity increases from high altitude to low altitude
(*c*) Diversity increases from high latitude to low latitude
(*d*) Diversity is maximum in tropical forests

207. Which character is not present in the hydrophytes :
(*a*) Poor roots
(*b*) Plentiful xylem and sclerenchyma
(*c*) Leaves with stomata on upper surface or absent
(*d*) Abundant aerenchyma

208. Which character is not present in the xerophytes :
(*a*) Thick cuticle
(*b*) Well developed mechanical tissue
(*c*) Well developed conducting tissues
(*d*) Spongy parenchyma

209. The leaves of desert plants are not torn away by high wind velocity because of :
(*a*) Spines
(*b*) Bending towards opposite side
(*c*) Sclerenchymatous tisssue that provides extra mechanical support
(*d*) Tearing of corners while the middle remains saved

210. Amongst hydrophytes finely dissected leaves occur in :
(*a*) Rooted floating leaved plants
(*b*) Submerged plants
(*c*) Emerged plants
(*d*) Free floating plants

211. The term biocoenosis was given by :
(*a*) Warming (*b*) Carl Mobius
(*c*) Tansley (*d*) Odum

212. Who proposed the term ecosystem :
(*a*) Odum (*b*) Gardner
(*c*) Warming (*d*) Tansley

213. The importance of ecosystem lies in :
(*a*) Cycling of materials
(*b*) Flow of energy
(*c*) Both (*a*) and (*b*)
(*d*) Its biomass

214. An ecosystem does not normally alter because it is in a state of :
(*a*) Homeostasis
(*b*) Imbalance
(*c*) Deficient light
(*d*) Deficient components

215. If 10 Kg food is *available at producer* level, then 0.1 kg food will be available to Peacock in which of the following chain?
(*a*) Plant-mice-snake-peacock
(*b*) Plant-snake-peacock
(*c*) Plant-mice-peacock-snake
(*d*) Plant-mice-cat-snake-peacock

216. In food chain, the largest population is that of :
(*a*) Producers
(*b*) Primary consumers
(*c*) Secondary consumers
(*d*) Tertiary consumers

217. Food levels of an ecosystem are known as :
(*a*) Producer levels (*b*) Herbivore levels
(*c*) Consumer levels (*d*) Trophic levels

218. Tropical dry deciduous forests occur in India in :
(*a*) Andamans
(*b*) Eastern Himalayas
(*c*) Madhya Pradesh
(*d*) Kerala

219. Plants of salty sea shore wet lands are :
(*a*) Heliophytes (*b*) Hydrophytes
(*c*) Halophytes (*d*) Saprophytes

220. *Eichhornia crassipes* is :
(*a*) Xerophyte (*b*) Hydrophyte
(*c*) Mesophyte (*d*) Parasite

221. Which one is the correct food chain :
(*a*) Eagle → Snake → Grasshopper → Grass → Frog
(*b*) Frog → Snake → Eagle → Grasshopper → Grass
(*c*) Grasshopper → Grass → Snake → Frog → Eagle
(*d*) Grass → Grasshopper → Frog → Snake → Eagle

222. Desert plants are able to tolerate water stress through :
(*a*) Root system reaching water table
(*b*) Stipular spines
(*c*) Absence of stomata
(*d*) Modification of stem into leaf like structures

223. Biome with broad-leaved resinous fire resistant drought enduring plants is :
(*a*) Savannah (*b*) Steppes
(*c*) Chapparal (*d*) Deciduous forest

224. Keystone species of an ecosystem are the ones which are :
(*a*) Most frequent
(*b*) Attain large biomass
(*c*) Present in maximum number
(*d*) Contribute to ecosystem properties

225. Which ecosystem has the highest gross primary productivity?
(*a*) Rain forests (*b*) Coral reefs
(*c*) Mangroves (*d*) Grasslands

226. During adverse season, therophytes survive through :
(*a*) Seeds (*b*) Bulbs
(*c*) Rhizomes (*d*) Corms.

227. Which is dominant in dessert?
(*a*) *Hyla* (*b*) Leopard
(*c*) Tiger (*d*) Lizard

228. Amount of energy transferred from one trophic level to next is :
(*a*) 1.5% (*b*) 10%
(*c*) 15% (*d*) 20%

229. Climatic and edaphic factors controlling distribution of a community constitute :
(*a*) Ecotone (*b*) Ecophene
(*c*) Epharmony (*d*) Ecological niche

230. *Acacia arabica* (= *A.nilotica*) is :
(*a*) Hydrophyte (*b*) Mesophyte
(*c*) Xerophyte (*d*) None of the above

231. Ecological pyramids are of types :
(*a*) Two (*b*) Three
(*c*) Four (*d*) Five

232. In an ecosystem, bacteria are :
(*a*) Microconsumers
(*b*) Macroconsumers
(*c*) Primary consumers
(*d*) Secondary consumers

233. Species diversity is lowest in ecosystem :
(*a*) Desert (*b*) Tundra
(*c*) Grassland (*d*) Deciduous forest

234. Concept of life forms was given by :
(*a*) Weaver (*b*) Clements
(*c*) Raunkier (*d*) Turesson

235. Homeostasis is :
(*a*) Tendency of biological systems to change with change in environment
(*b*) Tendency of biological systems to resist change
(*c*) Disturbance of self regulatory system and natural controls
(*d*) Biotic materials used in homeopathic medicines

236. The two components of an ecosystem are :
(*a*) Plants and animals
(*b*) Weeds, tress, animals and man
(*c*) Energy flow and mineral cycling
(*d*) Biotic and abiotic

237. Food chain is :
(*a*) Number of human beings forming a chain for food
(*b*) Animals near a source of food
(*c*) Transfer of food energy from producers to consumers
(*d*) None of the above

238. The driving force for an ecosystem is :
(*a*) Biomass
(*b*) Producers
(*c*) Carbohydrates in producers
(*d*) Solar energy

239. Ecosystem is :
(*a*) Always open
(*b*) Always closed
(*c*) Both open and closed depending upon community
(*d*) Both open and closed depending upon biomass

240. Energy entering an organism from outside is 100% efficient in case of :
(*a*) Unicellular green algae
(*b*) All green plants
(*c*) Some photosynthetic bacteria
(*d*) No photoautotroph

241. The major components of an ecosystem are :
(*a*) Food chain and decomposers
(*b*) Mineral cycling and energy flow
(*c*) Food chain and energy flow
(*d*) Energy flow and decomposers

242. Biotic components of an ecosystem include :
(*a*) Producers, consumers and decomposers
(*b*) Producers and consumers
(*c*) Producers only
(*d*) Consumers only

243. A food chain can have trophic levels :
(*a*) Three or four (*b*) Three
(*c*) Two (*d*) One

244. In a food chain, the initial organisms are :
(*a*) Top consumers
(*b*) Secondary consumers
(*c*) Primary consumers
(*d*) Photosynthates

245. In a food chain, herbivores/deer are :
(*a*) Primary producers
(*b*) Primary consumers
(*c*) Secondary consumers
(*d*) Decomposers

246. Green plants constitute :
(*a*) Complete food chain
(*b*) Second trophic level
(*c*) First trophic level
(*d*) Third trophic level

247. First link in food chain is green plant because :
(*a*) It alone can synthesise food
(*b*) It is fixed at one place
(*c*) It can pick up every thing
(*d*) It can eat every thing

248. What is true of ecosystem?
(*a*) Primary consumers are least dependent upon producers
(*b*) Primary consumers out-number producers
(*c*) Producers are more than primary consumers
(*d*) Secondary consumers are the largest and most powerful

249. Which one is not a trait of xerophytes :
(*a*) Thick cuticle
(*b*) Sunken stomata
(*c*) Aerenchyma
(*d*) Well developed mechanical tissue

250. In every ecosystem, the green plants are :
(*a*) Decomposers (*b*) Producers
(*c*) Consumers (*d*) None of the above

251. The factor related to structure of earth surface :
(*a*) Edaphic (*b*) Biotic
(*c*) Temperature (*d*) Topographic

252. Benthos of pond ecosystem are :
(*a*) Producers
(*b*) Primary consumers
(*c*) Secondary consumers
(*d*) Tertiary consumers

253. Lion is :
(*a*) Producer
(*b*) Primary consumer
(*c*) Predator
(*d*) Secondary consumer

254. Vegetation of Rajasthan is :
(*a*) Xerophytic (*b*) Alpine
(*c*) Arctic (*d*) Deciduous

255. During extreme aridity, Desert Rat :
(*a*) Stores water
(*b*) Uses metabolic water
(*c*) Saves water
(*d*) Does not use water

256. *Rhizophora* is an example of :
(*a*) Mesophyte (*b*) Hydrophyte
(*c*) Halophyte (*d*) Xerophyte

257. Which one lacks both roots and stomata :
(*a*) Hydrophytes (*b*) Mesophytes
(*c*) Hygrophytes (*d*) Halophytes

258. Which one is partially submerged and fixed in mud :
(*a*) *Marsilea* (*b*) *Cyperus*
(*c*) *Eichhornia* (*d*) *Typha*

259. 10% law for energy transfer in food chains was given by :
(*a*) Lindemann (*b*) Stanley
(*c*) Tansley (*d*) Weismann

260. Niche of a species is :
(*a*) Place of living
(*b*) Specific functions and competitive power
(*c*) Habitat and specific functions
(*d*) None of the above

261. Benthoic animals live :
(*a*) Deep is sea (*b*) Floating
(*c*) Submerged (*d*) Active swimmers

262. Major communities of the world are :
(*a*) Scrubs, jungles and gardens
(*b*) Ocean, fresh water and forest communities
(*c*) Grassland and desert communities
(*d*) Both (*b*) and (*c*)

263. Deciduous forests have :
(*a*) Variety of grasses
(*b*) Broad-leaved trees
(*c*) Narrow-leaved trees
(*d*) Variety of crocodiles

264. Which one is index of environmental conditions and changes :
(*a*) Individual
(*b*) Communities
(*c*) Niches
(*d*) Pollution

265. Increase in number of fauna and decrease in number of flora would be dangerous because of enhanced percentage of :
(*a*) Disease
(*b*) CO_2
(*c*) O_2
(*d*) Radioactive Pollution

266. Types of food chains are :
(*a*) Four (*b*) Three
(*c*) Two (*d*) One

267. Region of ocean which does not receive sunlight is :
(*a*) Abyssal zone
(*b*) Littoral zone
(*c*) Aphotic zone
(*d*) Photic zone

268. Match the followings :

A.	Diversification	1.	Stability
B.	Deeplakes	2.	Oligotrophic
C.	Continental shelf	3.	Bathyral zone
D.	Alpine tundra	4.	Mountain tops

Codes :

	A	B	C	D
(*a*)	1	2	3	4
(*b*)	4	3	2	1
(*c*)	2	3	1	4
(*d*)	1	4	3	2

269. Correct the matching :

A.	Taiga	1.	Conifers
B.	Tundra	2.	Tree less
C.	Chapparal	3.	Scrubs forest
D.	Abyssal zone	4.	Veldts
E.	Africa	5.	No light

Codes :

	A	B	C	D	E
(*a*)	1	2	5	3	4
(*b*)	1	2	5	4	3
(*c*)	1	2	3	5	4
(*d*)	2	1	3	5	4

270. **Chapparal** are evergreen broad leaved fire resistants drought evading scrub forests (sclerophyllous plants with hard thick leaves) found in mediterranean area, Africa, Australia and Chile. These are characterised by :
(*a*) heavy rain in summer and winter dry
(*b*) rain throughout year and no bush fire
(*c*) limited rain in winter, summer dry and bush fire
(*d*) little rain in summer and bush fire

271. Different trophic levels in an ecosystem are shown below. Line B in the graph represents :

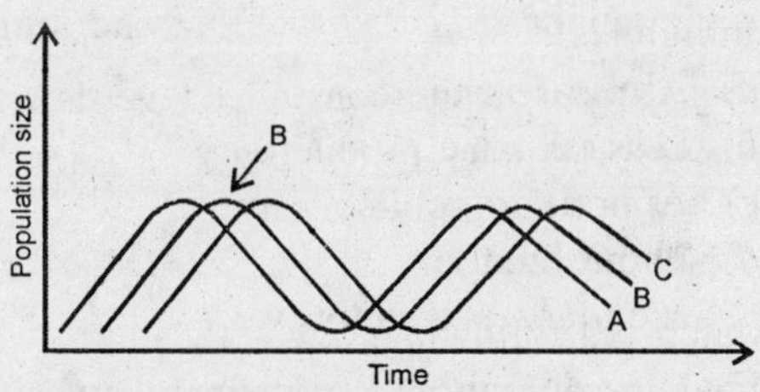

(*a*) primary consumer
(*b*) orimary producer
(*c*) secondary consumer
(*d*) tertiary consumer

272. Which is correct food cahin :
(*a*) Phytoplankton → Fishes → Zooplankton
(*b*) Zooplankton → Phytoplankton → Fishes
(*c*) Phytoplankton → Zooplankton → Fishes
(*d*) Fishes → Zooplankton → Phytoplankton

273. In European countries, the term for ecosystem is :
(*a*) Biogeocoenosis (*b*) Geobiocoenosis
(*c*) Biocoenosis (*d*) Microcosm

274. A synonym of term ecosystem, popular in Russia and given by Sukachev (1944) is :
(*a*) Geobiocoenosis (*b*) Microcosm
(*c*) Vernalization (*d*) Ecosphere

275. All the ecosystems show homeostasis. It is achieved through a number of controls called :
(*a*) Steady state (*b*) Entrophy
(*c*) Cybernetics (*d*) Entropy

276. Puddles in the nature, named as :
(*a*) macroecosystem
(*b*) microecosystem
(*c*) man made ecosystem
(*d*) monoculture agroecosystem

277. Decomposers are those which :
(*a*) operate to make chemical substance resulting in dead tissue
(*b*) operate in relay terms, simplifying step by step, the organic constituents of dead body
(*c*) attack plants and animals and kill them
(*d*) operate in living body and simplify step by step the organic constituent of the cell

278. Which is correct ?
(*a*) Most productive ecosystem is coral reef ecosystem
(*b*) Least productive ecosystem is deserts and deeplakes
(*c*) Sugarcane is most productive cropland agro ecosystem
(*d*) All of the above

279. The better idea of the productivity of an ecosystem can be obtained by :
(*a*) pyramid of numbers
(*b*) pyramid of biomass
(*c*) pyramid of energy
(*d*) All of the above

280. Which is correct food chain in Grassland :
(*a*) Grass → Snake → Insect → Deer
(*b*) Grass → Wolf → Deer → Buffalo
(*c*) Bacteria → Grass → Rabbit → Wolf
(*d*) Grass → Insect → Frog → Snake

281. Food chain in which micro-organisms breakdown the food formed by primary producers is :
(*a*) Parasitic food chain
(*b*) Detritus food chain
(*c*) Consumer food chain
(*d*) Predator food chain

282. A food chain comprises :
(*a*) Producers, herbivores and carnivores
(*b*) Producers, consumers and decomposers
(*c*) Producers and primary consumers
(*d*) Producers, carnivores and decomposers

283. Pick up the correct food chain :
(*a*) Grass → Chamelion → Insect → Bird
(*b*) Grass → Fox → Rabbit → Bird
(*c*) Phytoplankton → Zooplankton → Fish
(*d*) Fallenleaves → Bacteria → Insect larvae

284. Path of energy flow in an ecosystem is :
(*a*) Herbivores → Producers → Carnivores Decomposers
(*b*) Herbivores → Carnivores → Producers Decomposers
(*c*) Producers → Carnivores → Herbivores Decomposers
(*d*) Producers → Herbivores → Carnivores Decomposers

285. Biological equilibrium is equilibrium amongst :
(*a*) Producers and decomposer
(*b*) Producers and consumers
(*c*) Producers, consumers and decomposers
(*d*) Consumers and decomposers

286. An ecosystem is an interacting system of :
(*a*) Communities
(*b*) Communities and their physical environment
(*c*) Populations
(*d*) Individuals

287. Upper part of Sea/aquatic ecosystem contains :
(*a*) Plankton
(*b*) Nekton
(*c*) Both (*a*) and (*b*)
(*d*) Benthos

288. Energy transfer from organism to organism in a natural community develops :
(*a*) Biological control
(*b*) Food chain
(*c*) Natural barriers
(*d*) Food web

289. A group of interconnected food chains is :
(*a*) Complex of food chain
(*b*) Food cycle
(*c*) Food web
(*d*) Pyramid of energy

290. Which one is primary consumer :
(*a*) Carnivore (*b*) Scavenger
(*c*) Saprophyte (*d*) Herbivore

291. Decomposers of an ecosystem include :
(*a*) Microscopic animals
(*b*) Bacteria and fungi
(*c*) Both (*a*) and (*b*)
(*d*) Bacteria, fungi and macroscopic animals

292. Phytoplankton are destroyed. It will :
(*a*) Cause spurt in population of primary consumers
(*b*) Rapid growth of algae
(*c*) Affect the food chain
(*d*) Have no effect

293. In an aqueous environment, microscopic animals and plants are collectively known as :
(*a*) Plankton (*b*) Herbivore
(*c*) Commensals (*d*) Flora and fauna

294. Energy stored at the consumer level is :
(*a*) Gross primary productivity
(*b*) Net primary productivity
(*c*) Net productivity
(*d*) Secondary productivity

295. What is wrong about xerophytes :
(*a*) Sunken stomata
(*b*) Small spiny leaves
(*c*) Thick Cuticle
(*d*) Larger number of stomata

296. Mechanical tissue is undeveloped in :
(*a*) Xerophytes (*b*) Hydrophytes
(*c*) Halophytes (*d*) Mesophytes

297. Tropical forests occur in India :
(*a*) Jammu and Kashmir
(*b*) Rajasthan
(*c*) Kerala and Asom
(*d*) The forests do not occur in India

298. Which can be trophic level of a lion in forest ecosystem :
(*a*) T_3 (*b*) T_2
(*c*) T_4 (*d*) T_1

299. Which ones occurs at the same trophic level :
(*a*) Crow and Cow
(*b*) Snake and Earthworm
(*c*) Tiger and Wild Bear
(*d*) Deer and Bee

300. Which is correct :
(*a*) Least productive ecosystem is desert and deep lake
(*b*) Sugarcane is the most productive agroecosystem
(*c*) Most productive is coral reef system
(*d*) All of the above

301. Bulk CO_2 fixation occurs in :
(*a*) Crop plants
(*b*) Oceans
(*c*) Tropical rain forests
(*d*) Temperate forests

302. Desert biome does not support much vegetation as it lacks :
(*a*) Sufficient light
(*b*) Favourable temperature
(*c*) Sufficient water
(*d*) Sufficient nutrients

303. Animals that can tolerate a narrow range of salinity are :
(*a*) Stenohaline (*b*) Euryhaline
(*c*) Anadromous (*d*) Catadromous

304. Hygrometer is employed to measure :
(*a*) Wind velocity (*b*) Temperature
(*c*) Relative humidity (*d*) Turbidity

305. Stratification is more common in :
(*a*) Tropical rain forest
(*b*) Deciduous forest
(*c*) Temperate forest
(*d*) Tropical savannah

306. Importance of ecosystem lies in :
(*a*) Cycling of materials
(*b*) Flow of energy
(*c*) Both (*a*) and (*b*)
(*d*) None of the above

307. Number of primary producers per unit area would be maximum in :
(*a*) Forest ecosystem
(*b*) Pond ecosystem
(*c*) Desert
(*d*) Grassland ecosystem

308. A food chain begins with :
(*a*) Photosynthetic organisms
(*b*) Nitrogen fixing organisms
(*c*) Decomposers
(*d*) Consumers

309. The most stable ecosystem is :
(*a*) Forest (*b*) Mountain
(*c*) Desert (*d*) Ocean

310. In the absence of decomposers, ecosystem functioning is adversely affected due to :
(*a*) Blocking of energy flow
(*b*) Blocking of mineral cycling
(*c*) Blocking of solar energy to herbivores
(*d*) Rate of decomposition of other components will increase

311. Maximum number in pond ecosystem is of :
(*a*) Producers (*b*) Consumers
(*c*) Top consumers (*d*) Decomposers

312. Total energy fixed by an ecosystem is :
(*a*) Primary production
(*b*) Gross production
(*c*) Net production
(*d*) Secondary production

313. Savannahs are :
(*a*) Tropical rain forests
(*b*) Desert scrubs
(*c*) Grassland with scattered trees
(*d*) Dense forests with closed canopy

314. Which one has the maximum biomass :
(*a*) Temperate forest
(*b*) Tropical rain forest
(*c*) Alpine vegetation
(*d*) Taiga

315. Pyramid of numbers deals with number of :
(*a*) Species in an area
(*b*) Individuals in a community
(*c*) Individuals in a trophic level
(*d*) Subspecies in a community

316. Which ones lie at the level of primary consumers :
(*a*) Fishes (*b*) Eagles
(*c*) Cattle and insects (*d*) Snakes and frogs

317. Ecosystem creates :
(*a*) Food chains and food web
(*b*) Food web
(*c*) Habitats
(*d*) None of the above

318. In lake ecosystem, the pyramid of biomass is generally :
(*a*) Spindle-shaped (*b*) Inverted
(*c*) Upright (*d*) Horizontal

319. Carnivores represent :
(*a*) Primary consumers
(*b*) Secondary and tertiary consumers
(*c*) Secondary consumers
(*d*) Reducers

320. In a food chain, man is :
(*a*) Primary and secondary consumer
(*b*) Primary consumers
(*c*) Secondary consumer
(*d*) Producer

321. Pyramid of numbers in a pond ecosystem is :
(*a*) Irregular (*b*) Inverted
(*c*) Upright (*d*) Spindle shaped

322. Pyramid of numbers in a forest ecosystem is :
(*a*) Upright (*b*) Inverted
(*c*) Irregular (*d*) Linear

323. Species diversity increases as one proceeds from :
(*a*) High altitude to low altitude and high latitude to low latitude
(*b*) Low altitude to high altitude and high latitude to low latitude
(*c*) Low altitude to high altitude and low latitude to high latitude
(*d*) High altitude to low altitude and low latitude to high latitude

324. In grass-deer-tiger food chain, grass biomass is one tonne. The tiger biomass shall be :
(*a*) 100 kg (*b*) 10 kg
(*c*) 200 kg (*d*) 1 kg

325. In a biotic community the most important factor for survival of an animal is :
(*a*) Day length (*b*) Soil moisture
(*c*) Green food (*d*) Predators

326. In a food chain, the largest population is that of :
(*a*) Producers
(*b*) Decomposers
(*c*) Secondary consumers
(*d*) Primary consumers

327. Xeric environment is characterised by :
(*a*) Precipitation
(*b*) Low atmospheric humidity
(*c*) Extremes of temperature
(*d*) High rate of vapourisation

328. Second most important trophic level in a lake is :
(*a*) Zooplankton (*b*) Phytoplankton
(*c*) Benthos (*d*) Neuston

329. Which receives the maximum energy :
(*a*) Producers
(*b*) Decomposers
(*c*) Primary consumers
(*d*) Secondary consumers

330. *Nepenthes* belongs to the category of :
(*a*) Primary consumer
(*b*) Producer
(*c*) Secondary consumers
(*d*) Both (*b*) and (*c*)

331. Siddartha found a vegetarian field mouse being swallowed by snake which in turn formed the meal for a hawk. What is the position of snake in the food chain?
(*a*) Producer
(*b*) Primary consumer
(*c*) Secondary consumer
(*d*) Tertiary consumer

332. Where there is no difference :
(*a*) T_1 and herbivores
(*b*) Primary consumers and herbivores
(*c*) Primary carnivores and T_2
(*d*) Secondary consumers and herbivores

333. Abyssal zone in Ocean has :
(*a*) No sunlight but contains consumers and decomposers
(*b*) No sunlight but contains producers
(*c*) No sunlight but contains living beings
(*d*) Sunlight as well as producers

334. Flow of energy declines as it passes from lower to higher trophic level. This is explained by :
(*a*) First law of thermodynamics
(*b*) Second law of thermodynamic
(*c*) Newton's second law
(*d*) Newton's third law

335. A yound crocodile has eaten a lamb. A hawk attacks the crocodile and consumers the same In ecological terms, the hawk is :
(*a*) Producer
(*b*) Primary consumer
(*c*) Secondary consumer
(*d*) Tertiary consumer

336. If all the plants are to die, all the animals will also die due to deficiency of :
(*a*) Food (*b*) Carbon dioxide
(*c*) Oxygen (*d*) Timber

337. Pyramid of energy (in a forest/pond ecosystem) is :
(*a*) Always inverted
(*b*) Always upright
(*c*) Spindle-shaped
(*d*) Both upright and inverted depending upon ecosystem

338. In an ecosystem, which one shows one-way passage :
(*a*) Free energy (*b*) Carbon
(*c*) Nitrogen (*d*) Potassium

339. Pyramid of numbers in a grassland/true ecosystem is :
(*a*) Always inverted (*b*) Always upright
(*c*) Both (*a*) and (*b*) (*d*) Spindle-shaped

340. Suppose all the bacteria and fungi are destroyed. What will happen?
(*a*) There will be no disease and death
(*b*) No antibiotics would become available
(*c*) Dead bodies and excretions will pile up
(*d*) Soil will become depleted of all nutrients

341. Maximum human population can be supported if all the humans are :
(*a*) Carnivores
(*b*) Pure vegetarian
(*c*) Vegetarian alongwith use of milk
(*d*) Vegetarian alongwith use of milk and eggs

342. The pyramid which cannot be inverted in a stable ecosystem is that of :
(*a*) Biomass (*b*) Number
(*c*) Energy (*d*) All of the above

343. In a tree ecosystem, the pyramid of numbers is :
(*a*) Upright (*b*) Inverted
(*c*) Spindle like (*d*) Variable

344. Shallow lakes with abundant organic matter are :
(*a*) Saprotrophic (*b*) Oligotrophic
(*c*) Eutrophic (*d*) Heterotrophic

345. Animals in an ecosystem are called :
(*a*) Carnivores (*b*) Consumers
(*c*) Herbivores (*d*) Microconsumers

346. Biological equilibrium is an equilibrium amongst :
(*a*) Producers and decomposers
(*b*) Producers and consumers
(*c*) Producers, consumers and decomposers
(*d*) Consumers and decomposers

347. Energy and nutrients enter in a community by way of the :
(*a*) Herbivores (*b*) Scavangers
(*c*) Detritivores (*d*) Producers

348. The number of Primary producers within a specified area would be maximum in which ecosystem?
(*a*) Desert (*b*) Forest
(*c*) Grassland (*d*) Pond

349. Organisms which secrete digestive enzymes for breaking food into simpler components and then absorb it are known as :
(*a*) Osmotrophs (*b*) Phagotrophs
(*c*) Holotrophs (*d*) Autotrophs

350. Decomposers (microconsumers – also called reducers, transformers, osmotrophs, saprotrophs) are must in an ecosystem for :
(*a*) Flow of energy
(*b*) Cyclic exchange of minerals
(*c*) Both are correct
(*d*) All of these

351. Which is the most recently discovered ecosystem?
(*a*) Tundra (*b*) Iceberg
(*c*) Crater (*d*) Vent

352. Vegetarian field mouse is swallowed by snake which in turn by hawk. Then what is the position of snake in this food chain?
(*a*) Producer
(*b*) Primary consumer
(*c*) Secondary consumer
(*d*) Tertiary consumer

353. Deserts receive rainfall of less than 25 cm annually. How much area of land is desert?
(*a*) About 10 to 15%
(*b*) About 33%
(*c*) About 15 to 20%
(*d*) About 40%

354. The stability of a Grassland ecosystem depends upon :
(*a*) Carnivores (*b*) Grazers
(*c*) Both (*a*) and (*b*) (*d*) Neither (*a*) nor (*b*)

355. What ecological factors are strongest determining factors of various biomes?
(*a*) Light and wind
(*b*) Wind and edaphic
(*c*) *p*H and humidity
(*d*) Precipitation and temperature

356. Which grassland have richest and deepest soil and tall grasses?
(*a*) Prairies of Canada
(*b*) Pampas of South America
(*c*) Steppes of Eurasia
(*d*) Tussocks of New Zealand

357. Area towards the north and south poles where trees disappear and vegetation is meadow like is called :
(*a*) Tundra (*b*) Taiga
(*c*) Savannah (*d*) Rain forest

358. Plants growing in Savannahs biome are called :
(*a*) Eremophytes (*b*) Psamophytes
(*c*) Oxylophytes (*d*) Psilophytes

359. What is correct for pyramid of numbers?
(*a*) It may be upright or inverted or spindle like
(*b*) It is upright (vertical) in pond and grassland were predator and detritus food chains occur
(*c*) It is inverted in parasitic food chains and tree ecosystem
(*d*) All of the above

360. What is 'Pastures of the sea'?
(*a*) Estuaries (*b*) Coastal waters
(*c*) Antarctic zone (*d*) All of these

ANSWERS

1	2	3	4	5	6	7	8	9	10
(*d*)	(*d*)	(*c*)	(*b*)	(*c*)	(*c*)	(*c*)	(*d*)	(*d*)	(*b*)
11	**12**	**13**	**14**	**15**	**16**	**17**	**18**	**19**	**20**
(*a*)	(*c*)	(*b*)	(*c*)	(*d*)	(*c*)	(*d*)	(*d*)	(*a*)	(*b*)
21	**22**	**23**	**24**	**25**	**26**	**27**	**28**	**29**	**30**
(*c*)	(*b*)	(*a*)	(*c*)	(*d*)	(*d*)	(*c*)	(*d*)	(*d*)	(*c*)
31	**32**	**33**	**34**	**35**	**36**	**37**	**38**	**39**	**40**
(*c*)	(*b*)	(*d*)	(*a*)	(*d*)	(*a*)	(*b*)	(*c*)	(*d*)	(*a*)
41	**42**	**43**	**44**	**45**	**46**	**47**	**48**	**49**	**50**
(*b*)	(*d*)	(*d*)	(*d*)	(*c*)	(*a*)	(*c*)	(*c*)	(*a*)	(*a*)

51	**52**	**53**	**54**	**55**	**56**	**57**	**58**	**59**	**60**
(*c*)	(*c*)	(*c*)	(*c*)	(*b*)	(*b*)	(*a*)	(*a*)	(*b*)	(*a*)
61	**62**	**63**	**64**	**65**	**66**	**67**	**68**	**69**	**70**
(*d*)	(*d*)	(*c*)	(*c*)	(*b*)	(*d*)	(*b*)	(*a*)	(*c*)	(*b*)
71	**72**	**73**	**74**	**75**	**76**	**77**	**78**	**79**	**80**
(*b*)	(*a*)	(*b*)	(*b*)	(*c*)	(*c*)	(*d*)	(*d*)	(*a*)	(*a*)
81	**82**	**83**	**84**	**85**	**86**	**87**	**88**	**89**	**90**
(*a*)	(*b*)	(*d*)	(*a*)	(*a*)	(*c*)	(*c*)	(*b*)	(*b*)	(*b*)
91	**92**	**93**	**94**	**95**	**96**	**97**	**98**	**99**	**100**
(*a*)	(*a*)	(*c*)	(*c*)	(*b*)	(*a*)	(*b*)	(*c*)	(*b*)	(*b*)
101	**102**	**103**	**104**	**105**	**106**	**107**	**108**	**109**	**110**
(*d*)	(*d*)	(*c*)	(*a*)	(*c*)	(*b*)	(*b*)	(*d*)	(*a*)	(*c*)
111	**112**	**113**	**114**	**115**	**116**	**117**	**118**	**119**	**120**
(*b*)	(*c*)	(*a*)	(*b*)	(*c*)	(*d*)	(*b*)	(*d*)	(*c*)	(*b*)
121	**122**	**123**	**124**	**125**	**126**	**127**	**128**	**129**	**130**
(*d*)	(*b*)	(*d*)	(*c*)	(*d*)	(*b*)	(*a*)	(*d*)	(*c*)	(*c*)
131	**132**	**133**	**134**	**135**	**136**	**137**	**138**	**139**	**140**
(*a*)	(*c*)	(*c*)	(*d*)	(*a*)	(*d*)	(*a*)	(*d*)	(*d*)	(*d*)
141	**142**	**143**	**144**	**145**	**146**	**147**	**148**	**149**	**150**
(*c*)	(*d*)	(*b*)	(*a*)	(*c*)	(*b*)	(*b*)	(*c*)	(*a*)	(*d*)
151	**152**	**153**	**154**	**155**	**156**	**157**	**158**	**159**	**160**
(*d*)	(*a*)	(*d*)	(*a*)	(*b*)	(*c*)	(*a*)	(*b*)	(*b*)	(*a*)
161	**162**	**163**	**164**	**165**	**166**	**167**	**168**	**169**	**170**
(*c*)	(*c*)	(*d*)	(*c*)	(*b*)	(*d*)	(*c*)	(*b*)	(*c*)	(*d*)
171	**172**	**173**	**174**	**175**	**176**	**177**	**178**	**179**	**180**
(*b*)	(*a*)	(*b*)	(*a*)	(*a*)	(*c*)	(*b*)	(*a*)	(*c*)	(*b*)
181	**182**	**183**	**184**	**185**	**186**	**187**	**188**	**189**	**190**
(*a*)	(*d*)	(*a*)	(*c*)	(*d*)	(*d*)	(*c*)	(*a*)	(*c*)	(*b*)
191	**192**	**193**	**194**	**195**	**196**	**197**	**198**	**199**	**200**
(*d*)	(*a*)	(*a*)	(*d*)	(*d*)	(*a*)	(*d*)	(*a*)	(*b*)	(*d*)
201	**202**	**203**	**204**	**205**	**206**	**207**	**208**	**209**	**210**
(*b*)	(*a*)	(*a*)	(*c*)	(*c*)	(*a*)	(*b*)	(*d*)	(*c*)	(*b*)
211	**212**	**213**	**214**	**215**	**216**	**217**	**218**	**219**	**220**
(*b*)	(*d*)	(*c*)	(*a*)	(*a*)	(*a*)	(*d*)	(*c*)	(*c*)	(*b*)
221	**222**	**223**	**224**	**225**	**226**	**227**	**228**	**229**	**230**
(*d*)	(*d*)	(*c*)	(*d*)	(*b*)	(*a*)	(*d*)	(*b*)	(*d*)	(*c*)
231	**232**	**233**	**234**	**235**	**236**	**237**	**238**	**239**	**240**
(*b*)	(*a*)	(*b*)	(*c*)	(*b*)	(*d*)	(*c*)	(*d*)	(*c*)	(*d*)
241	**242**	**243**	**244**	**245**	**246**	**247**	**248**	**249**	**250**
(*b*)	(*a*)	(*a*)	(*d*)	(*b*)	(*c*)	(*a*)	(*c*)	(*c*)	(*b*)
251	**252**	**253**	**254**	**255**	**256**	**257**	**258**	**259**	**260**
(*d*)	(*b*)	(*c*)	(*a*)	(*b*)	(*c*)	(*a*)	(*d*)	(*a*)	(*c*)

261	**262**	**263**	**264**	**265**	**266**	**267**	**268**	**269**	**270**
(*a*)	(*d*)	(*b*)	(*c*)	(*b*)	(*b*)	(*a*)	(*a*)	(*c*)	(*c*)
271	**272**	**273**	**274**	**275**	**276**	**277**	**278**	**279**	**280**
(*a*)	(*c*)	(*c*)	(*a*)	(*c*)	(*b*)	(*b*)	(*d*)	(*b*)	(*d*)
281	**282**	**283**	**284**	**285**	**286**	**287**	**288**	**289**	**290**
(*b*)	(*a*)	(*c*)	(*d*)	(*c*)	(*b*)	(*a*)	(*b*)	(*c*)	(*d*)
291	**292**	**293**	**294**	**295**	**296**	**297**	**298**	**299**	**300**
(*b*)	(*c*)	(*a*)	(*d*)	(*d*)	(*b*)	(*c*)	(*c*)	(*d*)	(*d*)
301	**302**	**303**	**304**	**305**	**306**	**307**	**308**	**309**	**310**
(*b*)	(*c*)	(*a*)	(*c*)	(*a*)	(*c*)	(*b*)	(*a*)	(*d*)	(*b*)
311	**312**	**313**	**314**	**315**	**316**	**317**	**318**	**319**	**320**
(*a*)	(*b*)	(*c*)	(*b*)	(*c*)	(*c*)	(*a*)	(*b*)	(*b*)	(*a*)
321	**322**	**323**	**324**	**325**	**326**	**327**	**328**	**329**	**330**
(*c*)	(*a*)	(*a*)	(*b*)	(*c*)	(*a*)	(*b*)	(*a*)	(*a*)	(*d*)
331	**332**	**333**	**334**	**335**	**336**	**337**	**338**	**339**	**340**
(*c*)	(*b*)	(*a*)	(*b*)	(*d*)	(*c*)	(*b*)	(*a*)	(*b*)	(*c*)
341	**342**	**343**	**344**	**345**	**346**	**347**	**348**	**349**	**350**
(*b*)	(*c*)	(*b*)	(*c*)	(*b*)	(*c*)	(*a*)	(*d*)	(*a*)	(*b*)
351	**352**	**353**	**354**	**355**	**356**	**357**	**358**	**359**	**360**
(*d*)	(*c*)	(*c*)	(*b*)	(*d*)	(*a*)	(*a*)	(*d*)	(*d*)	(*b*)

5

BIOTIC RESOURCES

1. First '*Earth Summit*' at Rio-de-Janeiro (Brazil) held in 1992 was related to :
   (*a*) soil fertility
   (*b*) soil erosion
   (*c*) prevention of afforestation
   (*d*) conservation of environment
2. The most serious threat to migratory birds which are vulnerable species is :
   (*a*) destruction of habitats
   (*b*) deforestation
   (*c*) human settlements
   (*d*) pollution of oceans
3. The most important activity responsible for the extinction/diminishing of wildlife is :
   (*a*) pollution of air and water
   (*b*) hunting for wildlife products
   (*c*) introduction of alien species and lack of proper care
   (*d*) alteration and destruction of natural habitats
4. The cause of extinction of species is/are :
   (*a*) man made forest fire, deforestation hunting and pollution of air and water
   (*b*) conversion of natural habitats of wildlife into dams, reservoirs, crop lands, mining sides etc.
   (*c*) introduction of exotic species and over exploitation of organisms
   (*d*) All of the above
5. **Red data book** (RDB) published by IUCN provides :
   (*a*) information of threatened species of flora and fauna
   (*b*) information on wildlife
   (*c*) information on toxic plants
   (*d*) a book on biota red sea
6. International day for Biological Diversity is oberved on :
   (*a*) December 21 (*b*) December 29
   (*c*) June 5 (*d*) December 1
7. A species should be protected because :
   (*a*) species are lovely creatures of God
   (*b*) species are useful to us
   (*c*) species are studied by us
   (*d*) no one can recreate a species, if lost
8. Reason of diversity in living being is :
   (*a*) Mutation
   (*b*) Gradual change
   (*c*) Long term evolutionary change
   (*d*) Short term evolutionary change
9. What should we do to save the existing species of the wildlife?
   (*a*) Protection of endangered species
   (*b*) Protection of wildlife *in situ* and *ex situ*
   (*c*) Preservation of useful plants and animals in protected areas
   (*d*) All of these
10. *Ex situ* conservation of natural resources can be obtained by :
    (*a*) controlling natural habits
    (*b*) inducing variations
    (*c*) establishing sanctuaries
    (*d*) protecting wildlife in Zoos and Botanical gardens
11. *In situ* conservation of natural resources is :
    (*a*) protection of wildlife in natural habitat/ National parks
    (*b*) control of pollution
    (*c*) control of human interference in the biosphere
    (*d*) All of the above

12. To conserve wildlife, each state of India is alloted a species. Which plant is allocated to Karnataka?
(*a*) *Santalum indicum*
(*b*) *Cedrus deodara*
(*c*) *Ficus benghalensis*
(*d*) *Shorea robusta*

13. WWF is now called :
(*a*) world wildlife fund
(*b*) world wide fund for nature
(*c*) world wrestling federation
(*d*) wonder wash fabric

14. MAB launched in 1971 by UNESCO stands for :
(*a*) Man and Botany
(*b*) Man and Biosphere
(*c*) Man and Biotic community
(*d*) Man and Biomes

15. A hazardous waste is characterised by
(*a*) Ignitibility
(*b*) Reactivity
(*c*) Toxicity
(*d*) All of the above

16. Animals having high extinction prospects are :
(*a*) Lion and Leopard
(*b*) Tiger and Bustard
(*c*) Himalayan Bear and Musk deer
(*d*) Elephant and Crocodile

17. Which gene sanctuary has been created for an insectivorous plant?
(*a*) Nepenthes sanctuary
(*b*) Bori sanctuary
(*c*) Kumbhalgarh sanctuary
(*d*) All of the above

18. Dudhwa National Park is located in :
(*a*) Gujarat (*b*) UP
(*c*) Rajasthan (*d*) MP

19. How many hot spots have been identified in the world and Indian Subcontinent respectively ?
(*a*) 17, 2
(*b*) 12, 3
(*c*) 35, 2
(*d*) 17, 3

20. A society that cares for animals :
(*a*) Chipko
(*b*) Blue Cross
(*c*) MAB
(*d*) People For Animals

21. The state mammal of Himachal, Punjab, Haryana, UP and Delhi repectively :
(*a*) Musk deer, Black Buck, Nilgai, Leopard, Hanuman Langur
(*b*) Black Buck, Musk deer, Camel, Leopard, Monkey
(*c*) Musk deer, Black Buck, Donkey, Leopard, Nilgai
(*d*) Stag, Lion, Nilgai, Barasingha, Black Buck

22. Biological control of Pests is :
(*a*) Polluting (*b*) Expensive
(*c*) Self perpetuating (*d*) Toxic

23. Main cause of increase in salinity of arid land due to irrigation is :
(*a*) Contribution of solutes through irrigation
(*b*) Dissolution of solutes due to irrigation
(*c*) Solutes being brought up from lower soil horizon
(*d*) Contribution of solutes by plants grown with irrigation

24. Type of soil erosion taking place on the banks of fast running rivers is termed as :
(*a*) Gully erosion (*b*) Rill erosion
(*c*) Riparian erosion (*d*) Sheet erosion

25. Soil erosion is prevented by :
(*a*) afforestation
(*b*) overgrazing
(*c*) removal of weeds
(*d*) increasing bird population

26. Canes (rattans) are used in :
(*a*) furniture
(*b*) walking sticks
(*c*) ropes, sport goods
(*d*) All of these

27. Ecofriendly method is :
(*a*) Use of CNG (Compressed Natural Gas) in automobiles
(*b*) Energy plantation
(*c*) Both (*a*) and (*b*)
(*d*) Plantation of C_3 plants

28. The greatest damage to forests in hills is due to :
(*a*) excessive grazing (*b*) soil erosion
(*c*) pollution (*d*) leaching

29. Social forestry programme is :
(*a*) to make up for the loss of tree cover
(*b*) designed to prevent desertification
(*c*) meant to restore soil fertility
(*d*) to provide tree cover to meet daily needs of society

30. Wasteland reclamation is best brought by :
(*a*) Hybrid species of Eucalyptus
(*b*) *Prosopis*
(*c*) *Acacia*
(*d*) *Leucaena*

31. An example for *in situ* biological conservation method is to establish :
(*a*) Seed Banks
(*b*) Botanical Gardens
(*c*) Zoos
(*d*) Biosphere reserves

32. Which group of vertebrates comprises the highest number of endangered species?
(*a*) Reptiles (*b*) Birds
(*c*) Mammals (*d*) Fishes

33. Wildlife is conserved :
(*a*) *in situ*
(*b*) *ex situ*
(*c*) both (a) and (b)
(*d*) selective hunting of predators

34. The termwild life was coined by :
(*a*) William Hornday (*b*) August
(*c*) IUCN (*d*) UNESCO

35. Wildlife includes :
(*a*) animals, plants and microorganisms in their natural habitat
(*b*) cultivated plants and domestic animals
(*c*) wild animals in their natural habitat only
(*d*) wild plants in their natural habitat

36. Wildlife is important because :
(*a*) it balances population
(*b*) it maintains food chains and natural cycles
(*c*) it is the source of *gene bank* for breeding programme in agriculture
(*d*) All of the above

37. Wildlife, conservation means the protection and preservation of :
(*a*) wild flora
(*b*) wild fauna
(*c*) cultivated plants and domesticated animals
(*d*) all living in natural habitat

38. Conservation of living resources involves :
(*a*) maintenance of ecological processes and life supporting systems
(*b*) preservation of diversity of species
(*c*) sustainable utilization of species and ecosystems
(*d*) All of the above

39. The protected areas include :
(*a*) biosphere reserve (*b*) national parks
(*c*) sanctuaries (*d*) All of these

40. Which is correct for **threatened (T) species?**
(*a*) It is an endangered species like Rhino, Asiatic Lion, which is in danger of extinction
(*b*) It is rare species like wild Asiatic Ass with small population in certain geographical area
(*c*) It is a vulnerable species like Musk deer, black buck which is likely to move into endangered category in near future
(*d*) It is a species to be conserved to avoid its becoming rare, endangered or vulnerable species

41. Rare (R) species are :
(*a*) those with small population in certain geographical areas
(*b*) those which are found in silent valley of Kerala
(*c*) those which are likely to be endangered
(*d*) those which are in danger of extinction

42. Vulnerable (V) species are those :
(*a*) which are wild
(*b*) which live in National parks
(*c*) which are likely to be endanger of extinction in near future
(*d*) which require conservation

43. The taxa which are on the verge of extinction are called :
(*a*) wildlife
(*b*) endangered (E) species
(*c*) threatened (T) species
(*d*) vulnerable (V) species

44. Which programme is not for preservation of wildlife/forests in India?
(*a*) IUCN (*b*) MAB
(*c*) Project Tiger (*d*) NEERI

45. Plant/animals species should be present because :
(*a*) a species once lost can not be retrieved
(*b*) zoologists study them
(*c*) it can be useful to us
(*d*) it is a creature of nature

46. National 'Wildlife Protection Act' was enacted by our government to declare hunting as unlawful act in the year :
(*a*) 1979 (*b*) 1972
(*c*) 1962 (*d*) 1982

47. Conservation of plant diversity is an :
(*a*) genetic necessity
(*b*) environmental necessity
(*c*) economic necessity
(*d*) aesthetic necessity

48. Which of the following functions performed by a forest help most in controlling drought?
(*a*) Forests prevent soil erosion
(*b*) Forests act as water sheds
(*c*) Forests have lot of water plants
(*d*) Forests bring rainfall in monsoon

49. Soil erosion can be prevented by :
(*a*) not allowing grazing in the area
(*b*) increasing plantations/plant cover
(*c*) increasing soil fertility
(*d*) increasing the irrigation

50. U or V shaped valleys formed by swift running rivers is known as :
(*a*) sheet erosion (*b*) gully erosion
(*c*) rill erosion (*d*) slip erosion

51. Soil erosion is more in area where :
(*a*) rain fall is high (*b*) no rain fall
(*c*) low rain fall (*d*) moderate rain fall

52. Afforestation in relation to urban development is related to :
(*a*) Agroforestry
(*b*) Social forestry
(*c*) Integrated forest development
(*d*) Intergrated Pest Management

53. Rows of trees and plants raised to combat dessicating and eroding effects of winds on crop are known as :
(*a*) Green belts (*b*) Shelter belts
(*c*) Green field sites (*d*) Green ways

54. Shelter belt is growing of trees :
(*a*) along water channels
(*b*) trees in forests
(*c*) trees near hospitals
(*d*) All of these

55. The main causative factor of desertification is :
(*a*) Over grazing
(*b*) Human Developmental activities
(*c*) Irrigated agriculture
(*d*) Tourism

56. Tree and grass belts check advancements of :
(*a*) desert to fertile land
(*b*) fertile land to desert
(*c*) both (*a*) and (*b*)
(*d*) None of these

57. Communities more vulnerable to invasion by outside plants and wildlife animals :
(*a*) Mangrooves
(*b*) Oceanic islands
(*c*) Tropical evergreen forests
(*d*) Temperate forests

58. Maximum diversity is found in :
(*a*) Tropical forests (*b*) Coral reefs
(*c*) Estuaries (*d*) Sugarcane field

59. World's richest diversity of Birds is found in :
(*a*) India (*b*) Myanmar
(*c*) Colombia (*d*) Zaire

60. Man has altered biological communities mainly by :
(*a*) changing his own relationship with plants and other animals
(*b*) introducing alien species to an area
(*c*) destroying forests for industries
(*d*) All of the above

61. The book/magazine that gives information about rare plants growing in protected areas/ gardens is :
(*a*) Red Data Book (*b*) Green Book
(*c*) Sanctuary (*d*) WWF-N book

62. Biosphere reserves are being threatened with :
(*a*) Population growth
(*b*) Rains
(*c*) Pollution
(*d*) All of these

63. Which is responsible for extinction of wildlife :
(*a*) hunting
(*b*) pollution
(*c*) destruction of habitats
(*d*) All of these

64. Endemic plants are those plants which grow in :
(*a*) Fresh water lakes
(*b*) Shady places
(*c*) Tissues of other plants
(*d*) Geographically limited areas

65. One of the following langur is associated with Lord Hanuman and given special sanction :
(*a*) *Presbytis entellus*
(*b*) *Gazella gazella*
(*c*) *Hyalobates hoolock*
(*d*) *Macaco silenus*

66. Endangered plant species are conserved through :
(*a*) Herbarium
(*b*) Gene Library
(*c*) Gene Bank
(*d*) Reducing Pollution

67. The percentage of living species in danger is :
(*a*) 40 (*b*) 20
(*c*) 18 (*d*) 10

68. The number of plant species facing extinction is about :
(*a*) 2500 (*b*) 25000
(*c*) 35000 (*d*) 250

69. Number of endangered species of Angiosperms in India is about :
(*a*) 487 (*b*) 15000
(*c*) 5000 (*d*) 3000

70. Number of plant species identified as endangered in India is about :
(*a*) 1000 (*b*) 450
(*c*) 50 (*d*) 4000

71. The number of vertebrate species facing extinction is about :
(*a*) 108 (*b*) 1000
(*c*) 10000 (*d*) 500

72. The concept of biosphere reserve was evolved in 1986 by :
(*a*) MAB programme of UNESCO
(*b*) IUCN
(*c*) WWF-N
(*d*) Project Tiger

73. Where was the first biosphere reserve in India set up in 1986?
(*a*) Nokrek (*b*) Manas
(*c*) Gulf of Mannar (*d*) Nilgiri

74. We have 14 biosphere reserves covering 12 states. Multiple land use is permitted in such areas by dividing them into 3 zones. In which zone, limited human activity is allowed?
(*a*) Core zone
(*b*) Manipulation zone
(*c*) Buffer zone
(*d*) None of these

75. A biosphere reserve preserves :
(*a*) wild populations
(*b*) traditional life styles of tribals
(*c*) genetic resources of organisms
(*d*) All of the above

76. Which one of the following chemical species of mercury is highly toxic to living system ?
(*a*) Mercurous ion (*b*) Mercuric ion
(*c*) Organo mercurials (*d*) Atomic mercury

77. The objective/s of biosphere reserve is/are :
(*a*) conservation of wildlife
(*b*) research
(*c*) education and local involvement
(*d*) All of the above

78. New approach for the conservation of wildlife is the establishment of :
(*a*) Sanctuaries (*b*) Biosphere reserve
(*c*) National parks (*d*) Reserve forests

79. In which zone of biosphere reserve only wild life exists :
(*a*) Buffer zone
(*b*) Core zone
(*c*) Manipulation zone
(*d*) Any of these

80. A *national park* is an area reserved for betterment of wildlife (flora and fauna) where :
(*a*) activities of forestry, grazing and cultivation are prohibited
(*b*) grazing is allowed but forestry is prohibited
(*c*) cutting of trees is allowed but private ownership is not given
(*d*) All of these

81. National Park provides protection to :
(*a*) fauna only
(*b*) flora only
(*c*) both (*a*) and (*b*)
(*d*) entire ecosystem

82. The plant species which are going of become extinct are preserved in :
(*a*) Herbarium (*b*) Gene Bank
(*c*) National Park (*d*) Botanical Garden

83. In Wildlife sanctuary :
(*a*) only wild fauna (animals) are protected
(*b*) private ownership is allowed
(*c*) harvesting of trees for timber and forest products is permitted
(*d*) All of these

84. Animals and plants can be best protected in :
(*a*) National parks
(*b*) Sanctuaries
(*c*) Zoos
(*d*) Botanical gardens

85. **'Project Tiger'** was launched in April 1973. It is a :
(*a*) conservation programme
(*b*) afforestation programme
(*c*) biosphere reserve
(*d*) All of the above

86. The most important tanning bark used in our area is of :
(*a*) Arjun (*Terminalia*)
(*b*) Babul (*Acacia*)
(*c*) Amaltas (*Cassia*)
(*d*) Sal (*Shorea*)

87. Cutch (Katha) is obtained from :
(*a*) *Acacia arabica* (*b*) *A. senegal*
(*c*) *A. catechu* (*d*) *A. melanoxylon*

88. Uniform peeling away of soil surface by flowing H_2O is called :
(*a*) slip erosion
(*b*) sheet erosion
(*c*) rill erosion
(*d*) accelerated erosion

89. For soil conservation, what is required?
(*a*) Afforestation (*b*) Rain
(*c*) Overgrazing (*d*) Deforestation

90. Floods can be prevented by :
(*a*) making dams and planting trees on slopes
(*b*) cutting forests for making new buildings
(*c*) removing soil cover/fallen leaves in forests
(*d*) making land sloppy

91. Erosion due to over grazing is :
(*a*) sheet erosion (*b*) negative erosion
(*c*) rill erosion (*d*) positives erosion

92. Positive pollution of soil is due to :
(*a*) reduction in soil productivity
(*b*) addition of wastes on soil
(*c*) excessive use of fertilizer
(*d*) All of the above

93. Soil conservation means :
(*a*) prevention of spread of deserts
(*b*) prevention of soil from wind and water
(*c*) checking of soil erosion by afforestation/reforestation
(*d*) All of the above

94. Loss of fertility of soil is called :
(*a*) soil conservation (*b*) soil erosion
(*c*) soil conversion (*d*) mulching

95. Soil erosion is maximum in :
(*a*) sandy soil (*b*) loam soil
(*c*) clayey soil (*d*) All of these

96. Maximum soil erosion takes place in :
(*a*) grasslands (*b*) urban areas
(*c*) tropical forests (*d*) agricultural lands

97. One of the chief reasons of soil erosion in India is :
(*a*) drought conditions
(*b*) deforestation
(*c*) shifting cultivation
(*d*) non-awareness of ecological principles

98. Conservation is :
(*a*) not to use natural resources
(*b*) wise use of natural resources
(*c*) less use of natural non-renewable resources
(*d*) more use of our resources

99. In recent years, increasing incidence of floods in plains of Northern India is because :
(*a*) silting of dams has increased
(*b*) increased industrialization
(*c*) increased deforestation in catchment areas
(*d*) All of the above

100. Shifting cultivation is being practised by some tribals in Assam and Europe. It is one of the causes of deforestation as a forest area is cleared by slashing (cutting) and burning of trees for cultivation for 3 – 5 years and then a new forest area is cleared. The abandoned area invites erosion and wild vegetation. This cultivation is also called :
(*a*) Sweden cultivation
(*b*) Soil fertility
(*c*) Jhuming cultivation
(*d*) All of these

101. Jhoom cultivation refers to :
(*a*) cultivation of Jamun trees
(*b*) cultivation of medical plants by tribes
(*c*) tribal methods of shifting cultivation
(*d*) cultivation of terraces

102. Mulching helps in :
(*a*) Soil conservation
(*b*) Jhooming
(*c*) Moisture conservation
(*d*) All of these

103. Which one is the example of soil conservation by mechanical means to minimise soil erosion on hilly areas?
(*a*) Basin listing (*b*) Terracing
(*c*) Dams (*d*) All of these

104. The famous tiger Reserves of India :
(*a*) Dudhwa in UP
(*b*) Kanha and Indravati in MP
(*c*) Simlipal in Orissa
(*d*) All of the above

105. Natural gas is composed primarily of
(*a*) Methane
(*b*) n-butane
(*c*) n-octane
(*d*) A mixture of n-octane and nbutane

106. Which of the following is true regarding the Leopold interaction matrix used in Environmental Impact Assessment Process ?
(*a*) It can be expanded.
(*b*) It can be contracted.
(*c*) It can be contracted and expanded.
(*d*) It cannot be contracted and expanded.

107. Which of the following can be considered in Environmental Risk Assessment ?
(*a*) Exposure period
(*b*) Potency of a toxic material
(*c*) Quality of models
(*d*) All of the above

108. In India, Environmental Impact Assessment report of a proposed river valley project after environmental clearance is applicable for a maximal period of how many years ?
(*a*) 5 (*b*) 10
(*c*) 30 (*d*) 2

109. '*Save the crocodiles*' project for the protection and breeding of crocodiles in India was started in 1975 under the guidance of :
(*a*) Bustard (*b*) Salim Ali
(*c*) S. L. Bahuguna (*d*) S. L. Hora

110. Periyar wildlife sanctuary in Kerala is famous for the betterment of :
(*a*) Gaur (Bison)
(*b*) Nilgai
(*c*) Elephants and Otters
(*d*) Langurs and Gibbon

111. The first '**Zoo**' was established in :
(*a*) Boston, USA
(*b*) London, UK
(*c*) Paris, France
(*d*) Johannsberg, South Africa

112. India's largest National Park is :
(*a*) Corbett National Park, Uttarakhand
(*b*) Desert National Park, Rajasthan
(*c*) Nagarjuna Sagar National Park, Hyderabad AP.
(*d*) Sunderbans, W. Bengal

113. The *world's first* national park is :
(*a*) Manu National Park
(*b*) Yellow Stone National Park
(*c*) Rwenzori National Park
(*d*) Yosemite National Park

114. Which living beings were the first to receive attention for their protection and conservation at an international level?
(*a*) Reptiles
(*b*) Birds
(*c*) Microbes
(*d*) Estuaries and its animals

115. Which bird is the symbol of the **BNHS** (Bombay Natural History Society)?
(*a*) Horn bill (*b*) Erget
(*c*) Spoon bill (*d*) Sun bird

116. Which protected animal is the logo/symbol of **WWF-N**?
(*a*) Red Panda (*b*) Polar Baer
(*c*) Tiger (*d*) Giant Panda

117. Who is considered the Hindu Mythological Lord of the birds?
(*a*) Garuda (*b*) Peacock
(*c*) Swan (*d*) Owl

118. Which animal is seat of Lord Brahma?
(*a*) Swan (*b*) Peacock
(*c*) Garuda (*d*) Snake

119. Mahabharata mentions an animal as a teacher of Yudhisthra. It is :
(*a*) Mongoose (*b*) Eagle
(*c*) Dog (*d*) Ox

120. Which animal is the stead of Lord Indra :
(*a*) Elephant (*b*) Horse
(*c*) Scorpion (*d*) Peacock

121. Which animal is the stead of Lord Shiva :
(*a*) Ox (*b*) Bull
(*c*) Cow (*d*) Buffalo

122. Which animal is on the crest of the kings of England and Scotland?
(*a*) Lion (*b*) Crocodile
(*c*) Elephant (*d*) Horse

123. What is the Zodiac sign of cancer?
(*a*) Crab (*b*) Owl
(*c*) Fish (*d*) Spider

124. Which animal is the stead of Kartikeya?
(*a*) Peacock (*b*) Swan
(*c*) Mouse (*d*) Owl

125. Which one is *not correct* for the effects of deforestation?
(*a*) It leads to soil erosion
(*b*) It alters the weather pattern by decreasing rainfall
(*c*) It speeds up nutrient recycling
(*d*) It destroys natural habitats of wildlife

126. Deforestation (destroying of forests) leads to :
(*a*) diminishing/decrease in rainfall
(*b*) less water supply
(*c*) soil erosion and siltation in rivers
(*d*) All of the above

127. *Chipko Movement* consists of conservation of trees of :
(*a*) 3 Fs (*b*) 5 Fs
(*c*) 4 Fs (*d*) 6 Fs

128. *Chipko Movement* is the world's most known eco development programme, started by S.L.

Bahuguna in 1973 in Tehri Garhwal (now Uttrakhand). It is related with :
(*a*) plant/forest conservation
(*b*) afforestation
(*c*) conservation of natural resources
(*d*) population control

129. The destroying of forests results in :
(*a*) soil erosion
(*b*) floods and drought
(*c*) loss of wildlife
(*d*) All of these

130. Deforestation reduces the chances of :
(*a*) soil erosion (*b*) soil fertility
(*c*) rainfall (*d*) All of these

131. Destruction of forests will change one of the following parameters of the earth :
(*a*) shape (*b*) heat budget
(*c*) radiation budget (*d*) food budget

132. The largest rain forest in the world is in :
(*a*) Amazon basin (*b*) Congo basin
(*c*) Indonesia (*d*) Phillipines

133. Most of the forests are being damaged by :
(*a*) air pollution (*b*) water pollution
(*c*) acid rains (*d*) soil pollution

134. 1/3rd of all the world's rain forest is in :
(*a*) India (*b*) China
(*c*) Brazil (*d*) Zaire

135. Which type of forest is the most fertile reservoir of wildlife?
(*a*) Temperate forests
(*b*) Tropical rain forests
(*c*) Deciduous forests
(*d*) All of the above

136. The area of semirural, low density population is called :
(*a*) green area (*b*) green belt
(*c*) greenery (*d*) greenland

137. Quinine is obtained from the bark of a plant of peru origin. It is :
(*a*) bark of *Cinchona*
(*b*) bark of *Cassia*
(*c*) bark of *Eucalyptus*
(*d*) All of these

138. Newsprint making tree of India is :
(*a*) *Boswellia* (Salai)
(*b*) *Eucalyptus*
(*c*) *Diospyros* (Tendu)
(*d*) *Abies* (Fir)

139. Most prized essential oil is obtained from a forest tree :
(*a*) *Cedrus deodara* (*b*) *Abies balsamia*
(*c*) *Santalum album* (*d*) *Pinus longifolia*

140. The *bidi* leaf tree is :
(*a*) Sal (*b*) Dhak
(*c*) Tendu (*d*) *Butea*

141. Clove is the dried floral bud of :
(*a*) *Cinchona officinalis*
(*b*) *Syzygium aromaticum*
(*c*) *Cinnamomum zeylanicum*
(*d*) *Myristica fragrans*

142. Poor man's Timber is :
(*a*) Pines (*b*) Bamboos
(*c*) Firs (*d*) Junipers

143. Man of the tree is :
(*a*) Sunder Lal Bahuguna
(*b*) Baba Amte
(*c*) St. Barbe Baker
(*d*) Chandra Prakash Bhatt

144. A common gum yeilding tree is :
(*a*) *Boswellia* (*b*) *Acacia*
(*c*) *Pterocarpus* (*d*) All of these

145. Which is the largest bird ever known that is extinct now?
(*a*) Great Indian Bustard
(*b*) California Condor
(*c*) Aephorins
(*d*) Cassowary

146. What is common to Great Indian Bustard, Asiatic lion and *Cypripedium* orchid?
(*a*) E (endangered) species
(*b*) V (vulnerable) species
(*c*) R (Rare) species
(*d*) O (Out of Danger) species

147. The California Condor, the largest flying bird is the victim of :

(*a*) human activities changing its habitat
(*b*) marine pollution
(*c*) air pollution
(*d*) hunting

148. Which Indian state has named all its tourist resorts after birds?
(*a*) Haryana (*b*) Punjab
(*c*) Kerala (*d*) AP

149. Which one of the following animals has become extinct from India?
(*a*) Cheetah (*Acinonyx jubatus venaticus*)
(*b*) Lion (*Panthera leo-persica*)
(*c*) One horned Rhino (*Rhinoceros unicornis*)
(*d*) Snow Leopard (*Panthera uncia*)

150. The Indian one horned rhinoceros Rhinoceros *unicornis* is the most important protected species in .... National Park :
(*a*) Jim Corbett, Uttarakhand
(*b*) Kaziranga, Asom
(*c*) Bandipur, AP
(*d*) Gir, Gujarat

151. Which sanctuary is famous for one horned Indian Rhinoceros and where is it located?
(*a*) Kaziranga in Jorhat (Assam)
(*b*) Manas in Kamrup (Assam)
(*c*) Jaladapara in Jalpaiguri (West Bengal)
(*d*) All of the above

152. Which one is endangered species of Indian flora?
(*a*) Nepenthes (*Pitcher plant*)
(*b*) Rauwolfia (*Serpgandha*)
(*c*) Dioscorea (*Yam*)
(*d*) All of the above

153. Species on verge of extinction due to over exploitation :
(*a*) *Centella* (*b*) *Podophyllum*
(*c*) *Gloriosa* (*d*) All of the above

154. The endangered largest living lemur (*Idri-Idri*) is found in :
(*a*) Sri Lanka
(*b*) India
(*c*) Madagascar
(*d*) Mauritius and Fiji

155. Which one of the following types of animals does man chiefly protect?
(*a*) Feeble animals
(*b*) Harmless animals
(*c*) Useful animals
(*d*) Animals likely to Perish

156. Asiatic wild ass is a threatened species (rare species) due to hunting. It occurs in :
(*a*) Rann of Kutch
(*b*) Swamps of north-west Bengal and Assam
(*c*) Semi and lesser Panda/areas of Gujarat and Maharashtra
(*d*) Only in Bharatpur Sanctuary

157. The first recorded bird that is now no more was :
(*a*) Dodo of Mauritius
(*b*) Great Indian Bustard
(*c*) California Condor
(*d*) Flemingoes

158. Dodo (*Didus ineptus*-a passenger bird or foolish bird of Mauritius) as disappeared due to :
(*a*) hunting
(*b*) introduction of eyotic birds in Mauritius
(*c*) its fearlessness and it did not for its eggs
(*d*) Both (*a*) and (*c*)

159. A highly endangered bird :
(*a*) Dodo of Mauritius
(*b*) Great Indian Bustard of Rajasthan
(*c*) Pink headed duck of India
(*d*) All of these

160. Lesser Panda/Red Panda (*Ailurus fulgens*) is preserved at :
(*a*) Dachigam National Park, J and K
(*b*) Sasan Gir National Park, Gujarat
(*c*) Khangchend Zonga National Park, Sikkim
(*d*) Simlipal National Park, Orissa

161. Nandan-kanan Zoo Orissa is known for :
(*a*) Hippo (*b*) Nilgiri Tahr
(*c*) White Tiger (*d*) Both (*b*) and (*c*)

162. What percentage of total area in hilly regions does the National Forest Policy suggest to be under forests :
(*a*) 30% (*b*) 60%
(*c*) 33% (*d*) 66%

163. Which is wrong for forests that India has :
(*a*) tropical dry deciduous (38.7%)
(*b*) tropical moist deciduous (30.9%)
(*c*) tropical thorn forests (6.9%)
(*d*) None of the above

164. Social Forestry Programme (1976) includes raising of trees of multiple uses for the benefit of :
(*a*) Urban community
(*b*) Rural community
(*c*) Hills
(*d*) All of these

165. Planting trees on public and common land is known as :
(*a*) social forestry (*b*) farm forestry
(*c*) agroforestry (*d*) reforestation

166. Afforestation with purpose of environmental, aesthetic and economic development is known as :
(*a*) integrated afforestation
(*b*) social forestry
(*c*) agroforestry
(*d*) forest conservation

167. Planting of flower and fruit trees along road sides is included in :
(*a*) Agroforestry programme
(*b*) Social forestry programme
(*c*) Urban forestry programme
(*d*) Van Mahotsava

168. '*Trees means water, water means bread* and *bread is life*'. It is true as death of plants should result in death of animals also because :
(*a*) there will be no oxygen
(*b*) there will be no CO_2
(*c*) there will be deficiency of water
(*d*) All of the above

169. One of the following acts as soil binder :
(*a*) *Gram* (*b*) *Eucalyptus*
(*c*) *China rose* (*d*) *Helianthus*

170. According to our National Forest Policy, forests are divided into :
(*a*) 2 categories (*b*) 8 categories
(*c*) 5 categories (*d*) 3 categories

171. Forest products are of 2 types – minor and major. The contribution of minor forest produce to economy is not negligible. The minor forest produce are :
(*a*) minerals
(*b*) vegetables
(*c*) all forest products other than wood
(*d*) bamboos

172. Our forests are on the decline because of :
(*a*) soil erosion
(*b*) heavy floods
(*c*) no afforestation
(*d*) indiscriminate felling of trees and grazing

173. Tropical rain forests in India are found in :
(*a*) Tamil Nadu, Kerala
(*b*) Andaman and Assam
(*c*) Western Ghats
(*d*) All of these

174. Temperate forests in India are found in
(*a*) Himalayan range
(*b*) Gujarat
(*c*) Penninsular region
(*d*) Western Ghats

175. Forests near equator are :
(*a*) deciduous forests (*b*) tropical forests
(*c*) coniferous forests (*d*) grasslands

176. Forests growing at a height of more than 3567 m represent vegetation :
(*a*) Alpine (*b*) Temperate
(*c*) Taiga (*d*) Grassland

177. Which of the followings is an antiforest conservation activity?
(*a*) Selcetive feeling of trees
(*b*) Control on forest fires
(*c*) Clearing of fallen trees
(*d*) Protection of wildlife

178. The cause of deforestation is :
(*a*) population explosion of human and livestock

(*b*) increased demands of timber and fuel wood enhanced grazing
(*c*) human activities for settlements, dams, factories etc.
(*d*) All of the above

179. For which animals is Dachigam National Park famous?
(*a*) Hangul (Kashmir stag)
(*b*) Sambhar
(*c*) Musk deer
(*d*) Spotted deer and Black Buck

180. Which of the following is related with silent valley National Park in Kerala :
(*a*) Lion tailed Macaque
(*b*) Gharial
(*c*) Wild Ass
(*d*) Swamp deer

181. Hispid hare (*Caprologus hispidus*) is found only in :
(*a*) Manas National Park
(*b*) Dachigam National Park
(*c*) Kaziranga National Park
(*d*) Kanha National Park

182. In India, where one can found Siberian crane (*Grus leucogeranus*)?
(*a*) Keoladeo Bird Sanctuary, Bharatpur
(*b*) Sultanpur Lake Bird Sanctuary, Gurgaon, Haryana
(*c*) Ranganthittu Bird Sanctuary, Mysore
(*d*) Chilka Lake Sanctuary, Orissa

183. To famous forest/plant conservation movement in India is :
(*a*) Chipko Andolan
(*b*) Silent Valley Movement
(*c*) Both (*a*) and (*b*)
(*d*) MAB and IBP

184. Which is the only home for the protection conservation of Yellow maned Indian Lion?
(*a*) Jim Corbett National Park, Uttarakhand
(*b*) Gir Forests, Saurashtra, Gujarat
(*c*) Sariska Tiger Project, Rajasthan
(*d*) Kanha Forests, MP

185. The **Jewel** of Kanha National Park is :
(*a*) Tiger
(*b*) Swampdeer (Barasingha)
(*c*) Sambhar (Asiatic deer)
(*d*) Spotted deer (Cheetal)

186. The largest and most famous bird sanctuary of India is :
(*a*) Ghana Bird Sanctuary, Bharatpur (Raj.) (now called Keoladeo National Park)
(*b*) Ranganthittu Bird Sanctuary, Mysore
(*c*) Chilka Lake Bird Sanctuary, Balagaon (Orissa)
(*d*) Sultanpur Lake Bird Sanctuary, Gurgaon, (Haryana)

187. Great Indian Bustard (sarang) on endangered species is protected in :
(*a*) Desert National Park, Jaiselmer (Raj.)
(*b*) Kasera, Sanctuary, MP
(*c*) Great Indian Bustard Sanctuary, Maharashtra
(*d*) All of the above

188. Great Indian Bustard Sanctuary is located in :
(*a*) Rajasthan (*b*) Maharashtra
(*c*) Karera (MP) (*d*) Pakistan (Lahore)

189. Shivpuri Sanctuary in MP is asylum for :
(*a*) Birds (*b*) Tigers
(*c*) Lions (*d*) Snakes

190. Bhagwan Mahavir National Park is in :
(*a*) Rajasthan (*b*) MP
(*c*) Goa (*d*) Maharashtra

191. **Sukhna** sanctuary is situated in :
(*a*) Haryana (*b*) Chandigarh
(*c*) Delhi (*d*) UP

192. Sariska Tiger Project is in Rajasthan in :
(*a*) Alwar (*b*) Savai Madhopur
(*c*) Jaiselmer (*d*) Bharatpur

193. Where is Nalabana Bird Sanctuary located?
(*a*) Sultanpur Lake (*b*) Dal Lake
(*c*) Chilka Lake (*d*) Silsit Lake

194. Which park floats in a vast lake?
(*a*) Keibul Lamjao National Park, (Manipur)
(*b*) Keoladeo National Park, Bharatpur
(*c*) Chilka Lake Bird Sanctuary Orissa
(*d*) Nokrek National Park, Meghalaya

195. Where is the gene sanctuary for *Citrus* and other plants located?
(*a*) Nilgiri Biosphere reserve
(*b*) Sunderbans
(*c*) Garo Hills Megahalaya
(*d*) Gulf of Mannar

196. Which Indian bird sanctuary is essentially the hinterland of a saline laggon?
(*a*) Keoladeo (Raj.)
(*b*) Ranganthittu (Mysore)
(*c*) Point calimere (Tamil Nadu)
(*d*) Sultanpur (Haryana)

197. If we remove 1/2 of the forest cover of earth, the crisis that will occur :
(*a*) many wildilife would become extinct
(*b*) population, pollution and ecological imbalance will rise
(*c*) energy crisis will commence
(*d*) the rest of forest area will correct the imbalance

198. **Cultigens** are domestic animals and cultivated plants which can not survive without human care. Which of the following is a cultigen?
(*a*) Maize (*b*) Tomato
(*c*) Cabbage (*d*) All of these

199. When did Rachel Carson's book *Silent Spring* produce the worldwide awareness about nature conservation and environment?
(*a*) 1950 (*b*) 1971
(*c*) 1962 (*d*) 1942

200. World Environment Day is observed on :
(*a*) March 21st (*b*) Dec. 1st
(*c*) May 31st (*d*) June 5th

201. World Earth Day is observed on :
(*a*) April 22nd (*b*) June 5th
(*c*) March 21st (*d*) May 31st

202. World forest day is celebrated on :
(*a*) March 21st (*b*) April 7
(*c*) First week of Oct. (*d*) April 22

203. **Wildlife Week** is celebrated from/in :
(*a*) Monday of first week of Oct.
(*b*) Monday of second week of Oct.
(*c*) Any week of Oct.
(*d*) Any week in winter

204. Van Mahotsava is :
(*a*) festival of planting trees in open areas
(*b*) festival of taking oath to protect trees
(*c*) festival of worshiping trees
(*d*) festival to observe productivity of trees for future plantation

205. Van Mahotsava is celebrataed in 1st week of :
(*a*) February (*b*) July
(*c*) Both are correct (*d*) both are wrong

206. Which Indian army wing has taken up the task of preserving and restoring the ecology of the country?
(*a*) BSF (*b*) CRPF
(*c*) TASK (*d*) None of these

207. When was the Forest Conservation Act passed in India?
(*a*) 1960 (*b*) 1970
(*c*) 1980 (*d*) 1950

208. When was the Environment Protection Act enforced in India?
(*a*) 1980 (*b*) 1986
(*c*) 1982 (*d*) 1988

209. When was the National Forest Policy formulated?
(*a*) 1948 (*b*) 1980
(*c*) 1964 (*d*) 1952

210. When was National Environment Policy Act (NEPA) was passed?
(*a*) 1952 (*b*) 1969
(*c*) 1972 (*d*) 1989

211. Which forest area in India was first brought under control and protection?
(*a*) Malabar (*b*) Konkan
(*c*) Garhwal (*d*) Sunderbans

212. Which Indian King was fond of growing new plants and trees and watching birds?
(*a*) Bahadur Shah (*b*) Rama Raya
(*c*) Jahangir (*d*) None the these

213. Which Emperor in the past has done maximum plantation and established wildlife snactuaries?
(*a*) Ashoka (*b*) Bahadur Shah
(*c*) Akbar (*d*) Aggrasain

214. Where is the Indian Grassland and Fodder Research Institute (IGFRI) located?
(*a*) Patna (*b*) Bharatpur
(*c*) Jodhpur (*d*) Jnansi

215. Where is Central Arid Zone Reserach Institute (CAZRI) located?
(*a*) Jhansi (*b*) Karnal
(*c*) Jodhpur (*d*) Jaiselmer

216. Forests, called *Nation's Green Gold*, are important as :
(*a*) they provide timber and medicines
(*b*) they provide shelter to animal
(*c*) they prevent erosion of soil by binding soil particles and increasing the fertility and prevent pollution
(*d*) All of the above

217. An earthquake is rated as 'major' if its magnitude in Richter Scale is in the range of
(*a*) 4.0 – 4.9 (*b*) 7.0 – 7.9
(*c*) 6.0 – 6.9 (*d*) 5.0 – 5.9

218. Where is the snow leopard found?
(*a*) Arunachal Pradesh
(*b*) Laddakh
(*c*) Sikkim and Himachal Pradesh
(*d*) All of these

219. Which of the followings is fast disappearing from India?
(*a*) Cheetah (*b*) Wolf
(*c*) Leopard (*d*) Gaur

220. Guindy Park of Madras is famous for :
(*a*) Black Bucks (*Antelope cervicapra*)
(*b*) Cheetals (spotted deer, *Axis axis*)
(*c*) Deers
(*d*) All of the above

221. Famous snake garden of India is situated in :
(*a*) Mysore (*b*) Ooty
(*c*) Chennai (*d*) Trivandrum

222. Sanctuaries/parks in South India are basically for the protection of :
(*a*) Elephants
(*b*) Deers and Antelopes
(*c*) Bisons (Gaurs)
(*d*) All of these

223. **Valley of flowers** is located in :
(*a*) Garhwal (*b*) Mysore (South)
(*c*) Kashmir (*d*) MP

224. Identify the correct match between *tiger reserve* and its state :
(*a*) Bandipur – Tamil Nadu
(*b*) Palanau – Orissa
(*c*) Manas – Assam
(*d*) Jim Corbett – Madhya Pradesh

225. Flamingoes (Hansawar) are protected in :
(*a*) Bandipur National Park, Mysore
(*b*) Nagarahole Park, Mysore
(*c*) Shivpuri Sanctuary, MP
(*d*) Chilka Lake, Balagaon, Orissa

226. Marine invertebrates are protected in :
(*a*) Gulf of Mannar (*b*) Bay of Bengal
(*c*) Gulf of Cambay (*d*) Bombay High

227. Which is concerned with the nature and conservation of forests?
(*a*) Silent Valley (*b*) Kaziranga
(*c*) Gir (*d*) Ghana

228. A forest is a :
(*a*) biotic community
(*b*) population
(*c*) a protected area
(*d*) succession stage

229. For the best ecological balance, land mass of a country in plains covered with forests must be :
(*a*) 22% (*b*) 33%
(*c*) 30% (*d*) 35%

230. Forests control draught through :
(*a*) Lot of water plants
(*b*) Increasing rainfall
(*c*) Function as water shed
(*d*) Retention of water and prevention of soil erosion

231. Afforestation is useful for :
(*a*) increasing the fertility of soil
(*b*) reducing floods
(*c*) preventing soil erosion and spread of deserts
(*d*) All of these

232. In the developing countries, the heaviest demand on forests is for :
(*a*) fuel wood
(*b*) timber wood
(*c*) wood for agricultural tools
(*d*) medicines

233. Why is the *Silent Valley* so called?
(*a*) It is silent during the night
(*b*) It is silent during the day
(*c*) It has nothing to do with silence
(*d*) It is not a valley

234. Silent Valley of Kerala is preserved as :
(*a*) it contains valuable timber trees
(*b*) represents natural tropical rain forests with rich diversity
(*c*) it is reservoir of rare wildlife
(*d*) recreational value

235. About how much virgin landscape has been altered by man?
(*a*) 50% (*b*) 55%
(*c*) 33% (*d*) 23%

236. In your opinion which is the most effective way to conserve the plant diversity of an area?
(*a*) By creating botanical garden
(*b*) By creating biosphere reserve
(*c*) By developing seed bank
(*d*) By tissue culture technique

237. The maximum number of National Parks are located in :
(*a*) Madhya Pradesh (*b*) Tamil Nadu
(*c*) Maharashtra (*d*) Karnataka

238. Chipko movement is related to :
(*a*) Ganga water project
(*b*) Narmada dam project
(*c*) Tehri dam project
(*d*) Forest conservation

239. According to UNEP surveys, tropical forests are being destroyed at the rate of :
(*a*) 1,00,000 sq.km. annually
(*b*) 70,000 sq.km. annually
(*c*) 5,000 sq.km. annually
(*d*) 2,00,000 sq.km. annually

240. Wildlife refers to :
(*a*) living organisms in their natural habitats
(*b*) animals in the forests
(*c*) carnivorous animals such as lion, tiger, etc.
(*d*) plants in water and on land

241. Red data book is famous for :
(*a*) extinct plants
(*b*) endangered animals
(*c*) endangered plants
(*d*) endangerd plants and animals

242. Which of the following is not a plant product?
(*a*) Thein (*b*) Acetocarmine
(*c*) Ergotin (*d*) Morphine

243. 'Van Mahotsava' is practiced for :
(*a*) Forest destruction
(*b*) Forest cutting
(*c*) Forest planting
(*d*) None of the above

244. To prevent felling of trees, Chipko movement commenced in :
(*a*) Tehri – Garhwal district of Uttarakhand
(*b*) Mandi district of Himachal Pradesh
(*c*) Almora district of Uttarakhand
(*d*) Darjeeling district of West Bengal

245. Forests are :
(*a*) exhaustible but non-maintainable
(*b*) exhaustible but maintainable
(*c*) in exhustible natural resources
(*d*) None of the above

246. Which of the following is an antiforest conservation activity?
(*a*) Economy in lumbering
(*b*) Prevention of fires
(*c*) Preservation of wild animals
(*d*) Clear felling

247. What is the major cause of diminishing wildlife numbers?
(*a*) Habitat destruction
(*b*) Paucity of drinking water
(*c*) Felling of trees
(*d*) Cannibalism

248. In case forest cover is reduced to half, what is most likely to happen on a long term basis?
(*a*) Crop breeding programmes will suffer due to reduced availability of variety of germplasm

(*b*) Large area will become desert
(*c*) Tribals living in these areas will starve to death
(*d*) Cattle in forests and adjoining areas will starve to death

249. Importance of wildlife lies in :
(*a*) usefullness in breeding programmes
(*b*) balancing the population
(*c*) maintenance of food chains and natural cycles
(*d*) All of the above

250. Which of the following species are restricted to a given area?
(*a*) Endemic species
(*b*) Sympatric species
(*c*) Allopatric species
(*d*) Sibling species

251. In order to maintain proper ecological balance :
(*a*) trees must be cut as and when necessary because it is the underground part which performs useful purpose
(*b*) existing forests should be cleared and new ones are planted
(*c*) a tree should be planted in place of one that is cut for other uses
(*d*) some quick growing annuals should be planted if a tree cut for other uses

252. Wildlife is destroyed most when :
(*a*) natural habitat is destroyed
(*b*) natural calamity
(*c*) there is a lack of proper care
(*d*) mass scale hunting for foreign trade

253. The major reason for extinction of species is :
(*a*) hunting
(*b*) their use for food
(*c*) forest fire
(*d*) habitat destruction

254. Man and Biosphere programme (MAB) was launched by :
(*a*) WWF (*b*) UNESCO
(*c*) Govt. of India (*d*) IUCN

255. Which of the following biosphere is located in Uttarakhand?
(*a*) Valley of Flowers (*b*) Kaziranga
(*c*) Sunderbans (*d*) Kanha

256. Which of the following is a soap substitute :
(*a*) Tendu (*b*) Rudraksha
(*c*) Ritha (*d*) All of these

257. Deforestation may reduce the chances of :
(*a*) frequent landslides
(*b*) frequent cyclones
(*c*) erosion of soil surface
(*d*) rain fall

258. Aims of social forestry are :
(*a*) to utilize the waste land
(*b*) to meet the requirement of fuel wood and fodder
(*c*) to create an ecological balance
(*d*) None of these

259. Where do the tropical rain forests occur?
(*a*) Andamans
(*b*) Jammu and Kashmir
(*c*) Bihar
(*d*) Himachal Pradesh

260. A new approach to conservation is the establishment of :
(*a*) Sanctuaries
(*b*) Biosphere reserves
(*c*) National parks
(*d*) Reserve forests

261. Afforestation with the purpose of environmental, aesthetic and economic development is known as :
(*a*) social forestry
(*b*) integrated afforestation
(*c*) agro forestry
(*d*) forest conservation

262. Deforestation often leads to :
(*a*) growth of selected species of animals
(*b*) increased soil erosion
(*c*) development of new habitats
(*d*) availability of more soil for farming

263. Threatened species often include :
(*a*) vulnerable species
(*b*) rare species
(*c*) endangered species
(*d*) All of these

264. In the context of conservation, WWF stands for :
(*a*) World Wildlife Federation
(*b*) Water, Wastelands and Forestry
(*c*) World Wildlife Fund
(*d*) World Wildlife Forum

265. How many types of forests are found in India?
(*a*) Sixteen (*b*) Twelve
(*c*) Thirty two (*d*) Eight

266. The branch of science that deals with development of forest and utilization of forest products is :
(*a*) Pharmacognosy (*b*) Sericulture
(*c*) Silviculture (*d*) Horticulture

267. Had *Cinchona* has eliminated before its use was discovered, man world have been deprived of :
(*a*) valuable timber
(*b*) antimalarial drug
(*c*) tejpat used as spice
(*d*) use of its bark as dalchini

268. In an effort to preserve the species, special attention should be given to :
(*a*) those varieties that are most threatened and form usual flora and fauna
(*b*) prevention of extinction
(*c*) rare species overall the other types of threatened and form usual flora and fauna
(*d*) species that is the only representative of a family or genus

269. Bulk of our forests are composed of :
(*a*) tropical dry deciduous forests
(*b*) tropical thorn foests
(*c*) temperate deciduous forests
(*d*) tropical evergreen forests

270. Species which occur in small populations and are restricted to only certain geographical areas are palced under the category of :
(*a*) vulnerable species
(*b*) rare species
(*c*) endangered species
(*d*) All of these

271. The main causes of deforestation in India are :
(*a*) increased demand of timber and fuel wood
(*b*) expansion of croplands
(*c*) increase in human and livestock population
(*d*) All of the above

272. Conservation of living resources is a complex operation and is concerned with :
(*a*) all living organisms and non-living elements of the environments on which they depend
(*b*) plants, animals and microbes
(*c*) plants and animals
(*d*) protection of wildlife and the forests in which these inhabit

273. Destruction of species would be unethical because :
(*a*) it may still have certain unknown values
(*b*) it is a product of long evolutionary history
(*c*) it forms a rich biological diversity
(*d*) All of the above

274. The major forests product is :
(*a*) fibers (*b*) bamboos
(*c*) wood and timber (*d*) fuel wood

275. The best method for the conservation of the plant genetic resources is to :
(*a*) preserve them as seeds under completly dry condition
(*b*) preserve their genes in gene library
(*c*) cryopreserve them as seeds
(*d*) maintain them in their natural habitats

276. In order to reduce the cost of plantation of trees, a system of forest culture plus agriculture has been evolved. This system is called :
(*a*) dry farming
(*b*) taungya system
(*c*) shifting agriculture
(*d*) mixed farming

277. All the following are proper plans for increasing agricultural production except :
(*a*) cutting forests to add land for cultivation
(*b*) expansion of irrigation facilities

(*c*) mechanisation of various aspect of farming
(*d*) increase in fertilizer application

278. Which of the following is not a correct match?
(*a*) Grasslands – C_4 plants
(*b*) Deserts – C AM plants
(*c*) Tropical rain forest – Lianas and epiphytes
(*d*) Temperate deciduous forests – Managroove

279. If all green plants on the earth are destroyed :
(*a*) only pests shall die
(*b*) only herbivorous animals shall die
(*c*) all animals shall die ultimately
(*d*) nothing shall happen to animals

ANSWERS

1	2	3	4	5	6	7	8	9	10
(*d*)	(*a*)	(*d*)	(*d*)	(*a*)	(*b*)	(*d*)	(*c*)	(*d*)	(*d*)
11	**12**	**13**	**14**	**15**	**16**	**17**	**18**	**19**	**20**
(*a*)	(*a*)	(*b*)	(*b*)	(*d*)	(*c*)	(*a*)	(*b*)	(*c*)	(*b*)
21	**22**	**23**	**24**	**25**	**26**	**27**	**28**	**29**	**30**
(*a*)	(*c*)	(*c*)	(*c*)	(*a*)	(*d*)	(*c*)	(*b*)	(*d*)	(*b*)
31	**32**	**33**	**34**	**35**	**36**	**37**	**38**	**39**	**40**
(*d*)	(*c*)	(*c*)	(*a*)	(*a*)	(*d*)	(*d*)	(*d*)	(*d*)	(*d*)
41	**42**	**43**	**44**	**45**	**46**	**47**	**48**	**49**	**50**
(*a*)	(*c*)	(*b*)	(*d*)	(*a*)	(*b*)	(*a*)	(*b*)	(*b*)	(*b*)
51	**52**	**53**	**54**	**55**	**56**	**57**	**58**	**59**	**60**
(*a*)	(*c*)	(*b*)	(*a*)	(*a*)	(*a*)	(*b*)	(*b*)	(*c*)	(*d*)
61	**62**	**63**	**64**	**65**	**66**	**67**	**68**	**69**	**70**
(*b*)	(*c*)	(*d*)	(*d*)	(*a*)	(*c*)	(*d*)	(*b*)	(*d*)	(*b*)
71	**72**	**73**	**74**	**75**	**76**	**77**	**78**	**79**	**80**
(*b*)	(*a*)	(*d*)	(*c*)	(*d*)	(*c*)	(*d*)	(*b*)	(*b*)	(*a*)
81	**82**	**83**	**84**	**85**	**86**	**87**	**88**	**89**	**90**
(*d*)	(*d*)	(*d*)	(*a*)	(*a*)	(*b*)	(*b*)	(*b*)	(*a*)	(*a*)
91	**92**	**93**	**94**	**95**	**96**	**97**	**98**	**99**	**100**
(*b*)	(*d*)	(*d*)	(*b*)	(*c*)	(*d*)	(*b*)	(*b*)	(*c*)	(*d*)
101	**102**	**103**	**104**	**105**	**106**	**107**	**108**	**109**	**110**
(*c*)	(*d*)	(*d*)	(*d*)	(*a*)	(*c*)	(*d*)	(*b*)	(*a*)	(*c*)
111	**112**	**113**	**114**	**115**	**116**	**117**	**118**	**119**	**120**
(*c*)	(*c*)	(*b*)	(*b*)	(*a*)	(*d*)	(*a*)	(*a*)	(*a*)	(*a*)
121	**122**	**123**	**124**	**125**	**126**	**127**	**128**	**129**	**130**
(*b*)	(*a*)	(*a*)	(*a*)	(*c*)	(*d*)	(*b*)	(*a*)	(*d*)	(*c*)
131	**132**	**133**	**134**	**135**	**136**	**137**	**138**	**139**	**140**
(*b*)	(*a*)	(*a*)	(*c*)	(*b*)	(*b*)	(*a*)	(*a*)	(*c*)	(*c*)
141	**142**	**143**	**144**	**145**	**146**	**147**	**148**	**149**	**150**
(*b*)	(*b*)	(*c*)	(*d*)	(*c*)	(*a*)	(*a*)	(*a*)	(*a*)	(*b*)
151	**152**	**153**	**154**	**155**	**156**	**157**	**158**	**159**	**160**
(*d*)	(*d*)	(*b*)	(*c*)	(*d*)	(*a*)	(*a*)	(*d*)	(*b*)	(*c*)

161	**162**	**163**	**164**	**165**	**166**	**167**	**168**	**169**	**170**
(*d*)	(*b*)	(*d*)	(*b*)	(*a*)	(*b*)	(*c*)	(*a*)	(*b*)	(*d*)
171	**172**	**173**	**174**	**175**	**176**	**177**	**178**	**179**	**180**
(*c*)	(*d*)	(*c*)	(*a*)	(*b*)	(*a*)	(*c*)	(*d*)	(*a*)	(*a*)
181	**182**	**183**	**184**	**185**	**186**	**187**	**188**	**189**	**190**
(*a*)	(*a*)	(*c*)	(*b*)	(*b*)	(*a*)	(*d*)	(*c*)	(*b*)	(*c*)
191	**192**	**193**	**194**	**195**	**196**	**197**	**198**	**199**	**200**
(*b*)	(*a*)	(*c*)	(*a*)	(*c*)	(*c*)	(*b*)	(*d*)	(*c*)	(*d*)
201	**202**	**203**	**204**	**205**	**206**	**207**	**208**	**209**	**210**
(*a*)	(*a*)	(*a*)	(*a*)	(*c*)	(*c*)	(*c*)	(*b*)	(*d*)	(*b*)
211	**212**	**213**	**214**	**215**	**216**	**217**	**218**	**219**	**220**
(*a*)	(*c*)	(*a*)	(*d*)	(*c*)	(*d*)	(*b*)	(*d*)	(*b*)	(*d*)
221	**222**	**223**	**224**	**225**	**226**	**227**	**228**	**229**	**230**
(*c*)	(*d*)	(*a*)	(*b*)	(*d*)	(*a*)	(*a*)	(*a*)	(*b*)	(*d*)
231	**232**	**233**	**234**	**235**	**236**	**237**	**238**	**239**	**240**
(*d*)	(*a*)	(*a*)	(*d*)	(*b*)	(*b*)	(*a*)	(*d*)	(*a*)	(*b*)
241	**242**	**243**	**244**	**245**	**246**	**247**	**248**	**249**	**250**
(*d*)	(*b*)	(*c*)	(*a*)	(*b*)	(*d*)	(*a*)	(*b*)	(*d*)	(*a*)
251	**252**	**253**	**254**	**255**	**256**	**257**	**258**	**259**	**260**
(*d*)	(*a*)	(*d*)	(*b*)	(*a*)	(*c*)	(*d*)	(*b*)	(*a*)	(*b*)
261	**262**	**263**	**264**	**265**	**266**	**267**	**268**	**269**	**270**
(*a*)	(*b*)	(*d*)	(*c*)	(*a*)	(*c*)	(*b*)	(*d*)	(*a*)	(*b*)
271	**272**	**273**	**274**	**275**	**276**	**277**	**278**	**279**	
(*d*)	(*a*)	(*d*)	(*c*)	(*d*)	(*b*)	(*a*)	(*d*)	(*c*)	

6

ECOLOGY AND ECOLOGICAL FACTORS

1. The science of the relations of all organisms all their environments is :
(*a*) Ecology (*b*) Ecosystem
(*c*) Toxicology (*d*) Cytology

2. Term ecology was actually qoined by a German Ecologist :
(*a*) Clements (*b*) Haeckel
(*c*) Tansley (*d*) Reiter

3. Who first gave the definition of ecology?
(*a*) Reiter (*b*) Haeckel
(*c*) Odum (*d*) Tansley

4. In which year the term ecology was coined?
(*a*) 1885 (*b*) 1886
(*c*) 1883 (*d*) 1884

5. Father of plant ecology is Warming. Who is revered as father of ecology in India?
(*a*) Father H. Santapan
(*b*) W. Dudgeon
(*c*) Ramdeo Misra
(*d*) P. Maheshwari

6. Who is regarded as the first ecologist?
(*a*) Theopharastus (*b*) Haeckel
(*c*) Warming (*d*) Odum

7. The word Ecology (Oekologie) is derived from two Greek words which means :
(*a*) the study of wildlife
(*b*) the study of land and life
(*c*) the study of life
(*d*) the study of home

8. Term *bionomics* for relationship between organisms and their environment was used by :
(*a*) Hilaire (*b*) Reiter
(*c*) Lankester (*d*) Odum

9. *Oekologie* (*Oikos* = home; *Logos* = to study) was defined by Ernst Haeckel for the reciprocal relationships between animals and their environment. Term Oekology was used for the same study but for plants by :
(*a*) Kormondy
(*b*) Warming
(*c*) Theopharastus
(*d*) Weaver and Clements

10. Term **bioecology** to study plant and animal ecology as integral branch, was coined by :
(*a*) Odum
(*b*) Reiter
(*c*) Shelford and Clements
(*d*) Kormondy

11. The study of an individual or its population in relation to their environment in an area is called :
(*a*) Ecology (*b*) Autecology
(*c*) Synecology (*d*) Phytosociology

12. The study of structure and nature of communities or ecosystem is called :
(*a*) Autecology (*b*) Synecology
(*c*) Phytogeography (*d*) Ecology

13. The study of interaction between living organisms and their environment is called :
(*a*) Ecosystem (*b*) Phytogeography
(*c*) Phytosociology (*d*) Ecology

14. Study of plant environment is called :
(*a*) Phytosociology (*b*) Phytogeography
(*c*) Ecology (*d*) Biogeocoenosis

15. The definition of ecology is the study of relations between organisms and their environment. The study is :

(*a*) reciprocal (*b*) direct alone
(*c*) indirect alone (*d*) genetic alone

16. The aspect considered to be most important in ecology is :
(*a*) climate (*b*) soil
(*c*) environment (*d*) man

17. Species which are morphologically similar but vary in reproductive features are known as :
(*a*) sympatric species (*b*) allopatric species
(*c*) sub-species (*d*) sibling species

18. Silent Valley of Kerala is an asset because :
(*a*) It has rare species of plants and animals
(*b*) It has valuable teak trees
(*c*) It is a major tourist attraction in Kerala
(*d*) This region is rich in medicinal plants

19. Plants which can survive in narrow range of temperature are :
(*a*) euthermic (*b*) stenothermic
(*c*) hypothermic (*d*) helikothermic

20. Halophytes are peculiar in having :
(*a*) saline water
(*b*) velamen tissue
(*c*) pneumatophoric stem
(*d*) vivipary

21. Halophytes grow on physiologically dry soil due to the presence of :
(*a*) excessive salt in plants
(*b*) low water requirement
(*c*) excessive salt in water
(*d*) excessive humidity in the air

22. Broad leaved deciduous forests are typical of :
(*a*) Mid-altitude forests
(*b*) Mediterranean region
(*c*) Monsoon region
(*d*) Coniferous region

23. Which one of the following plant pigments prevents the leaves from damaging effects UV radiations?
(*a*) Xanthophyll
(*b*) Phycocyanin
(*c*) Chlorophyll
(*d*) Carotenoids

24. High velocity of winds bring about :
A. increase in rate of transpiration
B. soil erosion
C. shifting of sand dunes
D. dispersal of seeds and fruits
Which of the pairs is effected most by high wind velocity?
(*a*) A and B (*b*) A and C
(*c*) C and D (*d*) A and D

25. Which one has exclusive xerophytic adaptation?
(*a*) absence of stomata
(*b*) long tap root system
(*c*) stipular leaves
(*d*) spines

26. Desert can be converted into green land by :
(*a*) Oxylophytes (*b*) Psamophytes
(*c*) Halophytes (*d*) Tropical trees

27. Maximum transpiration occurs in :
(*a*) mesophytes (*b*) hydrophytes
(*c*) xerophytes (*d*) algae

28. Match the following :

Column A	Column B
A. Ecology	1. A science which concerns itself with the inter-relationship of living organisms, plants and animals and their environments.
B. Organism	2. An individual unit constituted to carry on the activities of life.
C. Habitat	3. The natural abode or lacality of an animal, plant or person.

Codes :

	A	B	C
(*a*)	3	2	1
(*b*)	2	3	1
(*c*)	1	3	2
(*d*)	1	2	3

29. Harmful effect is produced on vegetation by grazing of cattle. This aspect is studied under :
(*a*) biotic factors (*b*) temperature
(*c*) soil factor (*d*) light

30. *Rhododendron* is a characteristic component of vegetation in :
(*a*) Tropical forests
(*b*) Mangrooves
(*c*) Gangetic plains
(*d*) Alpine

31. An example of physiological xerophyte is :
(*a*) *Salvia* (*b*) *Euphorbia*
(*c*) *Salicornia* (*d*) *Agave*

32. Clay particles are :
(*a*) negatively charged
(*b*) neutral
(*c*) positively charged
(*d*) with no charge

33. A pond of :
(*a*) a biome
(*b*) a natural
(*c*) an artifical ecosystem
(*d*) All of the above

34. When food is derived by killing the host, this sort of interaction is :
(*a*) Predation (*b*) Parasitism
(*c*) Antibiosis (*d*) None of these

35. When a peacack eats snakes which eat insects thriving or green plants the peacock is :
(*a*) a final decomposer
(*b*) apex of the food pyramid
(*c*) primary decomposer
(*d*) All of the above

36. In ecological environment the behaviour of an organism is regulated by :
(*a*) raw materials and heredity
(*b*) environment and heredity
(*c*) raw materials and organisms
(*d*) genetic factors

37. In Ecology one can study :
A. association of a number of species
B. habitat
C. environment
D. light
The aim of ecology is explained by :
(*a*) A, B and C (*b*) B, C and D
(*c*) C, D and A (*d*) C, D and B

38. Alternative terms for ecology :
(*a*) Environmental Biology
(*b*) Bionomics
(*c*) Bioecology
(*d*) All of these

39. Branch dealing with distribution of plants on earth is called :
(*a*) Phytosociology
(*b*) Phytogeography
(*c*) Ecology
(*d*) Phytology

40. 'Act locally, think globally' is the concept given by :
(*a*) Kropotkin (*b*) Kelly
(*c*) William Gilpin (*d*) Anonymous

41. Plant ecology can not be studied without the help of :
(*a*) Morphology and Cytology
(*b*) Morphology and Physiology
(*c*) Morphology and Embryology
(*d*) Morphology and Taxonomy

42. Applied ecology deals with :
(*a*) individual species
(*b*) plant communities
(*c*) physiological and genetic potentialities
(*d*) man and bioshpere

43. Which tree is popular as Green Gold yet an ecological disaster?
(*a*) Apricot (*b*) Coconut
(*c*) *Eucalyptus* (*d*) *Eichhornia*

44. The distinct smell of sea is due to :
(*a*) NaCl
(*b*) Sodium phosphate
(*c*) H_2S
(*d*) Dimethyl sulphide

45. The 'Man of the trees' is :
(*a*) Bahuguna
(*b*) Chandi Prasad Bhatt
(*c*) Baba Amte
(*d*) St. Barbe Baker

46. The exotic species is :
(*a*) local species
(*b*) species with good characters

(*c*) a species brought into an area from other region
(*d*) a species of a selective region

47. Endemic species (indigenous plants) means
(*a*) plants cosmopolitan in distribution
(*b*) plants of a particular local/geographical region
(*c*) plants showing gregarious habit
(*d*) plants of Timberline

48. Chronobiology is :
(*a*) study of activities of animals in an area
(*b*) study of rhythmic periodicity in the activity of organisms
(*c*) study of factors on the growth and development of organisms
(*d*) None of the above

49. A troublesome American water weed in India called sorrow of Punjab is :
(*a*) *Typha* (*b*) *Trapa*
(*c*) *Cyperus* (*d*) *Eichhornia*

50. Fire has both positive and negative effect on forests. Study of fire ecology is called :
(*a*) Synecology (*b*) Hexicology
(*c*) Ecophyrology (*d*) Phytogeography

51. Environmentally induced morphological variants of a species which are genetically similar are called :
(*a*) ecotone (*b*) ecotype
(*c*) ecoline (*d*) ecophene

52. Flora/Fauna of an area is :
(*a*) listed
(*b*) only (*a*) is correct
(*c*) described
(*d*) both are correct

53. Which environment is rich in free oxygen?
(*a*) Warm water (*b*) Atmosphere
(*c*) Cold fresh water (*d*) Salt H_2O

54. The transitional zone where two different communities meet is called :
(*a*) ecoline (*b*) ecotone
(*c*) ecotype (*d*) niche

55. Which of the following terms is used to denote the living matter of the universe?
(*a*) Ecosystem (*b*) Lithosphere
(*c*) Biosphere (*d*) Atmosphere

56. Which one of the following interspecific interactions antagonistic relationship?
(*a*) Parasitism and predation
(*b*) Competition and antibiosis
(*c*) Parasitism and neutralism
(*d*) Competition and predation

57. Plants which can withstand wide range of temperature are called :
(*a*) Mesothermic (*b*) Monothermic
(*c*) Eurythermic (*d*) Stenothermic

58. Who amongst the following Indian scientists has contributed to the ecology :
(*a*) Ramdeo Misra (*b*) J.C. Bose
(*c*) P. Maheshwari (*d*) K.C. Mehta

59. *Argemone mexicana* (Prickly pear) is an ecological indicator of :
(*a*) poorly drained soil
(*b*) nitrate rich soil
(*c*) recently flooded soil
(*d*) iron rich soil

60. Soil salinity is measured by :
(*a*) Potometer
(*b*) Porometer
(*c*) Calorimeter
(*d*) Conductivity meter

61. Which is best for plant growth?
(*a*) loamy soil (*b*) sandy soil
(*c*) clayey soil (*d*) fine silt

62. Which soil is best for the growth of Jute?
(*a*) Clay (*b*) Sand
(*c*) Red soil (*d*) Loamy alluvial

63. Best soil for growth of plants in summers is :
(*a*) loamy (*b*) clayey
(*c*) sandy (*d*) silt

64. Soil in cold and wet temperate areas supporting dense coniferous forests with *p*H 3-5 is called :
(*a*) podsol soil (*b*) laterite soil
(*c*) chernozen soil (*d*) serpentine soil

65. Laterite soils are rich in :
(*a*) Aluminium (*b*) Silica
(*c*) Iron (*d*) All of the above

66. Laterization of soil is the process that result in :
(*a*) formation of soil
(*b*) degradation of soil
(*c*) sterilization of soil
(*d*) soil erosion

67. Latosol soil favours :
(*a*) tropical rain forests
(*b*) alpine forests
(*c*) shrubs
(*d*) no life

68. Regolith is the geological name of :
(*a*) top soil (*b*) loam
(*c*) sand (*d*) silt

69. Which is the acid associated with soil?
(*a*) Acetic acid (*b*) Nitric acid
(*c*) Humic acid (*d*) Sulphuric acid

70. Khadar alluvial soil is :
(*a*) recent and silting
(*b*) old and clayey
(*c*) rich in gravels and pebbles
(*d*) All of the above

71. Soil profile shows 4 distinct layers called :
(*a*) litter (*b*) horizons
(*c*) stratification (*d*) petition

72. The term subsoil is used for which horizon of soil profile :
(*a*) A (*b*) B
(*c*) D (*d*) C

73. Solum includes :
(*a*) Horizons A and B
(*b*) Horizon A only
(*c*) Horizons A_1 and A_2
(*d*) Horizons A_1 and B only

74. Soil formation in hot and humid climate is called :
(*a*) laterisation (*b*) podsolization
(*c*) gleization (*d*) calcification

75. Which is true for Humus?
(*a*) It has salts of P, S, Ca, K and N
(*b*) It has growth promoting humic acid
(*c*) It has 150 times more water holding capacity than clay and warm up soil being black in colour
(*d*) All of the above

76. Undecomposed organic matter in soil is called :
(*a*) litter (*b*) humus
(*c*) mull (*d*) duff

77. Soil humus that is slightly alkaline and rich in bacteria is called :
(*a*) Mor (*b*) Mull
(*c*) Peat (*d*) Litter

78. Humus is an example of :
(*a*) fertilizer
(*b*) organic colloid
(*c*) crystalloid
(*d*) component of soil

79. What is wrong for clay?
(*a*) Clay is heavy textured but has high water holding capacity
(*b*) Clay has negatively charged colloids and mineral cations
(*c*) Clay has positively charged colloids and mineral anions
(*d*) Clay is good to hold water

80. At permanent wilting, soil has about........% water.
(*a*) 10 (*b*) 20
(*c*) 5 (*d*) 3

81. Saline soils (kallar/Usar soil) can be reclamed by adding :
(*a*) Gypsum ($CaSO_4 . 2H_2O$)
(*b*) Molasses
(*c*) Mud of sugar factory
(*d*) All of the above

82. Which factors maintains the distinctiveness of characters among different species?
(*a*) Speciation
(*b*) Mutualism
(*c*) Co-operation
(*d*) Reproductive isolation

83. A man-made ecological factor is :
(*a*) Fire (*b*) Farming
(*c*) Grazing (*d*) Ploughing

84. Plants growing in shade are :
(*a*) Mesophytes (*b*) Heliophytes
(*c*) Xerophytes (*d*) Sciophytes

85. Heliophytes are plants growing in :
(*a*) shade
(*b*) full sunlight
(*c*) extreme dry conditions
(*d*) saline soil

86. Ecological factors generally work :
(*a*) in combination
(*b*) in complex combination by interacting and modifying one another
(*c*) without modifying the effect of other
(*d*) None of the above

87. Leaves of desert plants are not torn away by high wind velocity because :
(*a*) sclerenchymatous tissue that provides extra mechanical support
(*b*) leaves are modified into spines
(*c*) tearing of corners while the middle remains saved
(*d*) bending is in the direction of wind

88. Ecotype is :
(*a*) genetically different individuals with same phenotype
(*b*) genetically adapted ecological races of a local area
(*c*) genetically identical individuals with same phenotype
(*d*) transitional zone

89. A plant/animal form produced in response to a habitat, the adaptations not being heritable, is called :
(*a*) ecotype (*b*) life form
(*c*) ecad (*d*) ecophene

90. Regularly recurring, co-related with earth's 24 hours rotation is called :
(*a*) Circadian rhythm
(*b*) Metachronal rhythm
(*c*) Synchronal rhythm
(*d*) None of the above

91. Crocodiles taken sun bath at noon in winter, it is an example of :
(*a*) Hibernation
(*b*) Aestivation
(*c*) Periodic activity
(*d*) None of these

92. Swarming and spawning are co-related with :
(*a*) lunar activity (*b*) tidal activity
(*c*) seasonal changes (*d*) both (*a*) and (*b*)

93. About what per cent of earth's species will be destroyed, if all the tropical rain forests are destroyed?
(*a*) 10 (*b*) 20
(*c*) 50 (*d*) 90

94. The essentially automatic movement of an animal towards or away from a stimulus is :
(*a*) Taxis (*b*) Kinesis
(*c*) Reflex (*d*) Orientation

95. Foul smell in water of tanks and ponds is due to H_2S released by :
(*a*) anaerobiosis (*b*) aerobiosis
(*c*) psammophytes (*d*) biomagnification

96. Massive growth of *Eichhornia* indicates the chances of :
(*a*) flood (*b*) fire
(*c*) draught (*d*) deforestation

97. The reflectivity percentage of incident light on earth is meteorologically called as :
(*a*) Tornado (*b*) Albedo
(*c*) Refraction (*d*) Reradiation

98. Gloger/s rule refers to mammals, birds and insects of tropical region with their :
(*a*) body length
(*b*) size of body
(*c*) extremities
(*d*) dark pigmented body

99. Cyclomorphosis are changes in :
(*a*) shape (*b*) weight
(*c*) size (*d*) behaviour

100. Bergman's rule is related with :
(*a*) Pigmentation
(*b*) Avian and Mammalian life
(*c*) BMR in aves and mammals
(*d*) Size of fingers and number of vertebrae in animals living under different conditions

101. Bergman's rule states that :
(*a*) organisms of hotter area are darker in colour to reflect light
(*b*) mammals and birds of colder areas are larger than those of hot areas due to fat deposition
(*c*) mammals and birds of hotter areas show aestivation in summer
(*d*) aquatic animals are larger than terrestrial ones

102. The fishes found in water of low temperature tend to have more vertebrae and growth than those of warmer water as codfish has 56 vertebrae if hatching at 4-8°C and 54 vertebrae hatching at 10-11°C. This refers to :
(*a*) Jorden's rule (*b*) Gloger's rule
(*c*) Allen's rule (*d*) Bergman's rule

103. The birds of colder regions tend to have relatively narrow wings than the birds of warmer areas. This is :
(*a*) Rensch's rule (*b*) Gloger rule
(*c*) Cyclomorphosis (*d*) Batesian mimicry

104. BMR is more in animals of :
(*a*) warmer regions (*b*) caves
(*c*) arctic region (*d*) colder region

105. Extremites like tail, snout, (Fingers, eyes, ears and legs) of mammals are shorter in colder region than in warmer region. It was first noted in foxes and gazells. It is called :
(*a*) Allen's rule (*b*) Jorden rule
(*c*) Lindeman's rule (*d*) Gloger's rule

106. A habitat with long, severe winter and growing season restricted to a few months of summer forms :
(*a*) taiga (*b*) tundra ecosystem
(*c*) savannah (*d*) grassland

107. Physical and chemical conditions of soil are studied under :
(*a*) edaphic factors (*b*) biotic factors
(*c*) topographic factors (*d*) climatic factors

108. Ecologically fixed and genetically irreversed species are called :
(*a*) ecological equivalents
(*b*) ecotone
(*c*) ecotype
(*d*) None of these

109. In desert grassland which types of animals are relatively more abundant ?
(*a*) Arboreal (*b*) Diurnal
(*c*) Aquatic (*d*) Fossorial

110. Which of the following changes would likely to make terrestrial life on planet impossible?
(*a*) disappearance of the moon
(*b*) change in the atmosphere permitting all the solar radiations reaching the upper atmosphere to penetrate the surface of the earth (lithosphere)
(*c*) decrease in mean annual temperature by 10°C
(*d*) change in the orbit of the earth from an ellipse to a circle

111. Acidic soils are deficient in Ca and Mg salts. These can be reclamed by adding :
(*a*) calcium carbonate/quick lime/dolomite/ hydrate lime
(*b*) gypsum
(*c*) lime sulphur
(*d*) Any of the above

112. Alkali and Saline soils have percentage of soluble salts and deposition of chlorides, nitrates, sulphates and carbonates of Na, K, Ca and Mg. Which of the following soil is called Kallar or Thur or Reh?
(*a*) Alkali soil which is poor in soluble salts, contains carbonates and pH > 8.5
(*b*) Saline soil which is rich in soluble salts and contains no carbonates and pH 8.5
(*c*) Saline soil rich in soluble salts, pH 8.5, and Na exchanges percentage more than 15%
(*d*) acidic soils rich in $CaCO_3$

113. Limiting factor in soil nitrification is :
(*a*) Soil pH (*b*) Light
(*c*) Temperature (*d*) Air

114. Plants die in water logged soils due to :
(*a*) Nutrient leaching
(*b*) Stoppage of root respiration
(*c*) Dilution of cell sap
(*d*) Dilution of soil nutrients

115. Mulching helps in :
(*a*) increasing Nitrogenous content of soil
(*b*) moisture conservation of soil
(*c*) improving soil texture
(*d*) neutralization of acidity

116. Which of the following plants indicate the diamond in the soil :
(*a*) *Salvadora* (*b*) *Panicum*
(*c*) *Vallozia* (*d*) *Capparis*

117. Leaching and flushing processes of soil reclamation help in :
(*a*) levelling
(*b*) increasing fertility
(*c*) lowering salt contents
(*d*) increasing salt contents

118. To reclaim at the alkaline/saline soils, they are heavily irrigated and drained so that
(*a*) all the organic matter is removed
(*b*) all water soluble minerals are removed
(*c*) the soil becomes acidic
(*d*) excess amount of basic salts are removed

119. What is the proportion of the frequency of occurrence of La Nina compared to El Nino ?
(*a*) Half
(*b*) One-third
(*c*) Twice
(*d*) Two-third

120. This term refers to studies of groups of organisms associated to form a functional unit of an ecosystem :
(*a*) Autecology (*b*) Synecology
(*c*) Ecology (*d*) Ethology

121. Alpine tundra is found in :
(*a*) Siberia (*b*) Greenland
(*c*) Both (*a*) and (*b*) (*d*) Himalayas

122. Timber line is :
(*a*) edge of forest beyond which become shrubby and as such no trees occur
(*b*) boundary between forest and mountain
(*c*) latitude at which timber trees grow
(*d*) altitude beyond which trees occur in close canopy

123. Timber line in Western Himalayas occur at high altitude of :
(*a*) 3000 m (*b*) 3100-3600 m
(*c*) 4000 m (*d*) 3000-5100 m

124. Choose the correct pair :
(*a*) *Acacia arabica* : a xerophyte
(*b*) *Eichhornia* : a free floating hydrophyte
(*c*) *Capparis* : a xerophyte
(*d*) All of the above

125. A non-succulent xerophyte with thick leaves having white sticky waxy coating is :
(*a*) *Nerium* (*b*) *Calotropis*
(*c*) *Bryophyllum* (*d*) *Ruscus*

126. Drought resistance and succulents are connected with :
(*a*) well developed xylem
(*b*) fleshy mesophyll
(*c*) regulated stomatal movement
(*d*) high frequency of stomata

127. On sandy river banks there appears to be no scarcity of water, the plants growing there are called as :
(*a*) mesophytes (*b*) halophytes
(*c*) xerophytes (*d*) hydrophytes

128. Major source of water for the soil is :
(*a*) ground water (*b*) capillary water
(*c*) precipitation (*d*) combined water

129. The major characteristics of the vegetation of a locality are controlled by :
(*a*) mainly by climate
(*b*) animals only
(*c*) man only
(*d*) altitude of a place only

130. The grazing animals can change the type of vegetation by :
(*a*) bringing in plant pathogens
(*b*) cross pollination
(*c*) selective grazing
(*d*) bringing the seeds of other plants

131. Solubility and availability of plant nutrients are related to :
(*a*) Soil colour (*b*) Soil temperature
(*c*) Soil porosity (*d*) Soil *p*H

132. Which is the characteristic feature of a physiologically dry soil?

(*a*) Soil is stony
(*b*) There is a plenty of water in the soil
(*c*) Concentration of salts is very high in soil water
(*d*) Light available to the plenty is not sufficient

133. Any component of environment which effects directly or indirectly the function or form of the organism is called :
(*a*) climatic factor
(*b*) ecological factor
(*c*) biotic factor
(*d*) topographic factor

134. Geography in which India comes as a part of earth is :
(*a*) tropical (*b*) subtropical
(*c*) oriental (*d*) semi arid

135. Which one is biotic in origin
(*a*) soil texture (*b*) rainfall
(*c*) CO_2 in soil (*d*) light

136. The significant factor for living organisms is
(*a*) water (*b*) light
(*c*) RH (*d*) temperature

137. Most abundant gas on earth is :
(*a*) N_2 (*b*) O_2
(*c*) CO_2 (*d*) H_2

138. Which one are direct ecological factors, which determine vegetation of an area :
(*a*) Altitude, soil texture and wind
(*b*) Rain, soil and altitude
(*c*) Soil organisms, precipitation and altitude
(*d*) Temperature, light, soil, air and humidity

139. Vegetation of a locality is controlled by :
(*a*) man (*b*) climate
(*c*) altitude (*d*) edaphic factors

140. A microclimate is a local climate within a regional climate (macroclimate). It is controlled by :
(*a*) irregularities in land surface
(*b*) vegetation
(*c*) both are correct
(*d*) altitude and elevation

141. A leaf adapted to warm, dry climate is :
(*a*) large and thin (*b*) small and thin
(*c*) large and thick (*d*) small and thick

142. By growing close to ground, a Tundra plant :
(*a*) avoids wind
(*b*) avoids herbivores
(*c*) forms mutualistic relations with soil
(*d*) attracts pollinators

143. The leaves of Tundra plant resemble the leaves of a plant in a :
(*a*) tropical rain forest
(*b*) temperate deciduous forest
(*c*) northern coniferous forest
(*d*) desert

144. Red pigments in Tundra plants is for :
(*a*) increasing range of light for photosynthesis
(*b*) warming the plant
(*c*) tracking the sun
(*d*) measuring the time

145. An insect survives the cold of winter in a dormant stage by converting its glycogen to :
(*a*) ATP (*b*) Lactic acid
(*c*) Alcohol (*d*) BAT

146. A woody plant becomes hardened to the cold in preparation for winter. It lowers the freezing point of its cells and fluids by :
(*a*) increasing concentration of its solutes
(*b*) increasing TP
(*c*) making cell wall thick
(*d*) All of the above

147. With the coming of fall, yellow and orange pigments begin to appear in leaves as the :
(*a*) cold season is approaching
(*b*) abscission layer is formed
(*c*) leaves become old and heavy
(*d*) temperature lowers down the synthesis of chlorophyll and light destroys chlorophyll formation

148. Timberline is the line beyond which one of the followings ceases to grow :
(*a*) lichen (*b*) sedges
(*c*) trees (*d*) None of these

149. Photoperiodism is well developed in :
(*a*) polar plants (*b*) equator plants
(*c*) mangroove plants (*d*) All of these

150. Coniferous forests in India occur above an altitude of :
(*a*) 500 feet (*b*) 2000 feet
(*c*) 4000 feet (*d*) 6000 feet

151. A vegetation zone in Himalayas dominated by conifers is called :
(*a*) tropical (*b*) alpine
(*c*) chapparal (*d*) taiga

152. Temperate evergreen forests are found India in :
(*a*) Eastern and western Himalayan range
(*b*) Western ghats
(*c*) Assam
(*d*) Aravali range

153. Water left in soil after permanent wilting of plant is :
(*a*) ground water
(*b*) capillary H_2O
(*c*) gravitational H_2O
(*d*) hygroscopic H_2O

154. The portion of total soil water available to plant is :
(*a*) holard
(*b*) chresard
(*c*) echard
(*d*) wilting coefficient

155. Soil can be protected by :
(*a*) afforestation
(*b*) deforestation
(*c*) making a soil profile
(*d*) None of the above

156. The water present in between soil particles and available to plant roots is called :
(*a*) hygroscopic (*b*) capillary
(*c*) gravitational (*d*) combined water

157. Desert soils are rich in :
(*a*) Ca
(*b*) Mg
(*c*) Ca^{2+} and Mg^{2} both
(*d*) None of these

158. The sequence of humification and mineralization is :
(*a*) Plant/animal's dead organic matter → Litter → duff → humus → minerals
(*b*) Minerals → humus → litter → duff
(*c*) Dead organic matter → duff → litter → minerals → humus
(*d*) Humus → minerals → litter → duff

159. The composition of soil is :
(*a*) mineral + organic matter + water
(*b*) minerals + water + air
(*c*) organic matter + water
(*d*) organic matter + water + minerals + air

160. The soil having more than 40% of clay is called :
(*a*) clay soil (*b*) alluvial soil
(*c*) heavy soil (*d*) loamy soil

161. The loam soil has :
(*a*) sand 30-50%
(*b*) silt 30-50%
(*c*) clay not more than 20%
(*d*) All of the above

162. A soil deficient in plant nutrients is called :
(*a*) eutrophic (*b*) oligotrophic
(*c*) residual (*d*) transported

163. A best soil is that which :
(*a*) allows water to trickle through slowly and gradually
(*b*) allows water to pass quickly
(*c*) holds all water firmly
(*d*) allows limited water to enter it

164. Fertility of soil is measured by its ability to :
(*a*) hold water
(*b*) to retain nutrients
(*c*) to hold organic matter
(*d*) to support life

165. Soil having permanently wilted plants still has :
(*a*) hygroscopic water
(*b*) ground water
(*c*) capillary water
(*d*) gravitational water

166. Soil fertility is decreased by :
(*a*) decaying organic matter
(*b*) crop rotation
(*c*) intensive agriculture
(*d*) nitrification

167. Soil particles determine their :
(*a*) soil flora
(*b*) soil texture
(*c*) field capacity
(*d*) water holding capacity

168. The percentage of water left in the soil when a plant wilts is known as :
(*a*) wilting coefficient
(*b*) field capacity
(*c*) Holard
(*d*) water holding capacity

169. Soil carried by river is :
(*a*) alluvial (*b*) sandy
(*c*) laterite (*d*) clayey

170. Field capacity of soil is :
(*a*) its storage capacity
(*b*) storage capacity + capillary water
(*c*) storage capacity – hygroscopic water
(*d*) capillary water + hygroscopic water

171. In a fertile agricultural tract, surface soils appear deep coloured than the soil about one metre down. This is because the top soil :
(*a*) holds moisture
(*b*) is a recently formed layer
(*c*) is rich in humus organic matter
(*d*) is rich in iron and magnesium

172. The water holding capacity of soil is called :
(*a*) wilting coefficient
(*b*) field capacity
(*c*) soil profile
(*d*) pedology

173. Tropical evergreen forests receive a rainfall of :
(*a*) 50-100 cm (*b*) 150-225 cm
(*c*) 5-100 cm (*d*) 250-450 cm

174. Forests near equator are :
(*a*) tropical rain forests
(*b*) deciduous
(*c*) conifers
(*d*) grassland

175. Alpine plants growing at a height of more than 3567 m where wind velocity is high and temperature low show xerophytic characters like :
(*a*) rosette habit
(*b*) high O.P.
(*c*) reduced surface area, thick cuticle and long roots
(*d*) All of the above

176. Tropical rain forests in India are found in Assam, north-eastern Inida, Kerala, Western Ghats, Andaman and Nicobar. These are dense due to :
(*a*) high temperature and lesser rain
(*b*) high temperature and excess rain
(*c*) low temperature and excess rain
(*d*) wild animals and plants

177. Plants such as *Prosopis, Acacia* and *Capparis* represent examples of tropical :
(*a*) grasslands
(*b*) thorn (scrubland)
(*c*) deciduous forests
(*d*) evergreen forests

178. Terai forest is :
(*a*) Tropical
(*b*) Coniferous
(*c*) Deciduous
(*d*) Temperate deciduous

179. Alpine forests of Himalayans have :
(*a*) Tall evergreen coniferous trees
(*b*) Tall broad leaved evergreen trees
(*c*) Tall broad leaved deciduous trees
(*d*) Dwarf shrubby plants

180. The forests that colours in autumn is :
(*a*) Temperate evergreen
(*b*) Temperate deciduous
(*c*) Tropical evergreen
(*d*) Tropical deciduous

181. Difference between tropical and temperate rain forests is:
(*a*) Tropical forests have more of Angiosperms while temperate forests have more of gymnosperms
(*b*) Tropical forests are homogeneous while temperate forests are heterogeneous
(*c*) Plants of temperate forests are more of mesophytic
(*d*) Trees of temperate forests are taller than those of tropical forests

182. If tree is showing needle like leaves and scales, it might be growing in :
(*a*) desert (*b*) mountain
(*c*) saline soil (*d*) wamps

183. Seasonal periodicity is best seen in :
(*a*) evergreen forests
(*b*) evergreen scrub
(*c*) deciduous forests
(*d*) alpine forests

184. Water logged soils are :
(*a*) physically dry
(*b*) physiologically dry
(*c*) with great amount of water
(*d*) with less amount of water

185. Area having little summer precipitation but sufficient rainfall in winter produces :
(*a*) deciduous forests
(*b*) scrub forests
(*c*) grasslands
(*d*) deserts

186. Vegetation beyond timber line is tree less and called :
(*a*) Elfin scrub
(*b*) Alpine meadows
(*c*) Grassland
(*d*) Both (*a*) and (*b*)

187. Fall is a season in early October in Northern latitudes with programmed dropping of the leaves of trees. It is due to :
(*a*) longer day length promote hormone formation stimulating leaf fall
(*b*) short day length and low night temperature promote hormone formation stimulating leaf fall
(*c*) cold conditions stimulate leaf fall
(*d*) ageing of leaves

188. Leaves with drip trips and grooved veins are found in trees of :
(*a*) Tropical rain forest
(*b*) Deciduous forest
(*c*) Savannah
(*d*) Temperate forests

189. Commonest types of forests in India :
(*a*) Tropical dry deciduous
(*b*) Tropical moist deciduous
(*c*) Temperatre forests
(*d*) Tropical thorny forests

190. Competition of food, light and space is most severe between :
(*a*) closely related species growing in different habitats
(*b*) distantly related species occuping different habitats
(*c*) distantly related species occuping the same habitat
(*d*) closely related species growing in the same habitat

191. What is the best *p*H of the soil for cultivation of plants?
(*a*) 4.5 – 8.5 (*b*) 3.4 – 5.4
(*c*) 6.5 – 7.5 (*d*) 5.5 – 6.5

192. A plant species having different areas of geographical distribution are called :
(*a*) phytogeographic
(*b*) allopatric
(*c*) sympatric
(*d*) allelomorphs

193. Which of the following is important for speciation :
(*a*) Reproductive isolation
(*b*) Tropical isolation
(*c*) Seasonal isolation
(*d*) Behavioural isolation

194. Plant decomposers are :
(*a*) Fungi and plants
(*b*) Animalia and monera
(*c*) Protista and animalia
(*d*) Monera and fungi

195. The kind of soil water most useful to plant is :
(*a*) hygroscopic water
(*b*) gravitational water
(*c*) capillary water
(*d*) None of the above

196. The soil with poorest water holding capacity is :
(*a*) clay
(*b*) loam
(*c*) sand
(*d*) None of the above

197. The organic water in good soil should be :
(*a*) 25% (*b*) 50%
(*c*) 40% (*d*) 10%

198. The size of clay particles is :
(*a*) less than 0.002 mm
(*b*) more than 0.002 mm
(*c*) 0.2 mm to 2 mm
(*d*) None of the above

199. On the size of particles the soils are classified as :
A. sand B. loam
C. clay D. silt

On the size of soil particles which of the pairs has got maximum capacity of porosity?
(*a*) A and B (*b*) A and C
(*c*) A and D (*d*) B and C

200. From the above data, point out which of the pairs has got the maximum water holding capacity?
(*a*) A and B (*b*) A and C
(*c*) A and D (*d*) C and D

201. From the above data, point out which of the pairs has got maximum growth capacity?
(*a*) A and B (*b*) B and C
(*c*) C and D (*d*) D and A

202. Black soil is rich in :
(*a*) silt and earthworm
(*b*) clay and humus
(*c*) sand and Zn^{++}
(*d*) gravel and Ca^{++}

203. Major constituent of soil is :
(*a*) organic matter (*b*) inorganic matter
(*c*) soil air (*d*) soil water

204. Organic matter in soil is formed by :
(*a*) chemical weathering
(*b*) soil microorganisms
(*c*) consumers and herbivores
(*d*) plants

205. Formation of soil particles from rocks takes place by :
(*a*) weathering (*b*) pedogenesis
(*c*) paedogenesis (*d*) both (*a*) and (*b*)

206. The fertile part of soil is :
(*a*) mineral matter (*b*) soil air
(*c*) humus (*d*) soil water

207. Main source of water of the soil is :
(*a*) Canals
(*b*) rivers
(*c*) rain
(*d*) None of these

208. Maintenance of soil fertility without addition of nutrients is due to :
(*a*) crop residue
(*b*) microbial activity
(*c*) floods
(*d*) optimum temperature

209. Plants which grow on the slopes of hills face :
(*a*) physical drought
(*b*) physiological drought
(*c*) low wind action
(*d*) low water supply

210. Laterite soil (Latosol) is red due to oxides of :
(*a*) Fe (*b*) Al
(*c*) Silica (*d*) Mg and Cobalt

211. Best *p*H of fertile soil is :
(*a*) 6-7 (*b*) 5-7
(*c*) 4-7 (*d*) 7-8

212. Black soil is good for cotton. It is rich in :
(*a*) clay (*b*) organic matter
(*c*) aluminium (*d*) All correct

213. Clay soils are :
(*a*) heavy textured (*b*) light textured
(*c*) loose textured (*d*) porous

214. Which is halophyte of saline soil of Haryana and Rajasthan?
(*a*) *Salsola* (*b*) *Suaeda*
(*c*) *Salicornia* (*d*) All correct

215. Acidic soils occur in area of :
(*a*) high rainfall (*b*) low rainfall
(*c*) poor rainfall (*d*) moderate rainfall

216. Acidity of soil is due to :
(*a*) leaching of soluble basic salts of Ca, Mg, K and Na
(*b*) leaching of acidic salts and settling down of bases

(c) addition of oxides and silicates of Fe and Al in soil
(d) All of the above

217. Trees growing in windy places along sea shores and high mountain tops show :
(a) flag effect (b) edge effect
(c) giant effect (d) nanninism

218. The *flag effect* on trees near sea shore is because :
(a) Buds on the windward side of the trunk don's sprout
(b) Buds on seaward side of trunk sprout
(c) Wind action blows branches seaward
(d) Buds on both sides sprout quickly

219. At high altitude, the plants show nanninism *i.e.,* dwarfism because of :
(a) Windiness
(b) Scarcity of water and low temperature
(c) High light intensity
(d) Both (a) and (c)

220. Which of the following group of organisms are adapted to the arctic and alpine regions?
(a) Psychrophytes (b) Chersophytes
(c) Psilophytes (d) Therophytes

221. The plants found at top of mountains are called Alpine plants. They show :
(a) rosette habit
(b) xerophytic nature
(c) high sugar contents
(d) All of these

222. Layering or stratification is common in :
(a) tropical rain forests
(b) temperate forests
(c) deciduous forests
(d) tropical savannahs

223. Plants normally prefer temperature between :
(a) 10 – 20°C (b) 10 – 35°C
(c) below 20°C (d) above 40°C

224. Hekistotherms are plants of :
(a) extremely low temperature (10°C)
(b) high temperature plants
(c) cold soil plants
(d) shade loving plants

225. Temperature changes in the environment affect most of the animals which are :
(a) aquatic (b) desert living
(c) poikilothermal (d) homoeothermal

226. To avoid frost injury, plants show :
(a) conversion of fats into starch
(b) conversion of starch into fats and sugars
(c) formation of pentosans
(d) All of the above

227. High temperature results in leaf scorching and sunscald. Plants prevent themselves from high temperature injury by developing or forming :
(a) cork
(b) vertical orientation of leaves
(c) high contents of sugars/mucilage
(d) All of the above

228. The plants die at very low temperature because :
(a) cells rupture by pressure of ice
(b) dessication of cells
(c) precipitation of cell proteins
(d) All of these

229. Term *thermocline* deals with the region in a lake where there is :
(a) freezing temperature
(b) minimum fall in temperature
(c) maximum fall in temperature
(d) no effect of temperature

230. The response of plants to the rhythmic diurnal fluctuations in temperature is called :
(a) Thigmotropism
(b) Thermoperiodism
(c) Photoperiodism
(d) Tropism

231. The plants of warm habitat which require high degree of heat throughout the year like plants of desert are kept under :
(a) megatherms (b) mesotherms
(c) microtherms (d) hekistotherms

232. When rain fall is near uniform, change in temperature changes the flora of the area. It is called Schimpers :
(a) I Law (b) II Law
(c) III Law (d) No Law

233. Relative bilogical effectiveness (RBE) is usually referred to damages caused by :
(*a*) Low temperature (*b*) High temperature
(*c*) Pollution (*d*) Radiation

234. Plants which can withstand wide range of temperature tolerance are called :
(*a*) Stenothermic (*b*) Eurythermic
(*c*) Mesothermic (*d*) Heikistothermic

235. Submerged hydrophytes have thin dissected green leaves as shown by :
(*a*) *Hydrilla* (*b*) *Ceratophyllum*
(*c*) *Vallisneria* (*d*) *Potamogeton*

236. Amphibious plants have both xerophytic and hydrophytic characteristics, for example :
(*a*) *Hydrilla* and *Pistia*
(*b*) *Equisetum* and *Marsilea*
(*c*) *Vallisneria* and *Marsilea*
(*d*) *Potamogeton* and *Eichhornia*

237. In aquatic plants, usually seed formation does not occur because :
(*a*) humidity inhibits development of seeds
(*b*) humidity promotes production of sex organs
(*c*) of production of few propagules
(*d*) of continuation of favourable season

238. Usually vegetative reproduction is abundant in hydrophytes. This is due to the reason that humidity :
(*a*) inhibits production of sex organs
(*b*) promotes production of sex organs
(*c*) promotes profuse production of propagules
(*d*) inhibits production of propagules

239. Plants growing in humus rich soil which is poor in Ca^{++} :
(*a*) Calciphytes (*b*) Cryophytes
(*c*) Oxylophytes (*d*) Psammophytes

240. Elongated roots are found in :
(*a*) Mesophytes (*b*) Hydrophytes
(*c*) Xerophytes (*d*) Lichens

241. Plants found attached to stones and rocks are called :
(*a*) Lithophytes (*b*) Halophytes
(*c*) Aerophytes (*d*) Psammophytes

242. Acidity in acid plants (Oxylophytes) is less than 7. It is due to
(*a*) strong acids in them
(*b*) production of ammonium salt of organic acids
(*c*) both are correct
(*d*) None of these

243. Soil forms .... part of land.
(*a*) 1/5th (*b*) 2/5th
(*c*) 1/3th (*d*) 1/4th

244. Factor/s which relate the physical and chemical structure of soil are/is :
(*a*) edaphic (*b*) topographic
(*c*) biotic (*d*) topological

245. Soil determines the local distribution of plants directly or indirectly. It is :
(*a*) Schimper's second firsy law
(*b*) Schimper's first law
(*c*) Allen's Rule
(*d*) Gause principle

246. Factors related to the form and behaviour of earth surface are called :
(*a*) Topographic (*b*) Edaphic
(*c*) Biotic (*d*) Climatic

247. Edaphology is connected with :
(*d*) Plant + biosphere
(*b*) Soil + microorganisms
(*c*) Animals + ecosystem
(*d*) Soil + bioshpere

248. The formation of soil particles from rocks is called :
(*a*) Pedogenesis (*b*) Paedogenesis
(*c*) Mineralization (*d*) Weathering

249. The percentage of soil volume occupied by pore spaces is called porocity of soil. It is minimum in :
(*a*) sandy soil (*b*) loamy soil
(*c*) clay soil (*d*) silt

250. Salinity of soil can be corrected by the use of :
(*a*) $CaCO_3$ (*b*) lime
(*c*) fertilizers (*d*) sand

251. Which of the following factors affect plants and not animals?

(*a*) Temperature (*b*) Competition
(*c*) Altitude (*d*) Soil air

252. Which of the following soil is least porous?
(*a*) sandy soil (*b*) clay soil
(*c*) loam soil (*d*) silt soil

253. The thin film of water held tightly around soil particles by force of attraction and cohesion is :
(*a*) free water
(*b*) hygroscopic water
(*c*) crystalline water
(*d*) capillary water

254. Phytotron is a device by which :
(*a*) Proton are liberated
(*b*) Mutations are produced in plants
(*c*) Electrons are bombarded
(*d*) Plants are grown in controlled environment

255. In India, the temperate evergreen type of vegetation is found mostly in :
(*a*) Rajasthan and South Punjab
(*b*) Western ghats and Assam
(*c*) Eastern and Western Himalays less than 3,500 m
(*d*) Western Himalays above 3,500 m

256. When a soil has been thoughly wetted and then allowed to drain until the capillary movement of the water has stopped, the water content of the soil will give the estimate of its :
(*a*) field capacity
(*b*) capillary water
(*c*) storage capacity
(*d*) gravitational water

257. No organisms can survive beyond
(*a*) 40°C (*b*) 35°C
(*c*) 45°C (*d*) 75°C

258. In deserts, limiting factor for photosynthesis is :
(*a*) soil (*b*) temperature
(*c*) light (*d*) water

259. Which one of the following is the most characteristic feature of a xeric environment?
(*a*) Extremes of temperatures
(*b*) Low atmospheric humidity
(*c*) High rate of vapourisation
(*d*) None of the above

260. Hygrometer is used to measure :
(*a*) wind speed
(*b*) wind direction
(*c*) relative humidity
(*d*) temperature

261. Anemometer is used to measure :
(*a*) wind velocity (*b*) light
(*c*) temperature (*d*) RH

262. A de Candolle's plant group that tolerates polar regions beyond tree line is called :
(*a*) hekistotherms (*b*) microtherms
(*c*) megatherms (*d*) mesotherms

263. In which layer of lake, temperature change occurs?
(*a*) Epilimnion (*b*) Metalimnion
(*c*) Hypolimnion (*d*) Profundal

264. Effect of low temperature on flowering is studied in :
(*a*) phototropism (*b*) photoperiodism
(*c*) vernalisation (*d*) thermoperiodism

265. Secchi disc is used for the measurement of :
(*a*) turbility of H_2O
(*b*) BOD of H_2O
(*c*) light in H_2O
(*d*) flora and fauna of H_2O

266. Two areas getting equal rainfall still show different vegetation because :
(*a*) relative humidity is different
(*b*) rainfall is not only a criteria for vegetational type
(*c*) soil texture is different
(*d*) altitude is changed

267. Which one of the following would not make minerals more available to plants?
(*a*) Increasing rainfall in forests
(*b*) Raising pH of acidic soils
(*c*) Water logged soils
(*d*) Introducing fungi to form Mycorrhizae

268. Vegetation of an area is primarily determined by :

(*a*) amount of rainfall
(*b*) amount and periodicity of rain
(*c*) direction of rain
(*d*) All of the above

269. Heavy rainfall throughout the year results in
(*a*) luxurient evergreen forest
(*b*) deciduous forests
(*c*) scrub forests
(*d*) taiga forests

270. Moderate rain fall during summer and little in winter produces :
(*a*) grasslands (*b*) deserts
(*c*) scrub forests (*d*) deciduous forests

271. In Alpine zones, plants are killed by winter forst :
(*a*) low temperature
(*b*) dessication and injury
(*c*) stoppage of respiration
(*d*) plasmolysis and no photosynthesis

272. Three types of vegetation in the tropical and temperate areas is determined by the amount of seasonal distribution of rainfall and humidity of air. It is called Schimper's :
(*a*) I law (*b*) II law
(*c*) III law (*d*) None of these

273. Rainfall is determined largely by ;
(*a*) geography
(*b*) pattern of air movements
(*c*) both (*a*) and (*b*)
(*d*) rain shadow

274. Plants growing in shade conditions are :
(*a*) Sciophytes (*b*) Heliophobous
(*c*) Sciophilous (*d*) All of these

275. Shade plants show :
(*a*) long internodes and lower root/shoot ratio
(*b*) larger thinner leaves and amphistomatic condition
(*c*) less or no palisade and high rate of photosynthesis per unit area
(*d*) All of the above

276. Heliophytes (photophilous or heliophilous) are sun loving plants and have :
(*a*) well developed palisade
(*b*) smaller intercellular spaces
(*c*) stomata on lower surface
(*d*) All of the above

277. Plants of driest conditions are called :
(*a*) Pteridophytes (*b*) Xerophytes
(*c*) Chasmophytes (*d*) Epiphytes

278. Hydrophytes have well developed :
(*a*) root system (*b*) vascular system
(*c*) aerenchyma (*d*) exophytes

279. Amphibious plants (emergents) like *Typha polygonum* are found in
(*a*) shallow pond (*b*) stagnant water
(*c*) water (*d*) lakes

280. Root cap is absent in :
(*a*) Lithophytes (*b*) Xerophytes
(*c*) Hydrophytes (*d*) Mesophytes

281. Root is feebly developed and stem is soft and buoyant in :
(*a*) Hydrophytes (*b*) Halophytes
(*c*) Helophytes (*d*) Sciophytes

282. Hydrophytes have :
(*a*) poor root system
(*b*) reduced xylem vessels
(*c*) reduced stomata
(*d*) All of the above

283. Which is not a character of hydrophyte?
(*a*) Abundant aerencyhma
(*b*) Plentiful xylem and sclereids
(*c*) Leaves with stomata on upper side
(*d*) poor development of fruits

284. In hydrophytes, leaves are dissected :
(*a*) to increase surface
(*b*) decrease absorbing surface
(*c*) to decrease stomatal number
(*d*) all of the above

285. Submerged hydrophytes absorb water and exchange gases through :
(*a*) their general surface
(*b*) roots
(*c*) rhizoids
(*d*) hydathodes

286. Photosynthetic and respiratory gaseous exchange in hydrophytes occurs through :

(*a*) stomata (*b*) hydathodes
(*c*) lenticels (*d*) epidermis

287. Heterophylly is common in :
(*a*) free floating hydrophytes
(*b*) submerged hydrophytes
(*c*) rooted floating hydrophytes
(*d*) None of these

288. Cuticle and stomata are persent on the upper surface of the leaves of :
(*a*) *Salvinia* (*b*) *Wolffia*
(*c*) *Nymphaea* (*d*) *Lemna*

289. Additional aerenchyma stimulating the roots develop in :
(*a*) *Salvinia*
(*b*) *Ludwigia* (Jussiaea)
(*c*) *Eichhornia*
(*d*) *Trapa*

290. The example of an amphibious rooted hydrophyte is :
(*a*) *Vallisneria* (*b*) *Wolffia*
(*c*) *Typha* (*d*) *Zostera*

291. Submerged hydrophytes show :
(*a*) presence of cuticle and waxy epidermis on both surfaces
(*b*) presence of cuticle and stomata
(*c*) absence of stomata and waxy epidermis on submerged site
(*d*) absence of cuticle and stomata on any surface

292. *Vallisneria* does **NOT** have :
(*a*) cuticle and root
(*b*) cuticle and stomata
(*c*) root and stomata
(*d*) root and waxy epidermis

293. Absence of roots and cuticle can be observed in plants of :
(*a*) *Utricularia* and *Ceratophyllum*
(*b*) *Hydrilla* and *Nymphaea*
(*c*) *Nymphaea* and *Ceratophyllum*
(*d*) *Nymphaea* and *Wolffia*

294. The giant leaves of *Victoria amazonica* can hold the weight of a one year old baby due to the presence of :
(*a*) thick petiole with high buoyancy
(*b*) thin petiole with less buoyancy
(*c*) petiole with well developed mechanical tissue and less aerenchyma
(*d*) petiole without aerenchyma

295. Special mechanism for buoyancy can be seen in roots of :
(*a*) *Ludwigia* and *Neptunia*
(*b*) *Ludwigia* and *Hydrilla*
(*c*) *Neptunia* and *Ceratophyllum*
(*d*) *Neptunia* and *Wolffia*

296. Stomata are lacking in :
(*a*) *Victoria* (*b*) *Nymphaea*
(*c*) *Nelumbo* (*d*) *Ceratophylum*

297. The natural adaptations of muddy sea-shore plants are seen in :
(*a*) *Aloe* and *Ricinus*
(*b*) *Amaranthus* and *Rosa*
(*c*) *Argemone* and *Rice*
(*d*) *Avicennia* and *Rhizophora*

298. Higher root : shoot ratio is found in :
(*a*) Psammophytes (*b*) Halophytes
(*c*) Epiphytes (*d*) Hygrophytes

299. Extreme Xerophytic condition is shown best by :
(*a*) *Nerium* (*b*) *Capparis*
(*c*) *Cactus* (*d*) *Brassica*

300. Mucilaginous tissue and chlorenchymatous cortex are found in :
(*a*) Halophytic xerophytes
(*b*) Mesophytes
(*c*) Epiphytes
(*d*) Insectivorous plants

301. Desert plants are mostly :
(*a*) viviparous
(*b*) succulents
(*c*) heterophyllous
(*d*) herbaceous shrubs

302. Stomata are sunken and found in pits and protected by hairs in :
(*a*) xerophytes (*b*) hydrophytes
(*c*) hygrophytes (*d*) mesophytes

303. Plants with renewal bud near ground is called:
(*a*) cryptophyte (*b*) chamaephyte
(*c*) phanerophyte (*d*) hemicryptophyte

304. Plants which depend completely on ground water are :
(*a*) Psilophytes (*b*) Eremophytes
(*c*) Chersophytes (*d*) Phreatophytes

305. Plants growing below soil with underground buds :
(*a*) Cryophytes (*b*) Cryptophytes
(*c*) Endophytes (*d*) Ephemerals

306. Plants with buds exposed on shoots :
(*a*) crytophytes (*b*) phanerophytes
(*c*) geophytes (*d*) exophytes

307. Plants that colonise rock crevices/fissures are called :
(*a*) Lithophytes (*b*) Chasmophytes
(*c*) Psammophytes (*d*) Cryophytes

308. Plants which behave as mesophytes in rainy season and xerophytes in summers are called :
(*a*) Cryophytes (*b*) Trophophytes
(*c*) Tracheophytes (*d*) Halophytes

309. Stomata open at night are called :
(*a*) Photoactive (*b*) Scotoactive
(*c*) Statolith (*d*) Amphimictic

310. The cells for rolling down of lamina in grasses to reduce transpiration are :
(*a*) guard cells (*b*) subsidiary cells
(*c*) bulliform cells (*d*) sunken stomata

311. Plants completing its life cycle within 4-6 weeks before the onset of dry condition is said to be :
(*a*) Drought evading
(*b*) Drought escaping
(*c*) Drought resisting
(*d*) Drought enduring

312. Natural adaptations (adjustments) in deserts can be seen in :
(*a*) Orchids (*b*) *Capparis*
(*c*) Mangrooves (*d*) Pines

313. Ephemerals are a type of xerophytes :
(*a*) Drought escaping
(*b*) Drought resisting
(*c*) Drought enduring
(*d*) None of these

314. Water storage tissue has :
(*a*) large sized thin walled cells
(*b*) mucilage
(*c*) large sized vacuoles
(*d*) All of the above

315. There are perennial plants which can live under extremely unfavourable dry periods. Those plants are called :
(*a*) drought resistants
(*b*) drought evaders
(*c*) ephemerals
(*d*) drought endurers

316. Thickest cuticle on the fleshy leaves is found in :
(*a*) *Aloe* (*b*) *Euphorbia*
(*c*) *Opuntia* (*d*) *Calotropis*

317. Sunken stomata and schlerenchyma is found in leaf of :
(*a*) *Nerium* (*b*) *Eichhornia*
(*c*) *Bamboo* (*d*) Any of these

318. The factor governing structure of earth surface is :
(*a*) edaphic (*b*) temperature
(*c*) topographic (*d*) biotic

319. Which is the main causative factor of desertification?
(*a*) Overgrazing
(*b*) Irrigated agriculture
(*c*) Development activities
(*d*) Tourism

320. In India coniferous forests are found in :
(*a*) Himalayan region
(*b*) Rajasthan
(*c*) Satpura Hills
(*d*) Madhya Pradesh

321. Where do the tropical rain forests occur?
(*a*) Bihar
(*b*) Jammu and Kashmir
(*c*) Andamans
(*d*) Himachal Pradesh

322. Xerophytes have long roots :
(*a*) due to light
(*b*) to draw water from deep water beds
(*c*) to give mechanical support
(*d*) None of the above

323. Ephemerals are :
(*a*) drought evading plants
(*b*) drought enduring plants
(*c*) drought resisting plants
(*d*) drought escaping plants

324. Leaves of Sciophytes (Shade loving plants) :
(*a*) thin and broad
(*b*) thin and narrow
(*c*) thick and broad
(*d*) thick and narrow

325. Tall stems with long internodes are found in plants like :
(*a*) Xerophytes (*b*) Psammophytes
(*c*) Sciophytes (*d*) Heliophytes

326. Which of the following is not essential for seed germination?
(*a*) Water (*b*) Nutrients
(*c*) Light (*d*) Temperature

327. The relative volumes of palisade and spongy tissue in a leaf are determined by exposure of plant during development to :
(*a*) Temperature (*b*) Light
(*c*) Nutrients (*d*) Humidity

328. The arrangement of chloroplast is changed with change in light intensity. In moderate light, it is :
(*a*) Epistrophe (*b*) Parastrophe
(*c*) Apostrophe (*d*) Atrophe

329. The classification of plants into xerophytes, mesophytes and hydrophytes was given by :
(*a*) Warming
(*b*) Weaver and Clements
(*c*) Kormondy
(*d*) Odum

330. Epiphytes are common in areas where :
(*a*) rainfall is seasonal
(*b*) rainfall is scantly
(*c*) rainfall throughout the year
(*d*) temperature very low

331. Plants of saline soils are called :
(*a*) Halophytes (*b*) Helophytes
(*c*) Oxalophytes (*d*) Heliophytes

332. Plants near sea shores have thick leaves and other xerophytic characters, because :
(*a*) there is plenty of water
(*b*) there is too high concentration of salts to absorb sufficient water from soil
(*c*) soil is muddy and poor in air
(*d*) light is scantly

333. Which group of plants has to face physiological dryness?
(*a*) Halophytes
(*b*) Helophytes
(*c*) Lithophytes
(*d*) Epiphytes

334. Mangroove vegetation is found in :
(*a*) Western ghats
(*b*) Kullu valley
(*c*) Dehradun valley
(*d*) Sunderbans

335. Halophytes are peculiar in having :
(*a*) Pneumatophoric stems
(*b*) Velamon tissue
(*c*) Vivipary
(*d*) Saline soils

336. In sea "water water every where but not a drop to utilize" even then plants grow on its shore; such a group of plants are called as :
(*a*) mesophytes
(*b*) halophytes
(*c*) xerophytes
(*d*) hydrophytes

337. Mangrooves are rightly described as :
(*a*) Hydrophytes
(*b*) Xerophytes
(*c*) Pelophilous halophytes
(*d*) Lithophytes

338. Rhizophora/mangrooves of marshy/swampy Sunderbans is characterised by :
(*a*) Vivipary (*b*) Proproots
(*c*) Pneumatophores (*d*) All of the above

339. Halophytes grow on physiologically dry soil due to presence of :
(*a*) excessive salt in water
(*b*) excessive salt in plants
(*c*) excessive humidity outside
(*d*) dry soil

340. Pneumatophores are found in plants of :
(*a*) desert
(*b*) near river banks
(*c*) grasslands
(*d*) mountains

341. Plants are growing in :
A. Bombay sea shore
B. Sunderbans
C. Barmer Desert
D. National park

Which pairs from above show physiological drought condition?
(*a*) A and B (*b*) B and C
(*c*) C and D (*d*) D and A

342. In saline muddy swamps, plants mangrooves produces roots called :
(*a*) pneumatophores
(*b*) stilt roots
(*c*) sucking roots
(*d*) clinging roots

343. In mangroove vegetation, *branches* of the plants produce :
(*a*) Epiphytic roots
(*b*) Prop roots
(*c*) Still roots
(*d*) Pneumatophores

344. Which is not characteristic of intestinal symbionts?
(*a*) Feeding on extra food of host
(*b*) Providing vitamins to host
(*c*) Anaerobic respiration
(*d*) Aerobic respiration

345. Ecological succession on sand is :
(*a*) Psammomere
(*b*) Xerosere
(*c*) Halosere
(*d*) Hydrosere

346. Cause of mimicry is :
(*a*) concealment
(*b*) offence
(*c*) defence
(*d*) Both (*b*) and (*c*)

347. Which of the following insects mimics thin dry branches of the plant on which it lives?
(*a*) *Kalima parolecta*
(*b*) *Mantis religiosa*
(*c*) *Rhyllium frondosum*
(*d*) *Caraustus morosus*

348. The individual that shows mimicry is called :
(*a*) mimic (*b*) predator
(*c*) prey (*d*) parasite

349. Heterodon flattens its head, produces frequent hissing and strikes to advertise as if it is dangerous. This is an example of :
(*a*) alluring mimicry
(*b*) warning mimicry
(*c*) concealing mimicry
(*d*) batesian mimicry

350. In conscious mimicry :
(*a*) the organism behave as if they are dead bodies
(*b*) the organism become more conscious
(*c*) the organism catches its prey with a great ease
(*d*) None of the above

351. Which of the following resembles a dry leaf?
(*a*) *Phyllum*
(*b*) *Kallima paralecta*
(*c*) *Cryptolithodes*
(*d*) *Papilio machaon*

352. Which among the following is the primary function of mimicry prevalent is some animals?
(*a*) Warning (*b*) Concealment
(*c*) Allurement (*d*) Aggression

353. Succession in an ecosystem is the result of :
(*a*) occurrence of diseases
(*b*) changes in grazing habits of animals
(*c*) competition among animals
(*d*) adaptive ability to environmental changes

ANSWERS

1	2	3	4	5	6	7	8	9	10
(a)	(d)	(b)	(a)	(c)	(a)	(d)	(c)	(b)	(c)
11	12	13	14	15	16	17	18	19	20
(b)	(b)	(d)	(c)	(a)	(c)	(d)	(a)	(b)	(d)
21	22	23	24	25	26	27	28	29	30
(a)	(b)	(d)	(c)	(d)	(b)	(a)	(d)	(d)	(d)
31	32	33	34	35	36	37	38	39	40
(c)	(a)	(b)	(a)	(b)	(c)	(a)	(d)	(b)	(d)
41	42	43	44	45	46	47	48	49	50
(b)	(d)	(c)	(d)	(d)	(c)	(b)	(b)	(d)	(c)
51	52	53	54	55	56	57	58	59	60
(d)	(b)	(b)	(b)	(c)	(b)	(c)	(a)	(c)	(d)
61	62	63	64	65	66	67	68	69	70
(a)	(d)	(b)	(a)	(d)	(a)	(a)	(a)	(c)	(a)
71	72	73	74	75	76	77	78	79	80
(b)	(b)	(a)	(a)	(d)	(a)	(b)	(b)	(c)	(a)
81	82	83	84	85	86	87	88	89	90
(d)	(d)	(a)	(d)	(b)	(b)	(a)	(b)	(c)	(a)
91	92	93	94	95	96	97	98	99	100
(c)	(d)	(c)	(a)	(a)	(a)	(b)	(d)	(a)	(b)
101	102	103	104	105	106	107	108	109	110
(b)	(a)	(a)	(a)	(a)	(b)	(a)	(c)	(d)	(b)
111	112	113	114	115	116	117	118	119	120
(a)	(b)	(a)	(b)	(b)	(c)	(c)	(d)	(a)	(b)
121	122	123	124	125	126	127	128	129	130
(d)	(a)	(b)	(d)	(b)	(b)	(c)	(c)	(a)	(c)
131	132	133	134	135	136	137	138	139	140
(d)	(c)	(b)	(a)	(c)	(a)	(b)	(d)	(b)	(c)
141	142	143	144	145	146	147	148	149	150
(d)	(a)	(d)	(b)	(c)	(a)	(d)	(c)	(b)	(d)
151	152	153	154	155	156	157	158	159	160
(b)	(a)	(d)	(b)	(a)	(b)	(c)	(a)	(d)	(c)
161	162	163	164	165	166	167	168	169	170
(d)	(b)	(a)	(d)	(a)	(c)	(b)	(a)	(a)	(c)
171	172	173	174	175	176	177	178	179	180
(c)	(b)	(d)	(a)	(d)	(b)	(b)	(a)	(d)	(b)
181	182	183	184	185	186	187	188	189	190
(a)	(b)	(c)	(b)	(b)	(d)	(b)	(a)	(a)	(d)

191	192	193	194	195	196	197	198	199	200
(*c*)	(*b*)	(*a*)	(*d*)	(*c*)	(*c*)	(*d*)	(*a*)	(*a*)	(*d*)
201	**202**	**203**	**204**	**205**	**206**	**207**	**208**	**209**	**210**
(*b*)	(*b*)	(*b*)	(*b*)	(*d*)	(*c*)	(*c*)	(*b*)	(*b*)	(*a*)
211	**212**	**213**	**214**	**215**	**216**	**217**	**218**	**219**	**220**
(*a*)	(*d*)	(*a*)	(*d*)	(*a*)	(*a*)	(*a*)	(*a*)	(*d*)	(*a*)
221	**222**	**223**	**224**	**225**	**226**	**227**	**228**	**229**	**230**
(*d*)	(*a*)	(*b*)	(*a*)	(*c*)	(*d*)	(*d*)	(*a*)	(*c*)	(*b*)
231	**232**	**233**	**234**	**235**	**236**	**237**	**238**	**239**	**240**
(*a*)	(*a*)	(*b*)	(*b*)	(*b*)	(*b*)	(*a*)	(*c*)	(*c*)	(*c*)
241	**242**	**243**	**244**	**245**	**246**	**247**	**248**	**249**	**250**
(*a*)	(*b*)	(*a*)	(*a*)	(*a*)	(*a*)	(*b*)	(*a*)	(*a*)	(*b*)
251	**252**	**253**	**254**	**255**	**256**	**257**	**258**	**259**	**260**
(*d*)	(*b*)	(*b*)	(*d*)	(*c*)	(*a*)	(*d*)	(*d*)	(*b*)	(*c*)
261	**262**	**263**	**264**	**265**	**266**	**267**	**268**	**269**	**270**
(*a*)	(*d*)	(*b*)	(*c*)	(*a*)	(*b*)	(*a*)	(*b*)	(*a*)	(*a*)
271	**272**	**273**	**274**	**275**	**276**	**277**	**278**	**279**	**280**
(*b*)	(*c*)	(*a*)	(*d*)	(*d*)	(*d*)	(*b*)	(*c*)	(*a*)	(*c*)
281	**282**	**283**	**284**	**285**	**286**	**287**	**288**	**289**	**290**
(*a*)	(*d*)	(*b*)	(*a*)	(*a*)	(*c*)	(*c*)	(*c*)	(*b*)	(*c*)
291	**292**	**293**	**294**	**295**	**296**	**297**	**298**	**299**	**300**
(*d*)	(*b*)	(*a*)	(*a*)	(*a*)	(*d*)	(*d*)	(*a*)	(*c*)	(*a*)
301	**302**	**303**	**304**	**305**	**306**	**307**	**308**	**309**	**310**
(*b*)	(*a*)	(*b*)	(*d*)	(*b*)	(*b*)	(*b*)	(*b*)	(*b*)	(*c*)
311	**312**	**313**	**314**	**315**	**316**	**317**	**318**	**319**	**320**
(*b*)	(*b*)	(*a*)	(*d*)	(*a*)	(*a*)	(*a*)	(*c*)	(*a*)	(*a*)
321	**322**	**323**	**324**	**325**	**326**	**327**	**328**	**329**	**330**
(*c*)	(*b*)	(*d*)	(*a*)	(*c*)	(*c*)	(*b*)	(*a*)	(*a*)	(*c*)
331	**332**	**333**	**334**	**335**	**336**	**337**	**338**	**339**	**340**
(*a*)	(*b*)	(*a*)	(*d*)	(*c*)	(*b*)	(*c*)	(*d*)	(*a*)	(*b*)
341	**342**	**343**	**344**	**345**	**346**	**347**	**348**	**349**	**350**
(*a*)	(*a*)	(*b*)	(*d*)	(*a*)	(*b*)	(*b*)	(*a*)	(*b*)	(*a*)
351	**352**	**353**							
(*b*)	(*b*)	(*d*)							

7

ECOLOGICAL SUCCESSION

1. The inhibition of growth of *Parthenium* in the presence of *Vince rosea* is an example of :
   (*a*) Biological antagonism
   (*b*) Allelopathy
   (*c*) Competition
   (*d*) Mutualism
2. The interaction that does not promote coevolution?
   (*a*) Commensalism
   (*b*) Mutualism
   (*c*) Parasitism
   (*d*) Interspecific competition
3. Which of the following is wrong?
   (*a*) Lichens show mutualism
   (*b*) Epiphytes show commensalism
   (*c*) Sea Anemone and Hermitcrab show protocooperation
   (*d*) Mutualism, protocooperation and commensalism can not be included under symbiosis
4. Hyperparasite is parasite which :
   (*a*) kills its host
   (*b*) completes life cycle in one host
   (*c*) uses host machinery for reproduction
   (*d*) None of the above
5. Plants getting nourishments by haustoria are :
   (*a*) Epiphytes
   (*b*) Parasites
   (*c*) Xerophytes
   (*d*) Halophytes
6. Gause's hypothesis is related to :
   (*a*) Principle of competitive exclusion
   (*b*) Niche specialisation *i.e.*, one specialisation one niche
   (*c*) Inter specific competition between two *Paramecium* grown together in which one is eliminated
   (*d*) All of the above
7. Predation hepls in biological control of :
   (*a*) *Opuntia* weed by *Cactoblastis* insect in Australia
   (*b*) Red to cust menace by Mynah in Mauritius
   (*c*) Aphids by beetles
   (*d*) All of the above
8. Predation is :
   (*a*) source of flow of energy in ecosystem
   (*b*) basic to structure and function of ecosystem
   (*c*) essential for keeping number iof individuals of a species constant at a time in the ecosystem
   (*d*) All of the above
9. What is correct about cannibalism?
   (*a*) it is killing and consuming one's own kind
   (*b*) predator and prey belong to same species
   (*c*) it is intra specific predation
   (*d*) All of the above
10. Which one is prey as well as predator?
   (*a*) Sparrow (*b*) Frog
   (*c*) Lion (*d*) Elephant
11. Cuscuta is an example of :
   (*a*) Holostem parasite
   (*b*) Holoroot parasite
   (*c*) Partial root parasite
   (*d*) Partial item parasite

12. An organism carrying a disease from one organism to another is called :
(*a*) host (*b*) inoculum
(*c*) vector (*d*) parasite

13. The nature of interrelationship between corals and zooxanthellae is called :
(*a*) physiological symbiosis
(*b*) amensalism
(*c*) protocooperation
(*d*) commensalism

14. Population of ferocious red ant is kept under ckeck by :
(*a*) rufus wood pecker
(*b*) red billed oxpecker
(*c*) yellow billed oxpecker
(*d*) sparrow

15. Interaction between two species (+) and (O) is called :
(*a*) Amensalism
(*b*) Mutualism
(*c*) Commensalism
(*d*) Protocooperation

16. Industrial melanism is an example of :
(*a*) protective resemblance with the surroundings
(*b*) defensive adaptation of skin against ultraviolet radiations
(*c*) drug resistance
(*d*) darkening of skin due to smoke from industries

17. When the vegetation of any region reaches climatic climax, it is the climax community of a region is usually :
(*a*) hydrophytic (*b*) xerophytic
(*c*) lithophytic (*d*) mesophytic

18. The successful establishment of plants in a new locality is called :
(*a*) Migration (*b*) Colonisation
(*c*) Ecesis (*d*) Introduction

19. In a biotic community, the most important factor for the survival of an animal is
(*a*) green food (*b*) day length
(*c*) predators (*d*) soil moisture

20. The boundary/transition between two more cmmunities sharply defined, is called :
(*a*) Epilimnion (*b*) Biome
(*c*) Anticline (*d*) Ecotone

21. Species diversity increases as one proceeds from :
(*a*) low altitude to high altitude and from low latitude to high latitudes
(*b*) low altitude to high altitude and from high latitudes to low latitudes
(*c*) high altitude to low altitude and from low latitudes to high latitudes
(*d*) high altitudes to low altitude and from high latitude to low latitudes

22. The most threatened biotic community in the biosphere is :
(*a*) rainforest community
(*b*) desert community
(*c*) fresh water community
(*d*) Both (*a*) and (*c*)

23. Competition for food, space and light is most severe in :
(*a*) closely related species growing in same area
(*b*) closely related species growing in different habitat
(*c*) distantly related species growing in same habitat
(*d*) closely related plants and animals occupying different niche

24. Population of different species is kept under check by :
(*a*) birth rate
(*b*) food chain
(*c*) food web
(*d*) natural calamities

25. The population of each species is checked by :
(*a*) food chain (*b*) competition
(*c*) pyramids (*d*) niche

26. The dominating species living on this earth is :
(*a*) Man (*b*) Elephant
(*c*) Bacteria (*d*) Lion

27. The clear picture of sociological status of a species in the community is studied with the help of :
(*a*) phytograph (*b*) density
(*c*) quadrat (*d*) frequency

28. The two species having similar characters but different geographical area of distribution are called :
(*a*) sympatric (*b*) allopatric
(*c*) ecotone (*d*) commensal

29. Two species growing in the same area but with different characters are called :
(*a*) sympatric
(*b*) allopatric
(*c*) ecad
(*d*) None of these

30. Sympatric population can not be isolated by :
(*a*) behavioural barriers
(*b*) geographical barriers
(*c*) habit barrier
(*d*) seasonal barriers

31. The formation of new species from a single ancestral species by adapting to different habitats and modes of life is known as :
(*a*) adaptive convergence
(*b*) adaptive divergence
(*c*) adaptive radiation
(*d*) adaptive proper

32. In a condition when potential competitors accidently come together to share the same living place, extreme types from each population, those who might compete least are favoured, is a phenomenon called :
(*a*) competitive exclusion
(*b*) character displacement
(*c*) commensalism
(*d*) None of the above

33. Plant formation, including the animals, within the formation are called :
(*a*) biome (*b*) biochore
(*c*) biogeocenose (*d*) None of these

34. A smoother crop is the one which :
(*a*) does not require much irrigation
(*b*) easy to reap
(*c*) does not allow the weeds to grow
(*d*) immune to most diseases

35. Rhizosphere is denoted by soil which is :
(*a*) subjected to the influence of plant rhizoids
(*b*) attached to the surface of root hair only
(*c*) subjected to the influence of plant root
(*d*) attached to the surface of root only

36. The relationship between a cow and a snake is called :
(*a*) symbiosis
(*b*) protocooperation
(*c*) competition
(*d*) neutralism

37. Neutralism is a type of inter specific relationship where :
(*a*) One or both species are benefitted and neither species is harmed
(*b*) Atleast one of the species is harmed
(*c*) None of the two species is affected
(*d*) None of the above

38. Match the following :
A. Ecotone 1. a transitional zone between 2 communities
B. Ecesis 2. successful adjustment of a species in new area
C. Sere 3. a temporary community during succession
D. Niche 4. a habitat of a species

Codes :

	A	B	C	D
(*a*)	1	2	3	4
(*b*)	2	1	3	4
(*c*)	4	2	1	3
(*d*)	4	2	3	1

39. Primary succession refers to the development of communities on a :
(*a*) newly exposed habitat with no record of earlier vegetation
(*b*) pond freshly filled with water after a dry phase
(*c*) forest clearing after devastating fire
(*d*) freshly cleared crop field

40. Ecotone is :
(*a*) zone of transition between two adjacent communities
(*b*) zone with greater number of species
(*c*) related to Edge effect
(*d*) All of the above

41. Biota refers to :
(*a*) animals of a particular area
(*b*) plants of a particular area
(*c*) animals and plants of a particular area
(*d*) None of the above

42. Succession showing changes in communities at a place is called :
(*a*) biotic succession
(*b*) climatic succession
(*c*) geographical succession
(*d*) man made succession

43. Secondary succession is not completed if the barren area is invaded by :
(*a*) *Sphagnum* (*b*) *Lantana*
(*c*) *Eichhornia* (*d*) All of these

44. In a sal forest community, there are :
(*a*) only sal trees
(*b*) few sal trees
(*c*) more sal trees than any other species
(*d*) sal trees with other trees in nearly equal ratio

45. The termite and the flagellated protozoans relationship is an example of :
(*a*) predation
(*b*) facultative mutualism
(*c*) obligatory mutualism
(*d*) commensalism

46. The statement that best describes the climax stage in an ecological succession :
(*a*) it keeps changing
(*b*) it represents initial phases of plant succession
(*c*) it remains unchanged
(*d*) it is populated by plants only

47. Blue green algal lichens and mosses are invaders and observed in :
(*a*) Xerosere (*b*) Psamosere
(*c*) Hydrosere (*d*) Halosere

48. Biological weathering of rocks was initially brought about by Lichens that are :
(*a*) crustose (*b*) foliose
(*c*) fruticose (*d*) None of these

49. Domestic plants or animals living as escapes and subject to natural selection are called :
(*a*) feral
(*b*) living fossils
(*c*) fugitive species
(*d*) extinct species

50. Forb means
(*a*) small shrubs
(*b*) lianas
(*c*) small trees
(*d*) harbs other than grass

51. Population I and II are growing in the same habitat and are morphologically similar but these are intersterile. In terms of biological concept of species they may be considered as :
(*a*) one species
(*b*) two distinct species
(*c*) two sibling species
(*d*) None of the above

52. Sometimes in a locality, by chance a bird eats more dark moths than white moths and by chance, more eggs of dark moths are destroyed. This leads to increase in population of light moths. This is known as
(*a*) variation
(*b*) industrial melanism
(*c*) genetic drift
(*d*) ecological bomerang

53. The random change in distribution of genes in a population as the number of individuals in the population decreases is called :
(*a*) genetic variation
(*b*) genetic drift
(*c*) mutation
(*d*) gene jumping

54. The subspecies of the same species are :
(*a*) reproductively isolated
(*b*) partially isolated reproductively
(*c*) can exchange genes
(*d*) offspring partially fertile

55. In a small population the frequency of gene 'A' is 70% and its allele 'a' is 30%. After some time there is an abrupt change in gene frequency which becomes 40% for 'A' and 60% for 'a'. These results could be best explained by :
(*a*) mutation
(*b*) more mortality of organisms with 'A' genes
(*c*) selective migration of individuals with gene 'A'
(*d*) genetic drift

56. Genetic drift is an account of/caused by :
(*a*) mutation
(*b*) gene pool
(*c*) increase in population
(*d*) decrease in population

57. Genetic drift :
(*a*) is random change in gene frequencies
(*b*) has nothing in common with inbreeding
(*c*) is an orderly process of change in genes
(*d*) produces fluctuations in large populations

58. Different life forms among plants in relation to environment were given by :
(*a*) Reiter (*b*) Odum
(*c*) Raunkiers (*d*) Warming

59. Chamaephytes are small plants of less than 25-30 cm ht with renewal buds which are located from the soil surface to .... above it.
(*a*) more than 25 cm
(*b*) not more than 25 cm
(*c*) more than 100 cm
(*d*) buds are burried in the soil

60. Therophytes during adverse condition survive by :
(*a*) Perennating Buds
(*b*) Bulbs
(*c*) Rhizomes
(*d*) Seeds

61. Tropophytes are :
(*a*) plants whose conditions of life are according to the season of the year
(*b*) plants which are xerophytes in summer and become mesophyte during winter
(*c*) plants which shed their leaves and have underground stems
(*d*) All of the above

62. Tank epiphytes are those :
(*a*) that send their roots into soil
(*b*) that collect human within roots
(*c*) whose leaves act as roots to absorb water and salts
(*d*) None of these

63. Which of the following interactions will not promote coevolution :
(*a*) Competition
(*b*) Commensalism
(*c*) Mutualism
(*d*) Parasitism

64. Crocodile bird takes leeches from buccal cavity of crocodiles, it is an example of :
(*a*) commensalism
(*b*) scavenging
(*c*) cannibalism
(*d*) protocooperation

65. The mode of nutrition to get food with the help of fungi from humus is called :
(*a*) autotrophy
(*b*) heterotrophy
(*c*) mycotrophy
(*d*) mycorrhizy

66. Some saprophytic orchids take food directly from humus without the help of fungi. It is :
(*a*) *Wullschleigelia* (*b*) *Neottia*
(*c*) *Corallorhiza* (*d*) All of these

67. Model is an object with which a mimic resemble. It is :
(*a*) always a living organism
(*b*) always a non-living organism
(*c*) can be animate of inanimate object
(*d*) None of the above

68. *Opalina* lives in rectum of frog, it is an example of :
(*a*) symbiosis (*b*) commensalism
(*c*) parasitism (*d*) None of the above

69. Epiphytes are called space parasites and examplify :
(*a*) ectoparasite
(*b*) symbiosis
(*c*) ectocommensalism
(*d*) amensalism

70. The organism which suffers due to parasitism is called :
(*a*) predator (*b*) commensal
(*c*) model (*d*) None of these

71. The pedator cannot survive without its :
(*a*) host (*b*) parasite
(*c*) commensal (*d*) prey

72. Antagonistic interaction includes :
(*a*) scavenging (*b*) competition
(*c*) amensalism (*d*) Both (*b*) and (*c*)

73. The animals (like Rabbit) active only in twilight (dusk and dawn) are called :
(*a*) nocturnal animals
(*b*) diurnal animals
(*c*) crepuscular animals
(*d*) cursorial animals

74. Polyembryony is a :
(*a*) parasitic adaptation
(*b*) physiological adaptation
(*c*) ecological adaptation
(*d*) None of the above

75. Competition between two species with overlapping ecological niches is apt to lead to :
(*a*) stabilising selection
(*b*) disruptive selection
(*c*) hybridisation
(*d*) character displacement

76. Cooperative interaction is essential for perpetuation of :
(*a*) animals
(*b*) plants
(*c*) progeny of plants and animals
(*d*) neither plants nor animals

77. Female mosquitoes sucking human blood at intervals are :
(*a*) permanent parasite
(*b*) endoparasite
(*c*) hemiparasite
(*d*) intermittent parasite

78. Which one of the following is not a correct pair?
(*a*) Ecotone : Edge effect
(*b*) Foodwed : Stability of ecosystem
(*c*) *Acacia* : Myrenucophily
(*d*) *Parthenium* : Parasitism

79. Which of the following is a non-obligatory beneficial relationship :
(*a*) Commensalism (*b*) Mutualism
(*c*) Protocooperation (*d*) Parasitism

80. Gambusia fish is an example of :
(*a*) Biocontrol (*b*) Parasitism
(*c*) Hyperparasitism (*d*) None of these

81. In commensalism :
(*a*) both partners are benefitted
(*b*) both partners are harmed
(*c*) weaker and smaller one is benefitted while stronger and large one is unharmed
(*d*) None of the above

82. Mycorrhiza (a symbiotic association between higher plant roots and certain fungi)
(*a*) respiration
(*b*) water absorption
(*c*) nutrient absorption
(*d*) phosphate absorption

83. Phanerophytes are tree and shrubs in which perennating buds are present on the erect shoot :
(*a*) at more than 30 m above ground level
(*b*) at more than 25 m above ground level
(*c*) at more than 8 m above ground level
(*d*) plants grow on pebbles

84. Which of the following grasses is an indicator of water table at or near the surface soil?
(*a*) Wire grass (*b*) Blue grass
(*c*) Foverty grass (*d*) Salt grass

85. Cryoflora are :
(*a*) algae growing on sand
(*b*) algae growing on snow
(*c*) algae growing in hot water spring
(*d*) algae growing in sea water

86. What is a phytotron?
(*a*) Environment controlled house
(*b*) An instrument for measuring growth of plant
(*c*) An instrument for determining the calorific values of biological material
(*d*) An instrument for determining the rate of photosynthesis

87. A new species is formed when :
(*a*) an individual is a product of the phenotype and the environment
(*b*) individual variation reflect reproductive isolation among them
(*c*) phenotypes and genotypes are not related
(*d*) different species may have the same genotypes

88. Endemic plants are those which grow in :
(*a*) fresh water lakes
(*b*) shady places
(*c*) tissues of other plants
(*d*) geographically limited areas/bottom of sea

89. Insectivorous plants are usually adapted to :
(*a*) water rich soils
(*b*) soils deficient in sugars
(*c*) soil rich in trace elements
(*d*) soil deficient in nitrogenous compounds

90. Species having great power of dispersal and which always face competition are called :
(*a*) palaeoendemic (*b*) neoendemic
(*c*) fugitive species (*d*) None of these

91. Xerosere is :
(*a*) xerophyte
(*b*) halophyte
(*c*) ecological succession on rock
(*d*) None of the above

92. The scientific study on mimicry was first carried out by :
(*a*) Bates (*b*) Darwin
(*c*) Clark (*d*) Dobzanislay

93. Mimicry is an adaptation for :
(*a*) concealing from predator
(*b*) concealing from prey
(*c*) both (*a*) and (*b*)
(*d*) symbiosis to trap prey

94. Which one is not an example of concealing protective mimicry?
(*a*) Sea Dragon (Phyllopteryx) resembles sea weeds
(*b*) Geometrid moth's caterpillar resembles to small branches
(*c*) Preying mantis is green like green branches
(*d*) Leaf insect (*Phyllium*) looking like a green leaf

95. A protective device in animals :
(*a*) competition (*b*) mimicry
(*c*) commensalism (*d*) symbiosis

96. Palatable Viceroy Butterfly (*Limenitis archippus*) resembles a distasteful monarch butterfly (*Donasus plexippus*) for its protection. This is called :
(*a*) aggressive mimicry
(*b*) warming mimicry
(*c*) concealing mimicry
(*d*) alluring mimicry

97. When predator (mimic) remain hidden from prey to catch it suddenly as in preying mantis, it shows :
(*a*) concealing aggressive mimicry
(*b*) concealing protective mimicry
(*c*) warming mimicry
(*d*) alluring mimicry

98. Stick insect (*Carausium*) mimics like a thin dry branch and dead leaf or oak leaf butterfly (*Kallima*) looks like a dead leaf. It is :
(*a*) concealing protective mimicry
(*b*) warming mimicry
(*c*) concerning agressive mimicry
(*d*) None of these

99. Myrmecophyte is :
(*a*) a plant that has adaptation for housing ants for its benefit
(*b*) *Acacia sphaerocephala* showing myrmecophily (pollination by ants)
(*c*) both (*a*) and (*b*)
(*d*) None of these

100. Myremecophily is an association of :
(*a*) plants and moths (*b*) plants and bees
(*c*) plants and ants (*d*) plants and insects

101. Acacia tree provides nectar and nesting places for ants. These ants attack herbivores that attempt to feed on the trees. The relation between tree and ant is an example of :
(*a*) competition (*b*) mutualism
(*c*) social (*d*) protocooperation

102. Which of the following is an example of predation?
(*a*) Herbivory
(*b*) Carnivory
(*c*) Cannibalism insect parasitism
(*d*) All of these

103. In predation, predator captures the prey and kills it. Which one of the following show predation?
(*a*) *Dactylella* (loop fungus)
(*b*) *Drosera Nepenthes*
(*c*) Insectivorous (carnivorous) plants
(*d*) All of these

104. Insectivorous plants are carnivores as well as :
(*a*) primary producers
(*b*) secondary consumers
(*c*) auto and heterotrophs both
(*d*) All of these

105. The association between two species, each of which is benefitted by the presence of other but can live equally well without each other is called :
(*a*) Commensalism (*b*) Mutualism
(*c*) Protocooperation (*d*) Predation

106. Epiphytes and lianas show :
(*a*) commensalism (*b*) parasitism
(*c*) mutualism (*d*) protocooperation

107. Commensalism is found in :
(*a*) Barnacles and Whale
(*b*) Jackals and Lion
(*c*) *E. coli* and man
(*d*) All of the above

108. Protocooperation is seen in :
(*a*) Birds and and Cattles or Crocodiles
(*b*) Ox pecker or Tick birds and Rhinoceros
(*c*) Shrimps and fish of coral reefs
(*d*) All of the above

109. Mutualism (*reciprocal symbiosis*) is mutually benefitted relationship between two organisms (like nitrogen fixing *Anabaena* and water fern *Azolla*) which can not live independently. It is also seen in :
(*a*) Rhizobium and legume roots
(*b*) Sea anemone and hermit crab
(*c*) Zoolflagellates and termites/ruminants
(*d*) All of the above

110. *Escherichia coli* found in human intestine lives there as :
(*a*) parasite (*b*) saprobe
(*c*) commensal (*d*) predator

111. Hermitcrab and sea anemone (*Adamsia*) relationship is :
(*a*) Commensalism (*b*) Symbiosis
(*c*) Mutualism (*d*) None of these

112. Shrimps (Crustaceans) and fish in coral reef are example of :
(*a*) commensalism (*b*) protocooperation
(*c*) mutualism (*d*) predation

113. Which is holo-root parasite :
(*a*) *Orobanche*
(*b*) *Striga*
(*c*) *Rafflessia* and *Balanophora*
(*d*) All of the above

114. Perfect example of interdependence animal and plants upon each other is :
(*a*) *Yucca* plant and *Yucca Pronuba* moth
(*b*) flowers and man
(*c*) ants and fruits
(*d*) None of the above

115. A green Alga that lives mutually inside *Hydra* :
(*a*) *Zooxantheae* (*b*) *Zoochlorellae*
(*c*) *Zoopsis* (*d*) All of these

116. A butterfly of India when resting with folded wings resembles a dead leaf. This mechanism of protection is called :

(*a*) Mimicry (*b*) Hiding
(*c*) Congregation (*d*) Camouflage

117. When a palatable female butterfly (*e.g.*, Viceroy butterfly) copies an unpalatable species (Monarch butterfly) the type of adaptation is called :
(*a*) Batesian Mimicry
(*b*) Mullerian Mimicry
(*c*) Cryptic adaptation
(*d*) Warning colouration

118. When the mimic attracts its prey, it is called :
(*a*) warning mimicry
(*b*) alluring mimicry
(*c*) protective colouration
(*d*) camouflage

119. An accurate and deceivingly detailed resemblance to a member which is distasteful/ poisonous to a predator is a case of :
(*a*) Batesian mimicry
(*b*) Apatetic mimicry
(*c*) Mullerian mimicry
(*d*) Epigamic mimicry

120. The appearance of a stick insect is an example of :
(*a*) Apatetic mimicry
(*b*) Mullerian mimicry
(*c*) Batesian mimicry
(*d*) Epigamic mimicry

121. The presence of yellow and black bands on the body of an insect is :
(*a*) Mullerian mimicry
(*b*) Batesian mimicry
(*c*) Epigamic mimicry
(*d*) Apatetic mimicry

122. The colour changes which a chameleon exhibits with changing environment is :
(*a*) Camouflage
(*b*) Batesian mimicry
(*c*) Mullerian mimicry
(*d*) None of the above

123. Mimicry is :
(*a*) structural adaptation
(*b*) protective adaptation
(*c*) animal association adaptation
(*d*) regulatory process

124. Which of the following insects mimic a dry leaf?
(*a*) kalima (*b*) phyllium
(*c*) carausium (*d*) viceroy butterfly

125. An interesting modification of flower shape for insect pollination occurs in some orchids in which a male insect mistakes the pattern on the orchid flower for the female of his species and tries to copulate with it, thereby pollinating the flower. This phenomenon is called :
(*a*) Pseudoparthenocarpy
(*b*) Mimicry
(*c*) Pseudopollination
(*d*) Pseudocopulation

126. Succession is :
(*a*) gradual, convergent, directional and continuous process
(*b*) series of biotic communities that appear gradually in a barren area
(*c*) orderly process of community change till stability
(*d*) All of these

127. The first step towards succession is :
(*a*) ecesis (*b*) migration
(*c*) nudation (*d*) competition

128. In succession which of the following changes occur?
(*a*) habitat conditions changes from xerism or hydrism to mesis
(*b*) productivity Biomass (standing crop) ratio decreases
(*c*) biochemical diversity and stability increases but niche specialisation becomes narrow from broad
(*d*) All of the above

129. Plant succession on sandy area is called :
(*a*) Halosere (*b*) Psammosere
(*c*) Xerosere (*d*) Hydrosere

130. In ecological succession the seral stages are :
(*a*) regular
(*b*) irregular
(*c*) both (*a*) and (*b*)
(*d*) None of these

131. Primary succession takes much longer time than secondary succession because it involves :
(*a*) development of soil
(*b*) development by seeds bank
(*c*) colonization by organisms
(*d*) All of the above

132. A best and most successful parasite is that which :
(*a*) makes minimum demands on the host
(*b*) has life cycle only on one host
(*c*) is permanent parasite on host
(*d*) is highly specialised for host

133. Which volatiles guide insects?
(*a*) Phytochrome
(*b*) Pheromones
(*c*) Hormone ecdysone
(*d*) Progesterone

134. Lichen show a type of assocation between algae and fungi which is :
(*a*) commensalism
(*b*) symbiosis (mutualism)
(*c*) parasitism
(*d*) epiphytism

135. Association of animals belonging to different species where both partners are benefitted, is called :
(*a*) commensalism (*b*) colony
(*c*) mutualism (*d*) sympatry

136. Mycorrhiza is a symbiotic relationship (mutualism) between roots of higher plants and :
(*a*) virus
(*b*) blue green algae
(*c*) fungi
(*d*) bacteria

137. A high density of tiger population in an area can result in :
(*a*) predation
(*b*) interspecific (internecine) competition
(*c*) intraspecific (intranecine) competition
(*d*) protocooperation

138. When food is derived by killing the host, this interaction is called :
(*a*) Predation (*b*) Antibiosis
(*c*) Parasitism (*d*) Protocooperation

139. Inhibition of one species by another without getting any benefit is called
(*a*) Amensalism (*b*) Mutualism
(*c*) Commensalism (*d*) Competition

140. In a culture, Alexander Fleming found inhibition of bacteria (*staphylococus*) growth from the *Penicillium* growing in the same culture. It is an example of :
(*a*) Amensalism (*b*) Allelopathy
(*c*) Antibiosis (*d*) All of these

141. Amensalism avoids over crowding, it is commonly shown by :
(*a*) smoother crops (*b*) juglans
(*c*) *penicillium* (*d*) All of the above

142. Allelopathy is :
(*a*) a type of therapy
(*b*) phaging of materials by Lysosomes
(*c*) destructing of pollens
(*d*) effect of plants due to interaction

143. Allelopathy refers to :
A. seed dormancy due to presence of inhibitors on surface of seed coat
B. production of substances by one plant having harmful effect on other
C. helping in spacing of plants to reduce competition
D. helping the xerophytes to grow in small groups

Of these statements
(*a*) A,B,C are correct
(*b*) A and C are correct
(*c*) B and C are correct
(*d*) A and D are correct

144. The slow but efficient soil formers are :
(*a*) fungi
(*b*) lichens and mosses
(*c*) mosses
(*d*) fungi and lichens

145. Choose the correct statement :
(*a*) Symbiosis means association beneficial for both members
(*b*) Symbiosis means beneficial to one and harmful to other partner
(*c*) Commensalism means harmful for both
(*d*) Mutualism includes only symbiosis

146. Some ferocious ant take shelter and food from plants and in turn protect plants from other animals. In which of the south American plant, leaves secrete certain food substances (called Belts corpuscles) at the tips for ants and myrmecophily :
(*a*) *Acacia nilotica*
(*b*) *Acacia sphaerocephala*
(*c*) *Zizyphus jujuba*
(*d*) *Acacia melanoxylon*

147. The first community in an ecological succession is called :
(*a*) Pioneer community
(*b*) Climax community
(*c*) Seral community
(*d*) Ecosere

148. Stages of succession in salty water is termed :
(*a*) hydrochory (*b*) halosere
(*c*) hydrosere (*d*) psammosere

149. What changes occur during ecological succession?
(*a*) non-living organic matter and food chains increase
(*b*) diversity and stability increase
(*c*) biomass and energy flow increase
(*d*) All of the above

150. When succession occurs in an area where an early community has been damaged by fire/ flood etc. leaving considerable organic matter and few organisms, it is temed as :
(*a*) xerosere
(*b*) secondary succession (Subsere)
(*c*) primary succession (Prisere)
(*d*) heterotrophic succession

151. When the habitat is changed by some outside factor which induces the growth of other plants an inhibit the growth of existing plants, this type of succession is known as :
(*a*) autogenic (*b*) allogenic
(*c*) prisere (*d*) subsere

152. On barren, rocks pioneers early settlers of xerosere succession are :
(*a*) Moss (*b*) Lichens
(*c*) Algae (*d*) Fungi

153. The successful establishment of plants in a new locality is called :
(*a*) migration (*b*) ecesis
(*c*) colonisation (*d*) introduction

154. In ecological succession from pioneer to climax stage, the biomass shall :
(*a*) decrease
(*b*) increase continuously
(*c*) increase and then decrease
(*d*) No relation

155. Maximum diversity is found in :
(*a*) seral community
(*b*) pioneer community
(*c*) climax community
(*d*) psammosere

156. Minimum diversity is found in :
(*a*) seral community
(*b*) pioneer community
(*c*) climax community
(*d*) moss stage

157. Long term stability of a biotic community is governed by its :
(*a*) more diversity
(*b*) population
(*c*) pioneer community
(*d*) environment

158. Which seral stage in a succession takes maximum time?
(*a*) pioneer stage
(*b*) climax stage
(*c*) seral stage
(*d*) None of these

159. Regeneration of community is due to :
(*a*) primary succession
(*b*) secondary successeion
(*c*) climax community
(*d*) camouflage

160. Last succession in a sere is called :
(*a*) climatic climax
(*b*) seral community
(*c*) prisere
(*d*) ecological niche

161. A climax community is that which is :
(*a*) last stable community stable

(*b*) unstable
(*c*) permanent but seral community
(*d*) occupied by only one species

162. A climax community differs from subclimax one in having :
(*a*) more biomass
(*b*) self perpetuating and complex food chains
(*c*) species diversity
(*d*) All of the above

163. When the succession occurs in a barren area that was not previously inhabited by plant like sand dunes, seafloor, volcano lava sediments, it is called :
(*a*) secondary succession (subsere)
(*b*) primary succession (prisere)
(*c*) allogenic
(*d*) ecological succession

164. If the succession is caused by plants themselves. It is called :
(*a*) allogenic succession
(*b*) autogenic succession
(*c*) autotrophic
(*d*) heterotrophic

165. Sometimes ecological succession is due to forces other than effects of communities on environment such a succession is called :
(*a*) Autogenic (*b*) Allogenic
(*c*) Autotrophic (*d*) None of the above

166. Most wide spread succession is :
(*a*) Autotrophic (*b*) Autogenic
(*c*) Allogenic (*d*) None of the above

167. When the habitat is changed by some outside factor which induces the growth of other plants and inhibit the growth of existing plants, this type of succession is known as :
(*a*) autogenic (*b*) allogenic
(*c*) prisere (*d*) subsere

168. The ecosystem which has only one type of species is called :
(*a*) Tissue culture (*b*) Monoculture
(*c*) Pisciculture (*d*) Monoclone

169. Nature (= kind) of climax community in an area depends on area's :
(*a*) pool of colonists
(*b*) soil organism and water
(*c*) climate
(*d*) soil fertility

170. In succession, the deciding factor is :
(*a*) climate (*b*) organisms
(*c*) population (*d*) migration

171. The correct sequence of Hydrarch succession in pond of 6m depth is :
(*a*) Plankton stage → floating stage → reed swamp stage → wood land stage
(*b*) Plankton stage → submerged stage → floating stage → reeds → wood land → climax
(*c*) Plankton stage → reeds → marsh → meadow → submerged stage → wood land → climax
(*d*) Zooplankton stage → Hydrophytes → amphibious plants → climax community

172. The succession on bare rock (lithosere/ xerosere) involves following seral stages :
(*a*) Crustose lichen stage → Moss → Herbs → Shrubs → Scrubland → Trees
(*b*) Crustose lichens → Herbs → Amphibious plants → Shrubs → Climax (Tree)
(*c*) Foliose lichens → Herbs → Mossess → *Selaginella* → Tree
(*d*) Crustose → Fruticose → Foliose lichen → Moss → Shrubs → Trees

173. A dominant species (ecological dominants) in a succession are those :
(*a*) which are larger in size or larger in numbers most successful and control flow of energy
(*b*) which have major influence on the local physical environment
(*c*) which are not replaced by others easily
(*d*) All of the above

174. Keystone species in an ecosystem is that which is :
(*a*) present in maximum number
(*b*) are most frequent and most successful
(*c*) attaining a large biomass
(*d*) contributing to ecosystem properties

175. If the vegetation of a place is burnt, the first one to appear will be :
(*a*) Mosses and ferns (*b*) Lichens
(*c*) Liverworts (*d*) Grasses

176. Which one of the following statements is correct?
(*a*) The last succession in a series of biotic succession is called a *sere*
(*b*) Honey bees communicate among themselves by secreting pheromones
(*c*) The home range of the members of a species has a larger area than that of their territory
(*d*) The number of individuals of particular species present in a unit area at a given time is called its population size

177. What kind of relationship exists between a ramora or pilot fish and a shark?
(*a*) Commensal (*b*) Parasitic
(*c*) Mutualistic (*d*) None of these

178. An erget and a Rhino have often one of the following relationship with each other?
(*a*) Mutualistic (*b*) Commensalism
(*c*) Parasitism (*d*) Neutralism

179. The relationship between roots of higher plants and fungi is :
(*a*) symbiosis (*b*) commensalism
(*c*) parasitic (*d*) saprophytic

180. The assemblage of individuals of same kind inhabiting a particular geographical area is called :
(*a*) community (*b*) biome
(*c*) population (*d*) organisms

181. Assemblage of different living organisms sharing a common habitat is called :
(*a*) population (*b*) biotic community
(*c*) genus (*d*) biosphere

182. A community is not able to survive without :
(*a*) predator
(*b*) non-living components
(*c*) parasites
(*d*) decomposers

183. Study of plant communities is called :
(*a*) phytology
(*b*) ecosystem
(*c*) phytosociology
(*d*) population ecology

184. The basic unit in ecological studies is population. The sum of all of the population of the same kind of organisms form :
(*a*) community (*b*) species
(*c*) colony (*d*) genus

185. An association of individuals of different species sharing the same habitat and having functional interactions is called :
(*a*) ecosystem
(*b*) biotic community
(*c*) population
(*d*) ecological niche

186. An organism is often :
(*a*) distinct (*b*) indistinct
(*c*) both (*a*) and (*b*) (*d*) None of these

187. We are constituents of :
(*a*) ecosystem (*b*) biosphere
(*c*) environment (*d*) All of these

188. An ecological hierarchy is :
(*a*) individual organism → families → herds → tribes → breed → race → variety → population → species → communities
(*b*) population → families → herds → race → tribes → species → communities
(*c*) organism → population → species → bread → tribe → families → herds → communities
(*d*) ecosystem → community → species → population

189. Biotope is the :
(*a*) top of earth
(*b*) biosphere
(*c*) demarcated unit of environment where all forms of life are seen
(*d*) basic unit in biosphere

190. Biocoenosis means :
(*a*) communities in a biotype
(*b*) space occupied by living organisms
(*c*) association of plants and animals in relation to a given feeding area
(*d*) subunits of biotypes

191. The term biocoenosis to describe community was given by a European biologist :
(*a*) Ernst Haeckel (*b*) Karl Mobius
(*c*) Tansley (*d*) Elodum

192. The recurrence of daily and seasonal changes in a community is known as :
(*a*) stratification
(*b*) periodicity
(*c*) species divergence
(*d*) species dominance

193. To study quantitative characters of a plant community, the simplest method is :
(*a*) Raunkiaer system
(*b*) Quadrat method
(*c*) Biological spectrum
(*d*) None of these

194. Largest vegetational group is known as :
(*a*) association (*b*) consociation
(*c*) formation (*d*) ecosystem

195. Which can live in isolation?
(*a*) organisms or population
(*b*) communities
(*c*) ecosystems
(*d*) no one can live in isolation

196. Which is more stable from ecological point of view?
(*a*) herds (*b*) populations
(*c*) organisms (*d*) community

197. How many dominant species a climax comunity has?
(*a*) rarely one (*b*) two or more
(*c*) 12 or more (*d*) All correct

198. A climax community is recognisable because :
(*a*) it is uniform in composition
(*b*) it consist of trees and shrubs
(*c*) it is composed of trees
(*d*) None of these

ANSWERS

1	2	3	4	5	6	7	8	9	10
(b)	(a)	(d)	(d)	(b)	(d)	(d)	(d)	(d)	(b)
11	**12**	**13**	**14**	**15**	**16**	**17**	**18**	**19**	**20**
(a)	(c)	(a)	(a)	(d)	(a)	(d)	(c)	(a)	(d)
21	**22**	**23**	**24**	**25**	**26**	**27**	**28**	**29**	**30**
(d)	(a)	(a)	(b)	(b)	(a)	(a)	(b)	(a)	(b)
31	**32**	**33**	**34**	**35**	**36**	**37**	**38**	**39**	**40**
(c)	(b)	(a)	(c)	(c)	(d)	(c)	(a)	(a)	(d)
41	**42**	**43**	**44**	**45**	**46**	**47**	**48**	**49**	**50**
(c)	(a)	(d)	(c)	(c)	(c)	(a)	(a)	(a)	(d)
51	**52**	**53**	**54**	**55**	**56**	**57**	**58**	**59**	**60**
(c)	(c)	(b)	(c)	(d)	(d)	(a)	(c)	(b)	(d)
61	**62**	**63**	**64**	**65**	**66**	**67**	**68**	**69**	**70**
(d)	(c)	(d)	(d)	(c)	(a)	(c)	(b)	(c)	(d)
71	**72**	**73**	**74**	**75**	**76**	**77**	**78**	**79**	**80**
(d)	(d)	(c)	(a)	(a)	(c)	(d)	(d)	(c)	(a)
81	**82**	**83**	**84**	**85**	**86**	**87**	**88**	**89**	**90**
(c)	(c)	(b)	(d)	(b)	(a)	(b)	(d)	(d)	(c)
91	**92**	**93**	**94**	**95**	**96**	**97**	**98**	**99**	**100**
(c)	(a)	(c)	(c)	(b)	(b)	(a)	(a)	(c)	(c)

101	**102**	**103**	**104**	**105**	**106**	**107**	**108**	**109**	**110**
(*d*)	(*d*)	(*d*)	(*d*)	(*c*)	(*a*)	(*d*)	(*d*)	(*d*)	(*c*)
111	**112**	**113**	**114**	**115**	**116**	**117**	**118**	**119**	**120**
(*b*)	(*d*)	(*a*)	(*d*)	(*b*)	(*a*)	(*a*)	(*b*)	(*a*)	(*a*)
121	**122**	**123**	**124**	**125**	**126**	**127**	**128**	**129**	**130**
(*a*)	(*a*)	(*b*)	(*a*)	(*b*)	(*d*)	(*c*)	(*d*)	(*b*)	(*a*)
131	**132**	**133**	**134**	**135**	**136**	**137**	**138**	**139**	**140**
(*a*)	(*a*)	(*b*)	(*b*)	(*c*)	(*c*)	(*c*)	(*a*)	(*a*)	(*d*)
141	**142**	**143**	**144**	**145**	**146**	**147**	**148**	**149**	**150**
(*d*)	(*d*)	(*c*)	(*b*)	(*a*)	(*b*)	(*a*)	(*b*)	(*d*)	(*b*)
151	**152**	**153**	**154**	**155**	**156**	**157**	**158**	**159**	**160**
(*b*)	(*b*)	(*b*)	(*b*)	(*c*)	(*b*)	(*a*)	(*a*)	(*c*)	(*a*)
161	**162**	**163**	**164**	**165**	**166**	**167**	**168**	**169**	**170**
(*a*)	(*d*)	(*b*)	(*d*)	(*a*)	(*c*)	(*b*)	(*b*)	(*c*)	(*a*)
171	**172**	**173**	**174**	**175**	**176**	**177**	**178**	**179**	**180**
(*b*)	(*a*)	(*d*)	(*d*)	(*a*)	(*c*)	(*a*)	(*d*)	(*c*)	(*c*)
181	**182**	**183**	**184**	**185**	**186**	**187**	**188**	**189**	**190**
(*b*)	(*b*)	(*c*)	(*b*)	(*b*)	(*a*)	(*d*)	(*a*)	(*c*)	(*c*)
191	**192**	**193**	**194**	**195**	**196**	**197**	**198**		
(*b*)	(*b*)	(*b*)	(*b*)	(*d*)	(*d*)	(*d*)	(*c*)		

8

ENERGY AND ENVIRONMENT

1. Non-renewable sources of Energy and Renewable sources of Energy come under the ministry of :
   (a) Non-Conventional Energy, India
   (b) Environment and Forests, India
   (c) Coal and Petroleum, India
   (d) None of the above
2. A system that captures sunlight directly within a structure and converts it to low temperature heat for space heating is :
   (a) Passive Solar System
   (b) Active Solar System
   (c) Convection System
   (d) Radiation System
3. A system that specially designed collectors concentrate solar energy and store it as heat for space heating and heating water is
   (a) Passive Solar System
   (b) Active Solar System
   (c) Radiation System
   (d) Convection System
4. The **true** statement about solar energy heating space and water is :
   (a) The energy supply is free and naturally available on sunny days
   (b) The energy supply is not available at night and on cloudy days
   (c) The technology is well developed and can be installed quickly
   (d) All of the above
5. The instrument that converts solar energy into electrical energy by solar cells is :
   (a) Photovoltaic cells (b) AC generator
   (c) CD generator (d) None of these
6. The world's largest producer of electricity from hydropower is :
   (a) United States of America
   (b) India
   (c) Canada
   (d) Russia
7. Living communities and non-living environment are inseparable, interrelated and constantly interact energy each other in :
   (a) exchange of matter and energy
   (b) community
   (c) preservation of community
   (d) albedo
8. OTEC is :
   (a) Ocean Thymic Electrical Counter
   (b) Ocean Thermal Energy Conservation
   (c) Oriental Thermal Energy Conservation
   (d) Okahama Thermal Electronic Centre
9. Match the following :

	Column A	Column B
A.	Vast tracts of land covered with wind powered turbines.	1. Wind power
B.	It can either be used directly for heating buildings.	2. Geothermal Energy
C.	Ozone is an important component.	3. Stratosphere

Codes :

	A	B	C
(a)	2	3	1
(b)	1	3	2
(c)	2	1	3
(d)	1	2	3

10. Which statement is *TRUE*?

(*a*) Magneto-hydrodynamic generators convert solar radiation into electricity

(*b*) Coal can be converted to gaseous liquid or low sulphur, low ash solid fuels

(*c*) Sunlight depend on photosensitive layer

(*d*) None of the above

11. Electricity can be directly generated from solar radiation by using :

(*a*) photovoltaic cells

(*b*) solar collectors

(*c*) both of these

(*d*) None of these

12. The nature of resources :

(*a*) is same for all societies

(*b*) varies from society to society

(*c*) has no connection with society

(*d*) can not be predicted

13. The total amount of energy reaching the earth and the amount of energy leaving it is :

(*a*) energy budget of earth

(*b*) gross energy

(*c*) average energy

(*d*) GNP

14. Which of the following is a rich source of energy but never causes atomospheric pollution?

(*a*) Nuclear energy (*b*) Solar energy

(*c*) Coal (*d*) Wood

15. Biogas plants provide highly enriched :

(*a*) inorganic fertilizers

(*b*) organic fertilizers

(*c*) both (*a*) and (*b*)

(*d*) None of these

16. Biogas contains CH_4 (Methane) about :

(*a*) 50 – 68% (*b*) 2 – 10%

(*c*) 15 – 20% (*d*) None of these

17. Hydrogen (H_2) is a :

(*a*) non-renewable fuel

(*b*) renewable fuel

(*c*) both (*a*) and (*b*)

(*d*) None of these

18. Energy conservation and flow in the organisms within ecosystem is known as :

(*a*) radiation ecology

(*b*) microbial ecology

(*c*) space ecology

(*d*) ecological energetics

19. The population of *Homo sapiens* was 453 millions in :

(*a*) 1550 A.D.

(*b*) 4000 B.C.

(*c*) 1650 A.D.

(*d*) 8000 B.C.

20. Basic cause of continued urban growth is due to the :

(*a*) better transport facility

(*b*) better health facilities

(*c*) prosperity in cities

(*d*) entertainment facility

21. Increasing urbanisation causes :

(*a*) socio-economic problems

(*b*) overcrowding

(*c*) health and pollution hazards

(*d*) All of the above

22. Which of the following is/are **TRUE**?

(*a*) CO_2 tends to increase the temperature of the stratosphere by trapping their radiation

(*b*) CO_2 has long term effects due to its adsorption features

(*c*) CO_2 is released in nature by the oxidation of organic substances

(*d*) Both (*b*) and (*c*) only

23. Plant cells can withstand temperatures upto only :

(*a*) – 15°C

(*b*) – 30°C

(*c*) 45°C

(*d*) – 1°C

24. The heating value of wood is :

(*a*) 28,000 kJ/kg

(*b*) 26,000 kJ/kg

(*c*) 24,000 kJ/kg

(*d*) 19,000 kJ/kg

25. Match the following :

	Column A		**Column B**
A.	Solar energy	1.	Indirectly supplies all the energy required for sustaining life on earth
B.	Biogas	2.	An important solution to present energy crisis in rural areas
C.	Oil	3.	Largest source of commercial energy

Codes :

	A	B	C
(*a*)	2	3	1
(*b*)	1	3	2
(*c*)	1	2	3
(*d*)	2	1	3

26. Super thermal power stations are located near large coalfields because :

(*a*) cost of coal is low
(*b*) cost of generation is cheap
(*c*) it is cheaper to transport electricity than coal
(*d*) more land is available

27. Atomic power is derived from :

(*a*) Platinum (*b*) Gold
(*c*) Silver (*d*) Uranium

28. Match the columns :

	Column A		**Column B**
A.	Diesel mixture	1.	a fraction obtained between 270°C – 340°C and a of higher hydrocarbon
B.	Kerosene mixture	2.	a fraction obtained between 180°C – 250°C and a of decane to hexa-decane
C.	Petrol	3.	a fraction obtained between 40°C – 120°C and a mixture of pentane to octane

Codes :

	A	B	C
(*a*)	2	3	1
(*b*)	1	3	2
(*c*)	2	1	3
(*d*)	1	2	3

29. Petroleum products are more widely used than coal, because they :

(*a*) are cheaper than coal
(*b*) do not leave any residue
(*c*) are indispensible for transport on land, sea and air
(*d*) are easily available

30. Which of the following has highest carbon composition?

(*a*) Peat (*b*) Gasoline
(*c*) Diesel (*d*) Kerosene

31. Which of the following is a renewable resource?

(*a*) Soil (*b*) Minerals
(*c*) Forests (*d*) Fresh water

32. Petroleum is a mixture of :

(*a*) Hydrocarbons
(*b*) $CO + H_2$
(*c*) Sulphur and nitrogen
(*d*) Oxygen and water

33. The generation of hydroelectric power depends on :

(*a*) capital of country
(*b*) rainfall of the country
(*c*) slope of the valley
(*d*) load of the river

34. Of the following fractions of petroleum, the fraction having lowest boiling point is :

(*a*) gasoline (*b*) diesel
(*c*) kerosene oil (*d*) lubricating oil

35. In the proximate analysis of coal, the moisture is determined at a temperature of :

(*a*) 105°C (*b*) 500°C
(*c*) 25°C (*d*) 75°C

36. Anthracite is :
(*a*) a lowest rank coal
(*b*) a high percentage carbon molecule
(*c*) a high percentage volatile matter
(*d*) high calorific value and having high carbon percentage

37. The amount of nitrogen in coal is given by :
(*a*) its proximate analysis
(*b*) ultimate analysis
(*c*) burning it in the absence of air
(*d*) pyrolysis

38. Which of the following pairs regarding the composition of fuel substances is **FALSE**?
(*a*) Natural Gas → 4.5% Sulphur
(*b*) Petroleum → 3.5% Sulphur
(*c*) Lignites → 70% Carbon
(*d*) Anthracite → 92% Carbon

39. A good fuel should possess :
(*a*) better anti-knock properties
(*b*) poor anti-knock properties
(*c*) low calorific value
(*d*) None of the above

40. Which of the following is Biogas?
(*a*) Water gas (*b*) Coal gas
(*c*) Producer gas (*d*) Natural gas

41. Largest producer of Natural Gas in the world is :
(*a*) Russia (*b*) USA
(*c*) India (*d*) Bangladesh

42. Which of the following energy is the most important sources of energy?
(*a*) Nuclear energy
(*b*) Thermal energy
(*c*) Hydroelectric energy
(*d*) All of these

43. Petroleum refinery are situated near major ports mainly because :
(*a*) they posses technical manpower
(*b*) they have adequate facilities for handling tankers
(*c*) it is cheaper to impart crude oil than refined products
(*d*) All of the above

44. Petroleum products are indispensable for :
(*a*) manufacturing of variety of products
(*b*) lubricants of machines
(*c*) generation of thermal power
(*d*) internal combustion engines

45. Which amongst the following provides the largest source of commercial energy?
(*a*) Oil (*b*) Coal
(*c*) Natural Gas (*d*) Hydropower

46. Energy from the sun reaches the earth in large quantities, it is mostly used as :
(*a*) it can't be stored and used when needed
(*b*) it is in diffused state
(*c*) it is not available during nights
(*d*) it is costlier than solar energy

47. Which of the following terms related to Coal?
(*a*) Magnesite (*b*) Limonite
(*c*) Bituminous (*d*) Haematite

48. Hydroelectric power stations are generally located in mountainous regions, because :
(*a*) dams can be constructed easily
(*b*) rivers have steep gradients in these areas
(*c*) these receive heavy rainfall
(*d*) All of the above

49. A source of renewable power which can be developed with minimum cost is :
(*a*) mind mills
(*b*) tidal power
(*c*) geothermal energy
(*d*) biomass power

50. The future prospects of Nuclear energy in India is :
(*a*) block (*b*) bright
(*c*) doomed (*d*) can't say

51. An atomic explosion has the ability to make radioactive material :
(*a*) Iodine-131 (*b*) Cesium-137
(*c*) Strontium-90 (*d*) All of the above

52. Most solar cells are made from :
(*a*) Silicon (*b*) Zinc
(*c*) Lead (*d*) None of these

53. Geothermal reservoirs are :
(*a*) absorbed energy on the earth
(*b*) hot underground pools of water
(*c*) hot Magma under the earth
(*d*) None of the above

54. What percentage of energy coming from the sun is re-radiated space?
(*a*) 30% (*b*) 35%
(*c*) 20% (*d*) 25%

55. Which of the following is **NOT** a human related activity causing Global Warming?
(*a*) Volcanic eruptions
(*b*) Locomotives
(*c*) Power plants
(*d*) Coal combustion

56. Match the following :

	Column A		Column B
A.	Solar energy	1.	environmental clean source of energy
B.	Wind	2.	harnessing problems the solved
C.	Geothermal	3.	Underground heat

Codes :

	A	B	C
(*a*)	2	3	1
(*b*)	1	2	3
(*c*)	3	1	2
(*d*)	2	1	3

57. The geothermal every utilise potential of :
(*a*) the earth processes
(*b*) temperature underneath the earth surface
(*c*) magma of volcano
(*d*) volcanic eruptions

58. Ecological balance of a mining area is restored through :
(*a*) Conversion into agricultural area
(*b*) Revegetation of area
(*c*) Prevention of soil erosion
(*d*) Protection against grazing

59. The inexhaustible power is :
(*a*) tidal energy
(*b*) ocean energy
(*c*) hydroelectric power
(*d*) All of these

60. The process of ocean thermal energy conversion is based on :
(*a*) the utilisation of the potential of tidals
(*b*) the utilisation of the temperature differences between warm surface sea and cold deep sea water
(*c*) temperature underneath the surface of earth
(*d*) All of the above

61. At present, the generation of electricity is based mainly on the burning of :
(*a*) fossil fuels
(*b*) natural gas
(*c*) CNG
(*d*) garbage

62. Of the total water vapour potential of the world is :
(*a*) only 1/6th has so far been developed
(*b*) only 1/5th has so far been developed
(*c*) only 1/10th has so far been developed
(*d*) None of the above

63. The total potential water power of the world is estimated as :
(*a*) 496 million watt
(*b*) 969 million watt
(*c*) 171 million watt
(*d*) 200 million watt

64. A fuel having high ignition temperature is :
(*a*) wood (*b*) petrol
(*c*) LPG (*d*) CNG

65. The calorific value of fuel is expressed as :
(*a*) kcal/m^3 (*b*) kcal/cm^3
(*c*) Cal/m^3 (*d*) N/m^2

66. Natural gas is composed primarily of :
(*a*) *n*-butane
(*b*) *n*-octane
(*c*) methane
(*d*) a mixture of butame

67. Domestic cooking gas consists mostly of :
(*a*) methane and ethane
(*b*) ethylene and nylon
(*c*) acetylene and hydrogen
(*d*) CO + H_2

68. When petroleum is heat gradually, the first batch of vapour evolved will be rich in :
(*a*) diesel oil
(*b*) lubricating oil
(*c*) petroleum ether
(*d*) kerosene

69. Match the following :

Column A (Term)	Column B (Definition)
A. Energy	1. Ability to do work
B. Kinetic energy	2. Energy due to motion and mass
C. Potential energy	3. Energy due to position
D. Heat	4. Total energy due to all moving atoms or molecules in a given substance

Codes :

	A	B	C	D
(*a*)	4	3	1	2
(*b*)	1	2	3	4
(*c*)	2	1	4	3
(*d*)	3	1	2	4

70. Which is/are **true** statement?
(*a*) Supplemental commercial energy makes up remaining 1% of energy we use on earth
(*b*) Direct solar energy can also be captured by active solar energy systems
(*c*) Solar cells convert solar energy directly into electricity in one simple, non polluting step
(*d*) All of the above

71. "In all physical and chemical changes we can't create or destroy any of the atoms involved. All we can do is rearrange them into different spatial patterns or different combinations", it is the law of :
(*a*) Conservation of Energy
(*b*) Conservation of Matter
(*c*) Conservation of Mass
(*d*) Any of these

72. How much world's population would live in the scarcity of water?
(*a*) 10% (*b*) 35%
(*c*) 25% (*d*) 30%

73. All the following contribute to pollution *except* :
(*a*) Themal power plant
(*b*) Automobiles
(*c*) Hydroelectric power project
(*d*) Nuclear power plant

74. Value of a resorce is dependent on its :
(*a*) Qality
(*b*) Quantity
(*c*) Requirement by the society
(*d*) All of the above

75. The idea of OTEC was first proposed in the year :
(*a*) 1929 (*b*) 1880
(*c*) 1910 (*d*) 1950

76. Hydroelectric plants rarely need to be shut down, because they produce :
(*a*) No emission of CO_2 during operation
(*b*) CFC'S gases during operation
(*c*) SO_2 during operation
(*d*) None of these

77. Match the following :

Column A (Land Pollutant)	Column B (Control method)
A. Glass	1. Scrubbers and Cyclones
B. Gypsum	2. Precipitators and Scrubbers
C. Cement	3. Baghouses

Codes :

	A	B	C
(*a*)	2	3	1
(*b*)	1	3	2
(*c*)	1	2	3
(*d*)	2	1	3

78. Optimum forest cover for ecobalance should be :
(*a*) 23% (*b*) 33%
(*c*) 50% (*d*) 28%

79. Which resource is believed to exhaust first?
(*a*) Gold (*b*) Tin
(*c*) Coal (*d*) Natural gas

80. Which of the following resources is going to be exhausted by the end of this century?
(*a*) Lead (*b*) Gold
(*c*) Tin (*d*) All of these

81. The ultimate source of energy in an ecosystem is :
(*a*) Glucose (*b*) Sunlight
(*c*) ATP (*d*) Protein

82. The energy flows in an ecosystem is :
(*a*) cyclic (*b*) unidirectional
(*c*) multidirectional (*d*) square

83. The best source of renewable energy is :
(*a*) Coal (*b*) Petroleum
(*c*) Trees (*d*) Cattles

84. The process of splitting bigger hydrocarbon into smaller hydrocarbon molecules, is :
(*a*) combustion (*b*) pyrolysis
(*c*) cracking (*d*) decomposition

85. Main constituent of Natural gas is :
(*a*) CH_4 (*b*) C_2H_6
(*c*) CO_2 (*d*) H_2

86. Which of the following types of coal contains highest percentage of volatile matter?
(*a*) Anthracite (*b*) Peat
(*c*) Lignite (*d*) Bituminous

87. Suitability of a diesel fuel is determined by :
(*a*) Octane number
(*b*) Cetane number
(*c*) Percentage of carbon
(*d*) Length of hydrocarbon chain

88. Consider, which is **TRUE**?
(*a*) Half of the solar radiation is in the visible region
(*b*) Both sun and earth electromagnetic radiation
(*c*) The sun emits electromagnetic radiation like a black body
(*d*) All of these

89. Which of the following is still a very important source of energy for millions of Indians living in villages?
(*a*) Oil (*b*) Coal
(*c*) Fossil (*d*) Fuel wood

90. Which of the following is only source of energy which keeps natural ecosystems in a actual state?
(*a*) Nuclear power
(*b*) Sunlight
(*c*) Thermal power
(*d*) All of these

91. The first atomic bomb was thrown over :
(*a*) Nagasaki (*b*) Hiroshima
(*c*) Tokyo (*d*) Hong Kong

92. Atomic bomb was used during World War II in :
(*a*) 1941 (*b*) 1939
(*c*) 1943 (*d*) 1945

93. Maximum solar energy can be trapped by :
(*a*) growing grasses
(*b*) planting trees
(*c*) growing algae in large tanks
(*d*) more cultivation of crop plants

94. Incomplete combustion is judged by :
(*a*) measuring of oxygen in fuel gases
(*b*) excess air of fuel gases
(*c*) rainfall in the valley
(*d*) All of the above

95. The maximum temperature reached, when the coal is completely burnt in the air is :
(*a*) ignition temperature
(*b*) calorific intensity
(*c*) fusion temperature
(*d*) None of these

96. The calorific value of a coal sample is high, if its :
(*a*) fixed carbon is high
(*b*) moisture content is high
(*c*) volatile matter is high
(*d*) All of the above

97. Which of the following is **NOT** correctly matched?
(*a*) OTEC → Ocean Thermal Energy Conservation
(*b*) CNG → Compressed Natural Gas
(*c*) BOD → Biological Oxygen Demand
(*d*) LPG → Low Petroleum Gas

98. Important conventional source/s of energy in India is/are :
(*a*) Wood (*b*) Fossil fuels
(*c*) Hydropower (*d*) All of these

99. Which of the following is known as **Sink of the Energy**?
(*a*) Sun (*b*) Composers
(*c*) Autotrophs (*d*) Hetrotrophs

100. When the trees mature, they should be cut off for use, this process is called :
(*a*) deforestation
(*b*) improvement cutting
(*c*) selective cutting
(*d*) afforestation

101. The process of cutting of crooked and diseased are trees of no use is called :
(*a*) deforestation
(*b*) improvement cutting
(*c*) selective cutting
(*d*) afforestation

102. If we continue to cut the tropical rain forests at our present rate (100 acres per minute), they will be gone by the year :
(*a*) 2020 (*b*) 2100
(*c*) 2250 (*d*) 2500

103. Quick lime is obtained from
(*a*) sea weeds (*b*) fuel-minerals
(*c*) mollusk shells (*d*) None of these

104. Pearls of valuable jewellery are obtained from
(*a*) *Pinctada* (*b*) *Nautilus*
(*c*) *Octopus* (*d*) Water mussel

105. In social forestry programme, which slogan was adopted?
(*a*) Save Globe
(*b*) A tree for each child
(*c*) Save environment
(*d*) Society for clean environment

106. Existence of coal and petroleum may be detected with the study of :
(*a*) Palaeobotany (*b*) Ecology
(*c*) Embryology (*d*) Bacteriology

107. Fossil fuels, have been formed by a :
(*a*) Conventional process
(*b*) Natural process
(*c*) Non-conventional process
(*d*) None of the above

108. Who said; in nature there is enough for every one's seed, but too little for everyone's greed:
(*a*) Mumford (*b*) Thomas Mani
(*c*) M.K. Gandhi (*d*) S.L. Bahuguna

109. India has 15% of the total population of world but it uses only :
(*a*) 16% of the world's annual energy
(*b*) 2% of the world's annual energy
(*c*) 6% of the world's annual energy
(*d*) Both (*a*) and (*b*)

110. The energy storage at consumer level is :
(*a*) Secondary productivity
(*b*) Gross primary productvity
(*c*) Net productivity
(*d*) None of the above

111. The living organisms desire their energy and nutrients from :
(*a*) abiotic factors (*b*) sun
(*c*) lithosphere (*d*) green plants

112. Wildlife is :
(*a*) renewable resource
(*b*) non-renewable resource
(*c*) inexhaustible resource
(*d*) Both (*b*) and (*c*)

113. Liquid petroleum gas (LPG) used in domestic cooking gas cylinder is :
(*a*) Biogas (*b*) Fossil fuel
(*c*) Low pressure gas (*d*) Coal gas

114. Source of energy that does not evolve CO_2 is :
(*a*) Coal
(*b*) Oil
(*c*) Organic compounds
(*d*) Nuclear energy

115. Which of the following plants indicate the *diamond* in the soil
(*a*) *Salvadora* (*b*) *Panicum*
(*c*) *Vallozia* (*d*) *Capparis*

116. Which of the following types of plants usually produce raw humus that may cause podolization?
(*a*) Conifers (*b*) Algae
(*c*) Bryophytes (*d*) Fungi

117. A growth of tall and short grasses indicates that :
(*a*) Soil is fertile and good for agriculture
(*b*) Soil is fertile but unfit for agriculture
(*c*) Soil is not fertile
(*d*) Soil is Kallar and unfit for agriculture

118. The first geobotanical linkage between the growth of a plant and soil rich in metals was reported in :
(*a*) *Viola* (Zinc)
(*b*) *Equisetum* (Gold)
(*c*) *Ulex* (Aluminium)
(*d*) *Mosses* (Copper)

119. Extensive growth of *Eichhornia* indicates the possibility of :
(*a*) flood (*b*) fire
(*c*) afforestation (*d*) draught

120. Plants of wide limit of tolerance of heat are called :
(*a*) stenohydric (*b*) eurythermal
(*c*) stenothermal (*d*) thermotaxis

121. Requirements of life, available in normal environment, are called :
(*a*) non-renewable resources
(*b*) natural resources
(*c*) renewable resources
(*d*) ecosystem

122. Natural resources are components of biosphere essential for life. These are :
(*a*) materials and factors of nature used by man
(*b*) minerals and energy
(*c*) water and energy
(*d*) fossil fuels

123. A natural resource that has inherent capacity to replenish is called :
(*a*) renewable resource
(*b*) non-renewable resource
(*c*) exhaustible resource
(*d*) inexhaustible resource

124. Most of world's Gold and Platinum occur in :
(*a*) America (*b*) Canada
(*c*) India (*d*) South Africa

125. Iron and chromium would last upto :
(*a*) 2100-2200 A.D. (*b*) 2500-2800 A.D.
(*c*) 3500 A.D. (*d*) None of these

126. Molybdenum will last upto :
(*a*) 2100-2200 A.D. (*b*) 2500-2800 A.D.
(*c*) Zero A.D. (*d*) None of these

127. Of the 2000 minerals, how many we find in use :
(*a*) all 2000 (*b*) 230
(*c*) 100 (*d*) a few only

128. North America is rich in :
(*a*) molybdenum
(*b*) tungsten, tin and manganese
(*c*) silver
(*d*) gold and platinum

129. What is the estimated life span of crude oil :
(*a*) 2500-2800 A.D. (*b*) indefinite
(*c*) 2000 A.D. (*d*) 5000 A.D.

130. Oceans can be exploited for :
(*a*) food (*b*) minerals
(*c*) petroleum (*d*) All of these

131. Both power and manure is provided by :
(*a*) thermal plants
(*b*) nuclear plants
(*c*) biogas plants
(*d*) hydroelectric plants

132. Biogas can be good substitute for :
(*a*) fuel wood (*b*) petroleum
(*c*) coal (*d*) charcoal

133. For biogas production besides dung, which can be used?
(*a*) *Eichhornia* (*b*) *Parthenium*
(*c*) Sewage (*d*) *Leucaena*

134. In the recent years, which of the following plants has received attention as a source of fuel and food?
(*a*) *Deodar* (*b*) *Acacia*
(*c*) *Leucaena* (*d*) *Lasora*

135. The gasoline plant is :
(*a*) *Salvadora* (*b*) *Sterculia*
(*c*) *Thevetia* (*d*) *Euphorbia*

136. Agar-agar is obtained from :
(*a*) weeds (*b*) sea weeds
(*c*) mines (*d*) *sargassum*

137. *Argemone mexicana* is an ecological indicator of :
(*a*) Iron rich soil
(*b*) Poorly drained soil
(*c*) Nitrate rich soil
(*d*) Recently flooded soil

138. The latest weed (arrived in 1956 from America) to enter India responsible for changing the biotic community is :
(*a*) *Opunita*
(*b*) *Carrot grass* (*Parthenium*)
(*c*) *Lantana*
(*d*) *Water hyacinth* (*Eichhornia*)

139. One of the following plants found in India is an escape from the quarantine :
(*a*) Coffee plant (*b*) Congress weed
(*c*) Eichhornia (*d*) Cocoa

140. In many countries spread of *opuntia* was controlled by :
(*a*) DDT
(*b*) growing trees
(*c*) introducing insects
(*d*) letting loose cattles

141. Choose the correct pair :
(*a*) IUCN : Conservation of natural resources
(*b*) Energy cropping : Growing crops for getting alcohol
(*c*) Energy plantation : Growing fire wood trees on non-agricultural and non-forest lands
(*d*) Guano : A nitrogenous excrement of aquatic mammals

142. The inexhaustible non-conventional source of energy is :
(*a*) Solar radiation
(*b*) Nuclear energy
(*c*) Wind Power and sea tides
(*d*) All of the above

143. Sea tides can be used for :
(*a*) sun bath (*b*) energy
(*c*) shipping (*d*) algal sources

144. Main renewable source of energy is :
(*a*) forest/biomass
(*b*) fuel gas/petroleum
(*c*) cattle
(*d*) coal

145. Geothermal energy is produced in India from hot springs by a 5 KW geothermal power plant at :
(*a*) Manikaran (HP) (*b*) Puga (Ladhakh)
(*c*) Gulfs to Kutch (*d*) Ankleshwar

146. Where can tidal energy be developed?
(*a*) Gulf of Kutch (*b*) Puga
(*c*) Manikaran (*d*) Bombay High

147. Asia's largest wind will using wind waves for generating power is at :
(*a*) Kyota (Japan) (*b*) Lamba (Gujarat)
(*c*) Kazakistan (*d*) Pokhran (India)

148. Per capita daily consumption of energy is lowest in :
(*a*) USA (*b*) UK
(*c*) India (*d*) Russia

149. The common source of energy in villages is :
(*a*) coal (*b*) wood and dung
(*c*) sunlight (*d*) Both (*a*) and (*b*)

150. To meet energy crisis what other sources can be exploited :
(*a*) wind (*b*) tides
(*c*) nuclear (*d*) All of these

151. The biggest source of energy on earth's surface is :
(*a*) coal (*b*) tides
(*c*) atoms (*d*) solar radiations

152. Conservation of energy leads to :
(*a*) less pollution
(*b*) less cost
(*c*) conservation of resources
(*d*) All of these

153. When was the department of non-coventional energy sources established?

(*a*) 1975 (*b*) 1980
(*c*) 1988 (*d*) 1982

154. Oil, coal and natural gas constitute :
(*a*) renewable source (*b*) fossil fuel
(*c*) eontic fuel (*d*) None of these

155. For the production of biogas, the biogas plant requires :
(*a*) fire wood
(*b*) cattle dung
(*c*) agricultural waste
(*d*) kerosene

156. Where lies the highest concentration of ferromanganese nodules (**manganese nodules**)
(*a*) South Atlantic
(*b*) North Pacific ocean beds
(*c*) North Indian ocean beds
(*d*) North Atlantic ocean beds

157. **Guano** deposits, the excrement of **sea birds reptiles** and **bats** are the major source of
(*a*) phosphorus (*b*) sulphur
(*c*) zinc (*d*) nitrogen

158. The inexhaustive, non-conventional source of energy is/are
(*a*) solar radiations (*b*) wind power
(*c*) sea tides (*d*) All of these

159. Most important natural source of energy currently being used is :
(*a*) sunlight (*b*) fossil fuel
(*c*) biogas (*d*) atomic energy

160. Minerals, metals and fossil fuels are :
(*a*) renewable resources
(*b*) non-renewable resources
(*c*) biodegradable resources
(*d*) renewable as well as non-renewable resources

161. Match the following :

A.	Non-renewable	1.	Fossil fuels
B.	Reusable	2.	Wildlife
C.	Non reusable	3.	Wind power
D.	Immutable	4.	Soil fertility
E.	Renewable	5.	Gold

Codes :

	A	B	C	D	E
(*a*)	5	2	3	4	1
(*b*)	2	5	1	3	4
(*c*)	2	1	5	4	3
(*d*)	5	1	3	2	4

162. The renewable source is :
(*a*) trees
(*b*) agricultural products
(*c*) wildlife species
(*d*) Both (*a*) and (*b*)

163. The international/multinational natural resource/s is/are :
(*a*) sunlight and air
(*b*) migratory animals
(*c*) mineral
(*d*) land

164. Geothermal energy is :
(*a*) non-renewable, non-conventional source
(*b*) non-renewable conventional source
(*c*) renewable conventional source
(*d*) renewable non-conventional source

165. Which of the following is a renewable resource?
(*a*) Water
(*b*) Soil
(*c*) Forests and wildlife
(*d*) All of these

166. Which one of the following is most non-renewable source of energy?
(*a*) Forests
(*b*) Coal deposits
(*c*) Water
(*d*) Wildlife and Biogas

167. Depletion of scarce materials present within the ground can be prolonged by :
(*a*) restrictive use (*b*) substitution
(*c*) recycling (*d*) All of these

168. The land of wind mills using wind waves as a source of power is :
(*a*) Netherland (*b*) India
(*c*) Japan (*d*) Hong Kong

169. Exhaustible resources are :
(*a*) coal (*b*) fossil fuel
(*c*) minerals (*d*) All of these

170. Cultigens are :
(*a*) plants that require human protection
(*b*) that are protected by wildlife
(*c*) both are correct
(*d*) None of these

171. Animals like scorpions, cockroaches, lizards, mice sharing our abodes (homes) and food live in our homes, are called :
(*a*) Cultigens
(*b*) Inquilines
(*c*) Living fossil
(*d*) Domesticated

172. Biomass produced by plants in oceans accounts for :
(*a*) 85% (*b*) 75%
(*c*) 65% (*d*) 58%

173. Percentage land under forests in India is :
(*a*) 23% (*b*) 17%
(*c*) 33% (*d*) 13%

ANSWERS

1	2	3	4	5	6	7	8	9	10
(*a*)	(*a*)	(*b*)	(*d*)	(*a*)	(*a*)	(*a*)	(*b*)	(*d*)	(*b*)
11	**12**	**13**	**14**	**15**	**16**	**17**	**18**	**19**	**20**
(*a*)	(*b*)	(*a*)	(*b*)	(*b*)	(*a*)	(*b*)	(*d*)	(*c*)	(*c*)
21	**22**	**23**	**24**	**25**	**26**	**27**	**28**	**29**	**30**
(*d*)	(*d*)	(*a*)	(*d*)	(*c*)	(*c*)	(*d*)	(*d*)	(*c*)	(*b*)
31	**32**	**33**	**34**	**35**	**36**	**37**	**38**	**39**	**40**
(*c*)	(*a*)	(*b*)	(*a*)	(*a*)	(*d*)	(*b*)	(*a*)	(*a*)	(*a*)
41	**42**	**43**	**44**	**45**	**46**	**47**	**48**	**49**	**50**
(*a*)	(*b*)	(*c*)	(*b*)	(*a*)	(*b*)	(*c*)	(*b*)	(*d*)	(*b*)
51	**52**	**53**	**54**	**55**	**56**	**57**	**58**	**59**	**60**
(*d*)	(*a*)	(*b*)	(*a*)	(*a*)	(*b*)	(*b*)	(*b*)	(*d*)	(*b*)
61	**62**	**63**	**64**	**65**	**66**	**67**	**68**	**69**	**70**
(*a*)	(*b*)	(*a*)	(*a*)	(*a*)	(*c*)	(*a*)	(*c*)	(*b*)	(*d*)
71	**72**	**73**	**74**	**75**	**76**	**77**	**78**	**79**	**80**
(*b*)	(*b*)	(*c*)	(*c*)	(*b*)	(*a*)	(*c*)	(*b*)	(*b*)	(*d*)
81	**82**	**83**	**84**	**85**	**86**	**87**	**88**	**89**	**90**
(*b*)	(*c*)	(*c*)	(*c*)	(*a*)	(*b*)	(*b*)	(*d*)	(*d*)	(*a*)
91	**92**	**93**	**94**	**95**	**96**	**97**	**98**	**99**	**100**
(*b*)	(*d*)	(*c*)	(*a*)	(*b*)	(*a*)	(*d*)	(*d*)	(*a*)	(*c*)
101	**102**	**103**	**104**	**105**	**106**	**107**	**108**	**109**	**110**
(*b*)	(*a*)	(*c*)	(*a*)	(*b*)	(*a*)	(*c*)	(*c*)	(*b*)	(*a*)
111	**112**	**113**	**114**	**115**	**116**	**117**	**118**	**119**	**120**
(*a*)	(*a*)	(*b*)	(*d*)	(*c*)	(*a*)	(*a*)	(*a*)	(*a*)	(*b*)
121	**122**	**123**	**124**	**125**	**126**	**127**	**128**	**129**	**130**
(*b*)	(*a*)	(*a*)	(*d*)	(*b*)	(*a*)	(*b*)	(*a*)	(*c*)	(*d*)

131	132	133	134	135	136	137	138	139	140
(*c*)	(*b*)	(*a*)	(*c*)	(*d*)	(*b*)	(*d*)	(*b*)	(*b*)	(*c*)
141	**142**	**143**	**144**	**145**	**146**	**147**	**148**	**149**	**150**
(*d*)	(*d*)	(*b*)	(*a*)	(*a*)	(*a*)	(*b*)	(*c*)	(*b*)	(*d*)
151	**152**	**153**	**154**	**155**	**156**	**157**	**158**	**159**	**160**
(*d*)	(*d*)	(*d*)	(*b*)	(*b*)	(*b*)	(*a*)	(*c*)	(*b*)	(*b*)
161	**162**	**163**	**164**	**165**	**166**	**167**	**168**	**169**	**170**
(*b*)	(*d*)	(*a*)	(*a*)	(*d*)	(*b*)	(*d*)	(*a*)	(*d*)	(*a*)
171	**172**	**173**							
(*b*)	(*a*)	(*a*)							

9

WATER POLLUTION

1. Ganga Action plan was started in :
(*a*) 1947 (*b*) 1956
(*c*) 1982 (*d*) 1985

2. Fluoride pollution mainly affects :
(*a*) kidney (*b*) heart
(*c*) brain (*d*) teeth

3. *E. coli* is used as an indicator organism to determine pollution of water with :
(*a*) pollen of aquatic plants
(*b*) heavy metals
(*c*) faecal matter
(*d*) industrial effluents

4. BOD is a measure of :
(*a*) amount of oxygen needed by green plants during night
(*b*) industrial wastes poured into water bodies
(*c*) amount of CO inseparably combined with haemoglobin
(*d*) extent to which water is polluted with organic compounds

5. Frequent occurrence of water blooms in a lake indicates which of the following?
(*a*) Deficiency of nutrients
(*b*) Deficiency of oxygen
(*c*) Excessive availability of nutrients
(*d*) Absence of herbivores in the lake

6. The "solution to pollution is dilution". This can be best correlated to :
(*a*) air pollution
(*b*) water pollution
(*c*) noise pollution
(*d*) satiation pollution

7. Excess of nitrates in the field get mixed up with drinking water. It may result in :
(*a*) killing of intestinal bacteria
(*b*) upsetting enzyme production
(*c*) converting nitrates into nitrites which harms haemoglobin leading to anaemia
(*d*) producing more amino acids

8. Which of the following is the main factor of water pollution?
(*a*) Smoke (*b*) Industrial waste
(*c*) Ammonia (*d*) Detergents

9. Activated sludge is associated with management of waste and it is a kind of :
(*a*) chemical treatment
(*b*) mechanical means
(*c*) biological treatment
(*d*) nuclear means

10. Mottling of teeth is due to presence of an element in drinking water :
(*a*) Mercury (*b*) Fluorine
(*c*) Boron (*d*) Chlorine

11. Water pollution can be stopped best by :
(*a*) treating effluents to remove injurious chemicals
(*b*) rearing more fishes
(*c*) cultivating useful water plants
(*d*) spraying with DDT

12. Sewage water is purified by :
(*a*) Microorganisms (*b*) Light
(*c*) Fishes (*d*) Aquatic plants

13. Sewage infection of water will be demonstrated by cysts of :
(*a*) *Entamoeba*
(*b*) *Escherichia coli*
(*c*) *Pseudomonas*
(*d*) *Leishmania*

14. Sewage treatment in which a portion of decomposer bacteria present in waste is recycled into the beginning of the process :
(*a*) Cyclic treatment
(*b*) Activated sludge treatment
(*c*) Primary treatment
(*d*) Tertiary treatment

15. Water pollution causes :
(*a*) Increased photosynthesis
(*b*) Increased deoxygenation and turbidity
(*c*) Decreased trubidity
(*d*) Increased oxygenation

16. Water is often treated with chlorine to :
(*a*) Increase oxygen content
(*b*) Kill germs
(*c*) Remove hardness
(*d*) Remove suspended particles

17. Water blooms are formed by :
(*a*) *Lemna* (*b*) *Hydrilla*
(*c*) Water Hyacinth (*d*) Planktonic algae

18. BOD stands for :
(*a*) Biochemical Oxygen Demand
(*b*) Biotic Oxygen Dropping
(*c*) Biochemical Oxygen Dressing
(*d*) None of the above

19. Solutbility and availability of plant nutrients are more related to :
(*a*) Soil pH (*b*) Soil porosity
(*c*) Soil temperature (*d*) All of the above

20. Fresh water needed for humans, animals and plants is only provided by :
(*a*) rain (*b*) oceans
(*c*) precipitation (*d*) ground water

21. The precentage of fresh water form of water on the earth is :
(*a*) 9% (*b*) 7%
(*c*) 5% (*d*) 3%

22. The precipitation reaching the ground distribute in different ways as :
1. evaporate and reach the atmosphere
2. infiltrate the soil
3. detained in catchment area
4. bacome a form of run-off

Select the correct answer from the codes :
(*a*) 1, 2 and 3
(*b*) 2, 3 and 4
(*c*) 1, 3 and 4
(*d*) All the four

23. Natural water that exposed to limestone is :
(*a*) Calcareous water (*b*) Distill water
(*c*) Hard water (*d*) Any of these

24. The total concentration of ions in sea water is much higher than that in fresh water because :
(*a*) it has more water
(*b*) it has large amount of dissolved salts
(*c*) it has large area
(*d*) Any of these

25. Phenolpthalein alkalinity is also known as :
(*a*) Pure alkalinity
(*b*) Carbonate alkalinity
(*c*) Natural alkalinity
(*d*) Inpure alkalinity

26. The source of fresh water neded for humans is :
(*a*) ground water (*b*) rain water
(*c*) river water (*d*) oceans

27. The interception is :
(*a*) the condensation of water vapours
(*b*) holding of precipitation in environment
(*c*) running of precipitation from earth surface
(*d*) All of the above

28. Water is most common and most important chemical compounds for living organisms as:
1. the life has been originated in the waters of oceans
2. it makes a large proportions of the animal tissues
3. it has valency of + 4, + 2 etc.
(*a*) 1 and 2
(*b*) 1, 2 and 3
(*c*) 1 only
(*d*) 2 only

29. The total fresh water reserve of the earth is about :
(*a*) 2.2% (*b*) 0.001%
(*c*) 2.7% (*d*) 0.5%

30. Chemical Oxygen Demand is :
(*a*) the quantity of oxygen consumed in the oxidation of organic and inorganic matter in water under favourable conditions
(*b*) the quantity of biological oxygen used by the micro-organisms to live under water
(*c*) both of the above
(*d*) None of the above

31. Low levels of BOD in water bodies lead to the death of fishes and other micro-organisms due to :
(*a*) methane
(*b*) hydrogen sulphide
(*c*) offensive sludge
(*d*) All of these

32. The abundance and diversity of micro-organisms in any ecosystem are influenced by:
(*a*) oxygen demand
(*b*) sewage fungus
(*c*) gypsum quantity
(*d*) baghouses

33. Measurement of rate of oxygen utilisation by, a unit volume of water over period of time is to measure
(*a*) Fermentation
(*b*) Biogas generation
(*c*) Biosynthetic pathway
(*d*) Biological oxygen demand

34. The great ocean currents are set in motion by :
(*a*) rotation of moon
(*b*) rotation of sun
(*c*) dragging of wind over-vast areas of sea surface
(*d*) rise and cooling of air

35. Most of the clouds and the weather systems occurred in :
(*a*) mesosphere (*b*) troposphere
(*c*) Ionosphere (*d*) None of these

36. With an increase in altitude the temperature gradually :
(*a*) increase (*b*) decrease
(*c*) both (*a*) and (*b*) (*d*) None of these

37. Water pollution is due to :
(*a*) Agricultural discharges
(*b*) Sewage and other wastes
(*c*) Industrial effluents
(*d*) All of the above

38. Drained sewage has B.O.D. :
(*a*) More than that of water
(*b*) Less than that of water
(*c*) Equal to that of water
(*d*) None of the above

39. B.O.D. is connected with :
(*a*) Organic matter (*b*) Microbes
(*c*) Both (*a*) and (*b*) (*d*) None of the above

40. How much world's population would live in scarcity of water?
(*a*) 10% (*b*) 25%
(*c*) 35% (*d*) 40%

41. Fish die in water bodies polluted by sewage due to :
(*a*) Pathogens
(*b*) Clogging of gills by silt
(*c*) Reduction in oxygen
(*d*) Foul smell

42. Most poisonous pollutant in water is :
(*a*) Lead (*b*) Zinc
(*c*) Phosphate (*d*) Arsenic

43. Counter current flow of scrub solution and the gas stream is effective in trapping :
(*a*) liquid substances
(*b*) gaseous substances
(*c*) all kinds of pollutants
(*d*) All of these

44. If water pollution continues at its present rate it will eventually :
(*a*) stop water cycle
(*b*) make O_2^- molecule unavailable to water plants
(*c*) make NO_3^- molecule available for water cycle
(*d*) prevent precipitation and temperature rise

45. The rise in temperature in aquatic system has deterimental effects are as :
(*a*) reduction in D.O (*b*) increase in B.O.D.
(*c*) both (*a*) and (*b*) (*d*) None of these

46. 'Methaemoglobinaemia' disease is caused by the rising of :
(*a*) Lead levels in ground water
(*b*) Mercury levels in ground water
(*c*) Nitrate in ground water
(*d*) None of these

47. Fresh water freezes at 0°C, but the dissolved salts in sea water changes its properties so that it freezes at temperature :
(*a*) above 0°C
(*b*) below 0°C
(*c*) both (*a*) and (*b*)
(*d*) none of these

48. The maximum density of water is :
(*a*) 0°C (*b*) 4.0°C
(*c*) 100°C (*d*) 25°C

49. Addition of phosphates and nitrates/fertilizers into water leads to :
(*a*) Increased growth of decomposers
(*b*) Reduced algal growth
(*c*) Increased algal growth
(*d*) Nutrient enrichment/eutrophication

50. Fluoride pollution produces necrosis or chlorosis of :
(*a*) Leaf margin and tip
(*b*) Stem
(*c*) Petiole but not lamina
(*d*) Midrib

51. Geothermal reservoirs are :
(*a*) absorbed energy on the earth
(*b*) hot underground pools of water
(*c*) hot magma under the earth
(*d*) None of the above

52. The percentage of dissolved O_2 in the environment is :
(*a*) 22% (*b*) 18%
(*c*) 0.003% (*d*) 79%

53. Water treatment plants contribute major quantities of :
(*a*) dissolved oxygen
(*b*) O_2 –depleting substances
(*c*) CO_2–depleting substances
(*d*) All of these

54. Which will **not** cause any atmospheric pollution?
(*a*) Hydrogen (*b*) Sulphur dioxide
(*c*) Carbon dioxide (*d*) Any of these

55. The total concentration of ions in sea water is much higher than that in fresh water because it contains :
(*a*) dissolved oxygen
(*b*) oil and grease
(*c*) large quantities of dissolved salts
(*d*) None of these

56. Most important causative pollutant is :
(*a*) Plastic (*b*) Glass junk
(*c*) Iron junk (*d*) Detergents

57. The compounds that can promote eutrophication of water bodies :
(*a*) Cu- containing compounds
(*b*) N_2- containing compounds
(*c*) S- containing compounds
(*d*) O_2- containing compounds

58. All the following contribute to pollution except :
(*a*) Thermal power plant
(*b*) Automobiles
(*c*) Hydroelectric power project
(*d*) Nuclear power plant

59. Fluorosis can lead to :
(*a*) severe skeletal problems
(*b*) prevent dental caries
(*c*) stiffness and pain in joints
(*d*) (*a*) and (*c*) only

60. Goitre is an enlargement of :
(*a*) Pancreas (*b*) Thyroid gland
(*c*) Testes (*d*) Spleen

61. Which causes water pollution?
(*a*) Smoke/fly ash
(*b*) Automobile exhausts
(*c*) Aeroplanes
(*d*) 2, 4-D and pesticides

62. The capacity of the organic and biological matter in a sample of natural water to consume oxygen and the process catalysed by bacteria is :
(*a*) Chemical Oxygen Demand (COD)
(*b*) Biological Oxygen Demand (BOD)
(*c*) Bivariate Oxygen Demand (BOD)
(*d*) Complete Oxygen Demand (COD)

63. A lake receiving nutrients would be :
(*a*) Oligotrophic (*b*) Eutrophic
(*c*) Sink (*d*) Rich in fossils

64. In a polluted lake, the index of pollution is :
(*a*) *Daphnia* (*b*) Frog
(*c*) *Artemia* (*d*) None of these

65. Environment can be improved by :
(*a*) Wind erosion
(*b*) Excessive tree fall
(*c*) Conservation
(*d*) None of the above

66. Eutrophication causes reduction in
(*a*) Dissolved hydrogen
(*b*) Dissolved oxygen
(*c*) Dissolved salts
(*d*) All of the above

67. Continuous sewage flow into a stream would lead to :
(*a*) Eutrophication
(*b*) Algal bloom
(*c*) Depletion of oxygen
(*d*) Increase in temperature

68. Eutrophication is caused by :
(*a*) Lack of algae in a lake
(*b*) Abundant oxygen in ponds
(*c*) Run-off of fertilizers in lake
(*d*) Excess nekton in lake

69. If sea water is gradually evaporated, the first salt to precipatate is :
(*a*) $MgCl_2$ (*b*) KCl
(*c*) $CaCO_3$ (*d*) None of the above

70. Acid rain is a rainfall having pH of :
(*a*) greater than 7 (*b*) less than 5.0
(*c*) equal to 7 (*d*) equal to 5.5

71. Huge quantity of sewage is dumped in a river. The BOD will :
(*a*) Increase
(*b*) Decrease
(*c*) Slightly decreases
(*d*) Remain unchanged

72. Minamata disease is due to pollution of :
(*a*) Organic waste into drinking water
(*b*) Oil spill in water
(*c*) Industrial waste mercury into fishing water
(*d*) Arsenic into the atmosphere

73. Phosphate pollution is caused by :
(*a*) Weathering of phosphate rocks only
(*b*) Agricultural fertilizers
(*c*) Phosphate rocks and sewage
(*d*) Sewage and agricultural fertilizers

74. Common indicator organism of water pollution is :
(*a*) *Escherichia coil*
(*b*) *Cholera vibrio*
(*c*) *Salmonella typhi*
(*d*) *Entamoeba histolytica*

75. Many organic substances or organisms help in clearing the water when found in :
(*a*) high concentration
(*b*) low concentration
(*c*) moderate concentration
(*d*) neutral concentration

76. When pollution load is more in the lakes there cannot take place self purification because :
(*a*) There is no O_2 to sustain microbial activity
(*b*) No sunlight is present
(*c*) Microbes die
(*d*) Pollutants settle down automatically

77. Treatment of polluted water is carried out with the help of :
(*a*) Lichens (*b*) Fungi
(*c*) Ferns (*d*) Phytoplankton

78. Eutrophication is found in :
(*a*) Agricultural land near thermal plant
(*b*) Saline soil
(*c*) Lake
(*d*) Mountain

79. BOD (biological oxygen demand) is :
(*a*) Amount of oxygen consumed by microorganisms for decaying organic matter per unit volume of water
(*b*) Amount of CO_2 consumed by microorganisms per unit of sewage water
(*c*) Amount of oxygen required by aquatic plants for survival
(*d*) None of these

80. Sudden mass death of fish is more likely to occur in :
(*a*) Eutrophic lake (*b*) Mesotrophic lake
(*c*) Oligotrophic lake (*d*) Oxalotrophic lake

81. Which pollution causes jaundice :
(*a*) Water (*b*) Air
(*c*) Land (*d*) Thermal

82. Ganga water is believed not to be spoil because of the presence of :
(*a*) metals in it (*b*) phages in it
(*c*) pesticides in it (*d*) oils in it

83. Sewage water can be purified for recycling with the action of :
(*a*) penicillin (*b*) micro-organism
(*c*) fishes (*d*) aquatic plants

84. Thermal pollution of water bodies is due to discharge of :
(*a*) agricultural run-off water
(*b*) chemicals from industries
(*c*) wastes from mining
(*d*) heat from power plants

85. The average pH of surface ocean water is about :
(*a*) 5.2 (*b*) 10.5
(*c*) 7.0 (*d*) 8.1

86. NASA has launched a satellite named *Aqua* to :
(*a*) reduce the ozone hole
(*b*) study the green house gases
(*c*) study the effect of water in its various forms on climate
(*d*) none of these

87. A dental disease characterised by mottling of teeth is due to presence of a certain chemical elements in drinking water. Which is that element?
(*a*) Mercury (*b*) Fluorine
(*c*) Boron (*d*) Chlorine

88. Alum is used to purify water because it acts as :
(*a*) bacteriocide (*b*) deodorant
(*c*) coagulant (*d*) softner of water

89. Which of the following organisms is used as indicator of water quality?
(*a*) *Azospirilium* (*b*) *Escherichia*
(*c*) *Beggiatoa* (*d*) *Chlorella*

90. Melting point of water is :
(*a*) 5°C
(*b*) 3°C
(*c*) 0°C
(*d*) None of these

91. The fresh water we use comes from :
(*a*) ground water
(*b*) surface water runoff
(*c*) sea water
(*d*) (*a*) and (*b*) only

92. Minamata disease is a pollution related disease which results from :
(*a*) release of industrial waste mercury into fishing water
(*b*) oil spills into sea
(*c*) accumulation of arsenic in the atmosphere
(*d*) release of human organic wastes into drinking water

93. An element in soil will be considered as a trace element if its concentration is
(*a*) 1 – 2 wt %
(*b*) < 0.1 wt %
(*c*) > 2 wt %
(*d*) < 1 wt %

94. Lead in water can cause :
(*a*) kidneys damage
(*b*) hair falling
(*c*) eye disease
(*d*) minimata's disease

95. Warm ocean surge or Peru current that recurs after 5 – 8 years in East Pacific along South America is :
(*a*) El Nino (*b*) Aye Aye
(*c*) Mangox (*d*) Gulf Stream

96. B.O.D. is related to :
(*a*) Detergents
(*b*) Putrescibility
(*c*) Inorganic pollutants
(*d*) Organic pollutants

97. B.O.D. of a river was found to be very low, this means water :
(*a*) was clean
(*b*) was polluted
(*c*) contains algae
(*d*) contains other dissolved minerals

98. Indiscriminate use of fertilisers causes :
(*a*) Air pollution (*b*) Water pollution
(*c*) Land pollution (*d*) All of the above

99. Most abundant water pollutant is :
(*a*) Detergents (*b*) Pesticides
(*c*) Industrial wastes (*d*) Ammonia

100. Which of these has largest river basin?
(*a*) Brahmaputra (*b*) Ganga
(*c*) Godavari (*d*) Sutlej

101. National Institute of Oceanography is located at :
(*a*) Mumbai (*b*) Panaji
(*c*) Chennai (*d*) Lucknow

102. Major aerosol pollutant in jet plane emission is :
(*a*) Sulphur dioxide
(*b*) Carbon monoxide
(*c*) Methane
(*d*) Fluorocarbon

103. What will happen if our water resources are continued to be polluted by industrial wastes?
(*a*) Sufficient food will not be available to water organisms
(*b*) Sufficient O_2 will not be available to water organisms
(*c*) B.O.D. value of water will decrease
(*d*) Drinking water will not be available

104. Terrestrial life would become impossible with
(*a*) Change in orbit of earth
(*b*) Change in atmosphere permitting all solar radiations to reach lithosphere
(*c*) Disappearance of moon
(*d*) Decrease in mean annual temperature by 10°C

105. Disease aggravated by pollution is :
(*a*) Scurvy (*b*) Rheumatism
(*c*) Haemophillia (*d*) Bronchitis

106. Which one of the following has the highest surface tension :
(*a*) oil (*b*) water
(*c*) milk (*d*) None of the above

107. Biopiracy is related to which of the following?
(*a*) Bioresources
(*b*) Traditional knowledge
(*c*) Biomolecules are regarding bioresources genes isolated from bioresources
(*d*) All of the above

108. Which of the following statement is incorrect?
(*a*) Bioethics is a set of standards that may be used to regulate our activities in relation to biological world?
(*b*) A biowar is the case of biological weapor against humans and or their crops and animals
(*c*) Recombinant DNA technology is used to produce transgenic organisn
(*d*) Genetic engineering has failed in the development of crop varieties resistant to certain insects and diseases

109. Reservoir infection is :
(*a*) soil, water and air
(*b*) site where pathogens reside without causing any damage
(*c*) another animal
(*d*) another person who is suffering

110. Forest Research Institute is situated at :
(*a*) Shimla (*b*) Dehradun
(*c*) New Delhi (*d*) Coimbatore

111. Greatest problem in the water conservation is to reduce the amount of :
(*a*) Ground water (*b*) Precipitation
(*c*) Evaporation (*d*) Run off water

112. Water is resource considered to be most :
(*a*) renewable resource
(*b*) non renewable
(*c*) degradable but maintainable
(*d*) non-degradable

113. Largsest amount of fresh water occurs :
(*a*) as under ground water
(*b*) in lakes and streams
(*c*) as polar ice and glaciers
(*d*) in rivers

114. The largest amount of fresh water on our planet is *available* from to us :
(*a*) lakes and streams
(*b*) polar icecaps and glaciers
(*c*) rivers
(*d*) underground

115. Main source of water to soil is :
(*a*) river
(*b*) canals
(*c*) rain
(*d*) underground water

116. Reservoirs, lakes, ponds, rivers and canals contains how much precentage of fresh water :
(*a*) 77.2% (*b*) 22.4%
(*c*) 0.36% (*d*) 30.3%

117. Precentage of fresh water in hydrosphere is
(*a*) 10% (*b*) 25%
(*c*) 3% (*d*) 17%

118. Bio-indicator of underground waer is
(*a*) *Impatiens blasamina*
(*b*) *Prosopis cineraria.*
(*c*) *Astragalus*
(*d*) *Haplopappus*

119. Which of the plants is a hydrophyte?
(*a*) *Hydrilla* (*b*) Mango
(*c*) *Cuscuta* (*d*) *Opuntia*

120. Demineralised water is purified water free from :
(*a*) Cations
(*b*) Anions
(*c*) Both (*a*) and (*b*)
(*d*) All dissolved impurities

121. Which one of the following is universal solvent :
(*a*) Acetone (*b*) Chloroform
(*c*) Water (*d*) None of these

ANSWERS

1	2	3	4	5	6	7	8	9	10
(*d*)	(*d*)	(*c*)	(*d*)	(*c*)	(*b*)	(*c*)	(*b*)	(*b*)	(*b*)
11	**12**	**13**	**14**	**15**	**16**	**17**	**18**	**19**	**20**
(*a*)	(*a*)	(*a*)	(*b*)	(*b*)	(*b*)	(*d*)	(*a*)	(*d*)	(*a*)
21	**22**	**23**	**24**	**25**	**26**	**27**	**28**	**29**	**30**
(*d*)	(*c*)	(*a*)	(*b*)	(*b*)	(*a*)	(*a*)	(*a*)	(*d*)	(*a*)
31	**32**	**33**	**34**	**35**	**36**	**37**	**38**	**39**	**40**
(*d*)	(*b*)	(*d*)	(*c*)	(*a*)	(*c*)	(*d*)	(*a*)	(*c*)	(*c*)
41	**42**	**43**	**44**	**45**	**46**	**47**	**48**	**49**	**50**
(*c*)	(*c*)	(*d*)	(*b*)	(*c*)	(*c*)	(*b*)	(*b*)	(*d*)	(*a*)
51	**52**	**53**	**54**	**55**	**56**	**57**	**58**	**59**	**60**
(*b*)	(*a*)	(*b*)	(*a*)	(*c*)	(*d*)	(*c*)	(*c*)	(*b*)	(*a*)
61	**62**	**63**	**64**	**65**	**66**	**67**	**68**	**69**	**70**
(*d*)	(*b*)	(*b*)	(*a*)	(*c*)	(*b*)	(*c*)	(*c*)	(*c*)	(*b*)
71	**72**	**73**	**74**	**75**	**76**	**77**	**78**	**79**	**80**
(*a*)	(*c*)	(*d*)	(*a*)	(*b*)	(*c*)	(*d*)	(*c*)	(*a*)	(*a*)
81	**82**	**83**	**84**	**85**	**86**	**87**	**88**	**89**	**90**
(*a*)	(*b*)	(*b*)	(*d*)	(*d*)	(*c*)	(*a*)	(*c*)	(*d*)	(*c*)

91	92	93	94	95	96	97	98	99	100
(*d*)	(*a*)	(*b*)	(*a*)	(*a*)	(*d*)	(*a*)	(*b*)	(*c*)	(*b*)
101	**102**	**103**	**104**	**105**	**106**	**107**	**108**	**109**	**110**
(*b*)	(*d*)	(*b*)	(*b*)	(*d*)	(*b*)	(*a*)	(*d*)	(*b*)	(*b*)
111	**112**	**113**	**114**	**115**	**116**	**117**	**118**	**119**	**120**
(*c*)	(*c*)	(*c*)	(*d*)	(*c*)	(*c*)	(*c*)	(*b*)	(*a*)	(*c*)
121									
(*c*)									

10

AIR POLLUTION

1. Air pollution is maximum in :
   (*a*) Sewage and pesticides
   (*b*) Sewage and effluents
   (*c*) Detergents and pesticides
   (*d*) Automobile exhaust and chemicals from industries.

2. Air pollutant photochemical oxidants include :
   (*a*) Nitrous oxide, nitric acid and nitric oxide
   (*b*) Oxygen, chlorine and nitric acid
   (*c*) Ozone, peroxyacetyl nitrate and aldehydes
   (*d*) Carbon monoxide and sulphur dioxide

3. A person has impaired nervous system and signs of madness due to continued intake of metal contaminated water. The metal is :
   (*a*) Mercury (*b*) Calcium
   (*c*) Manganese (*d*) Lead

4. Methane gas producing field is :
   (*a*) Wheat field (*b*) Paddy field
   (*c*) Cotton field (*d*) Groundnut field

5. Photochemical smog is caused by :
   (*a*) CO (*b*) CO_2
   (*c*) O_3 (*d*) NO_2

6. "By burning fossil fuels, we release CO_2 and other heat absorbing gases that cause global warming and may bring about Sea Level rise and catastrophic climatic changes." The result will be :
   (*a*) Acid rain
   (*b*) Global warming
   (*c*) Meteroirites falling
   (*d*) None of these

7. Which of the following is damaging the layers in the stratosphere?
   (*a*) O_3 (*b*) CFCs
   (*c*) CF_2–CF_2 (*d*) $CaOCl_2$

8. Ozone day is :
   (*a*) January, 30 (*b*) September, 16
   (*c*) April, 21 (*d*) December, 25

9. Aerosols having carbon and fluorine compounds are chiefly released by :
   (*a*) Refineries (*b*) Automobiles
   (*c*) Industries (*d*) Jets

10. Oxides of sulphur and nitrogen are important pollutants of :
    (*a*) Water (*b*) Air
    (*c*) Soil (*d*) All of the above

11. Air pollution affects :
    (*a*) Leaves (*b*) Roots
    (*c*) Stem (*d*) Flowers

12. Which pollutant causes leaf curling?
    (*a*) CO (*b*) H_2S
    (*c*) O_3 (*d*) SO_2

13. How much gas an average adult human inhale?
    (*a*) 13.6 kg (*b*) 10 kg
    (*c*) $5m^3/kg$ (*d*) $6m^3/kg$

14. Any particles of dispersed matter, solid or liquid, that are larger than individual molecules, are :
    (*a*) SO_2 (*b*) Particulates
    (*c*) CFCs (*d*) Methane

15. Black lung, Urban emphysema etc. are mainly due to :
    (*a*) Methane (*b*) SO_2
    (*c*) Particulates (*d*) All of these

16. The main cause of acid rain (acid precipitation) is :
(*a*) SO_2 (*b*) NO_2
(*c*) CH_4 (*d*) All of these

17. Which is *true* regarding the contamination of human body with SO_2?
(*a*) Death can occur in just 30 seconds at very low conc. as 3 ppm
(*b*) Eyes can't see with 20 seconds of contact
(*c*) No effect can occur on skin
(*d*) All of the above

18. Technically, when we can term the rain as *acid rain* :
(*a*) when its pH is below 5.0
(*b*) when it has ($CH_4 + CO_2$)
(*c*) when its colour is yellow
(*d*) All of the above

19. Which will be more sensitive to acidity?
(*a*) Microbes (*b*) Algae
(*c*) Game fishes (*d*) None of these

20. Which is/are of the following corroding the vital support system on which all life depends?
(*a*) Over-exploitation of natural resources
(*b*) Pollution
(*c*) Both of the above
(*d*) None of the above

21. Which of the following air pollutants is the chief cause of acidic rains?
(*a*) H_2S (*b*) CO
(*c*) SO_2 (*d*) CO_2

22. During combustion of fuels, gases released are :
(*a*) CO_2 and CO
(*b*) CO, CO_2 and SO_2
(*c*) CO_2, CO, SO_2 and H_2O
(*d*) CO_2, CO, H_2S and SO_2

23. Air pollution causes :
(*a*) skin diseases (*b*) bronchitis
(*c*) blood cancer (*d*) blood pressure

24. The method for converting combustible gaseous compounds CO_2 and H_2O, halogen to HX and S to SO_2, is :
(*a*) Thermal Oxidation method
(*b*) Adsorption method
(*c*) Chemical conversion method
(*d*) Global warming

25. Chemical conversion processes are often employed for collection of :
(*a*) particulate (*b*) industrial wastes
(*c*) gaseous pollutants (*d*) All of the above

26. Growing more trees help to :
(*a*) reduce CO_2 and increase O_2 in environment
(*b*) reduce O_2 in the environment
(*c*) increase CO_2 in the environment
(*d*) reduce SO_2 in the environment

27. The presence of which of the following gases in the air checks the ultraviolet light from sunlight?
(*a*) SO_2 (*b*) O_3
(*c*) NO_2 (*d*) CO_2

28. Which of the following does *not* increase pollution?
(*a*) Plantation of trees
(*b*) Increase in human population
(*c*) Rapid urbanisation
(*d*) Rapid industrialisation

29. Component of smog is :
(*a*) O_3 (*b*) PAN
(*c*) PPN and PBN (*d*) Both (*a*) and (*b*)

30. In which industry, workers suffer from Byssinosis?
(*a*) Cardboard (*b*) Textile
(*c*) Plastic (*d*) Paper

31. Spraying of DDT on crops produces pollution of :
(*a*) air only (*b*) air and soil
(*c*) air, soil and water (*d*) air and water.

32. The most widely existing pollutant in the air is :
(*a*) CO (*b*) CO_2
(*c*) SO_2 (*d*) None of the above

33. Ozone layer is chiefly disturbed by :
(*a*) large number of automobiles
(*b*) large number of factories

(*c*) supersonic jets
(*d*) chimney exhausts

34. Carbon monoxide is a very harmful pollutant because it :
(*a*) inactivates nerves
(*b*) combines with oxygen
(*c*) forms a stable compound with haemoglobin
(*d*) inhibits Krebs' cycle

35. The pollutants emitted by jet aeroplanes in outer atmosphere as fluorocarbons are known as :
(*a*) photochemical oxidants
(*b*) aerosols
(*c*) smog
(*d*) None of these

36. SO_2 pollution can be controlled by all the methods except by :
(*a*) removing sulphur after combustion
(*b*) precombustion disulphurisation
(*c*) electricity
(*d*) photochemical oxidants

37. Automobiles discharge hydrocarbons and nitrous oxide in atmosphere which is further converted to :
(*a*) carbon monoxide
(*b*) ozone and other pollutants
(*c*) radioactive substance
(*d*) hydrochloric acid and nitrogen dioxide

38. In Kolkata adults are suffering from bronchitis TB, it is due to :
(*a*) impure water (*b*) adulterated food
(*c*) polluted air (*d*) polluted soil

39. Air pollution is highest in :
(*a*) Kolkata (*b*) Lucknow
(*c*) Panchmarhi (*d*) Bhopal

40. The presence of ozone in the atmosphere of earth :
(*a*) hinders higher rate of photosynthesis
(*b*) has been responsible for increasing the average global temperature in recent past
(*c*) helps in checking the ultra-violet rays to reach earth
(*d*) is advantageous since it supplies oxygen for people travelling in jets

41. In Bhopal gas tragedy, the gas released was :
(*a*) methyl isocyanate
(*b*) ethyl isocyanate
(*c*) sodium isocyanate
(*d*) potassium isocyanate

42. Aerosols are :
(*a*) chemicals released in air in the form of mist or vapour with force
(*b*) gases released from exhaust pump
(*c*) mixture of carbon particles and mist
(*d*) soluble effluents released in water

43. Component of living cell affected by pollutant SO_2 is :
(*a*) nucleus
(*b*) all cell membrane system
(*c*) cell wall
(*d*) membrane system

44. Which of the following helps in reducing the atmosphere burden of SPM?
(*a*) H_2O (*b*) CO_2
(*c*) CO (*d*) CFCs

45. Which can be the most destructive to the nervous system?
(*a*) SO_2 (*b*) CO
(*c*) Lead (*d*) All of these

46. Why did the human exposure to airborne lead decrease more than 90% since 2000 in India?
(*a*) Use of Lead-free petrol increased
(*b*) Use of Lead-free battery
(*c*) Both (a) and (b)
(*d*) None of these

47. Ozone is formed in the :
(*a*) Troposphere (*b*) Stratosphere
(*c*) Thermosphere (*d*) Mesosphere

48. Ozone is formed when high-energy .... splits O_2 into (O).
(*a*) UV radiation
(*b*) Infra-Red radiation
(*c*) Both of these
(*d*) None of these

49. Why the ozone in necessary?
(*a*) It facts as a shield that absorbs biologically dangerous UV-radiation
(*b*) It acts as a chemical reactant

(*c*) It is easily combined with CFCs
(*d*) All of the above

50. Ozone layer destroying chemicals are :
(*a*) Chlorofluorocarbons
(*b*) CH_4 and CO_2
(*c*) SO_2 and NO_2
(*d*) NO_2 and CH_4

51. In big cities automobiles are responsible for air pollution :
(*a*) 50% (*b*) 70%
(*c*) 80% (*d*) 100%

52. An important source of aerosol in upper atmosphere is :
(*a*) Sea
(*b*) Air
(*c*) Jet aeroplane emission
(*d*) Soil

53. Enriched air, if inhaled for long time, causes :
(*a*) allergy
(*b*) bronchitis
(*c*) disturbance of psychomotor function
(*d*) diarrhoea

54. Which wavelength of ultraviolet light of sunlight combine with ozone molecule?
(*a*) Ultraviolet-A (*b*) Ultraviolet-C
(*c*) Ultraviolet-B (*d*) Ultraviolet-D

55. Natural sink of stratospheric ozone is :
(*a*) Sulphuric dioxide
(*b*) Sulphur fluxes of oceans
(*c*) Freons
(*d*) HCFCs

56. Major source of methane in India is :
(*a*) Rice fields
(*b*) Sugarcane plantation
(*c*) Wheat fields
(*d*) Fruit orchards

57. Ozone hole is maximum over :
(*a*) Europe
(*b*) Antarctica
(*c*) India
(*d*) Africa

58. In coming years, skin related disorders will become more common due to :
(*a*) Excessive use of detergents
(*b*) Water pollution
(*c*) Air pollution
(*d*) Depletion of ozone layer

59. In particular, humans had been injecting enormous quantities of ozone-destroying substances into atmosphere, especially a class of chemical known as :
(*a*) Aerosol spray
(*b*) Chlorofluorocarbons
(*c*) Freons
(*d*) Radionuclides

60. Which of the following produce another air pollutant by reacting with oxides of nitrogen in presence of sunlight?
(*a*) O_3 (*b*) SO_2
(*c*) HCl (*d*) HCN gas

61. Sampling in which elements are grouped together because they share certain features :
(*a*) stratified sampling
(*b*) cluster sampling
(*c*) systematic sampling
(*d*) random sampling

62. The air pollutants react with lead based paints, causing decolouration is :
(*a*) SO_2 (*b*) H_2SO_4
(*c*) H_2S (*d*) HNO_3

63. The most severe pollutant of metals and materials is :
(*a*) SO_2 (*b*) HNO_3
(*c*) H_2SO_4 (*d*) $KMnO_4$

64. Aitken particles are :
(*a*) activated in humid air
(*b*) clouds condensed nuclei
(*c*) hygroscopic particles
(*d*) All of the above

65. The **true** statement/s about acid rain is/are :
(*a*) It has distinct effect on soil microbiology and environmental chemistry

(*b*) The acid pollutants emitted in one country may be deposited as acid precipitation in several countries
(*c*) Acid rain affects both aquatic system as well as vegetation
(*d*) All of the above

66. The major pollutant/parts in petrol based vehicles is/are :
(*a*) fuel tank (*b*) crankcase
(*c*) carburator (*d*) All of the above

67. Match the following :

Column A (Pollution)	Column B (Effects on Health)
A. Sulphur dioxide	1. Irritation of eyes, cough and breath problems
B. Carbon monoxide	2. Reduction in O_2 carrying capacity of blood
C. Ammonia	3. Irritation in mucus membrane
D. SPM	4. Respiratory diseases

Codes :

	A	B	C	D
(*a*)	4	3	1	2
(*b*)	2	3	1	4
(*c*)	4	1	3	2
(*d*)	1	2	3	4

68. Major health effects due to depletion of ozone layer is/are :
(*a*) increase in eye cataracts and mutation
(*b*) increase in skin cancer and melonema
(*c*) decrease in growth of ocean flora and fauna
(*d*) All of the above

69. The main source of CO in the atmosphere is :
(*a*) incomplete burning of automobile petrol
(*b*) conversion of limestone into cement
(*c*) decomposition of dead organic matter
(*d*) respiration and burning of fossil fuels

70. The main cause of Acid rain is
(*a*) SO_2 (*b*) NO_2
(*c*) CH_4 (*d*) All of the above

71. Which of the following is **TRUE** about cold front?
(*a*) They are least destructive
(*b*) They are associated with torrential rains
(*c*) It is the zone where cold air is invading warm air zone
(*d*) All of the above

72. Certain epiphytic lichens indicate changing levels of atmospheric pollution, specially of :
(*a*) SO_2 (*b*) CO_2
(*c*) NO_2 (*d*) SO_3

73. The biggest oil refinery in India is at :
(*a*) Vishakhapatnam
(*b*) Koyali
(*c*) Baruani
(*d*) Mathura

74. Every individual person inhales air daily about :
(*a*) 1 kg (*b*) 16 kg
(*c*) 100 litres (*d*) 1 litre

75. Colourless, odourless and non-corrosive air pollutants are :
(*a*) ozones (*b*) sulphur dioxide
(*c*) carbon dioxide (*d*) carbon monoxide

76. Catalytic incinerators are advantageous as :
(*a*) they cool the atmosphere
(*b*) they require lower temperature
(*c*) they require high temperature
(*d*) they require dissolved oxygen

77. Carbon monoxide is pollutant as it :
(*a*) Inactivates nerves
(*b*) Inhibits glycolysis
(*c*) Combines with oxygen
(*d*) Combines with haemoglobin

78. Air pollutants that produce photochemical oxidants include :
(*a*) CO_2, CO and SO_2
(*b*) Nitrous oxide, nitric oxide and nitric acid
(*c*) Oxygen, chlorine and nitric acid
(*d*) Ozone, chlorine and sulphur dioxide

79. Acid rains are produced by :
(*a*) Excess NO_2 and SO_2 from burning fossil fuels

(*b*) Excess production of NH_3 by industry and coal gas
(*c*) Excess release of carbon monoxide by incomplete combustion
(*d*) Excess formation of CO_2 by combustion

80. Carbon monoxide, emitted by automobiles, prevents transport of oxygen in body due to :
(*a*) Combining with oxygen to form carbon dioxide
(*b*) Destruction of haemoglobin
(*c*) Preventing reaction between oxygen and haemoglobin
(*d*) Forming stable compound with haemoglobin.

81. Most hazardous metal pollutant of automobile exhaust is :
(*a*) Mercury (*b*) Lead
(*c*) Cadmium (*d*) Copper

82. Photochemical smog always contains :
(*a*) Ozone (*b*) Methane
(*c*) Carbon monoxide (*d*) Carbon dioxide

83. Depletion of ozone layer is due to :
(*a*) Oxides of nitrogen
(*b*) Oxides of carbon
(*c*) Oxides of sulphur
(*d*) None of the above

84. Which of the following is a largest source of formaldehyde vapour pollution in a room?
(*a*) Utensil (*b*) Furniture
(*c*) Cooking range (*d*) Book

85. It is said **Taj** may be destroyed due to :
(*a*) flood in Yamuna river
(*b*) decomposition of marble as a result of high temperature
(*c*) air pollutants released from oil refinery of Mathura
(*d*) All of the above

86. Result of ozone hole is :
(*a*) Green house effect
(*b*) Global warming
(*c*) Acid rain
(*d*) UV radiations reach the earth

87. Necrosis is :
(*a*) the reduction of chlorophyll from leaf, that results in the disappearance of green colour
(*b*) the killing of tissues or destruction of leaf tissues or severe drying
(*c*) both of the above
(*d*) None of the above

88. Chlorosis is :
(*a*) the killing of tissues
(*b*) destruction of leaf tissues
(*c*) severe drying
(*d*) the reduction of chlorophyll from leaf

89. Lead is mainly comes from :
(*a*) Vehicular pollution
(*b*) Water pollution
(*c*) Increasing population
(*d*) All of the above

90. Meridional motions of air become zonal like trade winds, temperature and polar winds due to :
(*a*) wind transport of heat
(*b*) earth's rotation around its axis
(*c*) heating of earth
(*d*) gross energy of earth

91. In a small town, pasture is contaminated with air borne fluorides. Grazing animals of that area will suffer from :
(*a*) Goitre disease
(*b*) Thyroid disease
(*c*) Dental disease
(*d*) Beri-beri

92. A secondary pollutant is :
(*a*) CO (*b*) CO_2
(*c*) PAN (*d*) Aerosol

93. Ozone hole refers to :
(*a*) Hole in ozone layers
(*b*) Reduction in thickness of ozone layer in stratosphere
(*c*) Reduction of thickness of ozone in troposphere
(*d*) Increase concentration of ozone

94. Photochemical smog is related to pollution of :
(*a*) Air (*b*) Water
(*c*) Soil (*d*) Nostoc

95. The *correct* pair regarding the air quality *monitoring* technique is :
(*a*) O_3 → Utraviolet photometry
(*b*) SO_2 → Diffusion tube
(*c*) NO_2 → Infrared absorption
(*d*) C, N, Polyurethrane filter

96. Ozone layer of upper atmosphere is being destroyed by :
(*a*) Chlorofluorocarbon
(*b*) SO_2
(*c*) Photochemical oxidants/O_2 and CO_2
(*d*) Smog

97. SO_2 pollution is indicated by :
(*a*) *Deschampsia* (grasses)
(*b*) *Sphagnum* (mosses)
(*c*) *Usnea* (lichens)
(*d*) *Cucurbita* (climbers)

98. Increased asthmatic attacks in certain seasons are related to :
(*a*) Inhalation of seasonal pollen
(*b*) Eating of seasonal vegetables
(*c*) Low temperature
(*d*) Wet and dry environment

99. Peeling of ozone umbrella is due to :
(*a*) CFCs (*b*) PAN
(*c*) CO_2 (*d*) Coal burning

100. Ozone layer of stratosphere requires protection from indiscriminate use of :
(*a*) Fungicides, insecticides, bactericides and medicines
(*b*) Aerosols and high flying jets
(*c*) Atomic explosions and industrial wastes
(*d*) Baloons and turbo-prop aeroplanes

101. Which of the following is a secondary air pollutant?
(*a*) PAN (*b*) Aerosol
(*c*) NO_2 (*d*) SO_2

102. Smog produces :
(*a*) NO_2 (*b*) CH_4
(*c*) Aluminium ion (*d*) NO_2

103. The major thermal power station fed on natural gas is at :
(*a*) Lunej (*b*) Trombay
(*c*) Naharkatiya (*d*) Digboi

104. Acid rain is mainly caused by increased concentration (in atmosphere) of :
(*a*) NO_2 and SO_2 (*b*) NH_3 and SO_3
(*c*) Ozone and dust (*d*) CO and CO_2

105. Gases commonly referred to as green house gases are :
(*a*) Chlorofluorocarbons, CO_2, NH_3 and N_2
(*b*) CO_2, chlorofluorocarbons, CH_4 and NO_2
(*c*) CH_4, N_2, CO_2 and NH_3
(*d*) CO_2, O_2, NO_2 and NH_3

106. Today concentration of green house gases is high because of :
(*a*) deforestation
(*b*) increased combustion of oil and coal
(*c*) use of refrigerator
(*d*) All of the above

107. Some effects of SO_2 and its transformation production plants include :
(*a*) Golgibody destruction
(*b*) Chlorophyll destruction
(*c*) Plasmolysis
(*d*) None of these

108. Which is not a pollutant from exhaust of motor vehicle?
(*a*) Hydrocarbon gas (*b*) Fly ash
(*c*) SO_2 (*d*) CO

109. Which one of the following is not pollutant?
(*a*) CO_2 (*b*) CO
(*c*) SO_2 (*d*) NO_2

110. Acid rain is caused by :
(*a*) Excess production of coal gas
(*b*) Excess release of CO_2 due to increasing combustion and respiration
(*c*) Excess release of SO_2 and NO_2 from burning fossil fuels
(*d*) Excess production of gaseous hydrocarbons

111. SO_2 pollution is indicated by destruction of :
(*a*) Climbers (*b*) Lichens
(*c*) Mosses (*d*) Grasses

112. Freon is :
(*a*) Ferrous sulphide pollutant
(*b*) Chlorofluorocarbon
(*c*) Iron containing polycyclic hydrocarbons
(*d*) Metal fluoride

113. Maximum atmospheric NO_2 pollution is found in :
(*a*) Baroda (*b*) Chennai
(*c*) Nagpur (*d*) Mumbai

114. Photochemical smog brings about :
(*a*) Defoliation
(*b*) Bleaching and blazing of foliage
(*c*) Floral bud shedding
(*d*) Discolouration and curling of petals

115. Water soaked appearance of leaves due to sulphur dioxide pollution is caused by :
(*a*) Destruction of chlorophyll
(*b*) Damage to membranes
(*c*) Both (*a*) and (*b*)
(*d*) Corrosive action over metals

116. In addition to SO_2, metals and textiles are damaged by
(*a*) Nitrogen oxides (*b*) Fluorides
(*c*) Carbon monoxide (*d*) Aldehydes

117. Photochemical reaction of nitrogen oxides with unsaturation hydrocarbons produces :
(*a*) Methyl isocyanate (*b*) Phosgene
(*c*) Benzpyrene (*d*) Peroxy-acyl nitrates

118. Level of atmospheric CO_2 has increased from :
(*a*) 290 ppm to 340 ppm
(*b*) 250 ppm to 300 ppm
(*c*) 300 ppm to 350 ppm
(*d*) 330 ppm to 350 ppm

119. Which of the following is correct about attribute data in Geographic Information System ?
(*a*) Attributes are pieces of data that are connected or related to the points, lines or polygons mapped in the GIS.
(*b*) Attribute data can be analysed to determine patterns of importance.
(*c*) Attribute data is entered directly into a database where it is associated with element data.
(*d*) All of the above

120. Gravity settling tanks/porous filters are used to remove particles larger than :
(*a*) 2 μm (*b*) 50 μm
(*c*) 20 μm (*d*) 10 μm

121. Electrostatic precipitators are employed to remove particulate pollutants of the size of :
(*a*) 5 – 20 μm (*b*) 20 – 50 μm
(*c*) 50 μm and larger (*d*) 0.5 – 5.0 μm

122. Pollutant released by jet planes is :
(*a*) Fog (*b*) Aerosol
(*c*) Smog (*d*) Colloid

123. Carbon monoxide kills because it destroys :
(*a*) Haemoglobin (*b*) Phytochrome
(*c*) Cytochrome (*d*) Both (*a*) and (*b*)

124. Pollutant of automobile exhausts that affect nervous system/produces mental diseases is :
(*a*) Mercury (*b*) Lead
(*c*) Nitrogen oxide (*d*) Sulphur oxide

125. SO_2 and NO_2 produce pollution by increasing :
(*a*) Alkalinity (*b*) Acidity
(*c*) Neutrality (*d*) Buffer action

126. Major air pollutants in Mumbai and Kolkata are :
(*a*) Marsh gas and algal spores
(*b*) O_3
(*c*) Hydrocarbons and hot air
(*d*) CO and oxides of sulphur

127. Which will not cause atmospheric pollution?
(*a*) SO_2 (*b*) CO_2
(*c*) CO (*d*) H_2

128. Which pollutant is absent in automobile exhausts?
(*a*) Flyash
(*b*) Unburnt hydrocarbons
(*c*) Carbon monoxide
(*d*) Nitrogen oxides

129. Chlorofluorocarbon releases a chemical harmful to ozone :
(*a*) Fluorine (*b*) Chlorine
(*c*) Nitrogen peroxide (*d*) Sulphur dioxide

130. Air pollution is not caused by :
(*a*) Pollen grains
(*b*) Hydroelectric power
(*c*) Industries
(*d*) Automobiles

131. Carbon monoxide is harmful to human beings as it is :
(*a*) Carcinogenic
(*b*) Antagonistic to CO_2
(*c*) With higher affinity for haemoglobin as compared to oxygen
(*d*) Destructive to O_3

132. Gas causing maximum destruction of ozone is
(*a*) Liquid NH_3 (*b*) SO_2
(*c*) CH_4 (*d*) CO

133. Atmospheric carbon monoxide concentration becomes harmful at
(*a*) 0.5, 2 mm Hg (*b*) 0.4, 7 mm Hg
(*c*) 0.3, 5 mm Hg (*d*) 0.1, 0.7 mm Hg

134. At Nadir, the LISS – IV camera in IRS-P6 has a spatial resolution of
(*a*) 5.8 m (*b*) 5.9 m
(*c*) 5.7 m (*d*) 5.6 m

135. Which is not dangerous for life?
(*a*) Nuclear blast
(*b*) Deforestation
(*c*) Ozone layer
(*d*) Biopollutants

136. Heat islands are formed by :
(*a*) Water pollution (*b*) Air pollution
(*c*) Land pollution (*d*) All of the above

137. Main air pollutant is :
(*a*) CO (*b*) CO_2
(*c*) NO_2 (*d*) SO_2

138. Most inhabitants of Kolkata suffer from bronchitis. It is due to excess :
(*a*) Adulteration of food
(*b*) Impurity of water
(*c*) Polluted air
(*d*) Polluted soil

139. Atmospheric pollutants formed by human activities constitute of the total :
(*a*) 95% (*b*) 75%
(*c*) 25% (*d*) 0.05%

140. Most atmospheric pollutants do not rise above :
(*a*) 600 m (*b*) 1000 m
(*c*) 2000 m (*d*) 200 m

141. Aerosol is a system of colloidal particles having a size of :
(*a*) 5 μm (*b*) 1-2 μm
(*c*) Less than 1μm (*d*) More than 10 μm

142. A secondary pollutant is :
(*a*) O_3 (*b*) CO
(*c*) CH_4 (*d*) Pb

143. A colourless, non-irritant, highly toxic gas that impairs respiration is :
(*a*) SO_2 (*b*) NO_2
(*c*) CO_2 (*d*) CO

144. Lead pollution in Indian cities is mainly due to :
(*a*) Lead pencils
(*b*) Batteries
(*c*) Automobiles
(*d*) Electronic gadgets

145. Pollutant likely to deplete ozone layer is
(*a*) CO
(*b*) Nitrogen oxides
(*c*) Chlorofluorocarbons
(*d*) Both (*b*) and (*c*)

146. Atmospheric pollutant is :
(*a*) CO_2 (*b*) CO
(*c*) O_2 (*d*) N_2

147. Smog is produced due to :
(*a*) Air and metal dust
(*b*) Water and nitrogen oxide
(*c*) Smoke and fog
(*d*) None of the above

148. The photochemical smog is formed by :
(*a*) Nitrogen oxides
(*b*) Hydrocarbons
(*c*) Both (*a*) and (*b*)
(*d*) Solar radiations upon nitrogen oxides and hydrocarbons

149. O_3 promotes :
(*a*) Oxidation of biochemicals
(*b*) Destruction of chlorenchyma
(*c*) Both (*a*) and (*b*)
(*d*) Growth of plants

150. In metropolitan cities the automobiles cause air pollution :
(*a*) 80% (*b*) 60%
(*c*) 50% (*d*) 100%

151. Bhopal gas tragedy was due to :
(*a*) Air pollution (*b*) Soil pollution
(*c*) Water pollution (*d*) None of the above

152. Maximum air pollution is at :
(*a*) Delhi (*b*) Bhopal
(*c*) Kolkata (*d*) Mumbai

153. Lead is considered mainly :
(*a*) Soil pollutant (*b*) Water pollutant
(*c*) Air pollutant (*d*) Noise pollutant

154. Aerosols decrease primary productivity by
(*a*) Decreasing O_2 concentration
(*b*) Competing with CO_2
(*c*) Preventing N_2 fixation
(*d*) Reducing photosynthesis

155. Chief air pollutant which is likely to deplete ozone layer is :
(*a*) Sulphur dioxide
(*b*) Carbon dioxide
(*c*) Both (*a*) and (*b*)
(*d*) Nitrogen oxides and fluorocarbons

156. Which one is not a pollutant normally?
(*a*) Hydrocarbons (*b*) Carbon dioxide
(*c*) Carbon monoxide (*d*) Sulphur dioxide

157. Gas released during Bhopal tragedy was :
(*a*) Methyl isocyanate
(*b*) Potassium isothiocyanate
(*c*) Sodium isothiocyanate
(*d*) Ethyl isothiocyanate

158. Sulphur dioxide affects
(*a*) Cell wall
(*b*) Plasmodesmata
(*c*) All membrane systems
(*d*) Nucleus

159. Formation of ozone is maximum over :
(*a*) India (*b*) Africa
(*c*) Antarctica (*d*) Europe

160. Water pollution mainly caused by
(*a*) growth of phytoplanktons
(*b*) excessive rain
(*c*) industrial effluents
(*d*) decay of bodies of aquatic animals

161. PAN (peroxyacetyl nitrate)
(*a*) decreases the rate of photosynthesis
(*b*) increases the rate of photosynthesis
(*c*) decreases the rate of transpiration
(*d*) increases the rate of translocation

162. Natural sink of stratospheric ozone layer is :
(*a*) Freon
(*b*) Sulphur flux of oceans
(*c*) SO_2
(*d*) HCF

163. UNEP stands for :
(*a*) United Nations Educational Programme
(*b*) United Nations Environmental Programme
(*c*) United Nations Ecological Programme
(*d*) United Nations Ecotype Programme

164. Ozone depletion in stratosphere shall result in
(*a*) Forest fires
(*b*) Increased incidence of skin cancer
(*c*) Global warming
(*d*) None of the above

165. Which one of the following dissolves more rapidly in blood haemoglobin than oxygen?
(*a*) Ozone (*b*) Nitrous oxide
(*c*) Sulphure dioxide (*d*) Carbon monoxide

166. Which of the following forms a toxic substance in blood by combining with haemoglobin?
(*a*) Carbon dioxide (*b*) Carbon monoxide
(*c*) Oxygen (*d*) Methane

167. Jet aeroplane releases pollutants in air called
(*a*) Smog
(*b*) Photochemical oxidants
(*c*) Aerosols
(*d*) Algae and bacteria

168. Fertilizers, pesticides and insecticides may cause
(*a*) Air pollution (*b*) Water pollution
(*c*) Both (*a*) and (*b*) (*d*) None of the above

169. The gas released in Bhopal tragedy was :
(*a*) MIC (*b*) $COCl_2$
(*c*) Phosgene (*d*) None of the above

170. Pollutants directly emanating from human activities are
(*a*) Quantitative pollutants
(*b*) Qualitative pollutants
(*c*) Air pollutants
(*d*) Water pollutants

171. World Environment Day is :
(*a*) 5th June (*b*) 6th June
(*c*) 15th June (*d*) None of these

172. Checking of reradiating heat by atmospheric dust, water vapour, ozone, CO_2 etc. is known as :
(*a*) green house effect (*b*) ozone layer effect
(*c*) solar effect (*d*) radioactive effect

173. Which of the following is true?
(*a*) Reduction in fossil fuel buring will lessen the global warming
(*b*) Global warming is of no immediate concern
(*c*) Since many gases other than CO_2 are responsible for green house effect, deforestation will not decrease global warming
(*d*) Global warming is so imminent that nothing can be done

174. What do you understand by green house effect?
(*a*) decrease in temperature due to decrease in oxygen concentration
(*b*) decrease in temperature due to decrease in CO_2 concentration of the atmosphere
(*c*) increase in temperature due to increase in oxygen concentration of the atmosphere
(*d*) increase in temperature due to increase in CO_2 concentration of the atmosphere

175. All the following contribute to pollution except
(*a*) automobiles
(*b*) nuclear power plant
(*c*) hydroelectric power plant
(*d*) thermal power plant

176. Lichens are important in the studies on atmospheric pollution because they :
(*a*) are sensitive to pollutants
(*b*) can also grow in greatly polluted atmosphere
(*c*) can readily multiply in polluted atmosphere
(*d*) efficiently purify the atmosphere

177. Smog is
(*a*) smoke and fog
(*b*) other name for dust storm
(*c*) smoke
(*d*) moistened air gases

178. Taj Mahal is threatened due to the effect of :
(*a*) SO_2 (*b*) hydrogen
(*c*) chlorine (*d*) None of these

179. Which of the following is not produced as exhausts of vehicles?
(*a*) CO_2 (*b*) CO
(*c*) Flyash (*d*) SO_2

180. If there were no CO_2 in the earth's atmosphere, the temperature of earth surrounding would be
(*a*) less than the present
(*b*) higher than the present
(*c*) dependent on the amount of oxygen in the atmosphere
(*d*) the same

181. Plant which utilize some pollutants like CO_2, SO_2, etc. are referred to as :
(*a*) scavanger plants (*b*) keystone plants
(*c*) sink plants (*d*) indicator plants

182. Which of the following pollutants is not produced by exhaust of motor vehicles?
(*a*) CO (*b*) Hydrocarbon
(*c*) Flyash (*d*) SO_2

183. Which is *NOT* correctly matched?
(*a*) CNG → Compressed Natural Gas
(*b*) GDP → Gross Domestic Product
(*c*) GNP → Gross National Product
(*d*) LPG → Local Petroleum Gas

184. Ozone hole is caused by :
(*a*) Acetylene
(*b*) Ethylene
(*c*) Chlorofluorocarbons
(*d*) Methane

185. Atmospheric content of CO_2 is :
(*a*) 0.0034% (*b*) 0.034%
(*c*) 0.34% (*d*) 3.4%

186. Stratosphere is devoid of weather phenomena because
(*a*) it is free from moisture and dust
(*b*) it has a maximum temperature of –2°C
(*c*) all the atmosphere ozone is present in this layer
(*d*) All of the above

187. The lowest temperature in the atmosphere is :
(*a*) –90° (*b*) –100°
(*c*) –50° (*d*) None of these

188. Which of the following cities has the highest SO_2 pollution?
(*a*) Milan (*b*) Seoul
(*c*) New Delhi (*d*) New York

189. Increasing skin cancer and high mutation rate are due to :
(*a*) Acid rain (*b*) Ozone depletion
(*c*) CO pollution (*d*) CO_2 pollution

190. SO_2 pollution causes :
(*a*) Plasmolysis
(*b*) Destruction of cell wall
(*c*) Destruction of Golgi bodies
(*d*) Destruction of chlorophyll

191. Lichens indicate pollution by :
(*a*) O_3 (*b*) SO_2
(*c*) NO_2 (*d*) CO

192. SO_2 pollution affects :
(*a*) nucleus (*b*) mitochondria
(*c*) ribosomes (*d*) vacuole

193. Chlorofluoro carbons are air polluting agents. They are produced by :
(*a*) Acid batteries (*b*) Diesel trucks
(*c*) Aerosols (*d*) Jet planes

194. The persons working in Textile factories such as carpet weavers are exposed to which of the following occupational diseases?
(*a*) Asbestosis
(*b*) Asthma and Tuberculosis
(*c*) Silicosis
(*d*) Siderosis

195. Atmosphere of big/metropolitian cities is polluted most by :
(*a*) Automobile exhausts
(*b*) Pesticide residue
(*c*) Household waste
(*d*) Radioactive fall out

196. Which of the following species containing mercury is most toxic?
(*a*) CH_3Hg^+ (*b*) $HgCl_2$
(*c*) Hg_2Cl_2 (*d*) Hg metal

197. Which of the following oxides of nitrogen is not common air pollutant?
(*a*) NO_2 (*b*) N_2O
(*c*) NO (*d*) N_2O_5

198. Which one of the following particulates is most toxic?
(*a*) flyash
(*b*) soot
(*c*) inorganic compounds
(*d*) smog

199. Which of the following could act as a propellant for rockets?
(*a*) liquid nitrogen + liquid oxygen
(*b*) liquid hydrogen + liquid nitrogen
(*c*) liquid oxygen + liquid argon
(*d*) liquid hydrogen + liquid oxygen

200. Cooking gas supplied in cylinders by gas agencies is :
(*a*) solid (*b*) liquid
(*c*) solution (*d*) gaseous

201. The gas in atmosphere that helps burning is :
(*a*) Helium (*b*) Nitrogen
(*c*) Oxygen (*d*) Carbon dioxide

202. A gas which is not present in normal samples of air is :
(*a*) Chlorine (*b*) Carbondioxide
(*c*) Neon (*d*) Helium

203. Natural gas mainly consists of :
(*a*) CO_2 (*b*) H_2
(*c*) CH_4 (*d*) N_2

204. Which of the following is odd among others :
(*a*) CO (*b*) Co
(*c*) NO (*d*) CO_2

205. A gas which can be used as a anaesthetic is
(*a*) Nitrogen dioxide (*b*) Nitric oxide
(*c*) Nitrous oxide (*d*) Nitrogen

206. A gas that can not be collected over water is :
(*a*) N_2 (*b*) PH_3
(*c*) O_2 (*d*) SO_2

ANSWERS

1	2	3	4	5	6	7	8	9	10
(*d*)	(*c*)	(*d*)	(*b*)	(*d*)	(*b*)	(*b*)	(*b*)	(*d*)	(*b*)
11	**12**	**13**	**14**	**15**	**16**	**17**	**18**	**19**	**20**
(*a*)	(*d*)	(*a*)	(*b*)	(*c*)	(*a*)	(*a*)	(*a*)	(*c*)	(*c*)
21	**22**	**23**	**24**	**25**	**26**	**27**	**28**	**29**	**30**
(*c*)	(*c*)	(*b*)	(*b*)	(*a*)	(*a*)	(*b*)	(*a*)	(*d*)	(*b*)
31	**32**	**33**	**34**	**35**	**36**	**37**	**38**	**39**	**40**
(*c*)	(*a*)	(*c*)	(*c*)	(*b*)	(*c*)	(*d*)	(*c*)	(*a*)	(*c*)
41	**42**	**43**	**44**	**45**	**46**	**47**	**48**	**49**	**50**
(*a*)	(*a*)	(*b*)	(*a*)	(*c*)	(*a*)	(*b*)	(*a*)	(*a*)	(*a*)
51	**52**	**53**	**54**	**55**	**56**	**57**	**58**	**59**	**60**
(*c*)	(*c*)	(*c*)	(*b*)	(*c*)	(*a*)	(*b*)	(*d*)	(*b*)	(*a*)
61	**62**	**63**	**64**	**65**	**66**	**67**	**68**	**69**	**70**
(*a*)	(*a*)	(*c*)	(*d*)	(*d*)	(*d*)	(*d*)	(*d*)	(*b*)	(*a*)
71	**72**	**73**	**74**	**75**	**76**	**77**	**78**	**79**	**80**
(*c*)	(*a*)	(*a*)	(*b*)	(*b*)	(*b*)	(*d*)	(*b*)	(*a*)	(*d*)
81	**82**	**83**	**84**	**85**	**86**	**87**	**88**	**89**	**90**
(*b*)	(*a*)	(*a*)	(*b*)	(*c*)	(*d*)	(*b*)	(*d*)	(*a*)	(*b*)
91	**92**	**93**	**94**	**95**	**96**	**97**	**98**	**99**	**100**
(*d*)	(*c*)	(*b*)	(*a*)	(*a*)	(*a*)	(*c*)	(*a*)	(*a*)	(*b*)
101	**102**	**103**	**104**	**105**	**106**	**107**	**108**	**109**	**110**
(*b*)	(*c*)	(*c*)	(*a*)	(*b*)	(*d*)	(*b*)	(*b*)	(*a*)	(*c*)
111	**112**	**113**	**114**	**115**	**116**	**117**	**118**	**119**	**120**
(*b*)	(*b*)	(*a*)	(*b*)	(*c*)	(*a*)	(*d*)	(*a*)	(*d*)	(*b*)
121	**122**	**123**	**124**	**125**	**126**	**127**	**128**	**129**	**130**
(*a*)	(*b*)	(*a*)	(*b*)	(*b*)	(*d*)	(*d*)	(*a*)	(*b*)	(*b*)
131	**132**	**133**	**134**	**135**	**136**	**137**	**138**	**139**	**140**
(*c*)	(*d*)	(*d*)	(*a*)	(*c*)	(*b*)	(*a*)	(*c*)	(*d*)	(*a*)

141	**142**	**143**	**144**	**145**	**146**	**147**	**148**	**149**	**150**
(*c*)	(*a*)	(*d*)	(*c*)	(*d*)	(*b*)	(*d*)	(*d*)	(*c*)	(*a*)
151	**152**	**153**	**154**	**155**	**156**	**157**	**158**	**159**	**160**
(*a*)	(*c*)	(*c*)	(*d*)	(*d*)	(*b*)	(*a*)	(*c*)	(*d*)	(*a*)
161	**162**	**163**	**164**	**165**	**166**	**167**	**168**	**169**	**170**
(*b*)	(*d*)	(*d*)	(*b*)	(*d*)	(*b*)	(*c*)	(*c*)	(*a*)	(*b*)
171	**172**	**173**	**174**	**175**	**176**	**177**	**178**	**179**	**180**
(*a*)	(*a*)	(*c*)	(*d*)	(*c*)	(*a*)	(*d*)	(*a*)	(*a*)	(*d*)
181	**182**	**183**	**184**	**185**	**186**	**187**	**188**	**189**	**190**
(*a*)	(*c*)	(*d*)	(*c*)	(*b*)	(*c*)	(*b*)	(*a*)	(*b*)	(*d*)
191	**192**	**193**	**194**	**195**	**196**	**197**	**198**	**199**	**200**
(*b*)	(*b*)	(*c*)	(*b*)	(*a*)	(*a*)	(*d*)	(*b*)	(*d*)	(*b*)
201	**202**	**203**	**204**	**205**	**206**				
(*c*)	(*a*)	(*c*)	(*b*)	(*b*)	(*d*)				

11

SOIL : CHARACTERISTICS AND ITS POLLUTION

1. Pedology is a study of :
   (*a*) Locomotion of animals
   (*b*) Rocks
   (*c*) Soil
   (*d*) Crop diseases
2. When is a man a part of biotic community?
   (*a*) Always
   (*b*) Only when he lives in big cities
   (*c*) Only when he lives in a forest
   (*d*) Never
3. Laterite soil is rich in :
   (*a*) Calcium (*b*) Magnesium
   (*c*) Iron (*d*) Nitrogen
4. Amount of water available to the plants in the soil is called as :
   (*a*) Holard (E + C) (*b*) Chresard
   (*c*) Echard (*d*) None of these
5. Humus is defined as :
   (*a*) Physical texture of soil
   (*b*) Chemical composition of soil
   (*c*) Decomposed organic matter in soil
   (*d*) None of these
6. Almost decomposed organic matter in which original form is lost is in :
   (*a*) Duff (*b*) Litter
   (*c*) Leaf mould (*d*) None of these
7. Which of the following has smallest of soil particles?
   (*a*) Loam soil (*b*) Sand
   (*c*) Clay (*d*) Silt
8. Major constituent of soil is :
   (*a*) Organic matter (*b*) Inorganic matter
   (*c*) Soil air (*d*) Soil water
9. Formation of organic matter takes place by :
   (*a*) Chemical weathering
   (*b*) Soil micro-organisms
   (*c*) Herbivores
   (*d*) Soil water
10. Metallic minerals and fossil fuels are :
    (*a*) Non-renewable resources
    (*b*) Inexhaustible resources
    (*c*) Renewable
    (*d*) None of the above
11. The common source of energy in our villages is :
    (*a*) Coal
    (*b*) Wood and animal dung
    (*c*) Electricity
    (*d*) Sunlight
12. Edaphic factors are related to :
    (*a*) Soil (*b*) Man
    (*c*) Rainfall (*d*) Soil water
13. Which one of the following is not an edaphic factor?
    (*a*) Mineral matter (*b*) Organic matter
    (*c*) Rainfall (*d*) Soil water
14. The kind of soil water most useful to plant is :
    (*a*) Hygroscopic water
    (*b*) Gravitational water
    (*c*) Capillary water
    (*d*) None of the above

15. Formation of soil takes place by :
(*a*) Weathering (*b*) Pedogenesis
(*c*) Melting (*d*) Both (*a*) and (*b*)

16. Major use of petroleum is in :
(*a*) Industries
(*b*) Transport on land and air
(*c*) Factories
(*d*) Shipping

17. Soil fertility is determined by its ability to :
(*a*) decay organic matter
(*b*) hold organic matter
(*c*) retain nutrients
(*d*) support life

18. The soil with poorest water holding capacity is :
(*a*) Clay (*b*) Loam
(*c*) Sandy (*d*) None of the above

19. The organic matter of soil has the value :
(*a*) 25% (*b*) 50%
(*c*) 40% (*d*) 10%

20. The size of clay particles is :
(*a*) Less than 0.002 mm
(*b*) More than 0.002 mm
(*c*) 0.2 mm to 2 mm
(*d*) None of the above

21. Soil erosion is more where :
(*a*) Rainfall is high (*b*) No rainfall
(*c*) Low rainfall (*d*) None of the above

22. Layer of ozone is present in :
(*a*) Stratosphere (*b*) Thermosphere
(*c*) Troposphere (*d*) None of the above

23. The atmospheric stratum nearest to earth is :
(*a*) Thermosphere (*b*) Stratosphere
(*c*) Troposphere (*d*) None of the above

24. Which one of the following is renewable resource?
(*a*) Water (*b*) Metals
(*c*) Fossil fuel (*d*) All of the above

25. MAB stands for :
(*a*) Man and Biome
(*b*) Management and Biosphere
(*c*) Man and Biosphere
(*d*) Man and Biology

26. Afforestation results in :
(*a*) soil conservation
(*b*) destruction of forests
(*c*) soil erosion
(*d*) None of these

27. The best method to check the soil erosion is :
(*a*) plant cover (*b*) wind breaks
(*c*) terrace farming (*d*) shelter belts

28. Plantation of trees in short blocks to check soil erosion is called :
(*a*) Wind screen (*b*) Wind break
(*c*) Jhooming system (*d*) Shelter belt

29. Choose the correct statement from the following :
(*a*) Strip cropping helps to check the flow of water
(*b*) Contour farming help in storing the water in furrows
(*c*) Mulching is effective against both wind and water erosion
(*d*) All of the above

30. Finger-like groove formed due to rapid flow of water along the soil surface cause :
(*a*) water erosion (*b*) rill erosion
(*c*) gully erosion (*d*) sheet erosion

31. Sheet erosion is caused by :
(*a*) Glaciers (*b*) Wind
(*c*) Heavy rains (*d*) Fast running rivers

32. Soil can be conserved by :
(*a*) Mechanical methods
(*b*) Stream bank protection
(*c*) Biological methods
(*d*) All of the above

33. Which of the following types of erosions takes place along the banks of the fast flowing rivers?
(*a*) Riparian erosion (*b*) Rill erosion
(*c*) Sheet erosion (*d*) Gully erosion

34. Deforestation may be reduce the chances of :
(*a*) frequent land slides
(*b*) erosion of soil surface
(*c*) rain fall
(*d*) frequent cyclones

35. Soil erosion is greater when :
(*a*) rainfall is equally distributed
(*b*) soil is dry
(*c*) air is still
(*d*) rainfall is very heavy

36. Process of soil conservation involves :
(*a*) terracing (*b*) crop rotation
(*c*) floods (*d*) strip cropping

37. The loss of upper fertile layer of soil is known as :
(*a*) soil erosion (*b*) podsolization
(*c*) pedogenesis (*d*) None of the above

38. Soil erosion can be prevented by :
(*a*) removal of vegetation
(*b*) increasing grazing
(*c*) afforestation
(*d*) removal of vegetation

39. Desert can be converted into greenland by:
(*a*) tropical trees (*b*) halophytes
(*c*) oxylophytes (*d*) psamophytes

40. Terracing is an effective method of soil conservation in :
(*a*) plain areas (*b*) desert areas
(*c*) hilly areas (*d*) None of these

41. Soil fertility can be increased without addition of fertilizers by :
(*a*) floods (*b*) crop rotation
(*c*) strip cropping (*d*) terracing

42. Soil conservation means :
(*a*) sustained renewal of soil at any place
(*b*) soil protection only
(*c*) soil improvement only
(*d*) all of the above

43. Deforestation has a alarming effect on :
(*a*) weed control
(*b*) sunlight
(*c*) soil erosion
(*d*) increase in grazing area

44. IBP stands for :
(*a*) Indian Biogas Project
(*b*) International Biological Programme
(*c*) International Biotic Programme
(*d*) Indian Biological Programme

45. Which of the following is the best plant to check soil erosion?
(*a*) *Cyanodon dactylon*
(*b*) *Opunita*
(*c*) *Pteris*
(*d*) *Salvinia*

46. Soil transported by air is called :
(*a*) glacial (*b*) alluvial
(*c*) colluvial (*d*) eolian

47. Which of the following statements is not correct regarding the effects of deforestation?
(*a*) It speeds up nutrient recycling
(*b*) It leads to soil erosion
(*c*) It alters the local weather patterns
(*d*) It destroys the natural habitat of wild animals

48. A sharp decrease in the number of species in tropics is mainly due to :
(*a*) urbanization (*b*) soil erosion
(*c*) air pollution (*d*) deforestation

49. Which of the following is an antiforest conservation activity?
(*a*) Prevention of fires
(*b*) Lumbering economy
(*c*) Preservation of wild animals
(*d*) Clear felling

50. Overgrazing by animals result in
(*a*) gully erosion (*b*) mulching
(*c*) rill erosion (*d*) sheet erosion

51. Which of the following functions performed by a forest helps most in controlling drought?
(*a*) Forests bring rain
(*b*) Prevention of soil erosion
(*c*) Forests have many water plants
(*d*) Act as water sheds

52. The harmful effect of deforestation is :
(*a*) loss of soil fertility
(*b*) soil erosion
(*c*) recurring floods
(*d*) All of the above

53. Mulching is a process that helps in :
(*a*) moisture conservation
(*b*) soil fertility
(*c*) improvement of soil structure
(*d*) weed control

54. The floods and desert are the result of :
(*a*) overgrazing (*b*) wind erosion
(*c*) biotic interference (*d*) water erosion

55. The increased incidence of floods in the plains of northern India in recent years can be attributed to :
(*a*) increased deforestation in the catchment areas
(*b*) increased use of land farming
(*c*) increase in annual rainfall
(*d*) exceptionally high rate of silting of drains

56. Sea tides can be used for :
(*a*) Sufficient amout of sunlight stored
(*b*) A device to take sun bath
(*c*) An energy source
(*d*) All of the above

57. Part of earth covered by water is about :
(*a*) 73% (*b*) 50%
(*c*) 92% (*d*) 87%

58. Movement of air occurs in the atmosphere upto height of :
(*a*) 100 km (*b*) 50 km
(*c*) 25 km (*d*) 10 km

59. Peak concentration of ozone in the stratosphere (ozonosphere) lies at a height of :
(*a*) 10 km (*b*) 25 km
(*c*) 40 km (*d*) 50 km

60. Percentage of fresh water in the hydrosphere is :
(*a*) 3% (*b*) 30%
(*c*) 13% (*d*) 33%

61. Percentage of fresh water found in lakes, ponds, swamps, streams and rivers is :
(*a*) 22.4% (*b*) 77.2%
(*c*) 7.7% (*d*) 0.36%

62. The natural source of energy which is most important is :
(*a*) Atomic energy (*b*) Biogas
(*c*) Sunlight (*d*) Fossil fuels

63. Floods can be checked by :
(*a*) Making dams (*b*) Deforestation
(*c*) Reforestation (*d*) None of the above

64. Extinction of many wild animals is due to :
(*a*) Scarcity of food (*b*) Over-crowding
(*c*) Hunting (*d*) Deforestation

65. Maximum energy in world is used by the country :
(*a*) China (*b*) Japan
(*c*) America (*d*) U.K.

66. Oil, coal and natural gas constitute :
(*a*) Metals
(*b*) Renewable resource
(*c*) Fossil fuels
(*d*) None of the above

67. Which one is not a resource for Onge tribe?
(*a*) Water (*b*) Food
(*c*) Gold (*d*) Wood

68. Migratory birds are a resource that is :
(*a*) Inorganic (*b*) Multinational
(*c*) International (*d*) National

69. Underground water is :
(*a*) International Resource
(*b*) Non-renewable Resource
(*c*) Renewable Resource
(*d*) Mixed Resource

70. The energy required daily by hunter-gatherer humans was :
(*a*) 2000 – 4000 kcal
(*b*) 6000 – 10000 kcal
(*c*) 10000 – 70000 kcal
(*d*) 10000 – 12000 kcal

71. Which one of the following can be estimated by Flame Photometer ?
(*a*) Sodium and Potassium
(*b*) Cadmium and Cobalt
(*c*) Chlorine and Bromine
(*d*) Mercury and Arsenic

72. The contribution of CO2 towards global warming has been estimated to be about
(*a*) 57 – 60% (*b*) 60 – 75%
(*c*) 80 – 85% (*d*) 45 – 55%

73. Of the total fresh water, ground water constitutes :
(*a*) 90% (*b*) 10%
(*c*) 22.4% (*d*) 44.2%

74. Of the total water evaporated from oceans, precipitation returns :
(*a*) 100% (*b*) 90%
(*c*) 75% (*d*) 50%

75. Annual fish catch from Indian shores is :
(*a*) 2.9 million tonnes (*b*) 25 million tonnes
(*c*) 1 million tonnes (*d*) 10 million tonnes

76. Solid matter from land washed annually into oceans is :
(*a*) 330 million tonnes
(*b*) 3300 million tonnes
(*c*) 3.3 million tonnes
(*d*) 33 million tonnes

77. Land mass occupies about :
(*a*) 14 million hectares
(*b*) 140 million hectares
(*c*) 1400 million hectares
(*d*) 14000 million hectares

78. Arable land constitutes :
(*a*) 36.6% (*b*) 30%
(*c*) 22.0% (*d*) 11%

79. Soil forms the surface layer in percentage of land :
(*a*) 80% (*b*) 60%
(*c*) 50% (*d*) 30%

80. Land mass occupied by forests is :
(*a*) 40% (*b*) 22%
(*c*) 30% (*d*) 17%

81. Which metallic mineral is used both for nuclear reactors as well as stainless steel?
(*a*) Vanadium (*b*) Thorium
(*c*) Radium (*d*) Columbium

82. Soil salinity can be measured by :
(*a*) Calorimeter
(*b*) Potometer
(*c*) Porometer
(*d*) Conductivity meter

83. The total land under cultivation in India is :
(*a*) 51% (*b*) 80%
(*c*) 75% (*d*) None of these

84. Lead is :
(*a*) Air pollutant
(*b*) Soil pollutant
(*c*) Radioactive pollutant
(*d*) Noise pollutant

85. The soil near the surface is usually darker than about one meter down, it is because the top soil :
(*a*) is not so old
(*b*) is richer in Ca and Mg
(*c*) is drier than sub-soil
(*d*) contains more organic matter

86. Technique of soil conservation by constructing platforms across the slopes in :
(*a*) Basin listing (*b*) Bench terracing
(*c*) Both of these (*d*) None of these

87. Plants growing well in rock crevices are :
(*a*) Lithophytes (*b*) Eremophytes
(*c*) Chasmophytes (*d*) Halophytes

88. The removal of soil by the action of water and mind is :
(*a*) erosion (*b*) pollution
(*c*) gleization (*d*) None of these

89. Soil rich in soluble salts is :
(*a*) Halomorphic (*b*) Calcimorphic
(*c*) Laterite (*d*) None of the above

90. The pollutants which are already present in nature; but are released in substantial amounts by man are known as :
(*a*) Quantitative pollutants
(*b*) Qualitative pollutants
(*c*) Degradable pollutants
(*d*) Primary pollutants

91. Forest and Pasture land in India is :
(*a*) 183 million ha (*b*) 18 million ha
(*c*) 83 million ha (*d*) 143 million ha

92. In India, agriculture land comprises :
(*a*) 143 million ha (*b*) 123 million ha
(*c*) 166 million ha (*d*) 183 million ha

93. In India, land prone to soil erosion is :
(*a*) 16.73 million ha (*b*) 87 million ha
(*c*) 5.5 million ha (*d*) 8.7 million ha

94. Land degradation is a great challenge for India because of :
(*a*) the 83 mha forest land, over half is used to various degrees
(*b*) only 250 mha land of 330 mha posses any potential for production
(*c*) 406 million of livestock have to supported an 13 mha land
(*d*) All of the above

95. The term *sub-soil* is used for horizon :
(*a*) A (*b*) C
(*c*) D (*d*) B

96. Which **one** of the following is an indirect ecological factor?
(*a*) Soil structure (*b*) Wind
(*c*) Light (*d*) Altitude

97. Which of the following atmospheric pollutants is **NOT** produced by the exhaust of motor vehicle in Delhi?
(*a*) SO_2 (*b*) CO
(*c*) Flyash (*d*) Hydrocarbon gases

98. Which of the following is an example of primary minerals?
(*a*) Mica (*b*) Dolomite
(*c*) Clay (*d*) None of these

99. The structural formula of Montmorillonite is :
(*a*) $Al_4Si_4O_{10}(OH)_8$ (*b*) $Al_2Si_4O_{10}(OH)_2K$
(*c*) $Al_4Si_8O_{20}(OH)_4$ (*d*) None of these

100. Which of best for plant growth?
(*a*) Sandy soil (*b*) Loamy soil
(*c*) Gravel (*d*) Clayey soil

101. Solubility and availability of plant nutrients are more related to :
(*a*) soil pH (*b*) soil porosity
(*c*) soil temperature (*d*) All of the above

102. General formula of kaolinite is :
(*a*) $Al_2O_3.4SiO_2.H_2O$
(*b*) $Al_2O_3.2SiO_3 2H_2O$
(*c*) $Al_2Si_4O_{10}(OH)_2K$
(*d*) None of these

103. Metallic mineral that is used in both alloy steels and disinfectants is :
(*a*) Manganese (*b*) Magnesium
(*c*) Copper (*d*) Aluminium

104. A non-metallic mineral used in abrasives is :
(*a*) Asbestos (*b*) Corundum
(*c*) Sulphur (*d*) Fluorspar

105. Which one of the following is an example of metamorphic rocks :
(*a*) Lime stone (*b*) Shole
(*c*) Sand stone (*d*) Marble

106. Conservation is :
(*a*) Judicious use of natural resources
(*b*) Protection of natural resources
(*c*) Management of natural resources
(*d*) All of the above

107. Vegetation of a place is mainly determined by :
(*a*) Rainfall (*b*) Soil water
(*c*) Soil type (*d*) Amount of light

108. American water plant that has become a troublesome water weed in India is :
(*a*) *Cyperus rotundus*
(*b*) *Eichhornia crassipes*
(*c*) *Trapa latifolia*
(*d*) *Trapa bispinosa*

109. Regolith is formed by :
(*a*) A and B Horizons
(*b*) B and C Horizons
(*c*) A, B and C Horizons
(*d*) None of these

110. River water deposits :
(*a*) Loamy soil (*b*) Alluvial soil
(*c*) Laterite soil (*d*) Sandy soil

111. Alluvial soils are found in :
(*a*) Northern India
(*b*) Southern India
(*c*) Gangetic Jamuna plains
(*d*) Eastern India

112. A_o layer of the soil is made of :
(*a*) Decaying litter
(*b*) Rocky matter
(*c*) Soil mixed with organic matter
(*d*) Soil rich in inorganic matter

113. Development of soil from rocky matter is :
(*a*) Pedogenesis (*b*) Pedology
(*c*) Edaphic factors (*d*) Edaphic climax

114. Soil particles arranged in a series of increasing size is :
(*a*) Silt ⟶ Sand ⟶ Clay
(*b*) Sand ⟶ Silt ⟶ Clay
(*c*) Clay ⟶ Sand ⟶ Silt
(*d*) Clay ⟶ Silt ⟶ Sand

115. Soil best suited for plant growth is :
(*a*) Clay (*b*) Loam
(*c*) Sandy (*d*) Gravel

116. Good soil is the one which :
(*a*) Allows water to percolate slowly
(*b*) Allows water to pass quickly
(*c*) Allows limited amount of water into it
(*d*) Holds whole of water entering it

117. Least porous soil is :
(*a*) Clay soil (*b*) Sandy soil
(*c*) Loam soil (*d*) Gravelly soil

118. Deep black soil is productive due to high proportion of :
(*a*) Sand and Zinc
(*b*) Gravel and Calcium
(*c*) Clay and Humus
(*d*) Silt and Earthworm

119. Humus is good for plant growth because :
(*a*) It improves physical condition of soil
(*b*) It makes the soil porous
(*c*) It increases water holding and aeration of soil
(*d*) All of the above

120. Humus is important for plant growth as it is :
(*a*) Made of dead organic matter
(*b*) Derived from leaves
(*c*) Rich in nutrients and increases water holding capacity of soil
(*d*) Partially decomposed

121. Humus is example of :
(*a*) A fertilizer
(*b*) Component of soil structure
(*c*) Organic colloids
(*d*) Crystalloids

122. Excessive erosion of top soil :
(*a*) increase water holding capacity
(*b*) reduces water holding capacity
(*c*) neither reduces nor increases
(*d*) None of these

123. Fertility of soil is measured by its ability to :
(*a*) Retain nutrients
(*b*) Hold organic materials
(*c*) Hold water
(*d*) Support life

124. A fertile agricultural soil appears deep coloured at the surface as compared to soil one metre down. The reason for colour of top soil is :
(*a*) More moisture
(*b*) Rich in organic matter
(*c*) Rich in iron, calcium and magnesium
(*d*) Recent formation

125. Water holding capacity is highest in :
(*a*) Sandy soil (*b*) Silt soil
(*c*) Clay soil (*d*) Loam soil

126. Soil water available to roots is :
(*a*) Surface water
(*b*) Hygroscopic water
(*c*) Gravitational water
(*d*) Capillary water

127. Water held tightly by soil particles as a thin film over their surface is :
(*a*) Hygroscopic water
(*b*) Capillary water
(*c*) Chemical water
(*d*) Gravitational water

128. Which governs the solubility and availability of nutrients in the soil?
(*a*) Temperature (*b*) pH
(*c*) Aeration (*d*) Porosity

129. Water-logging commonly occurs in :
(*a*) Sandy soil (*b*) Gravelly soil
(*c*) Clayey soil (*d*) Loam soil

130. An area of soil thoroughly wetted and allowed to drain till percolation stops will have a water content called :
(*a*) Capillary water
(*b*) Storage water

(*c*) Field capacity
(*d*) Gravitational water

131. Amount of water a soil can hold against pull of gravity is called :
(*a*) Field capacity
(*b*) Gravitational water
(*c*) Storage water
(*d*) Hygroscopic water

132. Greatest problem in water conservation is to reduce the amount of :
(*a*) Ground water (*b*) Precipitation
(*c*) Runoff water (*d*) Evaporation

133. Soil conservation is :
(*a*) Conversion of sterile soil into fertile one
(*b*) Aeration of soil
(*c*) Erosion of soil
(*d*) Protection against loss

134. Removal of top fertile soil by wind or water is :
(*a*) Siltation
(*b*) Soil erosion
(*b*) Weathering of soil
(*d*) Leaching

135. Which of the following landscapes formed by the glacier?
(*a*) Drumlins
(*b*) Eskers
(*c*) Kames
(*d*) None of these

136. Overgrazing generally causes :
(*a*) Soil protection
(*b*) Soil erosion
(*c*) Soil improvements
(*d*) None of these

137. An isolated mass or rock near the coastline is called :
(*a*) Rias (*b*) Stacks
(*c*) Bars (*d*) Roofs

138. Maximum productivity (on global basis) is shown by :
(*a*) Forests
(*b*) Aquatic ecosystem
(*c*) Deserts
(*d*) Grasslands

139. Which one is biotic in origin?
(*a*) Texture and porocity of soil
(*b*) Rainfall
(*c*) Carbon dioxide content of soil
(*d*) Light intensity

140. Best source of renewable energy is :
(*a*) Cattle (*b*) Petroleum
(*c*) Coal (*d*) Trees

141. A non-conventional energy source is :
(*a*) Coal
(*b*) Petroleum
(*c*) Solar radiations
(*d*) Electricity from nuclear plants

142. A non-renewable resource is :
(*a*) Forest (*b*) Coal/Petroleum
(*c*) Water (*d*) Wildlife

143. Geothermal energy is :
(*a*) Non-renewable non-conventional energy source
(*b*) Non-renewable conventional energy source
(*c*) Renewable non-conventional energy source
(*d*) Renewable conventional energy source

144. Recurrence of floods in the plains of North India is due to excessive :
(*a*) Siltation of dams
(*b*) Rainfall
(*c*) Agriculture
(*d*) Deforestation in catchment area

145. The end product of weathering is :
(*a*) Soil (*b*) Gravel
(*c*) Rock (*d*) None of these

146. Eroded soils are :
(*a*) Devoid of plant nutrients
(*b*) Richer in plant nutrients
(*c*) Unaltered in plant nutrients
(*d*) Fit for agriculture

147. A depleting source of energy is :
(*a*) Sunlight (*b*) Water
(*c*) Wind (*d*) Fossil fuel

148. Renewable source of energy is
(*a*) Biomass (*b*) Coal
(*c*) Petroleum (*d*) Kerosene

149. Petroleum is a :
(*a*) Synthetic product
(*b*) Renewable resource
(*c*) Non-renewable resource
(*d*) Inconvenient resource

150. Minerals and metals are
(*a*) Biodegradable resources
(*b*) Renewable resources
(*c*) Non-renewable resources
(*d*) Both (*b*) and (*c*)

151. Main renewable source of energy is :
(*a*) Forest (*b*) Fuel gas
(*c*) Cattle (*d*) Coal

152. Biomass produced by plants in oceans accounts for :
(*a*) 85% (*b*) 75%
(*c*) 65% (*d*) 55%

153. Soil conservation is achieved through :
(*a*) Restricted human activities
(*b*) Good plant cover
(*c*) Wind screen
(*d*) Ploughing

154. Soil fertility is reduced by :
(*a*) Crop rotation
(*b*) Nitrogen fixing bacteria
(*c*) Decaying organic matter
(*d*) Intensive agriculture

155. Type of soil in Gangetic basin is :
(*a*) Eolian (*b*) Colluvial
(*c*) Residual (*d*) Alluvial

156. Soil particles determine its :
(*a*) Texture
(*b*) Field capacity
(*c*) Water holding capacity
(*d*) Soil flora

157. Soil showing permanently wilted plants has :
(*a*) Gravitational water
(*b*) Capillary water
(*c*) Hygroscopic water
(*d*) Ground water

158. The alluvial soils of India, deficiency of the following nutrient is most widespread?
(*a*) Zinc (*b*) Copper
(*c*) Iron (*d*) Manganese

159. Red soils of India are poor in
(*a*) Phosphorus (*b*) Nirtrogen
(*c*) Both (*a*) and (*b*) (*d*) None of these

160. Cation exchange capacity of mica is :
(*a*) 0 (*b*) 30-50
(*c*) 80-100 (*d*) 110-150

161. Sulphur soil testing is determined by using :
(*a*) $ZnSO_4$ (*b*) Hot water
(*c*) $CaCl_2$ (*d*) $NaHCO_3$

162. .... toxicity is probably the important growth limiting factor in acid soils, particularly when pH < 5.0 to 5.5.
(*a*) Fe (*b*) Cu
(*c*) Zn (*d*) Al

163. Which of the following soils have poor physical condition?
(*a*) Sodic (*b*) Saline
(*c*) Saline-alkali (*d*) None of these

164. Sodium adsorption ratio (SAR) can be calculated by using of formula :
(*a*) $SAR = Na^+ / \sqrt{Ca^{2+} + Mg^{2+}}$
(*b*) $SAR = Na^+ / \sqrt{Ca^{2+} + Mg^{2+}/2}$
(*c*) $SAR = Ca^{2+} + Mg^{2+} / \sqrt{Na^+}$
(*d*) $SAR = Na^+ / \sqrt{Ca^{2+} + K/2}$

165. Who isolated *Bacillus radiculata*, the organism responsible for *N* fixation in 1888?
(*a*) M.W. Beijerinck (*b*) J.B. Lawes
(*c*) Liebig (*d*) Milton Whitney

166. One ton is equal to (kg) :
(*a*) 1000 (*b*) 907
(*c*) 100 (*d*) None of these

167. The exchangeable sodium ratio (ESR) can be calculated as :
(*a*) ESR = Exchangeable Na^+ / $\sqrt{\text{Exchangeable } (Ca^{+2} + Mg^{2+})}$

(*b*) ESR = Exchangeable (Ca^{2+} + Mg^{2+}) / Exchangeable Na^+

(*c*) ESR = Exchangeable Na^+ / Exchangeable (Ca^{2+} + Mg^{2+})

(*d*) ESR = Exchangeable Na^+ / Exchangeable (Ca^{2+} + K^+)

168. Leaching requirement can be estimated by formula :

(*a*) $LR = EC_{iw} / EC_{dw}$

(*b*) $LR = D_{iw} / D_{dw}$

(*c*) $LR = EC_{dw} / EC_{iw} \times 100$

(*d*) None of these

169. It has been observed that soil pH increases in

(*a*) Summer

(*b*) Winter

(*c*) Post-monsoon season

(*d*) None of these

170. CEC for organic soils lies in range of :

(*a*) 10-20 meq/100g

(*b*) 150-200 meq/100g

(*c*) 20-50 meq/100g

(*d*) 50-100 meq/100g

171. The most minerals, the strength of cation adsorption or lyotropic series, is :

(*a*) $Al^{3+} > Ca^{2+} > Mg^{2+} > K^+ = NH_4^+ > Na^+$

(*b*) $Al^{3+} > Mg^{2+} > Ca^{2+} > K^+ = NH_4^+ > Na$

(*c*) $Ca^{2+} > Al^{3+} > Mg^{2+} > K = NH^4 > Na^+$

(*d*) $Mg^{2+} > Al^{3+} > Ca^{2+} > K^+ = Na^+ > NH_4^+$

172. Which extract is used for determination of CEC :

(*a*) 1 N KOAC (*b*) 1 N NH_4OAC

(*c*) 1 N $NaOHCO_3$ (*d*) None of these

173. Which of the following formula is used for calculation of base saturation :

(*a*) Total bases/CEC × 100

(*b*) CEC/total bases × 100

(*c*) CEC/exchangeable bases × 100

(*d*) Exchangeable bases/CEC × 100

174. The anion exchange capacity (AEC) increases as soil pH :

(*a*) increases

(*b*) decreases

(*c*) first increases then decreases

(*d*) remain unaffected

175. One acre of soil to a depth of 6 inch weight about :

(*a*) 2.25×10^6 kg (*b*) 2.25×10^6 lb

(*c*) 2×10^6 lb (*d*) 2×10^6 kg

176. Which of the following pairs is not correctly matched :

	Organic Substances	C/N ratio
(*a*)	Soil micro-organisms	8 : 1
(*b*)	Soil organic matter	10 : 1
(*c*)	Barnyard manure (rotted)	20 : 1
(*d*)	Saw dust	1000 : 1

177. For nitrification, the optimum pH is :

(*a*) 7.0 (*b*) 6.5

(*c*) 10.0 (*d*) 8.5

178. Unsolidated material overlying rocks is known as :

(*a*) Regolith (*b*) Solum

(*c*) Bed rocks (*d*) A horizon

179. Vertical section of a soil is known as :

(*a*) A soil (*b*) Profile

(*c*) Horizons (*d*) Solum

180. The solum is composed of :

(*a*) A, B and E horizons

(*b*) A^+ regolith

(*x*) A and B horizons

(*d*) A, B and C horizons

181. The organic soil commonly contain more than 50% organic matter by volume and at least ....% by weight basis.

(*a*) 30 (*b*) 25

(*c*) 58 (*d*) 20

182. Among primary minerals, most resistant to weathering is :

(*a*) Albite (*b*) Quartz

(*c*) Gypsum (*d*) Zinc

183. Least resistant mineral to weathering is :

(*a*) Quartz (*b*) Geothite

(*c*) Olivine (*d*) Anorthite

184. Which of the following is a secondary mineral
(*a*) Muscovite (*b*) Biotite
(*c*) Anorthite (*d*) Dolomite

185. Inorganic parent material transported by gravity is :
(*a*) Colluvial (*b*) Eolian
(*c*) Marine (*d*) Glacial

186. Wind blown materials, comprised primarily of silt with some fine sand and clay, are called :
(*a*) Eclian (*b*) Loess
(*c*) Moraine (*d*) Alluvial

187. Passive factor of soil formation includes :
(*a*) Climate (*b*) Organisms
(*c*) Parent materials (*d*) None of these

188. Which soil order derived from volcanic ejecta and dominated by allophane?
(*a*) Andisols (*b*) Alfisols
(*c*) Altisols (*d*) Histosols

189. CEC of which clay mineral is highest (120-150) cmol/kg) :
(*a*) Mica CEC (*b*) Chlorite
(*c*) Montmorillonite (*d*) Vermiculite

190. The negative charge on 2 : 1 clays is :
(*a*) pH dependent (*b*) pH independent
(*c*) both (*a*) and (*b*) (*d*) None of these

191. Lowest category of soil classification includes :
(*a*) Order (*b*) Great group
(*c*) Series (*d*) Family

192. Which one of the following is not correctly matched :

	Soil order	**Pronunciation**
(*a*)	Entisols	Recent
(*b*)	Aridisols	Arid
(*c*)	Histosols	Organic
(*d*)	Vertisols	Pedalfor

193. Which one of the following is not correctly matched :
(*a*) Feldspars : Potassium silicates
(*b*) Micas : Iron and aluminium silicates
(*c*) Gibbsite : Hydrous oxides of aluminium
(*d*) Geothite : Hydrous iron oxides

194. A clay soil must contains at least .... Clay separate, to be designated a clay.
(*a*) 70% (*b*) 80%
(*c*) 35% (*d*) 40%

195. Which type of structure is dominant in graslands :
(*a*) Spheroidal (*b*) Platy
(*c*) Columnar (*d*) Blocky

196. Per cent pore space can be calculated by using of which formula :
(*a*) $\% \text{ PS} = 100 - (D_p/D_b \times 100)$
(*b*) $\% \text{ PS} = (D_p/D_p \times 100)$
(*c*) $\% \text{ PS} = 100 - (D_b/D_p \times 100)$
(*d*) $\% \text{ PS} = 1 - (D_p/D_b \times 100)$

197. Which one of the following water potential in soil is always positive
(*a*) Gravitational potential
(*b*) Matric potential
(*c*) Osmotic potential
(*d*) None of these

198. In neutron moisture meter, source of fast neutrons is :
(*a*) Radium
(*b*) Americium-beryllium
(*c*) Both (*a*) and (*b*)
(*d*) None of these

199. How much quantity of total incoming solar radiation is absorbed by the soil and can be used to warm it :
(*a*) 20% (*b*) 25%
(*c*) 40% (*d*) 10%

200. The external surface area of 1 g of colloidal clay is at least .... times that of 1 g of coarse sand.
(*a*) 400 (*b*) 1000
(*c*) 500 (*d*) 100

201. Magnesium in octahedral sheet of clay mineral indicates:
(*a*) Dioctahedral (*b*) Trioctahedral
(*c*) Monohedral (*d*) Tetrahedral

202. Aluminium in octahedral sheet of clay mineral indicates :
(*a*) Dioctahedral (*b*) Tetrahedral
(*c*) Trioctahedral (*d*) None of these

203. *Nitrosomonas* and *Nitrobacter* cause nitrification are an obligate :
(*a*) Autotrophic bacteria
(*b*) Heterotrophic bacteria
(*c*) Both (*a*) and (*b*)
(*d*) Saprophytes

204. NH_4^+ fixation takes place in :
(*a*) Vermiculite and illite
(*b*) Chlorite and kaolinite
(*c*) Montmorillonite and kaolinite
(*d*) All of these

205. 'Peat' soil are generaly characterized as :
(*a*) Red light and acidic soil
(*b*) Black, heavy and acidic
(*c*) Black, heavy and nautral
(*d*) Black, light and alkaline soil

206. The inorganic and organic labile P fraction of soil are collectively called :
(*a*) Intensity factor (*b*) Quantity factor
(*c*) Capacity factor (*d*) None of these

207. What is the porosity percentage if the particle density of soil is 2.6 and bulk density is 1.3 :
(*a*) 50% (*b*) 35%
(*c*) 55% (*d*) None of these

208. Height of rise of water in a capillary tube is directly proportional to :
(*a*) Surface tension of water
(*b*) Viscosity of water
(*c*) Radius of capillary tube
(*d*) None of these

209. Availability of which micro-nutrient increases with increase in soil pH :
(*a*) Zn (*b*) B
(*c*) Fe (*d*) Mo

210. White alkali soils are
(*a*) Acid soil (*b*) Saline soil
(*c*) Saline sodic soil (*d*) Sodic soil

211. Which group of micro-organisms have highest biomass in soil :
(*a*) Bacteria (*b*) Algae
(*c*) Fungi (*d*) Actinomycetes

212. Humus fraction lightest in colour is :
(*a*) Fulvic acid (*b*) Humic acid
(*c*) Humin acid (*d*) None of these

213. The Water Holding Capacity (WHC) of humus on a mass basis is .... times that of the silicate clays.
(*a*) 2-3 (*b*) 4-5
(*c*) 9-10 (*d*) None of these

214. Which group of colloid have highest cation exchange capacity by volume basis :
(*a*) Vermiculite (*b*) Humus
(*c*) Kaolinite (*d*) Smectite

215. Select the wrong pair from the following given below :
(*a*) Strengite : $FePO_4 \cdot 2H_2O$
(*b*) Variscite : $AlPO_4 \cdot 2H_2O$
(*c*) Gibbsite : $Al_2O_3 \cdot 3H_2O$
(*d*) Hematite : FeOOH

216. Hill soils are generally :
(*a*) Alkaline (*b*) Neutral
(*c*) Acidic (*d*) None of these

217. The diagnostic surface horizons are called :
(*a*) Genetic horizons (*b*) Pedons
(*c*) Epipedons (*d*) Endopedons

218. Available W.H.C. is maximum in :
(*a*) Sandy clay loam (*b*) Clay loam
(*c*) Loam (*d*) Silty clay loam

219. Soil colour determination chroma refers to which of the following :
(*a*) Dominant spectral colour
(*b*) Lightness or darkness of the colour
(*c*) Purity or strength of colour
(*d*) None of these

220. Concentration of which one of the following element is highest in soil :
(*a*) Fe (*b*) O_2
(*c*) Cu (*d*) Zn

221. Which is incorrect match in the following :
(*a*) Soil bulk density : Hydrometer
(*b*) Particle size analysis of soil : Picnometer
(*c*) Soil moisture retention : Permeameter
(*d*) Soil moisture estimation : Potometer

222. Specific heat is higher in :
(*a*) Sand (*b*) Silt
(*c*) Humus (*d*) Clay

223. Laterization is a process of accumulation in soil :
(*a*) Iron and aluminium oxides
(*b*) Silica
(*c*) $CaCO_3$
(*d*) $CuSO_4$

224. Podzolization is a process of accumulation in soil :
(*a*) $CaCO_3$
(*b*) Iron and aluminium oxides
(*c*) Silica
(*d*) $CuSO_4$

225. The smallest volume that can be called 'a soil' is :
(*a*) Pedon (*b*) Pod
(*c*) Radon (*d*) None of these

226. Flame photometer is used in the determination of :
(*a*) Nitrogen (*b*) Zinc
(*c*) Potassium (*d*) Phosphorus

227. Pure clay is not suitable for plant growth because :
(*a*) it is chemically inert
(*b*) it is chemically active
(*c*) it forms a solid non-penetrable mass
(*d*) All of the above

228. Humus is an example of :
(*a*) Soil structure
(*b*) Crystalloids
(*c*) Organic colloids
(*d*) None of them

229. Restoration of ecological equilibrium in mined areas can be achieved through :
(*a*) Prevention of grazing
(*b*) Prevention of soil erosion
(*c*) Revegetation of the mined habitats
(*d*) Conversion of mined habitats into agricultural ecosystems

230. In Northern Indian plains, there is an increase in floods in recent times due to :
(*a*) Soil erosion in the plains
(*b*) Soil conservation on the hills
(*c*) Deforestation in the plains
(*d*) Deforestation in the catchment area

231. Laterization is a process that results in the :
(*a*) Degradation of soil
(*b*) Purification of water
(*c*) Formation of soil
(*d*) Sterilization of soil

232. In a geographic region the rainfall is low, temperature is high, the soil is loose and sandy with low water table. It is reasonable to expect there :
(*a*) a grassy land
(*b*) screw pine forest
(*c*) a xerophytic vegetation
(*d*) None of the above

233. Soil erosion can be prevented by :
(*a*) allowing herbivorous animals to graze excessively
(*b*) growing plants to form a soil cover
(*c*) making the land slopy
(*d*) increasing soil fertility

234. Micro-organsims are the agent of :
(*a*) Biological Weathering
(*b*) Physical Weathering
(*c*) Chemical Weathering
(*d*) None of these

235. India has immediate prospects of reclaiming 16.73 million hectares of :
(*a*) Ravines and gullies
(*b*) Current fallows
(*c*) Alpine soils
(*d*) Culturable wasteland

236. Which of the following soils cracks and shrinks most as it dries :
(*a*) Porous soil (*b*) Clay soil
(*c*) Loam soil (*d*) Sandy soil

237. What is the best *p*H of the soil for cultivation of plants :
(*a*) 3.4 – 5.4 (*b*) 6.5 – 7.5
(*c*) 4.5 – 8.5 (*d*) 5.5 – 6.5

238. Deforestation causes :
(*a*) Soil erosion
(*b*) Soil pollution
(*c*) Water pollution
(*d*) Noise pollution

239. Which are the dense forests?
(*a*) Tropical evergreen forests
(*b*) Tropical deciduous forests
(*c*) Tropical Savannahas
(*d*) Chapprah

240. Which of the following is the main reason for extinction of animals?
(*a*) Predation
(*b*) Pollution
(*c*) Destruction of habitat
(*d*) Felling of trees

241. The most serious cause of soil erosion in India
(*a*) deforestation
(*b*) drought conditions
(*c*) soil drifting by wind
(*d*) soil drifting by floods

242. Plants growing in cold soil are :
(*a*) Psychrophytes (*b*) Halophytes
(*c*) Oxylophytes (*d*) None of the above

243. Plants growing on rock surfaces are :
(*a*) Lithophytes (*b*) Halophytes
(*c*) Calciphytes (*d*) Any of the above

244. Plants growing in soils having sand and gravel are
(*a*) Lithophytes (*b*) Psammophytes
(*c*) Calciphytes (*d*) Halophytes

245. Maintenance of soil fertility without addition of nutrients is due to :
(*a*) floods
(*b*) crop residue
(*c*) favourable temperature
(*d*) activity of micro-organisms

246. Common type of soil found in India is :
(*a*) Sandy
(*b*) Alluvial and black soils
(*c*) Red soil
(*d*) Both (*b*) and (*c*)

247. Plants die in water-logged soils due to
(*a*) Nutrient leaching
(*b*) Stoppage of root respiration
(*c*) Dilution of soil nutrients
(*d*) Dilution of cell sap

248. Domestic cooking gas cylinder contains :
(*a*) Coal gas
(*b*) Liquid petroleum gas
(*c*) Diesel oil
(*d*) Alcohol

249. Possibility of coal in area is guessed through :
(*a*) Mining the area
(*b*) Economic survey
(*c*) Pollen grain analysis
(*d*) Ecology of the area

250. Multinational source of energy is :
(*a*) Soil (*b*) Water
(*c*) Sun (*d*) All of the above

251. Ecofriendly method is
(*a*) Plantation of C_3 plants
(*b*) Plantation of Sugarcane
(*c*) Energy plantation
(*d*) None of the above

252. In hilly areas, erosion is minimised by :
(*a*) Terracing (*b*) Manuring
(*c*) Ploughing (*d*) Mixed cropping

253. Fuel wood crisis can be overcome by :
(*a*) Better wooden stoves
(*b*) Efficient wood extraction
(*c*) Greater afforestation
(*d*) Using alternate energy source

254. Edaphology is connected with :
(*a*) Plant and biosphere
(*b*) Soil and living micro-organisms
(*c*) Animals and ecosystem
(*d*) Soil and biosphere

255. Top soil is darker and :
(*a*) Contains more Na and Mg
(*b*) Is drier than subsoil
(*c*) Contains more organic matter
(*d*) Is wetter than subsoil

256. A plant brought from America for controlling pollution has become a problem in India :
(*a*) *Aegilops* (*b*) *Eichhornia*
(*c*) *Opunita* (*d*) Klamath weed

257. Exfoliation is a :
(*a*) Chemical Process
(*b*) Biotic Process

(*c*) Physical Process
(*d*) None of these

258. Which of the natural process is predominent in arid and semiarid terrains?
(*a*) Chemical erosion (*b*) Wind erosion
(*c*) Stream erosion (*d*) Glacial

259. A renewable resource is
(*a*) Fossil fuel (*b*) Metals
(*c*) Sunlight (*d*) Both (*a*) and (*b*)

260. Animals like Mice, Lizards and Cockroach share their habitat with human dwellings. They are :
(*a*) Inquilines (*b*) Cultigens
(*c*) Transplants (*d*) Humus

261. Water covering soil particles and held over them by strong attractive forces is :
(*a*) Capillary (*b*) Gravitational
(*c*) Hydrophobic (*d*) Hygroscopic

262. Uniform soil erosion by running water is :
(*a*) Gully erosion (*b*) Rill erosion
(*c*) Riparian erosion (*d*) Sheet erosion

263. The most important determinant of resistance of rocks to weathering is rock :
(*a*) Hardness (*b*) Permeability
(*c*) Jointing (*d*) Porosity

264. After Na, K and Cl, sea water has higher concentration of :
(*a*) Mg (*b*) Zn
(*c*) Ca (*d*) Pb

265. Value of a resource is dependent on its :
(*a*) Quality
(*b*) Quantity
(*c*) Requirement and type of soceity
(*d*) All of the above

266. Water is a resource :
(*a*) Non-degradable non-maintainable
(*b*) Degradable maintainable
(*c*) Renewable
(*d*) Non-renewable

267. Main cause of soil erosion is :
(*a*) Afforestation
(*b*) Less rains
(*c*) Thinning of ozone layer
(*d*) Deforestation

268. Which is non-renewable resource?
(*a*) Water (*b*) Forest
(*c*) Mineral (*d*) Solar energy

269. Largest amount of fresh water is found in :
(*a*) Lakes and streams
(*b*) Underground
(*c*) Polar ice and glaciers
(*d*) Rivers

270. L.P.G. is :
(*a*) Low price gas
(*b*) Fossil fuel
(*c*) Low pressure gas
(*d*) Biogas

271. Bulk fixation of carbon through photosynthesis takes place in :
(*a*) Tropical rain forests
(*b*) Tropical rain forests and crop plants
(*c*) Crop plants
(*d*) Oceans

272. With the exception of water, which is most important accessory chemical used in industry :
(*a*) Ethanol (*b*) Petroleum
(*c*) Nitrogen (*d*) Rubber

273. Percentage of water present in oceans and seas is :
(*a*) 60% (*b*) 70%
(*c*) 80% (*d*) 95%

274. Inexhaustible, non-conventional source of energy is :
(*a*) Solar radiations (*b*) Sea tides
(*c*) Wind power (*d*) All of the above

275. Guano is the major source of :
(*a*) Nitrogen
(*b*) Phosphorus
(*c*) Sulphur
(*d*) Zinc

276. Sequence of humification and mineralisation is :

(*a*) Dead organic matter ⟶ Litter ⟶ Duff ⟶ Humus ⟶ Minerals
(*b*) Humus ⟶ Minerals ⟶ Litter ⟶ Duff
(*c*) Minerals ⟶ Humus ⟶ Litter ⟶ Duff
(*d*) Dead organic matter ⟶ Duff ⟶ Litter ⟶ Minerals ⟶ Humus

277. Soil is composed of :
(*a*) Mineral + Water + Air
(*b*) Mineral + Organic matter + Water
(*c*) Mineral + Organic matter + Air + Water
(*d*) Organic matter + Water

278. Source of energy which does not evolve CO_2 is :
(*a*) Coal
(*b*) Oil
(*c*) Organic compounds
(*d*) Nuclear energy

279. Which one is a non-renewable resource?
(*a*) Coal and minerals
(*b*) Plants and coal
(*c*) Water and natural gas
(*d*) Energy and water

280. Non-conventional source of energy is :
(*a*) Wood
(*b*) Biogas/Solar Energy
(*c*) Coal
(*d*) Petroleum

281. Fossil fuels have been formed by a :
(*a*) Conventional process
(*b*) Natural process
(*c*) Non-conventional process
(*d*) All of the above

282. Match the following :

Column A (Climatic Zone)	Column B (Rainfall)
A. Wet Zone	1. 200 cm
B. Dry Zone	2. 50-100 cm
C. Arid Zone	3. 50 cm
D. Intermediate Zone	4. 100 cm

Codes :

	A.	B.	C.	D.
(*a*)	1	2	3	4
(*b*)	2	3	1	4
(*c*)	4	3	1	2
(*d*)	4	1	2	3

283. Which of the following is **must to** determine the climate?
(*a*) Distance of earth from the sun
(*b*) Geometry of the earth-atmosphere system
(*c*) Movement of earth around the sun
(*d*) None of the above

284. The damage to land can be prevented by :
(*a*) preparing land data by remote sensing
(*b*) framing a time bound nation wide land use planning
(*c*) land management
(*d*) All of the above

285. The least porous soil among the following is
(*a*) Loam soil (*b*) Clay soil
(*c*) Sandy soil (*d*) Peaty soil

286. Which one is the most important causative pollutant of soil?
(*a*) Glass junk (*b*) Iron junk
(*c*) Detergents (*d*) Plastics

287. Soils which are transported by water are :
(*a*) Alluvial (*b*) Muck
(*c*) Peat (*d*) Colluvial

288. When the fertility of the soil is lost, it is :
(*a*) soil erosion (*b*) soil silting
(*c*) soil conservation (*d*) soil conversion

289. The pH of a fertile soil is usually around :
(*a*) 2 – 3 (*b*) 9 – 11
(*c*) 6 – 7 (*d*) 11 – 14

290. Soil is the :
(*a*) edaphic factor
(*b*) non-edaphic factor
(*c*) both of these
(*d*) None of these

291. Favourable soil temperature for soil micro-organisms is :
(*a*) 15 – 20°C

(*b*) 25 – 38°C
(*c*) 40 – 45°C
(*d*) None of these

292. Soil erosion can be prevented by :
(*a*) allowing herbivorous animals to graze exececssively
(*b*) growing plants to form a soil cover
(*c*) making the land slopy
(*d*) increasing soil fertility

293. The nature of igneous rocks found in India is :
(*a*) Acidic (*b*) Basic
(*c*) Neutral (*d*) None of these

294. The Earth capital is/are :
(*a*) Air, water and soil
(*b*) Wildlife, raw materials and minerals
(*c*) Energy resources and degradation
(*d*) All of the above

295. The "Unstable Earth" was written by :
(*a*) Walter Penk
(*b*) J.A. Steers
(*c*) Glibert
(*d*) Brukner

296. Plants requiring low calcium amount or found in acidic soil is :
(*a*) Calciphytes (*b*) Halophytes
(*c*) Oxylophytes (*d*) All of these

297. Geodesy is a science which studies of :
(*a*) The Space
(*b*) Earth Measurement
(*c*) The Earth's surface
(*d*) Interior of the Earth

298. Fertility of soil is reduced by :
(*a*) decaying organic matter
(*b*) crop rotation
(*c*) intensive agriculture
(*d*) addition of nitrogen fixing bacteria

299. Total land area of India is :
(*a*) 550 million hectares
(*b*) 390 million hectares
(*c*) 505 million hectares
(*d*) 305 million hectare

300. Man-land ratio in India is :
(*a*) 0.48 hectare per hand
(*b*) 2 hectare per hand
(*c*) 5 hectare per hand
(*d*) None of the above

301. Agriculture land in India is :
(*a*) 400 million hectares
(*b*) 162 million hectares
(*c*) 23 million hectares
(*d*) 50 million hectares

302. The side effects of heavy and constant grazing is that the :
(*a*) upper layers of the soil are loosened and are eroded
(*b*) lower layers are made more compact and root respiration is interfered with
(*c*) lower compact layers make root penetration difficult
(*d*) All of these

303. Which of the following factors is biotic
(*a*) CO_2 content of the soil
(*b*) rainfall
(*c*) texture and porosity of soil
(*d*) photoperiod

304. Plants absorb from the soil :
(*a*) Gravitational water
(*b*) Hygroscopic water
(*c*) Capillary water
(*d*) Both (*a*) and (*b*)

305. The soil which cracks and shrinks most as it dries is :
(*a*) Soil rich in minerals
(*b*) Sandy soil
(*c*) Chalky soil
(*d*) Clay soil

306. Soil particles arranged in order of increasing size are :
(*a*) Clay – silt – sand (*b*) Sand – silt – clay
(*c*) Silt – clay – sand (*d*) Clay – sand – silt

307. Soil that is made up of particles that have been carried in water and then deposited, is called :
(*a*) subsoil (*b*) silt
(*c*) loam (*d*) clay

308. Soil originates from rocks by erosion and fragmentation of rocks and accumulation of organic matter. The soil forming rocks are

(*a*) igneous
(*b*) sedimentary
(*c*) metamorphic
(*d*) All of the above

309. Soil is :
(*a*) inorganic and renewable
(*b*) organic and renewable
(*c*) mixture of inorganic and organic and is renewable
(*d*) inorganic and organic mixture and non-renewable

310. Macropores of soil (pore diameter > 20μ) are involved in :
(*a*) Holding water
(*b*) Percolation of water
(*c*) Holding air
(*d*) Both (*b*) and (*c*)

311. Common type of soil found in India :
(*a*) Black and alluvial soil
(*b*) Red soil
(*c*) Both (*a*) and (*b*)
(*d*) Red and black soil

312. The inexhaustible resources are
(*a*) air and light
(*b*) sand
(*c*) both are correct
(*d*) only (*a*) is correct

313. Availability of nutrients is related to :
(*a*) Soil porosity
(*b*) Soil *p*H
(*c*) Soil colour
(*d*) Soil temperature

314. A good soil is that which :
(*a*) allows little water to enter it
(*b*) allows extra water to percolate slowly
(*c*) holds all water entering into it
(*d*) allows water to pass quickly

315. Alluvial soil is brought by rivers in region of :
(*a*) South India
(*b*) Northern India
(*c*) Gangetic plains
(*d*) Eastern India

316. Jawar Kota (Rajasthan) is famous for
(*a*) Phosphate rocks
(*b*) Corundum
(*c*) Dolomite
(*d*) Gold and uranium mines

317. See tides can be used for sufficient amount of :
(*a*) sunlight stored
(*b*) sun bath
(*c*) a device to use sun rays as energy source
(*d*) All of these

ANSWERS

1	2	3	4	5	6	7	8	9	10
(*c*)	(*a*)	(*c*)	(*b*)	(*c*)	(*c*)	(*c*)	(*b*)	(*b*)	(*a*)
11	**12**	**13**	**14**	**15**	**16**	**17**	**18**	**19**	**20**
(*b*)	(*a*)	(*c*)	(*c*)	(*d*)	(*b*)	(*d*)	(*c*)	(*d*)	(*a*)
21	**22**	**23**	**24**	**25**	**26**	**27**	**28**	**29**	**30**
(*a*)	(*a*)	(*c*)	(*c*)	(*c*)	(*a*)	(*a*)	(*b*)	(*d*)	(*d*)
31	**32**	**33**	**34**	**35**	**36**	**37**	**38**	**39**	**40**
(*c*)	(*d*)	(*a*)	(*c*)	(*d*)	(*b*)	(*a*)	(*c*)	(*d*)	(*c*)
41	**42**	**43**	**44**	**45**	**46**	**47**	**48**	**49**	**50**
(*b*)	(*a*)	(*c*)	(*b*)	(*a*)	(*d*)	(*a*)	(*d*)	(*d*)	(*d*)
51	**52**	**53**	**54**	**55**	**56**	**57**	**58**	**59**	**60**
(*b*)	(*d*)	(*a*)	(*c*)	(*a*)	(*c*)	(*a*)	(*a*)	(*b*)	(*a*)

61	**62**	**63**	**64**	**65**	**66**	**67**	**68**	**69**	**70**
(*d*)	(*d*)	(*c*)	(*d*)	(*c*)	(*c*)	(*c*)	(*b*)	(*c*)	(*a*)
71	**72**	**73**	**74**	**75**	**76**	**77**	**78**	**79**	**80**
(*a*)	(*a*)	(*c*)	(*b*)	(*a*)	(*b*)	(*d*)	(*d*)	(*a*)	(*c*)
81	**82**	**83**	**84**	**85**	**86**	**87**	**88**	**89**	**90**
(*d*)	(*d*)	(*d*)	(*b*)	(*d*)	(*b*)	(*c*)	(*a*)	(*a*)	(*a*)
91	**92**	**93**	**94**	**95**	**96**	**97**	**98**	**99**	**100**
(*c*)	(*a*)	(*b*)	(*d*)	(*b*)	(*a*)	(*c*)	(*a*)	(*c*)	(*b*)
101	**102**	**103**	**104**	**105**	**106**	**107**	**108**	**109**	**110**
(*d*)	(*b*)	(*a*)	(*b*)	(*d*)	(*d*)	(*a*)	(*b*)	(*c*)	(*b*)
111	**112**	**113**	**114**	**115**	**116**	**117**	**118**	**119**	**120**
(*c*)	(*a*)	(*a*)	(*d*)	(*b*)	(*a*)	(*a*)	(*c*)	(*d*)	(*c*)
121	**122**	**123**	**124**	**125**	**126**	**127**	**128**	**129**	**130**
(*c*)	(*b*)	(*d*)	(*b*)	(*c*)	(*d*)	(*a*)	(*b*)	(*c*)	(*c*)
131	**132**	**133**	**134**	**135**	**136**	**137**	**138**	**139**	**140**
(*a*)	(*d*)	(*d*)	(*b*)	(*c*)	(*b*)	(*b*)	(*b*)	(*c*)	(*d*)
141	**142**	**143**	**144**	**145**	**146**	**147**	**148**	**149**	**150**
(*c*)	(*b*)	(*a*)	(*d*)	(*a*)	(*a*)	(*d*)	(*a*)	(*c*)	(*d*)
151	**152**	**153**	**154**	**155**	**156**	**157**	**158**	**159**	**160**
(*a*)	(*a*)	(*b*)	(*d*)	(*d*)	(*a*)	(*c*)	(*a*)	(*c*)	(*a*)
161	**162**	**163**	**164**	**165**	**166**	**167**	**168**	**169**	**170**
(*c*)	(*d*)	(*a*)	(*b*)	(*a*)	(*b*)	(*c*)	(*a*)	(*b*)	(*d*)
171	**172**	**173**	**174**	**175**	**176**	**177**	**178**	**179**	**180**
(*a*)	(*b*)	(*a*)	(*b*)	(*c*)	(*d*)	(*d*)	(*a*)	(*b*)	(*a*)
181	**182**	**183**	**184**	**185**	**186**	**187**	**188**	**189**	**190**
(*d*)	(*b*)	(*c*)	(*d*)	(*a*)	(*b*)	(*c*)	(*a*)	(*d*)	(*d*)
191	**192**	**193**	**194**	**195**	**196**	**197**	**198**	**199**	**200**
(*c*)	(*d*)	(*b*)	(*c*)	(*a*)	(*c*)	(*a*)	(*c*)	(*d*)	(*b*)
201	**202**	**203**	**204**	**205**	**206**	**207**	**208**	**209**	**210**
(*b*)	(*a*)	(*a*)	(*a*)	(*b*)	(*b*)	(*a*)	(*a*)	(*d*)	(*b*)
211	**212**	**213**	**214**	**215**	**216**	**217**	**218**	**219**	**220**
(*c*)	(*a*)	(*b*)	(*a*)	(*d*)	(*c*)	(*c*)	(*b*)	(*c*)	(*b*)
221	**222**	**223**	**224**	**225**	**226**	**227**	**228**	**229**	**230**
(*d*)	(*c*)	(*a*)	(*c*)	(*a*)	(*c*)	(*c*)	(*c*)	(*c*)	(*d*)
231	**232**	**233**	**234**	**235**	**236**	**237**	**238**	**239**	**240**
(*c*)	(*c*)	(*b*)	(*a*)	(*d*)	(*b*)	(*d*)	(*a*)	(*a*)	(*c*)
241	**242**	**243**	**244**	**245**	**246**	**247**	**248**	**249**	**250**
(*a*)	(*a*)	(*a*)	(*b*)	(*d*)	(*d*)	(*b*)	(*b*)	(*c*)	(*c*)
251	**252**	**253**	**254**	**255**	**256**	**257**	**258**	**259**	**260**
(*c*)	(*a*)	(*d*)	(*b*)	(*c*)	(*b*)	(*c*)	(*b*)	(*c*)	(*a*)
261	**262**	**263**	**264**	**265**	**266**	**267**	**268**	**269**	**270**
(*d*)	(*d*)	(*c*)	(*a*)	(*c*)	(*b*)	(*d*)	(*c*)	(*c*)	(*b*)

271	272	273	274	275	276	277	278	279	280
(*d*)	(*b*)	(*d*)	(*d*)	(*b*)	(*a*)	(*c*)	(*d*)	(*a*)	(*b*)
281	**282**	**283**	**284**	**285**	**286**	**287**	**288**	**289**	**290**
(*c*)	(*a*)	(*b*)	(*a*)	(*b*)	(*c*)	(*a*)	(*a*)	(*b*)	(*a*)
291	**292**	**293**	**294**	**295**	**296**	**297**	**298**	**299**	**300**
(*b*)	(*b*)	(*a*)	(*a*)	(*b*)	(*c*)	(*b*)	(*c*)	(*d*)	(*a*)
301	**302**	**303**	**304**	**305**	**306**	**307**	**308**	**309**	**310**
(*b*)	(*d*)	(*a*)	(*c*)	(*d*)	(*a*)	(*b*)	(*d*)	(*c*)	(*d*)
311	**312**	**313**	**314**	**315**	**316**	**317**			
(*c*)	(*c*)	(*b*)	(*b*)	(*c*)	(*a*)	(*c*)			

12

NOISE POLLUTION

1. Sound limits in industrial areas is :
   (*a*) 75 dB (*b*) 30 dB
   (*c*) 40 dB (*d*) 50 dB
2. Which of the following is a symbol of WWF?
   (*a*) Tiger (*b*) White Bear
   (*c*) Rhododendron (*d*) Red Panda
3. In cities 60 – 70% of noise may come from :
   (*a*) Road traffic
   (*b*) Radio and Microphones
   (*c*) Loudspeakers
   (*d*) Construction work
4. Green muffler is planting of trees and shrubs to reduce noise pollution. It is done :
   (*a*) along roads
   (*b*) on waste lands
   (*c*) along banks of canals
   (*d*) on the slopes of hills
5. Loud noise causes :
   (*a*) irritation
   (*b*) dilation of blood vessels
   (*c*) impairing of hearing
   (*d*) irrationality
6. The first effect of noise :
   (*a*) constriction of blood vessels
   (*b*) digestive spasm
   (*c*) anxiety and stress reactions
   (*d*) increased heart beat
7. Infrasonic (infrasound) frequencies are :
   (*a*) below 50 Hz (*b*) above 50 Hz
   (*c*) above 15000 Hz (*d*) None of these
8. Ultrasonic (ultrasound) frequencies are :
   (*a*) above 1500 Hz (*b*) above 15000 Hz
   (*c*) below 15000 Hz (*d*) None of these
9. The most significant attribute of noise is its
   (*a*) Duration
   (*b*) Unpleasant nature
   (*c*) Loudness
   (*d*) Frequency
10. Hearing ability of an individual is monitored by :
    (*a*) Audiometric test
    (*b*) Potentiometric test
    (*c*) Volumetric test
    (*d*) None of these
11. The hearing machinery of our body consists of :
    (*a*) three parts
    (*b*) two parts
    (*c*) four parts
    (*d*) None of these
12. Sound becomes hazardous noise pollution at level :
    (*a*) Above 30 dB (*b*) Above 80 dB
    (*c*) Above 100 dB (*d*) Above 120 dB
13. WHO's recommendations about the industrial noise limit is of :
    (*a*) 105 dB (*b*) 75 dB
    (*c*) 135 dB (*d*) None of these
14. Green muffler is related to pollution of :
    (*a*) Air (*b*) Soil
    (*c*) Noise (*d*) Water
15. Exposure to noise pollution causes :
    (*a*) Increased heart beat
    (*b*) Constriction of blood vessels
    (*c*) Dilation of pupil
    (*d*) All of the above

16. Noise pollution causes :
(*a*) deafness (*b*) increase in B.P.
(*c*) heart trouble (*d*) All the above

17. What is an ECO-MARK ?
(*a*) A scheme for labelling pollution free industrial unit
(*b*) A scheme for labelling environment friendly consumber product
(*c*) A cost-effective production technique
(*d*) An international certification – recognizing eco-friendly building

18. The concept of environments is based upon :
1. globalisation
2. environmental degradation
3. dimensions of totality of the environment of these
(*a*) 1, 2 are correct
(*b*) 1, 2 and 3 are correct
(*c*) only 2 is correct
(*d*) only 1 is correct

19. The standard permissible noise limits for refrigerator is :
(*a*) 60 dB (*b*) 46 dB
(*c*) 68 dB (*d*) 75 dB

20. The standard permissible noise limits for Diesel generator installed in household is :
(*a*) 50-60 dB (*b*) 70-80 dB
(*c*) 85-90 dB (*d*) None of these

21. Permanent loss of hearing occurs at .... due to continuous noise exposure.
(*a*) 40 dB (*b*) 60 dB
(*c*) 60 dB (*d*) 100 dB

22. Ambient noise standard in India for silence zone in day time is :
(*a*) 75 dB (*b*) 60 dB
(*c*) 50 dB (*d*) None of these

23. Ambient noise standard in India for residential area at night time is :
(*a*) 45 dB (*b*) 40 dB
(*c*) 60 dB (*d*) 55 dB

24. Sound levels .... dB cause plenty of discomfort, irritation and a variety of physiological disturbances.
(*a*) 50-60 (*b*) 60-65
(*c*) 70-80 (*d*) None of these

ANSWERS

1	2	3	4	5	6	7	8	9	10
(*a*)	(*d*)	(*a*)	(*d*)	(*c*)	(*c*)	(*a*)	(*b*)	(*c*)	(*a*)
11	**12**	**13**	**14**	**15**	**16**	**17**	**18**	**19**	**20**
(*a*)	(*b*)	(*d*)	(*c*)	(*d*)	(*d*)	(*b*)	(*a*)	(*b*)	(*c*)
21	**22**	**23**	**24**						
(*d*)	(*c*)	(*a*)	(*c*)						

13

WASTE AND ITS MANAGEMENT

1. The words trash, garbage, rubbish, refuse etc. are synonyms with :
(*a*) waste (*b*) hazard
(*c*) rubbish (*d*) All of these

2. The important categories of solid waste are :
(*a*) municipal wastes (*b*) industrial wastes
(*c*) hazardous wastes (*d*) All of these

3. Organic waste products :
(*a*) should be buried deep in the soil
(*b*) can be used for production of energy
(*c*) should be treated with chemicals to prevent breeding of organisms
(*d*) should be dumped into the sea

4. *Throwaway societies* are :
(*a*) today's advanced industrialised countries
(*b*) today's most polluting countries
(*c*) Asia and Australia
(*d*) Any of the above

5. Principles of Resource Recycling may be
(*a*) high-quality energy cannot be recycled
(*b*) disperse, or mix products that contain recyclable matter resources
(*c*) recycling matter always requires high-quality energy
(*d*) All of the above

6. The non-probability sampling is :
(*a*) cluster sampling
(*b*) stratified sampling
(*c*) correlation
(*d*) regression

7. The number of elements in the obtained sample is known as :
(*a*) sampling
(*b*) sample size
(*c*) sample distribution
(*d*) regression

8. Burning of fossil fuels is the main source of pollution :
(*a*) Nitrogen oxide (*b*) Nitric oxide
(*c*) Nitrous oxide (*d*) Sulphur dioxide

9. Modes of controlling pollution in large cities include :
(*a*) Cleanliness and less use of insecticides
(*b*) Proper disposal of organic wastes, sewage and industrial effluents
(*c*) Broader roads and shifting of factories out of the residential areas
(*d*) All of the above

10. Domestic waste constitutes :
(*a*) Non-biodegradable pollution
(*b*) Biodegradable pollution
(*c*) Effluents
(*d*) Air pollution

11. Main types of hauled container systems is/are :
(*a*) trash-trailer container
(*b*) tilt-frame container
(*c*) both (*a*) and (*b*)
(*d*) None of these

12. The process in which the trash and garbage are burned in large furnace, at high temperatures to get rid off much of the refuse as possible, is :
(*a*) landfills
(*b*) high ijection process
(*c*) incineration
(*d*) All of the above

13. The main problems with using the incineration process is/are :
(*a*) burning trash
(*b*) expelling huge amount of toxic pollution
(*c*) both (*a*) and (*b*)
(*d*) None of the above

14. Match the following :

	Column A		Column B
A.	Dioxin	1.	most toxic chemical ever manufactured by humans
B.	Dumps and landfills	2.	one of the most ancient and common ways of disposing of solid waste
C.	Sanitary landfills	3.	simplest closed dump

Codes :

	A	B	C
(*a*)	3	2	1
(*b*)	2	3	1
(*c*)	1	2	3
(*d*)	1	3	2

15. The *incorrect* pair is :
(*a*) Multistage inquiries → meant for big samples
(*b*) Area sampling → grouping the population of then selecting the groups
(*c*) Deliberate sampling → non-probability sampling
(*d*) None of the above

16. In testing of hypothesis, research and null hypothesis :
(*a*) are invalid (*b*) exist together
(*c*) one at a time (*d*) are same

17. Decomposition of domestic wastes under natural processes is known as :
(*a*) Industrial pollution
(*b*) Thermal pollution
(*c*) Biodegradable process
(*d*) Non-biodegradable process

18. Match the following :

	Column A		Column B
A.	Square matrix	1.	number of rows is equal to number of columns
B.	Triangular matrices	2.	elements below principle diagonal are zero
C.	Scalar matrix	3.	all the diagonal elements are equal

Codes :

	A	B	C
(*a*)	2	3	1
(*b*)	1	2	3
(*c*)	1	3	2
(*d*)	3	1	2

19. Disposal of flyash is carried out in :
(*a*) ash ponds (*b*) air tumbler
(*c*) thermal plants (*d*) None of these

20. The important steps in solid waste management are :
(*a*) waste generation and collection
(*b*) on-site handling, storage and processing
(*c*) transport and disposal
(*d*) All of the above

21. A waste is classified as hazardous if it shows :
(*a*) toxicity and ignitability
(*b*) corrosivity
(*c*) reactivity
(*d*) All of these

22. The factors that influence the quantity of municipal waste generated include :
(*a*) Collection frequency
(*b*) Geographic location
(*c*) Salvaging and recycling
(*d*) All of these

23. The factors that must be considered in the on-site storage of solid wastes is/are :
(*a*) type of container
(*b*) location of container
(*c*) public health and collection
(*d*) All of these

24. The statistical device helps in analysing covariation of two or more variables :
(*a*) Correlation
(*b*) Regression
(*c*) Median
(*d*) Standard deviation

25. The sampling method chosen when the members of a special population are difficult to locate is :
(*a*) dimensional sampling
(*b*) snowball sampling
(*c*) cluster sampling
(*d*) All of these

26. Match the following :

Column A	**Column B**
A. Labour	1. physical and mental talents of people
B. Natural resources	2. plants, animals, water, air nutrients etc.
C. Intermediate goods	3. tools, machinery, factory, building, etc.

Codes :

	A	B	C
(*a*)	1	2	3
(*b*)	3	2	1
(*c*)	2	3	1
(*d*)	2	1	3

27. Which is of the following element found mostly in earth's crust?
(*a*) Oxygen (*b*) Silicon
(*c*) Aluminium (*d*) Gold

28. The other two states other than states of matter (gas, liquid and solid) are :
(*a*) Plasma and EPS
(*b*) Plasma and Hb
(*c*) Moser and Plasma
(*d*) None of these

29. The typical composition of management of solid wastes do ***not*** depend on :
(*a*) landuse (*b*) locality
(*c*) season of year (*d*) None of these

30. Which of the following cause damage to blood?
(*a*) Iron (*b*) Lead
(*c*) Calcium (*d*) Arsenic

31. The three "Rs" of waste management hierarchy is/are :
(*a*) Reduce, Reuse and Recycle
(*b*) Reduce, Redox and Reoxidation
(*c*) Reuse, Reimburse and Regain
(*d*) Regain, Recycle and Resend

32. Examples of organic compounds :
(*a*) Hydrocarbons
(*b*) Chlorinated hydrocarbons
(*c*) Simple Sugars
(*d*) All of the above

33. Larger and more complex organic compounds are known as :
(*a*) monomers (*b*) polymers
(*c*) proteins (*d*) All of these

34. Nucleic acids have important genetic materials these are :
(*a*) Genes (*b*) Chromosomes
(*c*) Both (*a*) and (*b*) (*d*) None of these

35. Inorganic compounds are :
(*a*) NaCl, H_2O (*b*) SO_2, NH_3
(*c*) H_2SO_4, CO (*d*) All of the above

36. Which of the following is a rich source of energy but never causes atmospheric pollution?
(*a*) Nuclear energy (*b*) Solar energy
(*c*) Coal (*d*) Wood

37. Ultraviolet radiation from sunlight causes the reaction that produces :
(*a*) SO_2 (*b*) O_3
(*c*) CO_2 (*d*) CO

38. The 'Love Canal Incidence' is concerned with :
(*a*) Chemical plant accident
(*b*) River pollution
(*c*) Toxic waste dump
(*d*) Man-made bacteria

39. The physical treatment of hazardous wastes include :
(*a*) Screening and Sedimentation
(*b*) Flotation and Filtration
(*c*) Centrifugation and Dialysis
(*d*) All of the above

40. The chemical treatment of hazardous wastes include :
(*a*) neutralisation and precipitation
(*b*) ion exchange and dechlorination
(*c*) oxidation-reduction
(*d*) All of the above

41. The biological treatment of hazardous wastes include :
(*a*) sludge process and aerated lagoon
(*b*) trickling filters and stabilisation ponds
(*c*) anaerobic digestion
(*d*) All of the above

42. The Bhopal Disaster occurred on :
(*a*) December 3, 1984
(*b*) Jan. 4, 1984
(*c*) August 14, 1984
(*d*) no date known

43. The newspaper contains one of the following toxic material. It is :
(*a*) Cd (*b*) Pb
(*c*) Mg (*d*) Hg

44. Most harmful type of environmental pollutants are :
(*a*) Human orgaic wastes
(*b*) Natural nutrients in excess
(*c*) Waste animal feed
(*d*) Non-biodegradable chemicals

45. National Environmental Planning Engineering Organisation at Nagpur is
(*a*) NEERI (*b*) CPHER
(*c*) ICAR (*d*) CSIR

46. Cyclone collector is used for minimising :
(*a*) Radioactive pollution
(*b*) Air pollution
(*c*) Noise pollution
(*d*) Water pollution

47. Pollution can be checked through :
(*a*) Reducing discharge of waste
(*b*) Increasing industrial development
(*c*) Throwing wastes in open spaces
(*d*) All of the above

ANSWERS

1	2	3	4	5	6	7	8	9	10
(*a*)	(*d*)	(*b*)	(*d*)	(*d*)	(*a*)	(*b*)	(*d*)	(*d*)	(*b*)
11	**12**	**13**	**14**	**15**	**16**	**17**	**18**	**19**	**20**
(*c*)	(*c*)	(*b*)	(*c*)	(*d*)	(*c*)	(*c*)	(*b*)	(*a*)	(*d*)
21	**22**	**23**	**24**	**25**	**26**	**27**	**28**	**29**	**30**
(*d*)	(*d*)	(*d*)	(*a*)	(*b*)	(*a*)	(*a*)	(*b*)	(*d*)	(*b*)
31	**32**	**33**	**34**	**35**	**36**	**37**	**38**	**39**	**40**
(*a*)	(*d*)	(*b*)	(*c*)	(*d*)	(*b*)	(*b*)	(*c*)	(*d*)	(*d*)
41	**42**	**43**	**44**	**45**	**46**	**47**			
(*d*)	(*a*)	(*b*)	(*d*)	(*a*)	(*b*)	(*a*)			

14

PESTICIDE POLLUTION

1. Fungicides are used to kill :
   (*a*) Fungal pathogens of plants
   (*b*) Viral pathogens of plants
   (*c*) Bacterial pathogens of plants
   (*d*) None of these
2. DDT is pesticide which is a :
   (*a*) Organophosphate
   (*b*) Organosulphur
   (*c*) Organochlorine
   (*d*) None of these
3. Which of the following is organophosphorus insecticide :
   (*a*) Dieldrin (*b*) Aldrin
   (*c*) Carbaryl (*d*) Malathion
4. Which one of the following is used as fumigants :
   (*a*) Aluminium phosphide
   (*b*) B.H.C.
   (*c*) DDT
   (*d*) None of these
5. Avicides used to kills :
   (*a*) Herbs (*b*) Weeds
   (*c*) Rodents (*d*) Birds
6. Which of the following acts as nerve poison :
   (*a*) Phosphine
   (*b*) CO
   (*c*) Chlorinated hydrocarbons
   (*d*) HCN
7. Which of the following is a aphyxiants :
   (*a*) Nitrogen gas (*b*) Rock phosphate
   (*c*) Silica gel (*d*) None of these
8. Celphos (Phostoxin) is known as :
   (*a*) Zinc phosphide
   (*b*) Aluminium phosphide
   (*c*) Warfarin
   (*d*) None of these
9. Which of the following is a herbicide?
   (*a*) BHC (*b*) DDT
   (*c*) EDB (*d*) 2, 4-D
10. Carbofuran is a/an :
    (*a*) Fumigants
    (*b*) Organo-phsophorus insecticide
    (*c*) Carbamates
    (*d*) None of these
11. Triazines (derivatives of urea) are :
    (*a*) Bacteriocides (*b*) Fungicides
    (*c*) Insecticides (*d*) Herbicides
12. Bordeaux mixture (mixture of copper sulphate and calcium hydroxide) used for controlling?
    (*a*) Viral diseases in plants
    (*b*) Bacterial diseases in plants
    (*c*) Fungal diseases in plants
    (*d*) None of these
13. Which one of the following is an insect repellant?
    (*a*) 2, 4-D (*b*) DDT
    (*c*) BHC (*d*) Azadirachtin
14. Which one of the following is identified as a highly potential biosorbent material for heavy metal pollution control :
    (*a*) *Thiobacillus ferroxidans*
    (*b*) *Ganoderma lucidum*
    (*c*) *Alnus incana*
    (*d*) *Alanus japanica*
15. Which of the following can be controlled by using biopesticides :

(*a*) insects (*b*) diseases
(*c*) weeds (*d*) All of the above

16. Match the object given in Column I with the product listed in Column II :

	Column I		Column II
A.	2, 4-D	1.	Virus resistance
B.	Coat Protein gene	2.	Somatic hybridization
C.	PEG	3.	Callus culture
D.	Cry gene	4.	Insect resistance
		5.	Haploid plants

Codes :

	A	B	C	D
(*a*)	3	1	2	4
(*b*)	3	1	4	2
(*c*)	3	2	1	4
(*d*)	3	4	1	2

17. Which of the following is used in biowar?
(*a*) a pathogen
(*b*) toxin from a pathogen
(*c*) a delivery system for the bioweapon agent
(*d*) All of the above

18. The biological control of agricultural pests, unlike chemical controls :
(*a*) toxic (*b*) very expensive
(*c*) polluting (*d*) self perpetuating

19. The neem is used as a natural insecticide because :
(*a*) It is rapidly degradable in nature
(*b*) Its cost of production is not high
(*c*) The extract of neem contains azadirachtin which acts as an antifeedant compound
(*d*) It is significantly most effective than other pesticides

20. Biological control component is central to advanced agricultural production. Which of the following is used as a third generation pesticides :
(*a*) Insect repellents
(*b*) Insect hormone analogues
(*c*) Pathogens
(*d*) Pheromones

21. Biocontrol of larvae of mosquito is done by :
(*a*) Lady bird (*b*) Aphids
(*c*) Gambusia fish (*d*) Rohu fish

22. Antifeedant property is found in :
(*a*) Parthenium (*b*) Sesbania
(*c*) Margosa (*d*) Chrysanthemum

23. Sporeine was developed in :
(*a*) U.S.A. (*b*) Germany
(*c*) Russia (*d*) France

24. Biopesticide include :
(*a*) Bioinsecticides
(*b*) Bioherbicides
(*c*) Both (*a*) and (*b*)
(*d*) Bioherbicides, Bioinsecticides and Biofertilizers

25. 'Devine' and 'Collego' are two agricultural substances that are used as :
(*a*) Bioherbicides
(*b*) Insect hormones
(*c*) Biofertilizers
(*d*) Natural insecticides

26. Which of the following alkaloids are good plant insecticides?
(*a*) Cinerin (*b*) Pyrethrum
(*c*) Nicotine (*d*) All of these

27. An ideal pesticide is one which :
(*a*) is non-toxic and biodegradable
(*b*) is non-persistence
(*c*) brings about complete control of a specific pest
(*d*) All of these

28. The over-growth of Cacti was checked by the introduction of :
(*a*) Mycoherbicide (*b*) Preying mantis
(*c*) Cochineal insect (*d*) None of these

29. Pick up the natural insecticide prepared by Chinese :
(*a*) An alkaloid prepared from *Datura*
(*b*) Azadirachtin extract from neem plant
(*c*) Rotenones from roots *Derris eliptica*
(*d*) None of the above

30. Thurioside is a :
(*a*) bioherbicide
(*b*) biofertilizer
(*c*) chemical pesticide
(*d*) proteinaceous toxin of bacterial origin

31. Confusion technique is used in :
(*a*) developing resistance
(*b*) eliminating weeds
(*c*) reducing harmful insects
(*d*) increasing population of predators

32. Cochineal insects have been employed in checking overgrowth of :
(*a*) Cacti (*b*) Weeds
(*c*) Scale insects (*d*) None of these

33. Materials of biological origin which are commonly used to maintain and improve soil fertility are :
(*a*) biofertilizers (*b*) green manures
(*c*) bioinsecticides (*d*) Both (*a*) and (*b*)

34. As it passes into food chain, the concentration of DDT :
(*a*) Remains same (*b*) Decreases
(*c*) Increases (*d*) Unpredictable

35. A persistent insecticide is :
(*a*) Organophosphates
(*b*) Carbamates
(*c*) Thiocarbamates
(*d*) Chlorinated hydrocarbons

36. An organochlorine insecticide is :
(*a*) DDT/aldrin
(*b*) Malathion
(*c*) Tetraethyl pyrophosphate
(*d*) Thiocarbamate

37. The level of tolerance of DDT is 10 ppm in case of *Daphnia*, therefore *Daphnia* :
(*a*) can live upto this concentration
(*b*) will die if concentration is lower than this
(*c*) can tolerate ten times more concentration of DDT than 10^2 ppm
(*d*) cannot tolerate DDT at all

38. Better method of pest control is :
(*a*) the use of chemical pesticide
(*b*) the use of radioactive substance
(*c*) by using pesticide taking into account number and composition of pest population
(*d*) use of steam

39. Drawback of DDT as pesticide is :
(*a*) It becomes ineffective after some time
(*b*) It is less effective than others
(*c*) It is not easily/rapidly degraded in nature
(*d*) Its high cost

40. The biological amplification of DDT in the various trophic levels is known as :
(*a*) Green house effect
(*b*) Biomagnification
(*c*) Eutrophication
(*d*) Pollution

41. Spraying DDT on crops shall produce pollution of :
(*a*) Air and water
(*b*) Air and soil
(*c*) Crops and air
(*d*) Soil and water

42. DDT concentration recorded in human body has been :
(*a*) 0.3 – 0.7 ppm
(*b*) 1.3 – 3.1 ppm
(*c*) 13 – 31 ppm
(*d*) 30 – 70 ppm

43. Match the following :

A. Global warming	1. SO_2
B. DDT	2. biological magnification
C. PAN	3. CO, CO_2
D. Acid Rain	4. smog

Codes :

	A	B	C	D
(*a*)	3	2	4	1
(*b*)	2	3	1	4
(*c*)	3	4	2	1
(*d*)	4	3	1	2

44. Highest DDT deposition shall occur in :
(*a*) Phytoplankton (*b*) Sea Gull/Birds
(*c*) Crab (*d*) Eel

45. Among pollutants which has the most lasting effect :
(*a*) Carbon monoxide
(*b*) Pesticides
(*c*) Sulphur dioxide
(*d*) Smoke from chimneys

46. Now-a-days DDT is not effective for killing mosquitoes because :
(*a*) mosquito population has become strong
(*b*) DDT is adulterated
(*c*) DDT has selection pressure on the genetic variability
(*d*) mosquitoes have developed adaptive resistance to pesticides

47. The form of mercury (H_g), which is most toxic to organisms is :
(*a*) elemental (*b*) molecular
(*c*) atomic (*d*) All of these

48. DDT is a :
(*a*) Non-biodegradable pollutant
(*b*) Biodegradable pollutant
(*c*) Antibiotic
(*d*) All of the above

49. Spraying of DDT produces pollution of :
(*a*) Air (*b*) Air and water
(*c*) Air and soil (*d*) Air, water and soil

50. Which of the following is a qualitative pollutant?
(*a*) CO_2 (*b*) Insecticide
(*c*) Plastic (*d*) Both (*b*) and (*c*)

51. Aluminium is more dangerous and poisonous at a pH of :
(*a*) 5 (*b*) 7
(*c*) 5.7 (*d*) 6

52. The population of hawks and eagles is declining because :
(*a*) of food scarcity
(*b*) of game lovers
(*c*) of excessive use of poisoned pesticides
(*d*) very few dead animals are found in the fields

53. *Opuntia* was a menace a few decades back in India. It was almost eradicated by :
(*a*) spraying DDT
(*b*) using tractors
(*c*) cochineal insect introduction
(*d*) using 2, 4-D

54. Photochemical smog is caused by formation of:
(*a*) aluminium ions
(*b*) methane
(*c*) sulphur
(*d*) free radicals of oxygen

55. Which of the following cause damage to the blood?
(*a*) Ca (*b*) Pb
(*c*) Mg (*d*) Ar

56. Most poisonous pollutant in water is :
(*a*) Zn (*b*) PO_4
(*c*) Ar (*d*) CO_2

57. Use of leaded gasoline in internal combustion engines causes :
(*a*) more pollution
(*b*) no pollution
(*c*) less pollution
(*d*) smoke emission

58. A pollutant is any substance, chemical or other factor, that changes :
(*a*) natural geochemical cycles
(*b*) the natural balance of our environment
(*c*) the natural flora of our environment
(*d*) the natural wildlife of our region

59. Strengthening of concept of environmental monitoring is due to concern for the :
(*a*) quality of environment
(*b*) quantity of environment
(*c*) quality of monitor
(*d*) pure air

60. Mudball technique has been proposed by :
(*a*) Central Rice Research Institute, Cuttack
(*b*) CSIR, New Delhi
(*c*) Punjab Agriculture University, Ludhiana
(*d*) The International Rice Research Institute in Philippines

61. Biomagnification is a process of :
(*a*) magnification of animals
(*b*) enlargement of aquatic animals
(*c*) concentration of dangerous chemical into body of members of food web
(*d*) None of the above

62. Environmental monitoring helps in all except in :
(*a*) identifying pollution problem
(*b*) prescribing environmental quality standards
(*c*) predicting pollution abatement strategies
(*d*) planning pollution abatement strategies

63. Disease caused by eating fish found in water contaminated with industrial waste having mercury is :
(*a*) Minamata disease
(*b*) Bright's disease
(*c*) Hashimoto's disease
(*d*) Osteosclerosis

64. Where did the epidemic bone softening disease '*Itai Itai*' occurred first?
(*a*) Myanmar (*b*) Japan
(*c*) South Korea (*d*) U.S.A.

65. Non-biodegradable toxic pollutants, as they pass through food webs, undergo biological :
(*a*) oxidation (*b*) reduction
(*c*) magnification (*d*) hydratic

66. Biodegradable pollutant is :
(*a*) Plastic (*b*) Asbestos
(*c*) Sewage (*d*) Mercury

67. The deficiency disease of cadmium is :
(*a*) Itai Itai (*b*) Minimata
(*c*) Kidney failure (*d*) Diabetes

68. Match of following :

	Column A		**Column B**
A.	Volcano	1.	a rent through which molted substances comes out
B.	Earthquake	2.	tremors produced by the passage of vibratory waves through the rocks earth
C.	Flood	3.	excess rain and uneven distribution of water

Codes :

	A	B	C
(*a*)	2	1	3
(*b*)	1	2	3
(*c*)	1	3	2
(*d*)	3	1	2

69. Cadmium pollution is associated with disease :
(*a*) Anaemia
(*b*) Itai-Itai
(*c*) Minamata
(*d*) Pneumoconiosis

70. Main toxic substance in Bhopal disaster was :
(*a*) methyl isocyanide
(*b*) methyl isocyanate
(*c*) BHC
(*d*) DDT and BHC both

71. Use of lichens in case of pollution is :
(*a*) Treatment of pollutant water
(*b*) Bioindicators of pollution
(*c*) Promote pollution
(*d*) Lichens have no relation with pollution

72. Remote Sensing is done by :
(*a*) interacting between incident radiation and the target of interest
(*b*) acquiring information about the earth
(*c*) sensing and recording reflected or emitted and processing, analysing and applying that information
(*d*) All of the above

73. Copper is an essential trace element, necessary for oxidation and absorption of iron and vitamin C in :
(*a*) kidneys (*b*) lungs
(*c*) digestive system (*d*) heart

74. Calcium is an important constituents of living organisms are it is found in :
(*a*) brain cells (*b*) nervous system
(*c*) lungs (*d*) bones and shells

ANSWERS

1	2	3	4	5	6	7	8	9	10
(*a*)	(*c*)	(*d*)	(*a*)	(*d*)	(*c*)	(*a*)	(*b*)	(*d*)	(*c*)
11	**12**	**13**	**14**	**15**	**16**	**17**	**18**	**19**	**20**
(*d*)	(*c*)	(*d*)	(*b*)	(*d*)	(*a*)	(*d*)	(*d*)	(*c*)	(*b*)
21	**22**	**23**	**24**	**25**	**26**	**27**	**28**	**29**	**30**
(*c*)	(*c*)	(*b*)	(*c*)	(*a*)	(*d*)	(*d*)	(*c*)	(*c*)	(*d*)
31	**32**	**33**	**34**	**35**	**36**	**37**	**38**	**39**	**40**
(*c*)	(*a*)	(*d*)	(*c*)	(*d*)	(*a*)	(*a*)	(*d*)	(*c*)	(*b*)
41	**42**	**43**	**44**	**45**	**46**	**47**	**48**	**49**	**50**
(*d*)	(*c*)	(*a*)	(*b*)	(*b*)	(*d*)	(*a*)	(*a*)	(*d*)	(*d*)
51	**52**	**53**	**54**	**55**	**56**	**57**	**58**	**59**	**60**
(*a*)	(*c*)	(*c*)	(*c*)	(*b*)	(*c*)	(*a*)	(*b*)	(*a*)	(*d*)
61	**62**	**63**	**64**	**65**	**66**	**67**	**68**	**69**	**70**
(*c*)	(*c*)	(*a*)	(*a*)	(*b*)	(*c*)	(*a*)	(*b*)	(*b*)	(*b*)
71	**72**	**73**	**74**						
(*b*)	(*c*)	(*c*)	(*d*)						

15

RADIATION AND ENVIRONMENT

1. The phenomenon of radioactivity was discovered by :
(a) Madam Curie (b) Pierre Curie
(c) Henry Becquerrel (d) Rutherford

2. The most penetrating radiations are :
(a) α-rays
(b) β-rays
(c) γ-rays
(d) all are equally penetrating

3. Cobalt 60 is used in the treatment of :
(a) leukaemia (b) thyroid disorders
(c) cancer (d) pneumonia

4. The isotope used for dating acheological finding is :
(a) $^{3}_{1}H$ (b) $^{14}_{6}C$
(c) $^{18}_{8}O$ (d) $^{235}_{92}U$

5. The reaction $^{8}_{5}B \longrightarrow ^{8}_{4}Be$ takes place due to :
(a) α-decays (b) beta-decay
(c) electron capture (d) positron decay

6. Which of the following radiation can be stopped easily by air?
(a) α-rays (b) β-rays
(c) γ-rays (d) X-rays

7. Which of the following does not contain material particles?
(a) α-rays (b) β-rays
(c) anode rays (d) γ-rays

8. The equipment used to carry out nuclear reaction in a controlled manner is called :
(a) Breeder reactor
(b) Nuclear reactor
(c) Thermonuclear fusion
(d) Cyclotron

9. Which of the following is used as a neutron absorber in the nuclear reactor?
(a) Water (b) Deuterium
(c) Cadmium (d) None of these

10. The heaviest particle is :
(a) Meson (b) Neutron
(c) Proton (d) Electron

11. Which of the following is correct?
(a) Atom bomb and H-bomb both are examples of nuclear fission
(b) Nuclear reaction are markedly affected by temperature
(c) Electron and positron both have same mass
(d) The lesser the half-life, the lesser is the number of atoms undergoing decays in a given time

12. Which of the following is used as a moderator in nuclear reactor?
(a) H_2O (b) D_2O
(c) Alums (d) Any of these

13. β-particle is emitted in radioactivity
(a) by conversion of proton to neutron
(b) from outermost orbit
(c) by conversion of neutron to proton
(d) β-particle is not emitted

14. A radioisotope will not emit :
(a) α and β-rays simultaneously
(b) β and γ-rays simultaneously
(c) γ and α-rays simultaneously
(d) γ-rays only

15. Radiocarbon dating was discovered by :
(*a*) G.N. Lewis (*b*) J. Williard Gibbs
(*c*) W.F. Libby (*d*) W. Nerst

16. If radium and chlorine combine to form radium chloride, the compound is :
(*a*) No larger radioactive
(*b*) Twice as radioactive as radium
(*c*) Half as radioactive as radium
(*d*) As radioactive as radium

17. The chemical which causes damage to WBC, bone marrow, spleen, lymph, nodes and lungs is :
(*a*) Iodine-131 (*b*) Calcium
(*c*) Strontium-90 (*d*) Iodine-127

18. Name the chemicals which cause bone cancer and tissue degeneration :
(*a*) Iodine-131 (*b*) Strontium-90
(*c*) Iodine-127 (*d*) Calcium

19. Nuclear explosion causes mainly :
(*a*) noise pollution (*b*) soil pollution
(*c*) water pollution (*d*) air pollution

20. UV radiations to disinfect polluted water is not generally recommended because :
(*a*) it has no residual germicidal effect
(*b*) it is not effective against most micro-organism
(*c*) colour and turbidity of water reduces its disinfection potential
(*d*) Both (*a*) and (*c*)

21. UV radiations from sunlight cause the reaction that produce :
(*a*) CO (*b*) SO_2
(*c*) O_3 (*d*) NO_2

22. What was the cause of "Yusho" disease which occurred in 1968 from a leak in canning factory?
(*a*) DBCP (*b*) PCB
(*c*) Formaldehyde (*d*) Mercury

23. Term 'nuclear winter' is associated with :
(*a*) nuclear war
(*b*) nuclear disarmament
(*c*) nuclear weapon testing
(*d*) aftermath of a nuclear holocaust

24. The atmosphere is essential in maintaining the heat balance of the earth as it helps to :
(*a*) radiate long waves
(*b*) radiate energy
(*c*) trap the heat of sun
(*d*) trap the water

25. The **FALSE** statement is :
(*a*) all the short wave radiations are absorbed by the atmospheric gases
(*b*) earth surface emits long wavelength radiation
(*c*) the heat carried by the water vapour is transmitted to the air
(*d*) All of the above

26. Effect of to-day's radioactive fall out will be more on future children than children living to-day due to :
(*a*) Infant susceptibility to radiations
(*b*) Increase of susceptibility to radiations with age
(*c*) Mutated genes are usually recessive
(*d*) Radiations have delayed effect

27. What percentage of solar energy/radiation is used in photosynthesis?
(*a*) 2% (*b*) 4%
(*c*) 6% (*d*) 10%

28. Radium emits :
(*a*) electron (*b*) X-rays
(*c*) α- and γ-rays (*d*) None of these

29. X-rays are modified :
(*a*) Protons (*b*) Neutrons
(*c*) Positrons (*d*) Electrons

30. Centenary year for X-rays is :
(*a*) 1995 (*b*) 2000
(*c*) 1996 (*d*) 2001

31. Missed IUCD is recognised by
(*a*) CT scan (*b*) Ultrasound
(*c*) Barium meal (*d*) X-rays

32. Which of the following does not use ionising radiations?
(*a*) Contrast X-rays (*b*) CT scanning
(*c*) NMR (*d*) None of these

33. Which of the following is used by surgeons as a "light knife"?
(*a*) Lasers (*b*) X-rays
(*c*) Gamma rays (*d*) All of these

34. Which of the following is not type of laser?
(*a*) Neon laser (*b*) CO_2 laser
(*c*) Argon laser (*d*) Hydrogen laser

35. Who discovered X-rays?
(*a*) Rene Laennec
(*b*) Willhelm Roentgen
(*c*) William Stocker
(*d*) Hens Berger

36. The most abundant source of protons in the body are :
(*a*) Hydrogen atoms (*b*) Nitrogen atoms
(*c*) Oxygen atoms (*d*) All of these

37. X-rays imaging is commonly employed for diagnosing diseases of :
(*a*) Lungs (*b*) Bones
(*c*) Heart (*d*) All of these

38. PET is a diagnostic technique based on :
(*a*) X-rays radiations
(*b*) Medical lasers
(*c*) Positively charged electrons
(*d*) All of these

39. A positron emitting isotope is :
(*a*) Nitrogen 13 (*b*) Oxygen 16
(*c*) Carbon 14 (*d*) None of these

40. The principle of nuclear magnetic resonance was first described by :
(*a*) Cormack (*b*) Bloch
(*c*) Hounsfield (*d*) Domadian

41. The unit of magnetic field strength in MRI is :
(*a*) Megahertz (*b*) Ren
(*c*) Hounsfield (*d*) Tesla

42. Radiation is not used in
(*a*) NMR
(*b*) Cat scan
(*c*) Thyroid scan
(*d*) Digital substraction scanning

43. NMR imaging technique is based on gyromagnetic property of :
(*a*) Neutron (*b*) Positron
(*c*) Electron (*d*) Proton

44. All the following are used in radiotherapy except :
(*a*) Alpha rays (*b*) Beta rays
(*c*) Gamma rays (*d*) X-rays

45. X-rays were discovered in the year
(*a*) 1868 (*b*) 1895
(*c*) 1854 (*d*) 1865

46. Cell most sensitive to radiation is :
(*a*) Lymphocyte (*b*) Platelets
(*c*) Basophil (*d*) Neutrophil

47. The least radio sensitive tissue is :
(*a*) Bone (*b*) Kidney
(*c*) Thyroid (*d*) Nervous tissue

48. The tissue most resistant radioactivity is :
(*a*) Rectum (*b*) Vagina
(*c*) Colon (*d*) Cervix

49. Which is the most sensitive tissue to radiation :
(*a*) Skin (*b*) Spleen
(*c*) Liver (*d*) Gonads

50. Unit of magnetic induction is :
(*a*) Curie (*b*) Tesla
(*c*) Rad (*d*) Ren

51. Relative Biological Effectiveness (RBE) is related to :
(*a*) Radiation (*b*) Water
(*c*) Soil (*d*) Pollution

52. Most common tumour due to radiation arises from :
(*a*) Liver (*b*) Bone
(*c*) Lung (*d*) Breast

53. Earliest bone metastatis can be detected by :
(*a*) Plain X-rays
(*b*) Tomography
(*c*) Computed tomography
(*d*) Radioisotope bone scan

54. Radiation exposure occurs in all except :
(*a*) MRI (*b*) Plain X-rays
(*c*) CT scan (*d*) None of these

55. Stage III carcinoma cervix is best managed by :
(*a*) Palliative surgery
(*b*) Radiotherapy
(*c*) Surgery
(*d*) Both (*b*) and (*c*)

56. Which is not mutagenic :
(*a*) UV rays (*b*) X-rays
(*c*) Beta rays (*d*) Ultrasound

57. Laser was discovered by :
(*a*) Kolff (*b*) Maimah
(*c*) Berger (*d*) Roentgen

58. LASER is an acronym for :
(*a*) Light amplification by stimulated emission of radiation
(*b*) Low atomic serial energy resonance
(*c*) Lead and sulphur emission radiation
(*d*) Low amplitude simultaneous emission of radiation

59. Barium X-ray examination is useful to investigate the :
(*a*) Reproductive tract
(*b*) Excretory tract
(*c*) Digestive tract
(*d*) Circulatory system

60. The highest radioactive element is :
(*a*) Uranium (*b*) Protium
(*c*) Radium (*d*) Tritium

61. The radiant energy of sun is due to :
(*a*) Combustion (*b*) Nuclear Fission
(*c*) Nuclear Fusion (*d*) Disintegration

62. Maximum background radiation is found in :
(*a*) Kerala beach (*b*) M.P.
(*c*) Delhi (*d*) U.P.

63. The difference in the wavelength regions of solar and terrestrial radiation is of fundamental improtance to :
(*a*) energy balance of the earth-atmosphere system
(*b*) heat balance of earth
(*c*) energy balance of earth
(*d*) tropic level to be high

64. The magnitude of solar radiation reaching the surface of the earth depends on :
(*a*) orientation of land surface w.r. to sun
(*b*) time of year
(*c*) time of day
(*d*) All of these

65. The radiant energy falling perpendicular to the sun's rays at the earth's mean distance from the sun is :
(*a*) Equilibrium constant
(*b*) Solar constant
(*c*) Chemical equilibrium
(*d*) None of these

66. The value of *Solar Constant* is :
(*a*) 3.8×10^{23} watt/m^2
(*b*) 3.8×10^{23} kilowatt/m^2
(*c*) 1.34×10^{3} watt/m^2
(*d*) 6.67×10^{-23} watt/m^2

67. Match the following :

	Column A		**Column B**
A.	Cold weather season	1.	Atmospheric temperature goes very down
B.	Hot weather season	2.	Temperature rises and humidity decreases
C.	Rainy season	3.	Sets in middle of June and upto to beginning of July

Codes :

	A	B	C
(*a*)	1	2	3
(*b*)	2	3	1
(*c*)	1	3	2
(*d*)	3	2	1

68. Most outstanding danger at present for the survival of living beings on the earth is :
(*a*) radiation hazard
(*b*) automobiles
(*c*) industrial effluents
(*d*) detergents

69. What does the term 'over kill' deal with?
(*a*) Pesticide poisoning
(*b*) Soil erosion
(*c*) Nuclear holocaust
(*d*) Global warming

70. Radiation is health hazard because it causes :
(*a*) Haemophilia (*b*) Leukaemia
(*c*) Pneumonia (*d*) Polio

71. Which pigment protects plants from UV damage?
(*a*) Chlorophyll (*b*) Xanthophyll
(*c*) Carotenoids (*d*) Phycocyanin

72. Chernobyl nuclear tragedy occurred on which date?
(*a*) 9th August 1945
(*b*) 10th August 1945
(*c*) April 1986
(*d*) 3rd December 1984

73. Which is a **TRUE** statement?
(*a*) The planet earth is also called geosphere
(*b*) Earth receives 380000 Megawatt energy/sec.
(*c*) Only 30% of all energy radiated by the sun is utilised at the earth
(*d*) All of the above

74. The earth system is highly :
(*a*) static (*b*) complex
(*c*) dynamic (*d*) unidirectional

75. The presence of O_3 in atmosphere of earth :
(*a*) has been responsible for increasing average global temperature in recent years
(*b*) is advantageous since it supplies O_2 for people travelling in jets
(*c*) hinders higher rate of photosynthesis
(*d*) helps in checking the penetration of ultraviolet rays to earth

76. U.V. radiations from sunlight causes a reaction that produces :
(*a*) Ozone (*b*) SO_2
(*c*) CO_2 (*d*) None of these

77. Radioactive pollution causes :
(*a*) cancer of any types
(*b*) lethal mutation
(*c*) speeded senescence
(*d*) Any of the above

78. What causes the temperature differences between land and sea when heated by solar radiations?
(*a*) Due to high specific heat of H_2O
(*b*) Absorbance of high CO_2
(*c*) Both of the above
(*d*) None of the above

79. Strontium of radioactive fall out is :
(*a*) Sr-90 (*b*) Sr-95
(*c*) Sr-85 (*d*) Sr-80

80. Ultraviolet radiations are lethal because of inactivation of :
(*a*) Proteins, nucleic acids and pigments
(*b*) Minerals, air and water
(*c*) Carbohydrates, fats an vitamins
(*d*) Water, carbon dioxide and oxygen

81. Nuclear power genereates :
(*a*) photochemical pollution
(*b*) SO_2 pollution
(*c*) air pollution
(*d*) thermal pollution

82. As a general rule, ionizing radiation is most damaging to :
(*a*) mature, stable cells
(*b*) actively dividing cells
(*c*) highly specialized cells
(*d*) cells in which food is stored

83. Environmental pollutant that can cause birth defects is :
(*a*) SO_2 (*b*) CO
(*c*) Smog (*d*) Radioactivity

84. Contamination with radioactivity is dangerous because it causes :
(*a*) biological magnification
(*b*) gene mutation
(*c*) photochemical smog
(*d*) ozone destruction

85. UV radiations bring about :
(*a*) Skin cancer (*b*) Mouth cancer
(*c*) Lung cancer (*d*) Liver cancer

86. Which one is not biodegradable :
(*a*) Radioactive substances
(*b*) Bagasse
(*c*) Molasses
(*d*) Agricultural wastes

87. Which wavelength of ultraviolet light of sunlight combine with ozone molecule?

(*a*) Ultraviolet-A (*b*) Ultraviolet-C
(*c*) Ultraviolet-B (*d*) Ultraviolet-D

88. The molecular action of ultraviolet light is mainly reflected through :

(*a*) photodynamic action
(*b*) destruction of hydrogen bonds between DNA strands
(*c*) formation of pyrimidine
(*d*) destruction of ester bonds

89. Non-ionising radiations with specific biological effects are :

(*a*) UV radiations (*b*) Beta-rays
(*c*) Gamma rays (*d*) X-rays

90. Which part of human body is first to be affected by nuclear radiations?

(*a*) Bone marrow (*b*) Liver
(*c*) Lungs (*d*) Ear

91. The most dangerous radioactive air pollutant is :

(*a*) Strontium-90 (*b*) P-32
(*c*) S-35 (*d*) Ca-40

92. Ultraviolet light causes :

(*a*) Formation of pyrimidines
(*b*) Sticky metaphases
(*c*) Photodynamic action
(*d*) Destruction of hydrogen bonds between complementary DNA strands

ANSWERS

1	2	3	4	5	6	7	8	9	10
(*c*)	(*c*)	(*c*)	(*b*)	(*c*)	(*a*)	(*d*)	(*b*)	(*c*)	(*b*)
11	**12**	**13**	**14**	**15**	**16**	**17**	**18**	**19**	**20**
(*c*)	(*b*)	(*c*)	(*d*)	(*c*)	(*d*)	(*a*)	(*b*)	(*d*)	(*b*)
21	**22**	**23**	**24**	**25**	**26**	**27**	**28**	**29**	**30**
(*c*)	(*b*)	(*d*)	(*c*)	(*a*)	(*c*)	(*d*)	(*c*)	(*d*)	(*a*)
31	**32**	**33**	**34**	**35**	**36**	**37**	**38**	**39**	**40**
(*b*)	(*c*)	(*a*)	(*d*)	(*b*)	(*a*)	(*d*)	(*c*)	(*a*)	(*b*)
41	**42**	**43**	**44**	**45**	**46**	**47**	**48**	**49**	**50**
(*d*)	(*a*)	(*d*)	(*d*)	(*b*)	(*a*)	(*d*)	(*b*)	(*d*)	(*b*)
51	**52**	**53**	**54**	**55**	**56**	**57**	**58**	**59**	**60**
(*a*)	(*d*)	(*d*)	(*a*)	(*b*)	(*d*)	(*b*)	(*a*)	(*c*)	(*d*)
61	**62**	**63**	**64**	**65**	**66**	**67**	**68**	**69**	**70**
(*c*)	(*a*)	(*a*)	(*a*)	(*b*)	(*c*)	(*a*)	(*a*)	(*c*)	(*b*)
71	**72**	**73**	**74**	**75**	**76**	**77**	**78**	**79**	**80**
(*d*)	(*c*)	(*a*)	(*c*)	(*d*)	(*d*)	(*d*)	(*a*)	(*a*)	(*a*)
81	**82**	**83**	**84**	**85**	**86**	**87**	**88**	**89**	**90**
(*d*)	(*b*)	(*d*)	(*b*)	(*a*)	(*a*)	(*b*)	(*b*)	(*a*)	(*a*)
91	**92**								
(*a*)	(*d*)								

16

BIODIVERSITY AND ITS CONSERVATION

1. The term biodiversity refers to :
   (*a*) totality of species of a region
   (*b*) totality of ecosystem of a region
   (*c*) totality of genes of a region
   (*d*) All of the above
2. An American plant that has become a waterweed in India is :
   (*a*) *Eichhornia crassipes*
   (*b*) *Typha latifolia*
   (*c*) *Cyperus rotundus*
   (*d*) *Trapa bispinosa*
3. Endemic plants are those which are :
   (*a*) found in alpine region
   (*b*) gregarious in habit
   (*c*) cosmopolitan in distribution
   (*d*) restricted to a specified area
4. Planting of flower and fruit trees along road sides is included in :
   (*a*) Agroforestry programme
   (*b*) Social forestry programme
   (*c*) Urban forestry programme
   (*d*) Van Mahotsava
5. Decline in our forests is due to :
   (*a*) soil erosion
   (*b*) no afforestation
   (*c*) afforestation
   (*d*) indiscriminate felling of trees and grazing
6. What is cause of destruction of biologically rich and unique habitats?
   (*a*) Increasing human population
   (*b*) Consumption of resources
   (*c*) Pollution
   (*d*) All of the above
7. Ginkgo has been removed from the list of endangered species due to :
   (*a*) gene bank
   (*b*) extensive cultivation
   (*c*) *in-situ* cultivation
   (*d*) *ex-situ* cultivation
8. What is the approximate number of species of fish described all over the world?
   (*a*) 4780 (*b*) 26959
   (*c*) 43000 (*d*) 1550
9. Which of the following levels of biodiversity are interrelated?
   I Genetic diversity
   II Species diversity
   III Community and ecosystem diversity
   (*a*) I and II (*b*) II and III
   (*c*) I and III (*d*) I, II and III
10. What is the basis of speciation?
    (*a*) Amount of genetic variation
    (*b*) Kinds of variation
    (*c*) Variation in ecosystem and community
    (*d*) Species diversity
11. Alpha diversity refers to :
    (*a*) diversity of organism sharing the same habitat
    (*b*) rate of replacement of species along a gradient of habitat
    (*c*) diversity of the habitat over the geographical area
    (*d*) All of the above

12. From which of the following plant, medicine is obtained used as analgesic?
(*a*) *Cinchona ledgeriana*
(*b*) *Taxus brevifolia*
(*c*) *Papaver somniferum*
(*d*) *Taxus baccata*

13. Anthropogenic extinction is caused by :
(*a*) environmental changes
(*b*) human activities
(*c*) catastrophes
(*d*) Both (*a*) and (*b*)

14. Planting trees on public and common land is known as :
(*a*) social forestry (*b*) farm forestry
(*c*) agroforestry (*d*) reforestation

15. An example for *in-situ* biological conservation method is to establish :
(*a*) Seed banks
(*b*) Botanical gardens
(*c*) Zoos
(*d*) Biosphere reserve

16. The Earth Summit held at Rio de Janeiro in 1992 resulted into :
(*a*) Compilation of Red List
(*b*) Establishment of Biosphere Reserves
(*c*) Convention on Biodiversity
(*d*) IUCN

17. Approximate percentage of enaemic flowering plants in India is :
(*a*) 23% (*b*) 33%
(*c*) 53% (*d*) 63%

18. Select the correct statement :
(*a*) Biodiversity increases from the poles to the equator
(*b*) 925 animal species and 1014 plant species in India are characterized as Critically Endangered in the Red List
(*c*) As on September 2002, India had 581 protected areas
(*d*) All of the above

19. Which of the following is correct?
(*a*) Biodiversity refers to the totality of genes, species and ecosystem of a region
(*b*) Within-community diversity is called alpha diversity
(*c*) National parks are traditional protected areas
(*d*) All of the above

20. Which of the following is incorrect?
(*a*) Exotic species have large impact especially in island ecosystems
(*b*) Between-community diversity is called beta community
(*c*) Western Ghats and Eastern Himalayas in India are among the 25 global biodiversity hot spots of world
(*d*) None of the above

21. MAB stands for :
(*a*) Man and Biosphere
(*b*) Man, Antibiotic and Bacteria
(*c*) Man and Biotic community
(*d*) Mayer, Andersand and Bisby

22. Kaziranga wildlife sanctuary is famous for :
(*a*) Tiger (*b*) Rhino
(*c*) Elephant (*d*) Muskdeer

23. The 'threatened species' refers to the species which are :
(*a*) Endangered (*b*) Rare
(*c*) Vulnerable (*d*) All of the above

24. The number of vertebrate species facing danger of extinction is about :
(*a*) 10 (*b*) 100
(*c*) 1000 (*d*) 10,000

25. The concept of "Biosphere Reserve" was conceived by :
(*a*) ZSI (*b*) BSI
(*c*) UNESCO (*d*) Govt. of India

26. Which of the following animals has become almost extinct in India?
(*a*) Wolf (*b*) Rhinoceros
(*c*) Cheetah (*d*) Hippopotamus

27. Whales when washed ashore will die because:
(*a*) Their body temperatures will increase :
(*b*) They cannot respire
(*c*) Their skin will crack
(*d*) Their bones will be crushed because of weight of body

28. The famous Chipko movement was started by:
(*a*) S.L. Bahuguna (*b*) Rajiv Gandhi
(*c*) Menaka Gandhi (*d*) Salim Ali

29. When was MAB launched by UNESCO?
(*a*) 1971 (*b*) 1975
(*c*) 1981 (*d*) 1972

30. A species in immediate danger of extinction is :
(*a*) endangered (*b*) vulnerable
(*c*) rare (*d*) None of the above

31. Identify the correct match between tiger reserve and its state :
(*a*) Corbett - Madhya Pradesh
(*b*) Planau - Orissa
(*c*) Manas - Asom
(*d*) Bandipur - Tamil Nadu

32. First National Park of India is :
(*a*) Kanha N.P. (*b*) Periyar N.P.
(*c*) Corbett N.P. (*d*) Bandipur N.P.

33. Which of the following is matching pair of sanctuary and its main protected animals?
(*a*) North Eastern Himalayan Region - Samba
(*b*) Sunderban - Rhino
(*c*) Gir - Lion
(*d*) Kaziranga - Musk Deer

34. About what species of earth's species will be destroyed if all the tropical rain forests are destroyed?
(*a*) 10 (*b*) 20
(*c*) 50 (*d*) 90

35. Species most vulnerable to extinction from human activities are those with :
(*a*) low carrying capacity
(*b*) high population growth rates
(*c*) large niches
(*d*) many natural predators

36. Which of the following types of animals does man cheifly protect?
(*a*) Feeble animals
(*b*) Harmless animals
(*c*) Useful animals
(*d*) Animals likely to perish

37. Red panda is preserved at :
(*a*) Dachigam National Park (JK)
(*b*) Sasan Gir National Park (Gujarat)
(*c*) Kangchend National Park (Sikkim)
(*d*) Simlipal National Park (Orissa)

38. "Chipko Movement" is world's most known eco development programme started by Sunder Lal Bahuguna (1973). It is related with:
(*a*) Conservation of Forests
(*b*) Afforestation
(*c*) Planting
(*d*) Population

39. Which is correct for threatened (T) species :
(*a*) It is a species to be conserved to avoid its becoming rare, endangered or vulnerable species
(*b*) It is an endangered species like Rhino Asiatic Lion which is in danger of extinction
(*c*) It is a vulnerable species like musk deer, black buck which is likely to move into endangered category in near future
(*d*) It is a rare species like wild Asiatic Ass with a small population in certain geographical areas

40. Vulnerable (V) species are those :
(*a*) which live in National Park
(*b*) which are wild
(*c*) which require conservation
(*d*) which are likely to be in danger of extinction in near future

41. Rare (R) species :
(*a*) those which are in danger of extinction
(*b*) those with small population in certain geographical areas
(*c*) those which are found in Silent Valley of Kerala
(*d*) those which are likely to be endangered

42. A biosphere reserve preserves :
(*a*) Genetic resources of organisms
(*b*) Traditional life styles of tribals
(*c*) Wild population
(*d*) All of the above

43. Animals and plants can be best protected in :
(*a*) Sanctuaries
(*b*) Zoos
(*c*) National Parks
(*d*) Botanical gardens

44. Which of the following are exhaustible renewable resources?
(*a*) Water and Aquatic animals
(*b*) Soil fertility
(*c*) Natural vegetation and wildlife
(*d*) All of the above

45. Which of the following are non-renewable exhaustible natural resources?
(*a*) Minerals
(*b*) Biological species
(*c*) Hydropower
(*d*) Both (*a*) and (*b*)

46. Which of the following is not inexhaustible natural resources?
(*a*) Solar energy and wind power
(*b*) Rainfall
(*c*) Power of tides and hydropower
(*d*) Minerals

47. How much of the total water of earth's surface fresh water is frozen as polar or glacial ice?
(*a*) 2.5 per cent (*b*) 1.97 per cent
(*c*) 0.5 per cent (*d*) 0.001 per cent

48. Low lying areas covered with shallow water are called :
(*a*) estuaries (*b*) swamps
(*c*) wetlands (*d*) springs

49. Deforestation :
(*a*) causes extinction of plant, animal and microbial species
(*b*) induces regional and global climate change
(*c*) causes global warming
(*d*) All of the above

50. Wetland conservation programmes is/are based on :
(*a*) checking waste disposal in wetlands
(*b*) preparation of wetland inventories
(*c*) reduction of excessive inflow of nutrients and silt into wetlands
(*d*) All of the above

51. Planting of trees on unused farmland, community land, road and rail sides is called :
(*a*) commercial forestry
(*b*) social forestry
(*c*) agroforestry
(*d*) None of these

52. The average annual production of dry grass or hay in grasslands in India is about :
(*a*) 150 million tons (*b*) 250 million tons
(*c*) 300 million tons (*d*) 400 million tons

53. Wildlife (protection) Act, 1972 was amended in :
(*a*) 1982 (*b*) 1991
(*c*) 1999 (*d*) 2002

54. The principal aim of our National Forest Policy (1988) is to :
(*a*) ensure environmental stability
(*b*) maintenance of ecological balance
(*c*) maintaining atmospheric equilibrium
(*d*) All of the above

55. National goal of forest cover is :
(*a*) 33 per cent (*b*) 25 per cent
(*c*) 20 per cent (*d*) 30 per cent

56. Soil erosion can be prevented by :
(*a*) overgrazing
(*b*) removal of vegetation
(*c*) afforestation
(*d*) deforestation

57. Mild grazing in grassland by herbivores :
(*a*) retards growth of grasses
(*b*) arrests growth of grasses
(*c*) stimulates growth of grasses
(*d*) destroys vegetation

58. Deforestation generally decreases :
(*a*) rainfall (*b*) soil erosion
(*c*) drought (*d*) global warming

59. Forest area in India is about :
(*a*) 9% of geographical area
(*b*) 19% of geographical area
(*c*) 29% of geographical area
(*d*) 37% of geographical area

60. Which one of the following represents a renewable source of energy?
(*a*) Petroleum (*b*) Coal
(*c*) Nuclear fuel (*d*) Trees

61. Which of the following represents the regulative function of forest?
(*a*) Storage and release of gases
(*b*) Production of wood
(*c*) Production of essential oils
(*d*) Conservation of soil and water

62. The principal components of photochemical smog in urban areas are
(*a*) SO2 and NO2
(*b*) SPM and CO
(*c*) SPM and NO2
(*d*) Hydrocarbons and Ozone

63. Extensive planting of trees to increase forest cover is called :
(*a*) afforestation (*b*) agroforestry
(*c*) .deforestation (*d*) social forestry

64. Wetlands occupy :
(*a*) 6% of world's land
(*b*) 10% of world's land
(*c*) 12% of world's land
(*d*) 14% of world's land

65. Forest and wildlife are :
(*a*) non-renewable resources
(*b*) renewable natural resources
(*c*) inexhaustible resources
(*d*) None of the above

66. Which one of the following forests is more diverse?
(*a*) Coniferous evergreen
(*b*) Deciduous evergreen
(*c*) Tropical rain forest
(*d*) Subtropical rain forest

67. Deciduous forests are the characteristic of the region having :
(*a*) severe winter only
(*b*) warm summer only
(*c*) less winter and warm summer
(*d*) severe winter and warm summer

68. Which one of the following is most effective in controlling floods?
(*a*) Deforestation
(*b*) Reforestation
(*c*) Constructing dams
(*d*) Digging deep canals

69. Indian bustard bird is on the verge of extinction due to :
(*a*) deforestation (*b*) climate changes
(*c*) hunting (*d*) All of the above

70. Tropical evergreen forests are found in India in :
(*a*) Himachal Pradesh (*b*) Madhya Pradesh
(*c*) Asom (*d*) Tamil Nadu

71. Which of the following birds has gained importance as wildlife in recent years?
(*a*) Pheasants (*b*) Egrets
(*c*) Indian Bustard (*d*) Pelican

72. Jim Corbett National Park, first to be established, is present in:
(*a*) Uttarakhand and famous for tiger
(*b*) Rajasthan and famous for Black buck
(*c*) Punjab and home for Antelopes
(*d*) H.P. and famous for birds

73. Which of the following birds in India is on the verge of extinction?
(*a*) Pink headed duck
(*b*) Passenger pigeon
(*c*) Indian Bustard
(*d*) Sand piper

74. What percentage of approx total land area is covered by forests in India?
(*a*) 32% (*b*) 21%
(*c*) 23% (*d*) 25%

75. Conifers are dominant vegetation of :
(*a*) tropical zone
(*b*) cold temperate region
(*c*) polar region
(*d*) equitorial region

76. How many species of plants are threatened with extinction?
(*a*) 25,000 (*b*) 20,000
(*c*) 15,000 (*d*) 10,000.

77. With reference to conservation of wildlife, how many 'Project Tiger' areas have been selected :
(*a*) 17 (*b*) 18
(*c*) 19 (*d*) 20

78. In which state of India is the Gir Lion sanctuary situated?
(*a*) Maharashtra (*b*) M.P.
(*c*) Gujarat (*d*) Rajasthan

79. The most effective means of conservation is to :
(*a*) remove predators
(*b*) preserve habitat
(*c*) vaccination against diseases
(*d*) census the species during the breeding season

80. The bird 'Dodo' became extinc because of :
(*a*) its beautiful feathers
(*b*) hunting
(*c*) its curved beak
(*d*) its melodious songs

81. Which is the only home of yellow maned Indian Lion?
(*a*) Jim Corbett National Park, Uttarakhand
(*b*) Gir Forest, Gujarat
(*c*) Sariska Tiger Project
(*d*) Kanha Forest, M.P.

82. Indian Rhinoceros is the most protected species in National Park :
(*a*) Corbett (*b*) Kaziranga
(*c*) Bandipur (*d*) Gir

83. What for IUCN stands :
(*a*) International Understanding on Coal and Nuclear Fuel
(*b*) International Union for Controlling Noosphere
(*c*) International Union for Conservation of Nature
(*d*) International Union for Co-operation on Nuclear weapons

84. Small parks tend to support only :
(*a*) k-selected species
(*b*) r-selected species
(*c*) climax species
(*d*) species with small niches

85. All the following are proper plans for increasing agricultural production except :
(*a*) Expansion of irrigation facilities
(*b*) Increase in application of fertilizers
(*c*) Mechanisation of various aspects of farming
(*d*) Cutting of forests to add land for cultivation

86. Alluvial soil is mostly found in which region :
(*a*) Southern India
(*b*) Northern India
(*c*) Gangetic Jamuna Plains
(*d*) Eastern India

87. Laterite soil is rich in :
(*a*) Nitrogen (*b*) Iron
(*c*) Calcium (*d*) Magnesium

88. Amount of water a soil can hold against the pull of gravity is known as :
(*a*) Hygroscopic water
(*b*) Storage capacity
(*c*) Gravitational water
(*d*) Field capacity

89. Water remaining in the soil after a plant has permanently wilted is :
(*a*) Hygroscopic water
(*b*) Ground water
(*c*) Gravitational water
(*d*) Capillary water

90. Geothermal energy is :
(*a*) Non-renewable, conventional source of energy
(*b*) Non-renewable, non-conventional source of energy
(*c*) Renewable, non-conventional source of energy
(*d*) Renewable, conventional source of energy

91. Renewable source of energy is :
(*a*) Coal (*b*) Kerosene
(*c*) Petroleum (*d*) Biomass

92. The least porous soil among the following is:
(*a*) Sandy soil (*b*) Clayey soil
(*c*) Loamy soil (*d*) Gravel soil

93. The value of a resource depends upon :
(*a*) Quantity of resource
(*b*) Quality of resource
(*c*) Type of society and its needs
(*d*) All of the above

94. Water is considered to be :
(*a*) Renewable resource
(*b*) Non-renewable resource
(*c*) Degradable maintainable
(*d*) Non-degradable non-maintainable

95. Desertification is due to :
(*a*) Deforestation
(*b*) Soil-erosion due to water
(*c*) Soil-erosion due to wind
(*d*) Very high temperature and low rainfall

96. Which is the characteristic feature of a physiologically dry soil?
(*a*) Light available to plants is not sufficient
(*b*) There is plenty of water in the soil
(*c*) Concentration of salts is very high in the soil
(*d*) Soil is stony

97. The total solid matter washed into the sea is approximately :
(*a*) 300 million tonnes
(*b*) 1300 million tonnes
(*c*) 2300 million tonnes
(*d*) 3300 million tonnes

98. The best soil for healthy and vigorous growth of most plants is :
(*a*) Sandy soil (*b*) Loam soil
(*c*) Clay soil (*d*) None of these

99. Deforestation has an alarming effect on :
(*a*) Soil erosion
(*b*) Weed control
(*c*) Sunlight
(*d*) Increase in grazing area

100. Soil erosion can be prevented by :
(*a*) Grazing
(*b*) Deep ploughing
(*c*) Planting trees
(*d*) Increasing bird population

101. Which of the following functions performed by a forest help most in controlling drought?
(*a*) Forests prevent soil erosion
(*b*) Forests bring rainfall
(*c*) Forests have lot of water plants
(*d*) Forests act as water sheds

102. Water logging occurs in :
(*a*) Sandy soil (*b*) Gravel soil
(*c*) Loamy soil (*d*) Clay soil

103. A fertile soil is likely to have a pH value of :
(*a*) 3-4 (*b*) 8-9
(*c*) 6-7 (*d*) 10-11

104. Deep black soil is considered to be highly productive due to high proportion of :
(*a*) Silt and earthworm
(*b*) Clay and humus
(*c*) Gravel and Ca^{++}
(*d*) Sand and Zn

105. Main cause of extinction of wildlife is :
(*a*) Air pollution
(*b*) Water pollution
(*c*) Industrial gases
(*d*) Deforestation

106. Deforestation causes :
(*a*) Diseases (*b*) Epidemics
(*c*) Soil erosion (*d*) Rainfall

107. Quinine is obtained from :
(*a*) Cinchona plant (*b*) Bamboo plant
(*c*) Sandalwood (*d*) Rosha grass

108. Rare species are those :
(*a*) with small populations in world
(*b*) which are likely to become endangered
(*c*) which are in danger of extinction
(*d*) None of the above

109. Biologists celebrate every year 5th June as :
(*a*) Darwin's birthday
(*b*) World Environment Day
(*c*) World Health Organisation Day
(*d*) World Population Day

110. On which date Word Earth day is celebrated?
(*a*) July 15 (*b*) 22 April
(*c*) August 21 (*d*) December 16

111. Project tiger was launched in :
(*a*) 1972 (*b*) 1981
(*c*) 1975 (*d*) 1961

112. Nilgiri Biosphere Reserve Project is concerned with conservation scheme of :
(*a*) Tamil Nadu (*b*) Karnataka
(*c*) Kerala (*d*) All of the above

113. Biosphere reserve areas are :
(*a*) 13 (*b*) 17
(*c*) 19 (*d*) 25

114. Wildlife protection act was made in :
(*a*) 1982 (*b*) 1972
(*c*) 1988 (*d*) None of the above

115. In national parks which of the following are not allowed :
(*a*) Forestry
(*b*) Grazing
(*c*) Cultivation and private ownership
(*d*) All of the above

116. World forest day is observed on :
(*a*) 28th February (*b*) 6th October
(*c*) 21st March (*d*) 5th June

117. The concept of critical habitats is :
(*a*) territory of an animals
(*b*) breeding, nursing, feeding and resting area
(*c*) a boundary beyond which an animal will not move
(*d*) another name for wildlife sanctuary

118. The species which are in the immediate danger of extinction are called :
(*a*) Rare species
(*b*) Threatened species
(*c*) Endangered species
(*d*) All of the above

119. The percentage of endangered living species is :
(*a*) 40 (*b*) 18
(*c*) 20 (*d*) 10

120. Periyar Wildlife sanctuary is situated at :
(*a*) Balagaon– Orrisa
(*b*) Nilgiri– Tamil Nadu
(*c*) Idukki- Kerala
(*d*) Nainital– Uttarakhand

121. Ranthambore National Park is situated in :
(*a*) Punjab (*b*) Rajasthan
(*c*) Gujarat (*d*) Madhya Pradesh

122. Deforestation causes :
(*a*) Soil erosion
(*b*) Reduced rainfall
(*c*) More floods
(*d*) All of these

123. Quinine is :
(*a*) Plant product
(*b*) Animal product
(*c*) Synthetic drug
(*d*) Microbial product

124. White tigers are conserved in :
(*a*) Corbett National Park
(*b*) Kanha National Park–Mandla, Balaghat
(*c*) Tandoba National Park, Chandrapur
(*d*) Bandipur National Park, Mysore

125. Flamingoes in India are preserved at :
(*a*) Sambar Lake (*b*) Lake Mansarovar
(*c*) Rann of Kutch (*d*) Chilka Lake

126. Deforestation may reduce the chances of :
(*a*) frequent cyclones (*b*) soil erosion
(*c*) rainfall (*d*) landslides

127. Earth summit at Rio-de-Janeiro (Brazil) was related to :
(*a*) Land survey
(*b*) Soil fertility
(*c*) Conservation of genetic resources of animals and plants
(*d*) None of the above

128. Cultigens include :
(*a*) Domestic animals
(*b*) Wild animals
(*c*) Cultivated plants
(*d*) Both (*a*) and (*b*)

129. If environmental restoration is started right now, resolving the present man-made ecological crisis will take about :
(*a*) 100 yrs (*b*) 200 yrs
(*c*) 300 yrs (*d*) 50 yrs

130. Man disturbs natural food chains by :
(*a*) use of fossil fuel
(*b*) family planning
(*c*) introduction of exotic species
(*d*) All of the above

131. Silent valley of Kerala is being preserved because it has :
(*a*) Rare plants and animals
(*b*) Only natural forest of India
(*c*) Costly timber plants
(*d*) Recreational value

132. Afforestation should be with :
(*a*) Bamboos
(*b*) Eucalyptus
(*c*) Exotic species
(*d*) Indigenous species

133. To conserve wildlife, each state of India is allotted a species. Which plant is allocated to Karnataka?
(*a*) *Ficus benghalensis*
(*b*) *Shorea robusta*
(*c*) *Cedrus deodara*
(*d*) *Santalum indicum*

134. Bioshpere Reserve project was started in India during :
(*a*) 1984 (*b*) 1985
(*b*) 1988 (*d*) 1989

135. Recently a rice pest brown plant hopper (*Nilaparvata lugens*) threatened the entire rice cultivation. The genes for resistance to this pest were found in some old varieties of rice from :
(*a*) Mysore (*b*) A.P.
(*c*) Kerala (*d*) Haryana

136. The animal got extinct in recent years from India is :
(*a*) Nilgai (*b*) Cheetah
(*c*) Golden Langur (*d*) Hyena

137. Which is mainly responsible for extinction of wildlife?
(*a*) Hunting of flesh
(*b*) Destruction of habitats
(*c*) Pollution of air and water
(*d*) All of the above

138. Land mass occupied by forest is about :
(*a*) 11% (*b*) 22%
(*c*) 30% (*d*) 60%

139. A species restricted to a given area is :
(*a*) Endemic species
(*b*) Allopatric species
(*c*) Sympatric species
(*d*) Sibling species

140. The species of animal protected in Kaziranga sanctuary is :
(*a*) *Rhinoceros unicornis*
(*b*) *Panthera* leo
(*c*) *Panthera tigris*
(*d*) *Macaca mulatta*

141. Biosphere reserves are being threatended with
(*a*) Population growth
(*b*) Rains
(*c*) Pollution
(*d*) All of the above

142. *Idri-idri* occurs in :
(*a*) India (*b*) Mauritius
(*c*) Fiji (*d*) Madagascar

143. Number of Endangered species of Angiosperms in india :
(*a*) 487 (*b*) 15,000
(*c*) 5,000 (*d*) 3,000

144. World wildlife Fund was organised by UNESCO in :
(*a*) 1961 (*b*) 1983
(*c*) 1931 (*d*) 1915

145. Todaba National Park is located in :
(*a*) Mumbai (*b*) Cochin
(*c*) Chennai (*d*) Chandrapura

146. The species of animal protected in Biligiri Rangaswamy National Park is :
(*a*) Panther
(*b*) Different species of birds
(*c*) Tiger
(*d*) Elephant

147. The most threatening factor for survival of plant biodiversity is :
(*a*) destruction of natural habitat
(*b*) biosphere reserve
(*c*) vulnerable ecosystem like mangroves and wetlands
(*d*) inaccesibility of habitat

148. In bioreserves .... is allowed.
(*a*) Restricted human population
(*b*) Private operations
(*c*) No human population
(*d*) Permanent human population

149. Which endangered animal is the source of world's finest lightest warmest and most expensive wool-the shahtoosh?
(*a*) Chiru (*b*) Nilgai
(*c*) Cheetal (*d*) Kashmiri goat

150. According to Indian Forest Policy, what percentage of land area should be under forest cover?
(*a*) 13 per cent (*b*) 23 per cent
(*c*) 33 per cent (*d*) 43 per cent

151. Conservation of wildlife is essential to :
(*a*) Protect ecosystem
(*b*) Safeguard environment of earth
(*c*) Protect threatened wild life
(*d*) All of the above

152. Symbol of WWF is :
(*a*) Tiger (*b*) Rhododendron
(*c*) White Bear (*d*) Red Panda

153. Threatened species often include :
(*a*) endangered species
(*b*) vulnerable species
(*c*) rare species
(*d*) All of the above

154. Species which occur in small populations and are restricted to only certain geographical areas are placed under the category :
(*a*) endangered species
(*b*) vulnerable species
(*c*) rare species
(*d*) All of these

155. Conservation of living resources is a complex operation and is concerned with :
(*a*) plants and animals
(*b*) all living organisms and non-living elements of the environment on which they depend
(*c*) protection of wildlife and the forests in which these inhabit
(*d*) plants, animals and microbes

156. Which one of the following would be more appropriate in producing high yielding varieties?
(*a*) More application of fertilizers irrigation and use of pesticides
(*b*) Breeding with wild varieties of organisms with genetic potentiality to respond to improved inputs
(*c*) Development of disease resistant varieties of plants
(*d*) Selection of wild organisms and their subsequent preservation

157. What is the major cause of diminishing wildlife numbers :
(*a*) Cannibalism
(*b*) Habitat destruction
(*c*) Felling of trees
(*d*) Paucity of drinking water

158. Which of the following communities is more vulnerable to invasion by outside animals and plants?
(*a*) Temperate forests
(*b*) Tropical evergreen forests
(*c*) Oceanic island communities
(*d*) Mangroves

159. Dhudhawa National Park is located in :
(*a*) Madhya Pradesh (*b*) Himachal Pradesh
(*c*) Andhra Pradesh (*d*) Uttar Pradesh

160. Plant species on verge of extinction due to over exploitation is :
(*a*) Gloriossa
(*b*) *Centella*
(*c*) *Podophyllum*
(*d*) All of the above

161. Had *Cinchona* been eliminated before its use was discovered, man would have been deprived of :
(*a*) use of its bark as dalchini
(*b*) tejpat used as a spice
(*c*) antimalarial drug
(*d*) valuable timber

162. Kanha Biosphere reserve is to be established in :
(*a*) UP (*b*) MP
(*c*) Meghalaya (*d*) Orissa

163. Cold deserts of India occurs in :
(*a*) Rann of Kutch and Gujarat
(*b*) Thar
(*c*) N.E. States
(*d*) Lahul Spiti and Ladakh

164. In wildlife sanctuary :
(*a*) Harvesting of trees for timber and forest products is permitted
(*b*) Only wild fauna are protected
(*c*) Private ownership is allowed
(*d*) All of the above

165. If the standard deviation of a population is 20 and the standard error of mean is 4, then the sample size is
(*a*) 25 (*b*) 80
(*c*) 5 (*d*) 100

166. Marine invertebrates are protected in :
(*a*) Gulf of Mannar (*b*) Gulf of Cambay
(*c*) Bay of Bengal (*d*) All of the above

167. WWF-N is logo for conservation of :
(*a*) Red Panda (*b*) Giant Panda
(*c*) Polar Bear (*d*) Tiger

168. Which one of the following statements is appropriate for "Red Data Book" :
(*a*) It provides data on the effects of red light on photosynthesis
(*b*) It is a list of plants and animals present in Red sea
(*c*) It is the list of red pigmented plants
(*d*) It provides data on species threatened with extinction

169. In a National Park protection is provided to :
(*a*) Fauna only
(*b*) Flora only
(*c*) Entire ecosystem
(*d*) Flora and Fauna

170. Forests take part in :
(*a*) Control of atmospheric pollution
(*b*) Maintenance of natural balance
(*c*) Prevention of soil erosion
(*d*) All of these

171. The last succession in a series is known as :
(*a*) Climax (*b*) Climate climax
(*c*) Community (*d*) Either (*a*) or (*b*)

172. The relation between tick bird and *Rhinoceros* is called :
(*a*) commensalism (*b*) proto-cooperation
(*c*) antibiosis (*d*) neutralism

173. The organisms, preying upon other species of animals, are known as :
(*a*) parasites
(*b*) predators
(*c*) cannibals
(*d*) primary consumers

174. A sucker fish, attached to the body of shark, would exemplify :
(*a*) cooperation (*b*) commensalism
(*c*) mutualism (*d*) parasitism

175. The phenomenon, in which an organism is benefitted, without affecting the other, is called :
(*a*) parasitism (*b*) commensalism
(*c*) symbiosis (*d*) predation

176. Species diversity generally increases as one proceeds from :
(*a*) low altitude to high altitude, and from low latitudes to high latitudes
(*b*) high altitude to low altitude, and from low latitudes to high latitudes
(*c*) high altitude to low altitude, and from high latitudes to low latitudes
(*d*) low altitude to high altitude, and from high latitudes to low latitudes

177. The study of interrelationship of different groups of organisms is known as :
(*a*) community ecology
(*b*) population ecology
(*c*) synecology
(*d*) autecology

178. An animals, which referred to as ecotherms, is :
(*a*) frog (*b*) snake
(*c*) labeo (*d*) All of the above

179. Most of the desert animals are active during night time, because they :
(*a*) can see well only at night
(*b*) get a lot of food at night
(*c*) face less competition for food at night
(*d*) can conserve a lot of water at night

180. The 'niche' of a species is meant for :
(*a*) specific place where an organism lives
(*b*) specific species functions and its competitive power
(*c*) habitat and specific functions of a species
(*d*) None of these

181. A parasite living within the tissue of host is :
(*a*) Epiphyte (*b*) Endophyte
(*c*) Ectophyte (*d*) Ectoparasite

182. A bird introduced from another countries became a serious pest due to :
(*a*) more sexual reproduction
(*b*) better nesting habitats
(*c*) absence of natural competitions
(*d*) better adaptation to a new area

183. Which is a part of symbiosis in lichens?
(*a*) Alga-fungus
(*b*) Alga-alga
(*c*) Fungus-fungus
(*d*) Fungus-gymnosperm

184. Which of the following is an example of mutualism?
(*a*) *Spirogyra* (*b*) *Selaginella*
(*c*) *Lichen* (*d*) *Riccia*

185. The water plants, in a pond, provide to animals food and :
(*a*) water (*b*) oxygen
(*c*) nitrogen (*d*) phosphorus

186. If green plants are removed from an aquarium, the fishes will :
(*a*) Die
(*b*) Increase in number
(*c*) Decrease in size
(*d*) Not to be affected

187. Which of the following is wrong?
(*a*) Lichen, an association of fungus and alga, is an example of mutualism
(*b*) Epiphytes, using other plants for support only and not for water or food, show commensalism
(*c*) Sea Anemone and Hermit Crab association is an example of protocooperation
(*d*) Mutualism, protocooperation and commensalism cannot be included under symbiosis

188. Which is not a primary coloniser?
(*a*) Viruses (*b*) Lichens
(*c*) Blue-Green Algae (*d*) Mosses

189. Fungal association of roots of higher plants in mycorrhiza is known as :
(*a*) Parasitism (*b*) Hyperparasitism
(*c*) Mutualism (*d*) Commensalism

190. Hyperparasite is a kind of parasite which :
(*a*) Kills its host
(*b*) Completes life cycle in one host
(*c*) Uses host machinery for reproduction
(*d*) None of the above

191. Plants obtaining nourishment from other plants by haustoria are :
(*a*) Mesophytes (*b*) Parasites
(*c*) Xerophytes (*d*) Halophytes

192. A successful parasite is the one which :
(*a*) Grows rapidly
(*b*) Reproduces fast
(*c*) Sticks to host for long
(*d*) Makes minimum demands from its host

193. Which of the following statements is correct regarding the two organisms in commensalism?
(*a*) No one is harmed
(*b*) Both the partners are harmed
(*c*) One partner is benefitted whether another suffers
(*d*) One partner is benefitted and other remains unharmed

194. Which one of the following groups constitutes the fossil fuels?
(*a*) Coal, wood pieces and soil
(*b*) Coal, oil and natural gas
(*c*) Natural gas, oil and wood pieces
(*d*) Oil, wood pieces and dry dung

195. Which of the following is a non-renewable resource ?
(*a*) Water (*b*) Forest
(*c*) Wildlife (*d*) Fossil fuels

196. Most important plants which helped coal formation are :
(*a*) Angiosperms (*b*) Gymnosperms
(*c*) Pteriodophytes (*d*) Thallophytes

197. Large oceanic studies are concentrated upon to :
(*a*) get energy from sea tides
(*b*) get fuel, minerals and other substances
(*c*) get more food
(*d*) All of the above

198. Which of the following industry is not forest based?
(*a*) Lac (*b*) Paper
(*c*) Cement (*d*) Sports good

199. If more trees are grown in the industrial towns :
(*a*) there will be more rains
(*b*) inhabitants will have more shades
(*c*) oxygen will be replenished
(*d*) they will provide more fuel and food

200. Gobar gas contains mainly :
(*a*) ethylene
(*b*) methane
(*c*) hydrogen and ethylene
(*d*) hydrogen and oxygen

201. Depletion of forests results in :
(*a*) less rainfall (*b*) erosion
(*c*) loss of fertility (*d*) All of the above

202. Chipko movement started in the year :
(*a*) 1973 (*b*) 1975
(*c*) 1977 (*d*) 1980

203. The most crucial event in nature governing nutrient balance is :
(*a*) primary production
(*b*) secondary production
(*c*) nutrient cycle
(*d*) gross production

204. Burning of fossil fuels is the main cause of :
(*a*) nitrogen oxide pollution
(*b*) nitrous oxide pollution
(*c*) nitric oxide pollution
(*d*) sulphur dioxide pollution

205. The secondary source of carbon in nature is through :
(*a*) methanogenic archaebacteria
(*b*) methanotrophic bacteria
(*c*) methangenic fungi
(*d*) methanotrophic slime moulds

206. When a volcano erupts, one of the following cycles in nature is disturbed :
(*a*) Phosphorus (*b*) Nitrogen
(*c*) Carbon (*d*) None of the above

207. Which one of the following is an example of both organic and inorganic resource :
(*a*) Metallic ferrous ores
(*b*) Microbes
(*c*) Soil
(*d*) Air

208. Which one of the following gives better idea of productivity an an ecosystem?
(*a*) Pyramid of biomass
(*b*) Pyramid of energy
(*c*) Pyramid of number
(*d*) All of the above

209. The most important natural resource of energy is :
(*a*) electricity (*b*) atomic fission
(*c*) fossil fuels (*d*) biogas

210. Number of forest types found in India are :
(*a*) 16 (*b*) 10
(*c*) 12 (*d*) 24

211. Percent of water on the world's surface representing fresh water is
(*a*) 97 (*b*) 50
(*c*) 10 (*d*) 3

212. Major forest types in India are :
(*a*) Tropical evergreen and tropical thorn
(*b*) Temperate mixed and tropical deciduous
(*c*) Tropical dry deciduous and tropical moist deciduous
(*d*) Tropical evergreen and tropical moist deciduous

213. In India, Sal and Teak are planted in forest area :
(*a*) 5% (*b*) 23%
(*c*) 20% (*d*) 13%

214. The power obtained from a horizontal wind turbine operating at maximum efficiency is proportional to its diameter (d) as
(*a*) D (*b*) D^2
(*c*) $D^{3/2}$ (*d*) D

215. Tropical rain forests of world which were 1600 million hectares in 1900, now occupy :
(*a*) 938 million ha (*b*) 700 million ha
(*c*) 160 million ha (*d*) 538 million ha

216. Chipko movement originated in
(*a*) Silent Valley of Kerala
(*b*) Kangra Valley of Himachal Pradesh
(*c*) Tehri Garwal of Uttarakhand
(*d*) Pachmari of M.P.

217. Percentage of land covered by forests in India
(*a*) 9–18% (*b*) 18–27%
(*c*) 27–36% (*d*) More than 50 %

218. Conservation is :
(*a*) Protection of natural resources
(*b*) Management of natural resources
(*c*) Proper use of natural resources
(*d*) All of the above

219. Overgrazing causes :
(*a*) Negative pollution
(*b*) Positive pollution
(*c*) Soil erosion
(*d*) Reduction in crop yield

220. Extinction of numerous wild animals is due to :
(*a*) Hunting (*b*) Deforestation
(*c*) Overcrowding (*d*) Scarcity of food

221. First biosphere reserve was established in 1986 at :
(*a*) Nilgiri
(*b*) Nanda Devi
(*c*) Little Rann of Kutch
(*d*) Sunderbans

222. Limited private operations are allowed in :
(*a*) Zoos (*b*) Botanical gardens
(*c*) National Parks (*d*) Sanctuaries

223. A threatened species is :
(*a*) Endangered (*b*) Rare
(*c*) Vulnerable (*d*) All of the above

224. Wildlife Act was enacted in India in :
(*a*) 1950 (*b*) 1962
(*c*) 1972 (*d*) 1986

225. Forest management is related to :
(*a*) Silviculture (*b*) Sericulture
(*c*) Apiculture (*d*) Olericulture

226. Forests control drought through :
(*a*) Lot of water plants
(*b*) Increasing rainfall
(*c*) Retention of water and prevention of erosion
(*d*) Functioning as water shed

227. Deforestation brings about :
(*a*) Increased sunlight
(*b*) Soil erosion
(*c*) Weed control
(*d*) Increased grazing area

228. Common source of energy in Indian villages is :
(*a*) electricity
(*b*) coal
(*c*) wood and dry animal dung
(*d*) sun

229. Metallic minerals are :
(*a*) renewable resources
(*b*) non-renewable resources
(*c*) ineshaustible resources
(*d*) None of the above

230. Aluminium, cobalt and manganese will last up to :
(*a*) End of present century
(*b*) 2100-2200 A.D.
(*c*) Upto end of 2100
(*d*) Eternity

231. Most of world's gold and platinum occurs in :
(*a*) North America (*b*) South Africa
(*c*) India (*d*) Canada

232. In the following four countries which country has the highest per capita consumption of energy :

(*a*) India (*b*) Japan
(*c*) Mexico (*d*) Canada

233. Maximum petroleum is used in :
(*a*) mechanised agriculture
(*b*) shipping
(*c*) industries
(*d*) transport on land and air

234. Which of the following is a non-renewable resource?
(*a*) Forests (*b*) Coal deposits
(*c*) Water (*d*) Wildlife

235. Life supporting earth's surface is known as :
(*a*) lithosphere (*b*) stratosphere
(*c*) biosphere (*d*) ecotone

236. North America is rich in :
(*a*) Molybdenum (*b*) Tin
(*c*) Tungsten (*d*) Gold

237. The final step of material cycle consists of :
(*a*) mineral extraction
(*b*) their conversion into metals, ceramics and chemicals
(*c*) manufacture of public utility goods
(*d*) their return to environment as waste refuse

238. The ultimate source of H_2 for biological conservation of solar energy is :
(*a*) air (*b*) solar radiations
(*c*) water (*d*) plant body itself

239. Visible gas on denitrification is produced by the action of :
(*a*) Bacillus sp.
(*b*) *Nitrococcus sp.*
(*c*) *Chromobacterium lividium*
(*d*) *Rhizobium sp.*

240. Example of renewable resources is :
(*a*) air (*b*) clay
(*c*) fossil (*d*) biogas

241. The most important function of *Rhizobium* is :
(*a*) N_2 assimilation (*b*) N_2 fixation
(*c*) Ammonification (*d*) Nitrification

242. *Nitrosomonas* and *Nitrococcus* promote :
(*a*) anaerobic reduction of ammonia
(*b*) anaerobic oxidation of ammonia
(*c*) aerobic reduction of ammonia
(*d*) aerobic oxidation of ammonia

243. Which of the following sources of energy is virtually inexhaustible?
(*a*) Nuclear fusion (*b*) Coal
(*c*) Oil (*d*) Natural gas

244. A problem with monoculture is that they provide
(*a*) an environment for the growth of plant tumor
(*b*) a lot of calories but a few nutrients
(*c*) less energy than is used to produce darker
(*d*) a high carrying capacity for their insect harbivores

245. In a good agricultural field surface soil is usually darker than soil about one metre down. It is because the top soil :
(*a*) contains less organic matter
(*b*) is not so old
(*c*) contains more organic matter
(*d*) is richer in Ca and Mg

246. Plants are killed in winter by frost becasue :
(*a*) water in plants freezes
(*b*) water expands and breaks the cells
(*c*) of desiccation of vascular tissue
(*d*) no photosynthesis takes place at low temperature

247. Humus accumulates in Tundra because :
(*a*) there is no fire
(*b*) low temperature inhibits bacterial action
(*c*) low temperature favours conversion of leaves into humus
(*d*) the conditions are extremely dry to prevent bacterial action

248. Physiological dryness is faced by :
(*a*) pond plants (*b*) dry soil plants
(*c*) bog plants (*d*) epiphytes

249. Tundra soils are characteristics of :
(*a*) moderately cold climate
(*b*) warm and humid climate
(*c*) extremely cold climate
(*d*) warm and dry climate

250. Podzols are found in :
(*a*) tropical zones (*b*) temperate zones
(*c*) polar zones (*d*) subtropical zones

251. Plants can absorb capillary water only because :
(*a*) it does not allow air to circulate
(*b*) it allows air to circulate
(*c*) it is present in all types of soils
(*d*) it has dissolved oxygen in it

252. Good soil is one which has :
(*a*) 50% organic salts and 50% inorganic salts
(*b*) 50% of sand and 50% of clay
(*c*) 50% organic and inorganic salts and
(*d*) 50% of porous air and water

253. Which of the following means endemic?
(*a*) Indigenous (*b*) Exotic
(*c*) Ubiquitous (*d*) Naturalized

254. Those species whose populations have been seriously depleted and whose ultimate security is not assured are known as :
(*a*) Threatened species
(*b*) Endangered species
(*c*) Vulnerable species
(*d*) Rare species

255. Chipko movement is related to :
(*a*) Forest conservation
(*b*) Preventing soil pollution
(*c*) Preserving threatened species
(*d*) None of the above

256. The average life of a crop variety is :
(*a*) 25 – 50 years (*b*) 5 – 15 years
(*c*) 15 – 25 years (*d*) 1 – 5 years

257. Gene for resistance to Brown Plant Hopper (*Nilaparvata lugens*) of modern Rice has been obtained from
(*a*) Wild Rice
(*b*) African Rice
(*c*) Old Rice varieties from Kerala
(*d*) IR–8

258. *Cinchona* tree belongs to :
(*a*) India (*b*) England
(*c*) China (*d*) Peru

259. Living species in danger of extinction amount to :
(*a*) 10% (*b*) 20%
(*c*) 35% (*d*) 50%

260. Dodo, an extinct flightless bird, belonged to :
(*a*) Mauritius (*b*) Lakshadweep
(*c*) Canada (*d*) Iceland

261. Cheetah (*Acinonyx jubatus*) has become extinct from :
(*a*) Srilanka (*b*) India
(*c*) Africa (*d*) Malaysia

262. Which one is a troublesome weed of agricultural fields?
(*a*) *Chenopodium album*
(*b*) *Cyperus rotundus*
(*c*) *Parthenium hysterophorus*
(*d*) *Eichhornia crassipes*

263. An endangered bird is :
(*a*) Passenger Pigeon
(*b*) Pink-headed Duck
(*c*) Great Indian Bustard
(*d*) Vulture

264. Noise of 90 dB for 8 hours represents 100% dose. If the noise of 93 dB is for 1 hour duration, it represents a dose of
(*a*) 25% (*b*) 50%
(*c*) 75% (*d*) 100%

265. In India, cold desert occurs in :
(*a*) Mount Abu (*b*) Gujarat
(*c*) Rann of Kutch (*d*) Ladakh and Spiti

266. Scale lengths associated with mesoscale phenomenon in atmosphere are typically in the range
(*a*) 10 – 500 m (*b*) 1 – 200 km
(*c*) 100 – 1000 km (*d*) 1000 – 10,000 km

267. When an atmosphere has an isothermal profile, it is
(*a*) very stable
(*b*) slightly stable
(*c*) unstable
(*d*) very unstable (turbulent)

268. The wavelength range of UV-C radiation is
(*a*) 320 – 400 nm (*b*) 280 – 320 nm
(*c*) 100 – 1500 nm (*d*) 240 – 280 nm

269. 'Valley of Flowers' is found in :
(*a*) Nilgiri Hills
(*b*) North Eastern Himalayas
(*c*) North Western Himalayas
(*d*) Satpura Hills

270. Congress Grass is :
(*a*) *Cynodon dactylon*
(*b*) *Digitaria purpurea*
(*c*) *Cymbopogon citratus*
(*d*) *Parthenium hysterophorus*

271. Consumption of wood as fuel is estimated at :
(*a*) 1700 million m^3 (*b*) 100 million m^3
(*c*) 10000 million m^3 (*d*) 4500 million m^3

272. Poor man's timber is :
(*a*) Mango wood (*b*) Bamboo
(*c*) Acacia wood (*d*) Eucalyptus wood

273. Tendu/Kendu leaves used as wrappers for 'bidis' are got from :
(*a*) *Diospyros ebenum*
(*b*) *Dipterocarpus indicus*
(*c*) *Dipterocarpus tuberculatus*
(*d*) *Diospyros exsculpta*

274. The plant yielding Sola Pith (*Aeschynomene aspera*) is :
(*a*) Large sized tree
(*b*) Herb
(*c*) Perennial shrub with spongy floating stem
(*d*) Palm like monocot

275. A rough idea of the deficiency of an essential element in the soil without performing soil tests can be obtained by :
(*a*) analysing the ash of a plant growing in the soil
(*b*) noticing the typical morphology symptoms of deficiency shown by plants growing in it
(*c*) observing the physical texture of soil
(*d*) determining the dry weight of the plant

276. Soil erosion means :
(*a*) breaking up of rock by water streams
(*b*) deposition of new soil layers
(*c*) removal of top soil layers by wind or water
(*d*) decomposition of organic matter and development of the soil

277. Soil conservation is the process whereby :
(*a*) sterile soil is converted into fertile soil
(*b*) soil is protected against loss
(*c*) soil erosion is allowed
(*d*) soil is aerated

278. To rectify acid soil one of the following is used :
(*a*) Urea (*b*) Phosphate
(*c*) Nitrate (*d*) Lime

279. Loam soils are considered to be highly productive because of their proper proportion of :
(*a*) clay and humus
(*b*) sand and zinc
(*c*) sand, clay, silt and humus
(*d*) minerals and water

280. The aggregates of fine soil particles improve the characteristics of soil by :
(*a*) increasing permeability of soil to water and air
(*b*) increasing permeability of soil to the roots and root hair
(*c*) increasing the water and nutrient holding capacity of the soil
(*d*) All of the above

281. Saprobial index relates to :
(*a*) level of water in ecosystem
(*b*) extent of litter decomposition
(*c*) status of terrestrial system
(*d*) status of water body

282. A very rich source of Phosphorus (Phosphate rocks) has been discovered in :
(*a*) Gwalior M.P.
(*b*) Ranchi (Jharkhand)
(*c*) Jawar Kota (Rajasthan)
(*d*) Murad Nagar (U.P.)

283. What is ground water reserve of Inida?
(*a*) 17 million km^3 (*b*) 27 million km^3
(*c*) 37 million km^3 (*d*) 47 million km^3

284. Waterlogging occurs in :
(*a*) sandy soil (*b*) gravel soil
(*c*) loamy soil (*d*) clayey soil

285. Soil conservation is the process where :
(*a*) soil is aerated
(*b*) soil erosion is allowed

(*c*) sterile soil is converted into fertile soil
(*d*) soil is protected against loss

286. Minerals and metals are :
(*a*) Renewable resources
(*b*) Non-renewable resources
(*c*) Renewable as well as non-renewable resources
(*d*) Biodegradable resources

287. Petroleum is considered as :
(*a*) renewable resource
(*b*) an unconventional energy resource
(*c*) a non-renewable resource
(*d*) a synthetic product

288. Deep black soil is considered to be highly productive due to high proportion of :
(*a*) Salt and earthworm
(*b*) Clay and humus
(*c*) Gravel and Ca^{++}
(*d*) Sand and Zn

289. Both power and manure is provided by :
(*a*) Nuclear plants
(*b*) Thermal plants
(*c*) Biogas plants
(*d*) Hydroelectric plants

290. Out of the following four countries which counrty has the highest per capita consumption of energy :
(*a*) Pakistan (*b*) India
(*c*) USA (*d*) Korea

291. Example of renewable resource is :
(*a*) Clay (*b*) Sand
(*c*) Water (*d*) Fossil fuels

292. Soil covered by peaty fibrous layer is :
(*a*) Glei (*b*) Podsol
(*c*) Laterite (*d*) Chernozem

293. Which of the following is most important natural resource of energy?
(*a*) Electricity (*b*) Biogas
(*c*) Fossil fuels (*d*) Atomic fission

294. Reservoirs, lakes, ponds, rivers and canals contain percentage of fresh water :
(*a*) 77.2% (*b*) 22.4%
(*c*) 0.36% (*d*) 30.3%

295. Which one of the following groups constitute the fossil fuels?
(*a*) Natural gas, oil and wood pieces
(*b*) Oil, wood pieces and dry lung
(*c*) Coal, wood pieces and oil
(*d*) Coal, oil and natural gas

296. Red soils of India are :
(*a*) Laterite soils
(*b*) Deficient in lime, Mg, P and K
(*c*) Rich in iron and organic matter
(*d*) All of the above

297. When biosphere turns into human dominated environment, it is called :
(*a*) Noosphere (*b*) Troposphere
(*c*) Mesosphere (*d*) Thermosphere

298. Which one is endangered species?
(*a*) *Cuscuta* (*b*) *Acacia nilotica*
(*c*) *Nepenthes* (*d*) Both (*b*) and (*c*)

299. Dachigam sanctuary is associated with conservation of :
(*a*) Hangul (*b*) Rhino
(*c*) Barking Deer (*d*) Both (*b*) and (*c*)

300. Afforestation in relation to urban development is component of :
(*a*) Social forestry
(*b*) Integrated forest development
(*c*) Agro forestry
(*d*) Fuel forestry

301. Wildlife is conserved :
(*a*) *In situ*
(*b*) *Ex situ*
(*c*) Both (*a*) and (*b*)
(*d*) Selective hunting of predators

302. Organisation responsible for maintaining Red Data Book is :
(*a*) IUCN (*b*) BNHS
(*c*) IBWL (*d*) WWF

303. Jim Corbette National Park is known for :
(*a*) Lions (*b*) Tigers
(*c*) Black Buck (*d*) Rhino

304. Rajaji National Park is located in
(*a*) Delhi (*b*) Uttarakhand
(*c*) Tamil Nadu (*d*) Karnataka

305. Which one is endangered animal :
(*a*) Lion Tailed Macaque
(*b*) Hanuman Monkey
(*c*) Langur
(*d*) Antelope

306. Macropores of soil (diameter more than 20 mm) take part in :
(*a*) Holding air
(*b*) Holding air and percolation of water
(*c*) Percolation of water
(*d*) Holding of capillary water

307. Which resource is believed to exhaust first?
(*a*) Gold (*b*) Tin
(*c*) Coal (*d*) Natural gas

308. Pearls of valuable jewellery are of from :
(*a*) *Pinctada* (*b*) *Nautilus*
(*c*) *Octopus* (*d*) Water mussel

309. The gasoline plant is :
(*a*) *Salvadora* (*b*) *Sterculia*
(*c*) *Thevitia* (*d*) *Euphorbia*

310. Most of world's Gold and Platinum occur in :
(*a*) South Africa (*b*) India
(*c*) Russia (*d*) U.S.A.

311. Main source of water to soil is :
(*a*) River (*b*) Rain
(*c*) Canals (*d*) Underground

312. Noosphere is :
(*a*) Component of ecosystem
(*b*) Water filled areas of earth
(*c*) Human dominated biosphere
(*d*) Part of atmosphere above mesosphere

313. The largest amount of fresh-water on our planet is available in :
(*a*) Lakes and streams
(*b*) Polar ice caps and glaciers
(*c*) Rivers
(*d*) Underground

314. Forests are :
(*a*) Exhaustible resource
(*b*) Non-renewable resource
(*c*) Inexhaustible resource
(*d*) Non-degradable resource

315. Fertility of the soil is reduced by :
(*a*) Decaying organic matter
(*b*) Crop rotation
(*c*) Intensive agriculture
(*d*) Addition of nitrogen fixing bacteria

316. Stratosphere is characterised by :
(*a*) Fall in temperature with height
(*b*) Lack of water vapours and dust particles
(*c*) Rise in temperature with height
(*d*) Both (*b*) and (*c*)

317. Where lies the highest concentration of ferro-manganese nodules?
(*a*) North Pacific ocean beds
(*b*) South Atlantic ocean beds
(*c*) North Indian ocean beds
(*d*) North Atlantic ocean beds

318. Ionosphere is a component of :
(*a*) Thermosphere
(*b*) Mesosphere
(*c*) Stratosphere
(*d*) Troposphere

319. Percentage amount of fresh water is :
(*a*) 10% (*b*) 25%
(*c*) 3% (*d*) 17%

320. Match the different items of column I to the appropriate items in column II.

Column I	Column II
A. Inexhaustible type of resources	1. Water, wood, natural pastures
B. Renewable	2. Fossil fuels, copper, iron, and other ones
C. Non-renewable	3. Air, sand and clay
D. Quality of environment can be improved by	4. Air, water and copper
	5. Conservation
	6. Agroforestry

Codes :

	A	B	C	D
(*a*)	3	1	2	5
(*b*)	3	1	5	2
(*c*)	6	2	3	4
(*d*)	3	1	2	4

321. The plants commonly sown for crop rotation are :
(*a*) *Cajanus* and *Dalbergia*
(*b*) *Cajanus* and *Aeschyomene*
(*c*) *Dalbergia* and *Trigonella*
(*d*) *Trigonella* and *Trifolium*

322. If the same crop is repeatedly grown in a field :
(*a*) Nitrogen starvation may result
(*b*) Specific mineral deficiency may rise
(*c*) Soil will become prone to diseases
(*d*) Water level in soil will recede

323. Over all mineral level of the soil recedes due to :
(*a*) Leaching only
(*b*) Utilization by plants
(*c*) Both of these
(*d*) Chemical reactions

324. The amount of soil lost to sea each year due to rain fall is :
(*a*) 3,000 million tons
(*b*) 3,00,000 million tons
(*c*) 3,00,00000 million tons
(*d*) 3,00,000 billion tons

325. Soil erosion in plains consequent to rain fall is initiated by :
(*a*) Rill erosion (*b*) Sheet erosion
(*c*) Gully erosion (*d*) All of these

326. The Soil erosion on slopes proceeds in the following manner :
(*a*) Gully → Rill → Ravine
(*b*) Rill → Ravine → Gully
(*c*) Rill → Gully → Ravine
(*d*) Ravine → Rill → Gully

327. Which of the following plants are used as wind breaks?
(*a*) *Zizyphus* and *Calotropis*
(*b*) *Dalbergia* and *Delonix*
(*c*) *Delonix* and *Albizia*
(*d*) *Morinda* and *Anona*

328. Stone dams are made to control the :
(*a*) Rill and gullies
(*b*) Sheet erosion
(*c*) Gullies and ravines
(*d*) All of these

329. The chief cause of accelerated erosion is :
(*a*) Excessive rains
(*b*) Wind storms
(*c*) Overfelling and overgrazing
(*d*) All of these

330. National Park associated with *Rhinoceros* is :
(*a*) Kaziranga (*b*) Ranthambore
(*c*) Corbett (*d*) Valley of Flowers

331. Deforestation does not lead to :
(*a*) Quick nutrient cycling
(*b*) Soil erosion
(*c*) Alteration of local weather conditions
(*d*) Destruction of natural habitat of wild animals.

332. Forests take part in :
(*a*) Control of atmospheric pollution
(*b*) Prevention of soil erosion
(*c*) Maintenance of natural balance
(*d*) All of the above

333. Forest destruction results in :
(*a*) Loss of wildlife
(*b*) Floods and drought
(*c*) Soil erosion
(*d*) All of the above

334. Afforestation should be with :
(*a*) Exotic species
(*b*) Indigenous species
(*c*) Bamboos
(*d*) Eucalyptus

335. Animals and plants are best protected in :
(*a*) Botanical gardens (*b*) Zoos
(*c*) National Parks (*d*) Sanctuaries

336. Troublesome American water weed found in India is :

(*a*) *Eichhornia* (*b*) *Trapa*
(*c*) *Cyperus* (*d*) *Typha*

337. Kanha National Park is famous for :
(*a*) *Rhinoceros* (*b*) Tiger
(*c*) Birds (*d*) Crocodiles

338. Identify the correct match for tiger reserve and its state :
(*a*) Palamau – Orissa (*b*) Bandipur – T.N.
(*c*) Manas – Assam (*d*) Corbett – M.P.

339. Which one is matching sanctuary?
(*a*) Gir – Lion
(*b*) Kaziranga – Musk Deer
(*c*) Sunderbans – Rhino
(*d*) N.E. Himalayan region – Sambar

340. National Wildlife Protection Act was formulated during :
(*a*) 1972 (*b*) 1974
(*c*) 1976 (*d*) 1978

341. Breeding place of Flamingo (Hansawar) in India is :
(*a*) Chilka Lake (*b*) Sambar Lake
(*c*) Rann of Kutch (*d*) Ghana Vihar

342. If we remove half of the forest cover of earth, the crisis that will occur :
(*a*) Many species would become extinct
(*b*) Population, pollution and ecological imbalance will rise
(*c*) Energy crisis will commence
(*d*) The remaining forest will correct the imbalance

343. Decreased rainfall in northern areas is due to
(*a*) Changes in sun
(*b*) Global phenomenon
(*c*) Deforestation in catchment areas
(*d*) Deforestation in evaporation area near equator

344. Bandipur (Karnataka) National Park is site of :
(*a*) Deer project (*b*) Peacock project
(*c*) Elephant project (*d*) Tiger project

345. Biosphere reserve project was started in India during :
(*a*) 1984 (*b*) 1985
(*c*) 1986 (*d*) 1989

346. Decrease in species diversity in tropical countries is mainly due to :
(*a*) Urbanisation (*b*) Pollution
(*c*) Deforestation (*d*) Soil erosion

347. Lightening in the atmosphere produces
(*a*) NO (*b*) CO
(*c*) CO_2 (*d*) NH_3

348. Siberian Crane is a regular visitor of bird sanctuary :
(*a*) Ranganathittoo (Karnataka)
(*b*) Bharatpur (Rajasthan)
(*c*) Vedanthgol (T.N.)
(*d*) Lalbagh (Karnataka)

349. Plant species on verge of extinction due to over-exploitation is :
(*a*) *Centella* (*b*) *Podophyllum*
(*c*) *Gloriosa* (*d*) All of the above

350. The soil binding is done in the best way by :
(*a*) *Algae* (*b*) *Mycorrhizae*
(*c*) Grasses (*d*) All of these

351. All the following are proper plans for increasing agricultural production except :
(*a*) Expansion of irrigation facilities
(*b*) Increase in application of fertilizers
(*c*) Mechanisation of various aspects of farming
(*d*) Cutting of forests to add land for cultivation

352. Alluvial soil is mostly found in which region :
(*a*) Southern India
(*b*) Northern India
(*c*) Gangetic Jamuna Plains
(*d*) Eastern India

353. Laterite soil is rich in :
(*a*) Nitrogen (*b*) Iron
(*c*) Calcium (*d*) Magnesium

354. Increased incidence of floods in the plains of North India are due to?
(*a*) Increased deforestation in catchment areas

(*b*) Increase in incidence of rainfall
(*c*) Silting of dams
(*d*) More area under cultivation

355. 'Red Data Book' provides data on :
(*a*) Biota of Red Sea
(*b*) Effect of red light or photosynthesis
(*c*) Red pigmented plants
(*d*) Threatened species

356. Soil erosion can be prevented by :
(*a*) Restricted human activity
(*b*) Good plant cover
(*c*) Checking movement of animals
(*d*) Wind screen alone

357. Kanha National Park is located in :
(*a*) Assam (*b*) Rajasthan
(*c*) Uttar Pradesh (*d*) Madhya Pradesh

358. Which communities are more vulnerable to invasion by outside plants and animals?
(*a*) Tropical evergreen forests
(*b*) Temperate forests
(*c*) Mangroves
(*d*) Oceanic island communities

359. Adherence to two-children norm shall help in
(*a*) Improving food web
(*b*) Checking pollution
(*c*) Stabilising ecosystem
(*d*) Fertility of soil

360. Which of the following has high extinction prospects?
(*a*) Himalayan Bear and Musk Deer
(*b*) Lion and Leopard
(*c*) Tiger and Bustard
(*d*) Crocodile and Elephant

361. Which of the following will help most in conservation of wildlife?
(*a*) Making stringent laws
(*b*) Making numerous zoos
(*c*) Making numerous sanctuaries
(*d*) All of the above

362. Jhoom cultivation refers to :
(*a*) Cultivation of Jamun trees
(*b*) Cultivation of medicinal plants by tribes
(*c*) Tribal method of shifting cultivation
(*d*) Cultivation of terraces

363. Kajiranga National Park is located in the state of :
(*a*) Assam (*b*) West Bengal
(*c*) Kerala (*d*) Karnataka

364. Animal species protected in Kaziranga National Park is :
(*a*) *Panthera leo*
(*b*) *Rhinoceros unicornis*
(*c*) *Panthera tigris*
(*d*) *Macaça mulatta*

365. Which is not characteristic of intestinal symbionts?
(*a*) Freeding on extra food of host
(*b*) Providing vitamins to host
(*c*) Anaerobic respiration
(*d*) Aerobic respiration

366. Ecological succession on sand is :
(*a*) Psammomere (*b*) Xerosere
(*c*) Halosere (*d*) Hydrosere

367. Cause of mimicry is :
(*a*) concealment (*b*) offence
(*c*) defence (*d*) Both (*b*) and (*c*)

368. Which of the following insects mimics thin dry branches of the plant on which it lives?
(*a*) *Kalima parolecta*
(*b*) *Mantis religiosa*
(*c*) *Rhyllium frondosum*
(*d*) *Caraustus morosus*

369. The individual that shows mimicry is called :
(*a*) mimic (*b*) predator
(*c*) prey (*d*) parasite

370. Heterdon flattens its head, produces frequent hissing and strikes to advertise as if it is dangerous. This is an example of :
(*a*) alluring mimicry
(*b*) warning mimicry
(*c*) concealing mimicry
(*d*) batesian mimicry

371. In conscious mimicry :
(*a*) the organism behave as if they are dead bodies

(*b*) the organism become more conscious
(*c*) the organism catches its prey with a great ease
(*d*) None of the above

372. Which of the following resembles a dry leaf ?
(*a*) *Phyllum* (*b*) *Kallima paralecta*
(*c*) *Cryptolithodes* (*d*) *Papilio machaon*

373. Which among the following is the primary function of mimicry prevalent in some animals?
(*a*) Warning (*b*) Concealment
(*c*) Allurement (*d*) Aggression

374. Succession in an ecosystem is the result of :
(*a*) occurrence of diseases
(*b*) changes in grazing habits of animals
(*c*) competition among animals
(*d*) adaptive ability to environmental changes

375. Silent Valley has been preserved as it has :
(*a*) Recreational value
(*b*) Valuable timber plants
(*c*) Natural forest
(*d*) Rare plants and animals

376. Silent Valley having rare plants and animals is located in :
(*a*) Kerala
(*b*) Karnataka
(*c*) Jammu and Kashmir
(*d*) Andhra Pradesh

377. Which one is connected with conservation of forests ?
(*a*) Gir (*b*) Silent Valley
(*c*) Kaziranga (*d*) Bharatpur

378. Deforestation will decrease
(*a*) Soil erosion (*b*) Land slides
(*c*) Soil fertility (*d*) Rainfall

379. Black Buck is not allowed to be hunted by :
(*a*) Bishnois (*b*) Bhils
(*c*) Ahirs (*d*) Jats

380. New approach to conservation is establishment of :
(*a*) Reserve forests
(*b*) Sanctuaries
(*c*) Biosphere reserves
(*d*) National Parks

381. Gir National Park is famous for :
(*a*) Tiger (*b*) Asiatic Lion
(*c*) Panthar (*d*) Musk Deer

382. Social forestry is :
(*a*) Management of forests by cooperative societies
(*b*) Growing and management of useful plants on common lands
(*c*) Growing one type of trees
(*d*) Growing different types of plants together

383. Deforestation is the major causal agent of :
(*a*) Depletion of natural resources
(*b*) Environmental pollution
(*c*) Desertification of habitat
(*d*) Genetic erosion

384. In a National Park protection is provided to :
(*a*) Entire ecosystem (*b*) Flora and fauna
(*c*) Fauna only (*d*) Flora only

385. Ranganathitoo Sanctuary (Mysore) is known for population of :
(*a*) Bison (*b*) Tiger
(*c*) Goats (*d*) Birds

386. Which animal should be protected?
(*a*) Harmless
(*b*) Economically useful
(*c*) Likely to perish
(*d*) Ferocious

387. Animal species should be protected because they are :
(*a*) Lovely creatures
(*b*) Useful to humans
(*c*) To be studied by zoologists
(*d*) Man cannot recreate a lost species

388. Lions are found in :
(*a*) Western Ghats
(*b*) Jim Corbett National Park
(*c*) Forests of Madhya Pradesh
(*d*) Gir forest

389. Wildlife is destroyed most when
(*a*) There is lack of proper care
(*b*) Mass scale hunting for foreign trade
(*c*) Its natural habitat is destroyed
(*d*) Natural calamity

390. Which of the following is correct?
(*a*) Population is a set of humans in a given area
(*b*) Population is a group of interbreeding individuals of same species which is isolated from other groups
(*c*) Population is a group of individuals of the same species inhabiting the same area and functioning as a unit of biotic communities
(*d*) All of the above

391. A set of local populations connected by dispersing individuals is called :
(*a*) ecotype (*b*) community
(*c*) metapopulation (*d*) All of the above

392. The increase in number of individuals in a population under given environmental condition is called :
(*a*) age distribution
(*b*) population density
(*c*) natality
(*d*) mortality

393. The inherent capacity of an organism to reproduce or increase in number is termed biotic potential designated by the symbol :
(*a*) K (*b*) *r*
(*c*) *t* (*d*) *d*

394. The J-shaped growth form is represented by which of the following exponential equation:
(*a*) $\frac{dt}{dN} = rN$ (*b*) $dt = \frac{dN}{rN}$
(*c*) $rN = \frac{dN}{dt}$ (*d*) $dN = \frac{rN}{dt}$

395. The nature of mimic action could be :
(*a*) aggressive (*b*) defensive
(*c*) offensive (*d*) Both (*a*) and (*b*)

396. The S-shaped sigmoid growth form is represented by which of the following equation, which includes an expression for environmental resistance :
(*a*) $\frac{dN}{dt} = rN\left(\frac{N-K}{K}\right)$
(*b*) $\frac{dt}{dN} = rN\left(\frac{K-N}{K}\right)$
(*c*) $\frac{dN}{dt} = rN\left(1-\frac{N}{K}\right)$
(*d*) $\frac{dN}{dt} = rN\left(1-\frac{K}{N}\right)$

397. Commensalism is a type of interaction which is :
(*a*) beneficial to one species and no effect on the other species
(*b*) beneficial to both the species
(*b*) beneficial to one and harmful to the other
(*d*) adverse effect on both the species

398. Which of the following interaction has adverse effect on both the species?
(*a*) Predation
(*b*) Parasitism
(*c*) Competition
(*d*) None of the above

399. One of the following is a functional association not merely living together :
(*a*) Mutualism (*b*) Parasitism
(*c*) Predation (*d*) Commensalism

400. Select the mismatch pair :
(*a*) Crab and Sea anemone – Commensalism
(*b*) Rhizobium and roots of pea plant – symbiosis
(*c*) Bacteria and gut of ruminants – Mutualism
(*d*) Tiger and deer – Predation

401. In terrestrial communities, which of the following are dominants?
(*a*) Shrubs (*b*) Tall trees
(*c*) Herbs (*d*) None of these

402. The species having much greater influence on community characteristics, relative to their low abundance or biomass are called :
(*a*) birth species

(*b*) ecotones
(*c*) key stone species
(*d*) edge species

403. Which of the following is pioneer in succession in hydarch?
(*a*) Marsh meadow stage
(*b*) Reed swamp stage
(*c*) Phytoplankton stage
(*d*) Scrub stage

404. Select the correct statement :
(*a*) The aggregation of individuals of species is called population
(*b*) The relationship where one organism is benefitted while the other is neither benefited nor harmed is referred to as commensalism
(*c*) Organisms preying on animals are called predator
(*d*) All of the above

405. An association of two species in which both species are benefitted is called......
(*a*) Commensalism
(*b*) Mutualism
(*c*) Protoco-operation
(*d*) Amenalism

406. Succession involves a turnover of species during :
(*a*) micro evolutionary time
(*b*) macro evolutionary time
(*c*) ecological time
(*d*) the seasons of the year

407. Select the statement, which best explains commensalims :
(*a*) One organism is benefitted
(*b*) Both the organisms ar benefitted
(*c*) One organism is benefited other is not affectted
(*d*) One organism is benefited other is affectted

408. Community is best defined as aggregation of:
(*a*) individuals of same kind
(*b*) individuals of different kinds
(*c*) individuals of a population
(*d*) population of different species

409. Parasite can be best explained as an organism which depends on :
(*a*) others for food
(*b*) others for shelther
(*c*) others for both food and shelter
(*d*) others for reproduction

ANSWERS

1	2	3	4	5	6	7	8	9	10
(*d*)	(*a*)	(*d*)	(*c*)	(*d*)	(*d*)	(*d*)	(*b*)	(*d*)	(*a*)
11	**12**	**13**	**14**	**15**	**16**	**17**	**18**	**19**	**20**
(*a*)	(*c*)	(*b*)	(*a*)	(*d*)	(*c*)	(*a*)	(*d*)	(*d*)	(*d*)
21	**22**	**23**	**24**	**25**	**26**	**27**	**28**	**29**	**30**
(*a*)	(*b*)	(*d*)	(*c*)	(*c*)	(*c*)	(*d*)	(*a*)	(*a*)	(*a*)
31	**32**	**33**	**34**	**35**	**36**	**37**	**38**	**39**	**40**
(*b*)	(*c*)	(*c*)	(*c*)	(*a*)	(*d*)	(*c*)	(*a*)	(*a*)	(*d*)
41	**42**	**43**	**44**	**45**	**46**	**47**	**48**	**49**	**50**
(*b*)	(*d*)	(*c*)	(*d*)	(*d*)	(*d*)	(*b*)	(*c*)	(*d*)	(*d*)
51	**52**	**53**	**54**	**55**	**56**	**57**	**58**	**59**	**60**
(*b*)	(*b*)	(*b*)	(*d*)	(*a*)	(*c*)	(*c*)	(*a*)	(*b*)	(*d*)
61	**62**	**63**	**64**	**65**	**66**	**67**	**68**	**69**	**70**
(*d*)	(*b*)	(*a*)	(*a*)	(*b*)	(*c*)	(*d*)	(*b*)	(*c*)	(*b*)

71	**72**	**73**	**74**	**75**	**76**	**77**	**78**	**79**	**80**
(*c*)	(*a*)	(*c*)	(*c*)	(*b*)	(*a*)	(*a*)	(*c*)	(*b*)	(*b*)
81	**82**	**83**	**84**	**85**	**86**	**87**	**88**	**89**	**90**
(*b*)	(*b*)	(*c*)	(*b*)	(*a*)	(*c*)	(*b*)	(*a*)	(*a*)	(*b*)
91	**92**	**93**	**94**	**95**	**96**	**97**	**98**	**99**	**100**
(*d*)	(*b*)	(*c*)	(*c*)	(*a*)	(*c*)	(*a*)	(*b*)	(*a*)	(*c*)
101	**102**	**103**	**104**	**105**	**106**	**107**	**108**	**109**	**110**
(*b*)	(*d*)	(*c*)	(*b*)	(*d*)	(*c*)	(*a*)	(*a*)	(*b*)	(*b*)
111	**112**	**113**	**114**	**115**	**116**	**117**	**118**	**119**	**120**
(*a*)	(*d*)	(*a*)	(*b*)	(*d*)	(*c*)	(*b*)	(*c*)	(*d*)	(*c*)
121	**122**	**123**	**124**	**125**	**126**	**127**	**128**	**129**	**130**
(*b*)	(*d*)	(*a*)	(*a*)	(*d*)	(*c*)	(*c*)	(*d*)	(*a*)	(*c*)
131	**132**	**133**	**134**	**135**	**136**	**137**	**138**	**139**	**140**
(*a*)	(*d*)	(*d*)	(*b*)	(*c*)	(*b*)	(*d*)	(*c*)	(*a*)	(*a*)
141	**142**	**143**	**144**	**145**	**146**	**147**	**148**	**149**	**150**
(*c*)	(*d*)	(*d*)	(*a*)	(*d*)	(*d*)	(*a*)	(*a*)	(*a*)	(*c*)
151	**152**	**153**	**154**	**155**	**156**	**157**	**158**	**159**	**160**
(*d*)	(*d*)	(*d*)	(*c*)	(*b*)	(*b*)	(*b*)	(*b*)	(*d*)	(*c*)
161	**162**	**163**	**164**	**165**	**166**	**167**	**168**	**169**	**170**
(*c*)	(*b*)	(*d*)	(*d*)	(*a*)	(*a*)	(*a*)	(*d*)	(*c*)	(*d*)
171	**172**	**173**	**174**	**175**	**176**	**177**	**178**	**179**	**180**
(*c*)	(*b*)	(*b*)	(*b*)	(*b*)	(*c*)	(*b*)	(*d*)	(*d*)	(*c*)
181	**182**	**183**	**184**	**185**	**186**	**187**	**188**	**189**	**190**
(*b*)	(*c*)	(*a*)	(*c*)	(*b*)	(*a*)	(*d*)	(*a*)	(*c*)	(*d*)
191	**192**	**193**	**194**	**195**	**196**	**197**	**198**	**199**	**200**
(*b*)	(*d*)	(*d*)	(*b*)	(*d*)	(*c*)	(*d*)	(*c*)	(*c*)	(*b*)
201	**202**	**203**	**204**	**205**	**206**	**207**	**208**	**209**	**210**
(*d*)	(*a*)	(*c*)	(*d*)	(*a*)	(*a*)	(*c*)	(*d*)	(*c*)	(*a*)
211	**212**	**213**	**214**	**215**	**216**	**217**	**218**	**219**	**220**
(*d*)	(*c*)	(*d*)	(*b*)	(*a*)	(*c*)	(*b*)	(*d*)	(*c*)	(*b*)
221	**222**	**223**	**224**	**225**	**226**	**227**	**228**	**229**	**230**
(*a*)	(*a*)	(*d*)	(*d*)	(*a*)	(*c*)	(*b*)	(*c*)	(*b*)	(*d*)
231	**232**	**233**	**234**	**235**	**236**	**237**	**238**	**239**	**240**
(*b*)	(*d*)	(*d*)	(*b*)	(*c*)	(*a*)	(*d*)	(*c*)	(*c*)	(*d*)
241	**242**	**243**	**244**	**245**	**246**	**247**	**248**	**249**	**250**
(*b*)	(*d*)	(*a*)	(*d*)	(*c*)	(*c*)	(*b*)	(*c*)	(*c*)	(*b*)
251	**252**	**253**	**254**	**255**	**256**	**257**	**258**	**259**	**260**
(*b*)	(*d*)	(*a*)	(*c*)	(*a*)	(*b*)	(*c*)	(*d*)	(*a*)	(*a*)
261	**262**	**263**	**264**	**265**	**266**	**267**	**268**	**269**	**270**
(*b*)	(*c*)	(*c*)	(*a*)	(*b*)	(*b*)	(*b*)	(*d*)	(*c*)	(*d*)
271	**272**	**273**	**274**	**275**	**276**	**277**	**278**	**279**	**280**
(*a*)	(*b*)	(*d*)	(*c*)	(*b*)	(*c*)	(*b*)	(*d*)	(*c*)	(*d*)

281	282	283	284	285	286	287	288	289	290
(*d*)	(*c*)	(*b*)	(*d*)	(*d*)	(*c*)	(*c*)	(*b*)	(*c*)	(*c*)
291	**292**	**293**	**294**	**295**	**296**	**297**	**298**	**299**	**300**
(*c*)	(*b*)	(*c*)	(*c*)	(*d*)	(*d*)	(*a*)	(*c*)	(*a*)	(*b*)
301	**302**	**303**	**304**	**305**	**306**	**307**	**308**	**309**	**310**
(*c*)	(*a*)	(*b*)	(*b*)	(*a*)	(*b*)	(*b*)	(*a*)	(*d*)	(*a*)
311	**312**	**313**	**314**	**315**	**316**	**317**	**318**	**319**	**320**
(*b*)	(*c*)	(*b*)	(*a*)	(*c*)	(*d*)	(*a*)	(*a*)	(*c*)	(*a*)
321	**322**	**323**	**324**	**325**	**326**	**327**	**328**	**329**	**330**
(*d*)	(*b*)	(*c*)	(*b*)	(*b*)	(*c*)	(*a*)	(*c*)	(*c*)	(*a*)
331	**332**	**333**	**334**	**335**	**336**	**337**	**338**	**339**	**340**
(*a*)	(*d*)	(*d*)	(*b*)	(*c*)	(*a*)	(*b*)	(*a*)	(*a*)	(*a*)
341	**342**	**343**	**344**	**345**	**346**	**347**	**348**	**349**	**350**
(*a*)	(*b*)	(*c*)	(*d*)	(*c*)	(*c*)	(*a*)	(*b*)	(*b*)	(*c*)
351	**352**	**353**	**354**	**355**	**356**	**357**	**358**	**359**	**360**
(*d*)	(*c*)	(*b*)	(*a*)	(*d*)	(*b*)	(*d*)	(*d*)	(*c*)	(*a*)
361	**362**	**363**	**364**	**365**	**366**	**367**	**368**	**369**	**370**
(*c*)	(*c*)	(*a*)	(*b*)	(*d*)	(*a*)	(*a*)	(*b*)	(*a*)	(*b*)
371	**372**	**373**	**374**	**375**	**376**	**377**	**378**	**379**	**380**
(*a*)	(*b*)	(*b*)	(*d*)	(*c*)	(*a*)	(*b*)	(*d*)	(*a*)	(*c*)
381	**382**	**383**	**384**	**385**	**386**	**387**	**388**	**389**	**390**
(*b*)	(*b*)	(*c*)	(*b*)	(*d*)	(*c*)	(*d*)	(*d*)	(*c*)	(*d*)
391	**392**	**393**	**394**	**395**	**396**	**397**	**398**	**399**	**400**
(*c*)	(*c*)	(*b*)	(*c*)	(*d*)	(*c*)	(*a*)	(*c*)	(*a*)	(*a*)
401	**402**	**403**	**404**	**405**	**406**	**407**	**408**	**409**	
(*b*)	(*c*)	(*c*)	(*d*)	(*b*)	(*c*)	(*c*)	(*d*)	(*c*)	

17

ENVIRONMENTAL BIOTECHNOLOGY

1. In natural immunity :
(*a*) body prepares antibodies against an antigen
(*b*) antibodies are present right from birth
(*c*) readymade antibodies are injected into the body
(*d*) All of the above

2. Malfunctioning of vitalorgans leads to :
(*a*) Congenital diseases
(*b*) Organic diseases
(*c*) Infective diseases
(*d*) Deficiency diseases

3. Hypersensitivity of tissue occur in :
(*a*) allergies (*b*) cancer
(*c*) malaria (*d*) haemophilia

4. Vehicle borne transmission of a disease is the transmission occurring through :
(*a*) certain vectors like arthropods
(*b*) agencies like water, food or blood
(*c*) articles like toys, clothes
(*d*) unclean hands and fingers

5. Which of the following organs is not involved in elicitation of immune response?
(*a*) Thymus (*b*) Brain
(*c*) Spleen (*d*) Lymph nodes

6. Reservoir of infection is :
(*a*) site where pathogens reside without causing any damage
(*b*) soil, water and air
(*c*) another animal
(*d*) another person who is suffering

7. Bacteria and viruses cause :
(*a*) Allergies
(*b*) Non-communicable diseases
(*c*) Degenerative diseases
(*d*) Infectious diseases

8. Virulence means :
(*a*) The entry of the pathogen into the body of the animal
(*b*) The symptoms of the disease are produced
(*c*) Degree of the damage which the pathogen causes to the host
(*d*) The period for which a pathogen stays in the host and continues to causes damage

9. Antibodies fight against :
(*a*) starvation (*b*) stress
(*c*) thirst (*d*) infection

10. Antigens are :
(*a*) The micro-organisms which are the source of disease in the body
(*b*) A foreign body which is harmful to the animal and evokes the generation of antibodies
(*c*) The substance generated in the body in response to the infection
(*d*) None of these

11. WBCs accumulate at the site of wounds as a result of :
(*a*) diapedesis
(*b*) homeostasis
(*c*) breaking capillaries
(*d*) phagocytic action

12. Passive immunity is achieved by injecting :
(*a*) vaccine
(*b*) readymade antibodies
(*c*) antibiotics
(*d*) antigens

13. Generally an antigen is :
(*a*) a protein prepared in the body
(*b*) a protein injected into body
(*c*) a protein or polysaccharide present on the surface of the cell wall of bacterium
(*d*) a polysaccharide on the surface of the pathogen

14. Active immunity means :
(*a*) resistance of body achieved after disease
(*b*) resistance developed before disease
(*c*) increasing amount of blood
(*d*) increasing rate of heart beat

15. Humoral immune system consists of :
(*a*) a family of diverse proteins present in body fluids
(*b*) some special type of cells which destroy the pathogens
(*c*) Both cells as well as polysaccharides
(*d*) All the above

16. How many principal lines of defence are present in the body?
(*a*) Two (*b*) Three
(*c*) Five (*d*) Innumerable

17. Which of the following is a correct statement?
(*a*) B-cells directly engulf the pathogenic bacteria
(*b*) B-cells produce antibodies soon after they are produced
(*c*) B-cells produce a large clone of plasma cells soon after it is formed
(*d*) The B-cells produce the plasma cells in the body only after they are triggered by a specific antigen

18. Antiserum is a serum containing :
(*a*) antigens (*b*) leucocytes
(*c*) active antibodies (*d*) None of the above

19. Interferon is a glycoprotein which possesses :
(*a*) antiviral activity
(*b*) antifungal activity
(*c*) antiparasitic activity
(*d*) antibacterial activity

20. Antibodies are :
(*a*) A large family of protein molecules produced by the body defence cells in the body fluids which neutralise the antigens
(*b*) The chemicals produced by the invading microbes which destroy and damage the body cells
(*c*) Certain substances enclosed in lymphocytes
(*d*) None of the above

21. The mode of transmission of communicable diseases is dealt by a branch of science named:
(*a*) Epidemiology (*b*) Immunology
(*c*) Etiology (*d*) Angiology

22. The degree of pathogenecity is called :
(*a*) Infestation (*b*) Infection
(*c*) Virulence (*d*) Resistance

23. Which one of the following disease is caused by bacteria?
(*a*) Chicken-pox (*b*) Poliomyelitis
(*c*) Measles (*d*) Tetanus

24. Yeast is a good source of :
(*a*) Carbohydrates (*b*) Vitamin B
(*c*) Proteins (*d*) Both (*b*) and (*c*)

25. The micro-orgaism involved in making bread is :
(*a*) Acetobacter
(*b*) Brewer's yeast
(*c*) *Saccharomyces cerevisiae*
(*d*) None of the above

26. Agar-agar is obtained from :
(*a*) moulds (*b*) algae
(*c*) sea weeds (*d*) egg protein

27. The conditions which favour fermentation are :
(*a*) temperature and air
(*b*) concentration
(*c*) presence of foreign substance
(*d*) All of the above

28. Penicillin is obtained from :
(*a*) Mushroom

(*b*) Viruses
(*c*) Bacteria and viruses
(*d*) *Penicillium notatum*

29. The vinegar means :
(*a*) Bitter wine (*b*) Sweet wine
(*c*) Sour wine (*d*) None of the above

30. Penicillin was first discovered by :
(*a*) Gratia
(*b*) Alexander Fleming
(*c*) L. Pasteur
(*d*) Buchner

31. Yeast is used in the production of :
(*a*) Acetic acid (*b*) Cheese
(*c*) Curd (*d*) Ethyl alcohol

32. First antibiotic isolated was :
(*a*) Terramycin (*b*) Neomycin
(*c*) Penicillin (*d*) Streptomycin

33. Streptomycin was first isolated in 1944-45 by :
(*a*) Leeuwenhoek
(*b*) Burkholder
(*c*) Alexander Fleming
(*d*) Waksman

34. In the production of leavened bread the following is used :
(*a*) Bacterium (*b*) Yeast
(*c*) Rhizopus (*d*) None of the above

35. Heating milk or any other liquid at 65°C and then sudden cooling is known as :
(*a*) Sterilization (*b*) Pasteurization
(*c*) Preservation (*d*) Fermentation

36. Most of the micro-organisms which produce antibiotics live in the soil because :
(*a*) Darkness favours synthesis of antibiotics
(*b*) By the phenomenon of antibiotics their growth, nutrition and survival value and enhanced in competitive world of microflora of the soil
(*c*) They cannot get nutrition outside the soil
(*d*) No one easily misuses their antibiotics

37. Streptomycin is produced by :
(*a*) *Streptomyces venezuele*
(*b*) *Streptomyces griseus*
(*c*) *Streptomyces scoleus*
(*d*) *Streptomyces fradie*

38. Who was the first to isolate streptomycin?
(*a*) Twort
(*b*) Alexander Flemming
(*c*) Selman Waksman
(*d*) Robert Koch

39. Chloramphenicol and erthyromycin (broad spectrum antibiotics) are produced by :
(*a*) *Streptomyces* (*b*) *Nitrobacter*
(*c*) *Rhizobium* (*d*) *Penicillium*

40. Chloromycetin is produced by :
(*a*) *Bordetella pertusis*
(*b*) *Streptomyces venezuelae*
(*c*) *Streptomyces rumosus*
(*d*) *Clostridium botulinum*

41. Terramycin is obtained from :
(*a*) *Streptomyces venezuelae*
(*b*) *Streptomyces aureofaciens*
(*c*) *Streptomyces rumosus*
(*d*) *Streptomyces griseus*

42. Enzymes can be immobilised by :
(*a*) Cross-linking enzyme molecules
(*b*) Covalently attaching to a solid support
(*c*) Entrapping them in gel
(*d*) All of the above

43. The number of enzymes known today is approximately :
(*a*) 1200 (*b*) 2200
(*c*) 3200 (*d*) 4200

44. Who of the following scientists showed that *Saccharomyces cerevisiae* caused fermentation products such as beer and buttermilk?
(*a*) Louis Pasteur
(*b*) Alexander Fleming
(*c*) Selman Waksman
(*d*) Sach

45. Which enzymes are used for converting corn starch into high fructose syrup?
(*a*) Glucoisomerases (*b*) Glucoamylases
(*c*) Amylases (*d*) All of these

46. A bioreactor refers to :
(*a*) Fermentation tank
(*b*) Organisms reacting to a stimulus
(*c*) Nuclear reactor for biological studies
(*d*) Tank of biochemical reactions

47. Germinating barley seeds are employed in the preparation of :
(*a*) Cheese (*b*) Wine
(*c*) Beer (*d*) Lactic acid

48. Cells obtained from cancerous tumours are known as
(*a*) Myelomas (*b*) Hybridomas
(*c*) Lymphocytes (*d*) Monoclonal cells

49. Hepatitis B vaccine is a :
(*a*) First generation vaccine
(*b*) Second generation vaccine
(*c*) Third generation vaccine
(*d*) An interferon

50. Which one of the following communicable diseases is not caused by becteria?
(*a*) Diphtheria (*b*) Typhoid
(*c*) Leprosy (*d*) Poliomyelitis

51. The causative organism of cholera is a :
(*a*) Bacterium (*b*) Protozoan
(*c*) Nematode (*d*) Virus

52. Tetanus is caused by :
(*a*) Bacterium (*b*) Fungus
(*c*) Protozoan (*d*) Virus

53. Poliomyelitis is caused by :
(*a*) Bacteria (*b*) Virus
(*c*) Protozoan (*d*) Nematodes

54. AIDS is caused by :
(*a*) Cocci (*b*) Bacilli
(*c*) TMV (*d*) HIV

55. Invention and study of effects of medicines on the organism is known as :
(*a*) toxicology (*b*) pharmacology
(*c*) pharmacy (*d*) haematology

56. DPT vaccine is given to infants to immunize them against :
(*a*) diphtheria, pneumonia and typhoid
(*b*) diphtheria, whooping cough and tetanus
(*c*) diarrhoea, pneumonia and tuberculosis
(*d*) diphtheria, whooping cough and typhoid

57. Dengue fever is caused by :
(*a*) Bacteria
(*b*) Plasmodium
(*c*) Virus
(*d*) *Entamoeba histolytica*

58. A virus caused contagious epidemic disease with high fever and rash all over the body. Its incidence is among children. Its one attack gives immunity. Which one is of the following?
(*a*) Mumps (*b*) Plague
(*c*) Brain fever (*d*) Measles

59. Syphilis is venereal disease. It is caused by :
(*a*) *Neisseria*
(*b*) *Vibrio*
(*c*) *Corynebacterium*
(*d*) *Treponema pallidium*

60. The contagious diseases are :
(*a*) measles (*b*) chicken pox
(*c*) whooping cough (*d*) All of the above

61. Where are the gametocytes of *Plasmodium* first formed and found?
(*a*) Liver of man
(*b*) Stomach of female mosquito
(*c*) Blood of man
(*d*) RBC of blood of man

62. *Entamoeba histolytica* has :
(*a*) well developed pseudopodia
(*b*) contractile vacuole
(*c*) Both (*a*) and (*b*)
(*d*) None of the above

63. Which mosquito actually transmits malaria and acts as intermediate host of *Plasmodium*?
(*a*) Male Anopheles
(*b*) Female Anopheles
(*c*) Male Culex
(*d*) Female Culex

64. The credit of working out the complicated life cycle of Plasmodium goes to :
(*a*) Louis Pasteur (*b*) John Snow
(*c*) Robert Koch (*d*) Ronald Ross

65. The symptoms of Malaria fever appear at their peak is a patient when :
(*a*) sporozoites enter liver
(*b*) merozoites enter red blood cells
(*c*) red blood cells rupture and haemozoin is released
(*d*) gametocytes are formed

66. Which of the following worms is viviparous?
(*a*) *Wuchereria bancroftir*
(*b*) *Ancylostoma dudoenale*
(*c*) *Ascaris lumbricodes*
(*d*) *Taenia solium*

67. The infective stage of plasmodium is :
(*a*) Trophozoite (*b*) Sporozoite
(*c*) Merozoite (*d*) Schizont

68. A chronic contagious eye disease, caused by virus is called :
(*a*) thrombosis (*b*) myopia
(*c*) conjunctivitis (*d*) night blindness

69. Region of the body where poliomyelitis virus multiplies is :
(*a*) nerve cells (*b*) muscle cells
(*c*) intestinal cells (*d*) None of the above

70. The disease 'filariasis' is caused by the worm :
(*a*) *Wuchereria bancrofti*
(*b*) *Ancylostoma dudoenale*
(*c*) *Trichinella spiralis*
(*d*) *Enterobius vermicularis*

71. The mode of transmission of the disease Filaria is :
(*a*) Bite of mosquito
(*b*) Eating unwashed eatables
(*c*) Eating unripe Pork
(*d*) Both (*b*) and (*c*)

72. Which mosquito aids in the transmission of the disease filaria?
(*a*) Male Anopheles
(*b*) Female Anopheles
(*c*) Culex
(*d*) Both (*a*) and (*b*)

73. A disease characterised by chronic sleeplessness is :
(*a*) insomnia
(*b*) jaundice
(*c*) sleeping sickness
(*d*) nervous breakdown

74. Trachoma is caused by the infection of :
(*a*) virus (*b*) fungus
(*c*) nematode (*d*) bacterium

75. Chicken pox can be easily identified from measles due to the :
(*a*) high fever
(*b*) irritation all over the skin
(*c*) dew drop like rashes
(*d*) sneezing and water discharge from nose

76. Varicella virus causes :
(*a*) Small pox (*b*) Chicken pox
(*c*) Measles (*d*) Influenza

77. Elephantiasis is caused by :
(*a*) Tapeworm (*b*) Wuchereria
(*c*) Ascaris (*d*) Culex

78. The incubation period of small pox is :
(*a*) 2 days (*b*) 12 days
(*c*) 12 hours (*d*) 2 to 12 days

79. Rennet enzyme was purified by :
(*a*) A. Fleming (*b*) S.A. Waksman
(*c*) Payen and Persoz (*d*) Christian Hansen

80. The enzyme diastase was indentified by :
(*a*) S.A. Waksman (*b*) A. Fleming
(*c*) Christian Hasen (*d*) Payan and Persoz

81. Which enzymes are used for manufacturing detergents?
(*a*) Proteases (*b*) Glucoamylases
(*c*) Amylases (*d*) Lactases

82. The enzyme TPA is used to :
(*a*) Maintain turgor pressure
(*b*) Strengthen tissues
(*c*) Increase plasma
(*d*) Dissolved blood clots

83. Hybridomas are employed for :
(*a*) Synthesis of antibiotics
(*b*) Killing cancer cells
(*c*) Synthesis of monoclonal antibodies
(*d*) Production of somatic hybrids

84. The method of growing micro-organisms as a thin layer on nutrient medium is known as :
(*a*) Thin layer growth system
(*b*) Support growth system
(*c*) Suspended growth
(*d*) None of these

85. Vitamin B_{12} is commercially obtained from :
(*a*) *Escherichia coli*
(*b*) *Closteridium butyricum*
(*c*) *Leuconostoc mesenteroids*
(*d*) *Streptomyces alivacaeus*

86. Vitamin B_2 is obtained from :
(*a*) *Acetobacter* (*b*) *Ashbya gossypi*
(*c*) *Penicillium* (*d*) *Aspergillus niger*

87. Vitamin B_1 was isolated by :
(*a*) Albert van Zent (*b*) Mellanby
(*c*) McCollum (*d*) Funk

88. Vitamin B_{12} is produced directly during the course of fermentation by :
(*a*) *Ashbya gossypii*
(*b*) *Rhizopus stolonifer*
(*c*) *Saccharomyces cerevisiae*
(*d*) *Propioni bacteria*

89. Pasteurization makes foodstuffs free from :
(*a*) All vegetative forms of bacteria
(*b*) Vegetative forms of all pathogenic microbes
(*c*) All living organisms
(*d*) All bacteria

90. Number of antibiotics isolated till today is :
(*a*) about 70 (*b*) about 700
(*c*) about 1700 (*d*) over 7000

91. Tissue plasminogen activator is :
(*a*) A vitamin
(*b*) An electric device
(*c*) An enzyme
(*d*) A chemical that stimulates tissue differentiation

92. For rapid production of alcohol, immobilised yeast cells are kept in :
(*a*) Silica gel
(*b*) Wire netting
(*c*) Porcelain columns
(*d*) Calcium alginate beads

93. Dextran is used in :
(*a*) Bleeding (*b*) Blood pressure
(*c*) Blood transfusion (*d*) Blood clotting

94. Which of these participates in the manufacturing of dextrans?
(*a*) Lactobacillus (*b*) Leuconostoc
(*c*) Pseudomonas (*d*) Mucor

95. Steroids are used in :
(*a*) Birth control
(*b*) Treatment of hormonal balance
(*c*) Treatment of auto-immune diseases
(*d*) All of these

96. Utility of fungi for steroid conversion was demonstrated by :
(*a*) Pasteur and Jaubert
(*b*) Kohler and Milstein
(*c*) Murray and Peterson
(*d*) Waksman and Woodruff

97. Humuline is :
(*a*) A form of chitin
(*b*) A powerful antibiotic
(*c*) A new digestive enzyme
(*d*) Human insulin

98. Humuline was launched by :
(*a*) An English firm (*b*) An American firm
(*c*) German firm (*d*) French firm

99. Which of the following organic acids was produced by fermentation?
(*a*) Oxalic acid (*b*) Lactic acid
(*c*) Citric acid (*d*) Propionic acid

100. Most of the Eubacteriale antibiotics come from :
(*a*) Bacillus (*b*) Rhizobium
(*c*) Pseudomonas (*d*) Streptococcus

101. Restriction enzyme was discovered by :
(*a*) Berg
(*b*) Smith and North
(*c*) Waksman
(*d*) Alexander Fleming

102. Hybridomas are a result of fusion of :
(*a*) Male reproductive cells
(*b*) Female reproductive cells
(*c*) Normal antibody producing cells with myeloma
(*d*) Abnormal antibody producing cells with myeloma

103. Kohler and Milstein developed Biotechology for the production of :
(*a*) Myelomas
(*b*) Steroid conversion
(*c*) Monoclonal antibodies
(*d*) Immobilised enzymes

104. Enzymes used in detergents are :
(*a*) Steroid conversion
(*b*) Lipases
(*c*) Proteases
(*d*) Glucoisomerases

105. The infective period of enteric fever is :
(*a*) 6 hours (*b*) 6 days
(*c*) 6 weeks (*d*) 6 minutes

106. Protection against poliomyelitis and tetanus is done simultaneously by :
(*a*) Sulpha drugs
(*b*) Gamma globulin inoculation
(*c*) Multiple vaccine
(*d*) Pasteur treatment

107. After floods the victims are usually attacked by :
(*a*) Appendicitis (*b*) Perionitis
(*c*) Rabies (*d*) Cholera

108. Rabies is also called :
(*a*) Infantile paralysis (*b*) Lock Jaw
(*c*) Hydrophobia (*d*) Amoebiasis

109. Rubeola virus causes :
(*a*) Small pox (*b*) Measles
(*c*) Chicken pox (*d*) Influenza

110. Black death or Great mortality is the name given to:
(*a*) Plague (*b*) Malaria
(*c*) Cholera (*d*) Cancer

111. A person with blood group 'O' can receive blood transfusion from persons with blood groups :
(*a*) O and A B (*b*) O, A and B
(*c*) O only (*d*) AB only

112. After which animal is the 'Rh' factor named?
(*a*) Dragon fly (*b*) Monkey
(*c*) Man (*d*) Rat

113. Universal recipient in blood transfusion belongs to group :
(*a*) A (*b*) O
(*c*) AB (*d*) B

114. Rh factor is connected with :
(*a*) Carbohydrate metabolism in the body
(*b*) Initiation of protein synthesis
(*c*) Blood clotting
(*d*) Blood of man

115. Haemophilia is a disease caused by deficiency of :
(*a*) water in plasma (*b*) RBCs
(*c*) WBCs (*d*) thromboplastin

116. Rh^- negative individuals are :
(*a*) Homozygous dominant (RR)
(*b*) Heterozygous (Rr)
(*c*) Homozygous recessive (rr)
(*d*) Possess only one gene (R or r)

117. Which of the following is a genetic trait?
(*a*) Albinism (*b*) Leucoderma
(*c*) Tuberculosis (*d*) Diphtheria

118. Rh factor was discovered by :
(*a*) William Harvey
(*b*) Landsteiner and Weiner
(*c*) James Watson
(*d*) Robert Hooke

119. Universal donor in blood transfusion belongs to blood group :
(*a*) A (*b*) O
(*c*) AB (*d*) B

120. A woman with blood group O marries a man with blood group A. The child conceived to such a woman will :

(*a*) survive with normal health
(*b*) survive with slight anaemic conditions
(*c*) will not survive long
(*d*) will die soon after birth

121. Which of the following is biologically incompatible marriage because of danger of erythroblastosis foetalis is?
(*a*) Rh^- man and Rh^- woman
(*b*) Rh^+ man and Rh^- woman
(*c*) Both Rh positive
(*d*) Both Rh negative

122. Down's Syndrome has karyotype make up as :
(*a*) 44 + 3x
(*b*) 44 + xxy
(*c*) 45 + xx in female
(*d*) 44 + xy or 44 + xx in female

123. If a man is Rh^+ and lady is Rh^- then :
(*a*) The first child will die
(*b*) The first child will survive
(*c*) No child will be born
(*d*) None of these

124. If a human mother has blood group 'O', the foetus in the womb would die, the blood group of the foetus is :
(*a*) A
(*b*) B
(*c*) AB
(*d*) No effect in any case

125. To a person of blood group AB blood group of A and B are given separately, what will happen :
(*a*) Clumping occurs with A
(*b*) Clumping occurs with B
(*c*) Clumping occurs with both
(*d*) Clumping does not occur

126. Which of the following diseases is genetically similar to haemophilia?
(*a*) Albinism (*b*) Colour blindness
(*c*) Phenylketonuria (*d*) None of the above

127. The disease *Erythroblastosis foetalis* in human embryo is caused due to :
(*a*) Disadjustment of blood groups
(*b*) Disadjustment of Rh factor
(*c*) Both of these
(*d*) None of these

128. ABO blood groups were discovered by :
(*a*) Landsteiner (*b*) Darwin
(*c*) Harvey (*d*) Weiner

129. The second Rh^+ child conceived to a Rh^- woman will :
(*a*) die immediately
(*b*) surely survive
(*c*) survive with serious malformations
(*d*) usually die at an early stage

130. Persons with blood group 'O' lack :
(*a*) antigens (*b*) antibody 'a'
(*c*) antibody 'b' (*d*) haemophilia

131. Foetal sex can be determined by examining cells from amnoitic fluid looking for :
(*a*) Barr bodies (*b*) Chiasmata
(*c*) Sex chromosome (*d*) Kinetochores

132. A plant part that is excised from its original location and used for initiating a culture is termed :
(*a*) callus
(*b*) explant
(*c*) suspension culture
(*d*) protoplast

133. Growth regulator commonly used in plant tissue culture is/are :
(*a*) 2, 4 – D
(*b*) BAP
(*c*) Auxins and cytokinins
(*d*) All of the above

134. Shoot regeneration is promoted by :
(*a*) NAA (*b*) BAP
(*b*) 2, 4 D (*d*) IBA

135. Which of the following is used to obtain single cell protein used as food or feed?
(*a*) Algae and fungi (*b*) Yeast
(*c*) Bacteria (*d*) All of the above

136. A West African plant produces a protein called *Pentadiplandra brazzeana* which is about 2000 times as sweet as sugar :

(*a*) saccharin (*b*) monelin
(*c*) brazzein (*d*) None of the above

137. Which of the following statement is incorrect?
(*a*) A biowar is the case of biological weapon against humans and or their crops and animal
(*b*) Bioethics is a set of standards that may be used to regulate our activities in relation to biological world
(*c*) Recombinant DNA technology is used to produce transgenic organism
(*d*) Genetic engineering has failed in the development of crop varieties resistant to certain insects and diseases

138. Which transgenic is used in organism in production of hirudin?
(*a*) *Bacillus thurinagiensis*
(*b*) *Brassica napus*
(*c*) *Flava savr*
(*d*) *Spirulina*

139. Protoplast of plant cell is obtained by working :
(*a*) Cellulase (*b*) Pectinase
(*c*) PEG (*d*) Both (*a*) and (*b*)

140. Ringworm of scalp is caused by :
(*a*) *Aspergillus* (*b*) *Microsporum*
(*c*) *Alternaria* (*d*) *Penicillium*

141. An enzyme used in cheese making is :
(*a*) Protease (*b*) Rennet
(*c*) Glucoamylase (*d*) Lactase

142. Biopiracy is related to which of the following?
(*a*) Traditional knowledge
(*b*) Biomolecules are regarding bioresources genes isolated from bioresources
(*c*) Bioresources
(*d*) All of the above

143. Which of the following is used in biowar?
(*a*) A pathogen
(*b*) Toxin from a pathogen
(*c*) A delivery system for the bioweapon agent
(*d*) All of the above

144. Which of the following is included in biopesticide?
(*a*) Viruses and bacteria
(*b*) Viruses, bacteria and fungi
(*c*) Viruses, bacteria, fungi, protozoa and mites
(*d*) Viruses, bacteria, fungi and protozoa

145. Which of the following can be controlled by using biopesticides?
(*a*) Insects (*b*) Diseases
(*c*) Weeds (*d*) All of the above

146. Biofertilizers include :
(*a*) Blue-green algae, rhizobia, other nitrogen fixing bacteria and mycorrhiza fungi
(*b*) Blue-green algae, rhizobia and other nitrogen fixing bacteria
(*c*) Rhizobia, other nitrogen fixing bacteria and mycorrhiza fungi
(*d*) Blue-green algae, rhizobia and mycorrhiza fungi

147. Which of the following risks are associated with genetically modified food?
I. Toxicity
II. Allergic reaction
III. Antibiotic resistance in microorganisms present in alimentary canal

Codes :
(*a*) I and II (*b*) All of the above
(*c*) I and III (*d*) II and III

148. Embryo culture is used for :
(*a*) establishing suspension culture
(*b*) recovery of interspecific hybrids
(*c*) somatic hybridization
(*d*) haploid production

149. A transgene expression can achieve which of the following?
(*a*) Prevent expression of a native gene
(*b*) Modify an existing biosynthetic pathway
(*c*) Produce a protein that itself produces the phenotype of interest or is the product of interest
(*d*) All of the above

150. Match the object given in Column I with the product listed in Column II.

	Column I	Column II
A.	2, 4 – D	1. Virus resistance
B.	Coat protein gene	2. Somatic hybridization
C.	PEG	3. Callus culture
D.	Cry gene	4. Insect resistance
		5. Haploid plants

Codes :

	A	B	C	D
(*a*)	3	1	2	4
(*b*)	3	1	4	2
(*c*)	3	2	1	4
(*d*)	3	4	1	2

151. The plant cells without cell wall is called :
(*a*) protoplasm (*b*) protoplast
(*c*) cytoplasm (*d*) Both (*a*) and (*b*)

152. During infection T-cells interact with :
(*a*) Macrophages (*b*) B-cells
(*c*) Infected cells (*d*) Erythrocytes

153. The following organism causes the African sleeping sickness :
(*a*) Amoeba (*b*) Paramecium
(*c*) Trypanosoma (*d*) Plasmodium

154. Match the columns :

	Column I	Column II
A.	Emphysema	1. Nervous system
B.	Ulcer	2. Circulatory system
C.	Arteriosclerosis	3. Respiratory system
D.	Epilepsy	4. Digestive system
		5. Excretory system

Codes :

	A	B	C	D
(*a*)	3	4	5	2
(*b*)	3	4	2	1
(*c*)	3	5	1	2
(*d*)	3	4	1	5

155. Some protection is provided against carcinogens by :
(*a*) Penicillic acid (*b*) Aflatoxin
(*c*) Streptomycin (*d*) Tocopherol/vit. E

156. A disease which causes maximum deaths in children is :
(*a*) Diphtheria
(*b*) Measles
(*c*) Tuberculosis
(*d*) Whooping cough

157. James Phipps and Ali Marvow are related to viral disease that has disappeared :
(*a*) Cow pox (*b*) Small pox
(*c*) Chicken pox (*d*) Tuberculosis

158. Which ones engulf foreign materials?
(*a*) Macrophages
(*b*) Plasma cells
(*c*) Mast cells
(*d*) Lymphocytes

159. Squeezing of leucocytes from capillary walls to fight foreign agents is called :
(*a*) Diakinesis (*b*) Diapedesis
(*c*) Diapause (*d*) Diaphysis

160. What is true for monoclonal antibodies?
(*a*) These antibodies obtained from one parent and for one antigen
(*b*) These obtained from different parents and for one antigen
(*c*) These obtained from one parent and for many antigens
(*d*) These obtained from many parents and for many antigens

161. Salmonella is related with :
(*a*) Typhoid (*b*) Polio
(*c*) T.B. (*d*) Tetanus

162. Which of the most infectious disease is :
(*a*) Hepatitis-B (*b*) AIDS
(*c*) Cough and cold (*d*) Malaria

163. Vaccination against small pox developed by :
(*a*) Edward Jenner
(*b*) Louis Pasteur
(*c*) Alexander Fleming
(*d*) Robert Koch

164. Match the common names of diseases listed under Column-I with their medical terms listed under Column-II; Choose the answer which gives the correct combination of the alphabets of the two columns.

Column-I (Common names)	Column-II (Medical terms)
A. Blood clotting in small capillaries	1. rhinitis
B. Valve defects	2. Stenosis
C. Hay fever	3. Parkinson's disease
D. Paralysis	4. Coronary thrombosis

Codes :

	A	B	C	D
(*a*)	4	2	1	3
(*b*)	2	4	3	1
(*c*)	3	4	2	1
(*d*)	4	1	3	2

165. For detection of cancer isotope used is :
(*a*) Iodine^{131} (*b*) Caesium^{60}
(*c*) Radium (*d*) Uranium^{238}

166. Which of the following disease is caused by virus?
(*a*) Polio (*b*) Diphtheria
(*c*) Typhoid (*d*) Tuberculosis

167. Common influenza is caused by :
(*a*) virus (*b*) bacteria
(*c*) fungi (*d*) protists

168. Radiations can easily destroy cancerous cells because they :
(*a*) are fast mutating
(*b*) are fast dividing
(*c*) get starved of nutrition
(*d*) start replicating fast

169. The term antibiotic was coined by :
(*a*) Alexander Fleming
(*b*) Edward Jenner
(*c*) Louis Pasteur
(*d*) Selman Waksman

170. Antibodies are produced by :
(*a*) RBC (*b*) thrombocytes
(*c*) monocytes (*d*) lymyphocytes

171. Trypanosoma causes :
(*a*) sleeping sickness (*b*) kala-azar
(*c*) typhoid (*d*) filariasis

172. *Torulopsis utilis* is :
(*a*) Food yeast
(*b*) An important intestinal commensal
(*c*) Micro-organism that yields third generation vaccines
(*d*) Employed for synthesis of citric acid

173. Antibiotics inhibit the growth of or destroy :
(*a*) Bacteria and fungi
(*b*) Bacteria and viruses
(*c*) Bacteria, algae and viruses
(*d*) Bacteria, fungi and viruses

174. If all the bacteria and fungi of the world are destroyed then :
(*a*) all living things will become immortal and there will be no disease left
(*b*) we shall be unable to obtain any antibiotics
(*c*) the soil will gradually become depleted of all nitrogen
(*d*) the world will become packed with dead bodies and excretions of all kinds of living organisms

175. *Streptomyces venezuelae* is used to obtain :
(*a*) Chloromycetin (*b*) Streptomycin
(*c*) Tetracycline (*d*) Aureomycin

176. Citric acid is produced by :
(*a*) *Aspergillus niger*
(*b*) *Streptococcus lactic*
(*c*) *Acetobacter suboxyitans*
(*d*) *Candida utilis*

177. The first commercial example of enzyme modification of a protein for human use is :
(*a*) the conversion of pig insulin to human insulin
(*b*) the conversion of goat insulin to human insulin
(*c*) the conversion of pig thyroxine to human thyroxine
(*d*) the conversion of pig aldosterone to human aldosterone

178. Which of the following is used for the diagnosis of disease caused by closely related pathogen?

(*a*) Immunoglobulins
(*b*) Monoclonal antibodies
(*c*) Interferon
(*d*) Vaccines

179. Utilization of living organisms/systems/ processes for producing materials useful to human society is known as :
(*a*) Applied biology
(*b*) Technology
(*c*) Biotechnology
(*d*) Biomedical engineering

180. Biotechnology utilizes new organisms developed from present organisms utilizing :
(*a*) mutations
(*b*) recombinant DNA technology
(*c*) both are correct
(*d*) None of these

181. Which of the following is not concerned with biotechnology?
(*a*) Biogas production
(*b*) Sewage treatment
(*c*) Biofertilizers
(*d*) Wood seasoning

182. Which of these is used in biotechnology :
(*a*) Cattle
(*b*) Yeast
(*c*) Both (*a*) and (*b*)
(*d*) Neither (*a*) nor (*b*)

183. Which of these participates in the manufacturing of dextrans :
(*a*) Mucor (*b*) Lactobacillus
(*c*) Leuconostoc (*d*) Pseudomonas

184. Which of the following is used for manufacture of cosmetics?
(*a*) Serotonin (*b*) Cholesterol
(*c*) Shikonin (*d*) Keratin

185. The technique by which virus detection can be made both in plants and animals is known as :
(*a*) Enzyme linked immunoabsorbent assay (ELISA)
(*b*) Electrophoresis
(*c*) Electron microsocopy
(*d*) Immunofluorescence

186. Streptokinase (TPA) helps in :
(*a*) clearing blood clots
(*b*) increasing plasma
(*c*) dissolving tissues
(*d*) increasing O.P. of cell

187. The enzyme diastase was identified by :
(*a*) Payen and Persoz
(*b*) Waksman
(*c*) Christian Hansen
(*d*) Alexander Fleming

188. The immoblization of enzyme is achieved by :
(*a*) killing the cells without affecting enzymes
(*b*) attaching the enzymes covalently to a solid support
(*c*) entrapping the living cells in gel
(*d*) All of these

189. Interferons are :
(*a*) Proteins released in minute quantities by animals or plant cells, on being infected with virus
(*b*) Proteins synthesized in large quantities by cells actively engaged in synthesis
(*c*) Hormones released by cells in small quantities which influenced some of the various physiological activities
(*d*) Defensive mechanism

190. Magic bullets are :
(*a*) interferons
(*b*) vaccines
(*c*) monoclonal antibodies
(*d*) antigen-antibody cells

191. Cheese contains :
(*a*) proteins 20-35%, fats 20-3%
(*b*) fats 20-35%, protein 20-30%
(*c*) proteins double than fats
(*d*) fats double than proteins

192. The hybridoma technique was developed by :
(*a*) Louis Pasteur
(*b*) Edward Jenner
(*c*) Georges Kohler and Caser Milstein
(*d*) Burnet

193. Skin and mucous membrane traps foreign micro-organisms and cilia propels micro-organisms out of body. It is a non-specific immunity comes under the category of :
(*a*) physiological barriers
(*b*) anatomic barriers
(*c*) phagocytic barriers
(*d*) inflammatory barriers

194. In response to infection which kind of cells are converted into macrophages?
(*a*) Lymphocytes (*b*) Monocytes
(*c*) Eosinophils (*d*) Basophils

195. Perforin lined pores created in the plasma membrane of virus infected cells or some tumour cells, killing of cell occurs by which method?
(*a*) Pores allow entry of interferons
(*b*) Pores allow entry of antibodies
(*c*) Pores allow entry of water which results in bursting of target cells
(*d*) Pores allow entry of killer cells which eat up the contents of target cells

196. There are more than 30 proteins which are a part of complement system. They participate in which type of immunity?
(*a*) Passive immunity
(*b*) Acquired immunity
(*c*) Innate immunity
(*d*) Both (*b*) and (*c*)

197. Which of the following is/are a unique features of adaptive or specific immunity?
(*a*) Specificity
(*b*) Diversity and memory
(*c*) Discrimination between self and non-self
(*d*) All of the above

198. A healthy human possesses about how many lymphocytes?
(*a*) 20,000 cells
(*b*) About a million cells
(*c*) About a billion
(*d*) About a trillion

199. Antibody mediated or humoral immunity is comprised by :
(*a*) B-cells (*b*) T-cells
(*c*) Antigens (*d*) Both (*a*) and (*b*)

200. Antigen binding sites of an antibody molecule are present on :
(*a*) variable region of light chain
(*b*) constant region of light chain
(*c*) variable region of heavy chain
(*d*) constant region of heavy chain

201. IgM class of immunoglobin functions :
(*a*) activation of B-cells
(*b*) mediator in allergic response
(*c*) stimulation of phagocyte
(*d*) as receptor

202. Which of the following immunoglobin class provides protection from inhaled and ingested proteins :
(*a*) Ig D (*b*) Ig A
(*c*) Ig E (*d*) Ig G

203. Which of the following antibodies are most abundant and cross placenta and provide specific immunity for foetus?
(*a*) Ig A (*b*) Ig D
(*c*) Ig G (*d*) Ig M

204. BCG vaccine is adminstered to :
(*a*) all babies of 2, 3 and 4 months of age
(*b*) all babies whose mothers or close family members have been infected with hepatitis B
(*c*) all babies of 2, 3 and 4 month of age at the same time as DTP-Hib
(*d*) all children between 10-14 years

205. Which of the following is not a component of innate immunity?
(*a*) Antibodies
(*b*) Interferons
(*c*) Complement proteins
(*d*) Phagocytes

206. HIV attacks which of the following?
(*a*) B-cells
(*b*) T-cells
(*c*) Antigen presenting cells
(*d*) T-helper cells

207. Which of the following property of acquired immunity is the basis of vaccination?
(*a*) Specificity
(*b*) Diversity
(*c*) Memory
(*d*) Discrimination between self and non-self

208. Immuno-deficiency can result from which of the following?
(*a*) Gene mutation (*b*) Infection
(*c*) Malnutrition (*d*) All of the above

209. Which of the following is an autoimmune disease?
(*a*) Cholera (*b*) Rheumatic fever
(*c*) Typhoid fever (*d*) Malaria

210. If one's own tissue is grafted to another part of the body, it is termed as :
(*a*) Isograft (*b*) Autograft
(*c*) Allograft (*d*) Xenograft

211. Immunity acquired after an infection is :
(*a*) active immunity (*b*) passive immunity
(*c*) innate immunity (*d*) Both (*b*) and (*c*)

212. The type of immunoglobulin, whose function is possible antigen recognition by B-cells, may be :
(*a*) Ig E (*b*) Ig A
(*c*) Ig D (*d*) Ig G

213. Which of the following is used for immune suppression for kidney transplantation.
(*a*) Monoclonal antibodies
(*b*) Interferon
(*c*) Antibiotics
(*d*) Vaccines

214. In one type of yeast fermentation, the entire medium with fermenting organism is removed from the bioreactor after reaching alcohol level of 10-12%. This process is called :
(*a*) continuous process
(*b*) batch process
(*c*) synchronous culture
(*d*) immobilised process

215. The potential use of protoplast fusion technology is :
(*a*) Production of somatic hybrids of genetically diverse species
(*b*) Transfer of cell organelles from one species to another
(*c*) Transfer of a few chromosomes or genes between divergent species
(*d*) All of the above

216. Biotechnology has applications in :
(*a*) Animal and human health care
(*b*) Genetic counselling
(*c*) Forensic medicine
(*d*) All of the above

217. Which is correct about vaccines?
(*a*) Vaccines produced by conventional methods are called first generation vaccines
(*b*) Second generation vaccines are made by genetic engineering
(*c*) Synthetic vaccines are pure, potent and form vaccines of third generation
(*d*) All of the above

218. Vaccine for Hepatitis B virus is :
(*a*) first generation vaccine
(*b*) second generation vaccine
(*c*) third generation vaccine
(*d*) an interferon

219. Which of the following are 'second-generation' vaccines?
(*a*) DPT
(*b*) Hepatitis A
(*c*) Vaccines produced by genetic engineering for hepatitis B and Herpes virus
(*d*) All of the above

220. Who established the scientific basis of vaccination?
(*a*) Edward Jenner (*b*) Louis Pasteur
(*c*) George Kohler (*d*) Cesar Milestein

221. 'Biolipsticks' is :
(*a*) Bioplastics (*b*) Haematoxylin
(*c*) Indigo (*d*) Shikonin

222. The corner-stone of biorevolution is :
(*a*) Protoplast culture

(*b*) Tissue culture technology
(*c*) Biotechnology
(*d*) Biotransformation

223. The first genetically engineered human insulin was launched in :
(*a*) America (*b*) India
(*c*) U.K. (*d*) China

224. A byeproduct of brewing industry is food yeast or vitaminised food. It contains :
(*a*) 40-50% of proteins
(*b*) vitamins of B complex
(*c*) fats
(*d*) All of these

225. The method of growing microorganims by suspending cells/mycelia in a liquid nutrient medium is called :
(*a*) batch process
(*b*) suspended growth system
(*c*) support growth system
(*d*) continuous process

226. Diastase was identified for the first time in 1933 by :
(*a*) Buchner brothers (*b*) Hofkins
(*c*) Peyen and Persoz (*d*) Wohler

227. Which of the following enzymes is used for removing nitrogenous stains?
(*a*) Proteases (*b*) Amylases
(*c*) Rennet (*d*) Lactases

228. The enzyme used in the beverage industry to flavour soft drinks and in the banking industry to sweeten biscuits and cakes is :
(*a*) Amylase
(*b*) Protease
(*c*) Glycoamylases
(*d*) Gluocoamylases and glucoisomerases

229. Shikonin is a :
(*a*) vitamin produced by genetic engineering
(*b*) enzyme produced in tissue culture
(*c*) a red dye produced in tissue culture for using in cosmetics
(*d*) steriod produced by biotechnology

230. Conversion of Cortexolone steroid into prednisolone drug involves a microbe mediated process called :
(*a*) dehydrogenation (*b*) hydroxylation
(*c*) hydrogenation (*d*) deoxygenation

231. Which organism serves as a biofertilizer?
(*a*) *Azolla* (*b*) *E. coli*
(*c*) *Spirogyra* (*d*) *Cassia*

232. *Azotobacter* and *Bacillus* polymyxa are :
(*a*) decomposers
(*b*) non-symbiotic nitrogen fixers
(*c*) symbiotic nitrogen fixers
(*d*) pathogenic bacteria

233. The sum total of genes in a population is known as :
(*a*) genome (*b*) gene bank
(*c*) gene store (*d*) gene pool

234. Which Institute in India is involved in the conservation of germplasm of *Pennisetum*, *Cicer* and others?
(*a*) ICCRISAT-Hyderabad
(*b*) CPRI-Shimla
(*c*) CCMB-Hyderabad
(*d*) NBRI-Lucknow

235. Passive immunity uses discovered by :
(*a*) Edward Jenner (*b*) Emil von Behring
(*c*) Robert Koch (*d*) Louis Pasteur

236. Influenza virus has :
(*a*) DNA
(*b*) RNA
(*c*) Both (*a*) and (*b*)
(*d*) Only proteins and no nucleic acids

237. A patient suffering from cholera is given saline drip becuase :
(*a*) Cl^- ions are important component of blood plasma
(*b*) Na^+ ions help to retain water in the body
(*c*) Na^+ ions important in transport of substance across membrane
(*d*) Cl^- ions help in the formation of HCl in stomach for digestion

238. Hypersensitivity to an allergen is associated with :
(*a*) Aberrant functioning of the immune mechanism
(*b*) Increase in ambient temperature
(*c*) Age of the individual
(*d*) Food habits

239. Syphilis is a sexualy transmitted disease caused by :
(*a*) *Pasteurella*
(*b*) *Leptospira*
(*c*) *Treponema pallidium*
(*d*) *Vibrio*

240. In which one of the following pairs of diseases both are caused by viruses :
(*a*) Tetanus and typhoid
(*b*) Whooping cough and sleeping sickness
(*c*) Syphilis and AIDS
(*d*) Measles and rabies

241. Which disease in children is caused by intensive use of nitrate fertilizer?
(*a*) Jaundice
(*b*) Methemoglobinemia
(*c*) Mumps
(*d*) Septicemia

242. AIDS (Acquired Immuno Deficiency Syndrome) is caused by :
(*a*) Blood cancer
(*b*) Human T-cell leukaemia virus
(*c*) Bacterium
(*d*) TMV

243. Infection of Ascaris usually occurs by :
(*a*) Eating imperfectly cooked pork
(*b*) Contaminated water and vegetables
(*c*) Mosquito bite
(*d*) Tse-tse fly

244. Arhenotoky is a type of :
(*a*) Parthenogenesis found in honey bees, wasp and ants
(*b*) Parthenogenesis found in every insect
(*c*) Parthenogenesis found in mosquito
(*d*) Parthenogenesis found in butterflies

245. Interferons are :
(*a*) Antiviral proteins
(*b*) Antibacterial proteins
(*c*) Anitcancer proteins
(*d*) Complex proteins

246. The immunity developed after the body has recovered from a disease is called :
(*a*) Active immunity (*b*) Passive immunity
(*c*) Both (*a*) and (*b*) (*d*) None of the above

247. Cancer is related to :
(*a*) Uncontrolled growth of tissues
(*b*) Old age
(*c*) Controlled division of tissues
(*d*) None of the above

248. Vaccination against small pox means the introduction into our body of :
(*a*) Leucocytes obtained from animals
(*b*) Antibodies produced in other animals
(*c*) Antibodies
(*d*) Attenuated small pox virus

249. Which one of the following is not a water borne disease?
(*a*) Asthma (*b*) Cholera
(*c*) Amoebiasis (*d*) None of these

250. Virus was discovered by :
(*a*) D. Iwanowski (*b*) Beijernick
(*c*) Stanley (*d*) Herelle

251. All living organisms are killed by heat treatment is known as :
(*a*) Pasteurization (*b*) Immunity
(*c*) Sterilization (*d*) None of these

252. Huntington's chorea is disease :
(*a*) Similar to diabetes
(*b*) Common in Korea
(*c*) Which affects the kidney
(*d*) In which there is a degeneration of nervous system leading to involuntary shaking of head, arms and legs

253. Events in body defence against infection is :
(*a*) Inflammation, chemotaxis, diapedesis, phagocytosis and digestion

(b) Inflammation, diapedesis, chemotaxis, phagocytosis and digestion
(c) Digestion, diapedesis, phagocytosis, chemotaxis and inflammation
(d) Diapedesis, chemotaxis, digestion, phagocytosis and inflammation

254. Which is not an immunological technique?
(a) Antibiotic injection
(b) Tetanus toxoid
(c) Gammaglobulin
(d) Small pox vaccination

255. AIDS, mumps, measles, chicken pox, polio, influenza and rabies are caused by :
(a) Fungi (b) Bacteria
(c) Viruses (d) Protozoa

256. Vaccination protects a person from disease becasue it :
(a) Helps in better digestion
(b) Increases RBC count
(c) Produces antibodies
(d) Corrects body heating system

257. Immunoglobulin that increases in number during allergy is :
(a) IgA (b) IgE
(c) IgG (d) IgM

258. The causes for disease like peptic ulcers, hypertension, coronary heart diseases, liver cirrhosis are :
(a) Certain viruses and bacteria
(b) Excess of fats in food
(c) Excessive use of alcoholic drinks
(d) Not yet identified

259. Trisomic condition of Down's syndrome arises due to :
(a) triploidy
(b) non-disjunction
(c) translocation
(d) dicentric bridge formation

260. Condition of sex chromosomes in male child of Down's syndrome will be :
(a) XY (b) XXY
(c) XX (d) XO

261. Phenylketonuria (PKU) is :
(a) A nutritional disorder due to the protein deficiency
(b) An inborn error of metabolism due to a recessive autosomal gene mutation
(c) A sex-linked disorder which is more common in males than in females
(d) None of the above

262. Chromosomes of Klinefelter's syndrome usually have :
(a) One X (b) XXY
(c) 2X only (d) no Y

263. XO chromosome abnormality is :
(a) Turner's syndrome
(b) Klinefelter's syndrome
(c) Criminal syndrome
(d) Down's syndrome

264. Tay Sach's disorder is :
(a) A chromosomal disorder in young children
(b) The result of severe protein deficiency in diet and damages the muscle development in growing children
(c) An inherited disorder in which the spinal cord and brain are severely damaged within a few months of birth leading to paralysis and mental retardation, and finally the infant's death in 3 or 4 years
(d) A genetic abnormality which appears at the age of 25-30 years and damages the bones

265. Active immunity is due to :
(a) Memory cells (b) Killer T-cells
(c) Helper T-cells (d) Suppressor T-cells

266. Passive immunity is provided through :
(a) Exogenous supply of antigens
(b) Exogenous supply of antibodies
(c) Endogenous supply of antigens
(d) Endogenous supply of antobodies

267. B-cells produce antibodies in response to instruction received from :
(a) Killer T-cells (b) Suppressor T-cells
(c) B-lymphocytes (d) All of the above

268. Opsonisation is carried out by :
(*a*) IgM (*b*) IgG
(*c*) IgA (*d*) IgD and IgE

269. Lysis of foreign cells is mediated through :
(*a*) IgM and IgG (*b*) IgG and IgA
(*c*) IgA and IgD (*d*) IgD and IgE

270. T-Cells have a life of :
(*a*) 4-5 days (*b*) 4-5 weeks
(*c*) 4-5 months (*d*) 4-5 years

271. Antigenic determinant sites bind to which portion of an antibody molecule?
(*a*) Light chains
(*b*) Heavy chains
(*c*) Intermediate chains
(*d*) Both (*a*) and (*b*)

272. The cells that actually release the antibodies are :
(*a*) Helper T-cells (*b*) Cytotoxic T-cells
(*c*) Mast cells (*d*) Memory cells

273. Types of T-cells are :
(*a*) Killer cells and helper cells
(*b*) Killer cells and suppressor cells
(*c*) Killer, helper and suppressor cells
(*d*) Killer, helper and depressor cells

274. Interferon is protein that :
(*a*) Inactivates a virus
(*b*) Protects unattacked cells from virus
(*c*) Prevents viruses from taking over the celluclar machinery
(*d*) All of the above

275. The most modern technique of vaccine preparation is :
(*a*) Extraction of antigens from pathogens
(*b*) Multiplication of antigens through DNA technique
(*c*) Weakening of pathogen through chemical treatment
(*d*) Attenuation of pathogen through heat

276. AIDS testing on normal individuals is done by :
(*a*) Separation of virus
(*b*) Reduction in immunity of the individual
(*c*) Identification of antibodies
(*d*) Identification of antigen-toxin

277. When people are born without B-cells or T-cells they suffer from :
(*a*) autoimmune diseases
(*b*) immunodeficiency diseases
(*c*) both of these
(*d*) None of these

278. Which of the following is incorrect :
(*a*) Skin is a tough outer layer, so it prevents entry of bacteria and viruses
(*b*) Skin secretes oil and sweat by the glands which makes the surfce basic and thus kills the microbes
(*c*) Skin secretes lysozyme along with sweat which prevents infection
(*d*) Some bacteria are present on the skin which release acids and other metabolic wastes that inhibit the growth of pathogens

279. Which one of the following diseases is due to an allergic reaction?
(*a*) Enteric fever (*b*) Hay fever
(*c*) Skin cancer (*d*) Goitre

280. Which one of the following micro-organisms is used for production of citric acic in industries?
(*a*) *Lactobacillus vulgaris*
(*b*) *Renicillium citrinum*
(*c*) *Aspergillus niger*
(*d*) *Rhizopus nigricans*

281. Important objective of biotechnology in agriculture sector is :
(*a*) To produce pest resistant varieties of plants
(*b*) To increase the nitrogen content
(*c*) To decrease the seed number
(*d*) To increase the plant weight

282. The main technique involved in agricultural biotechnology is called :
(*a*) Tissue culture (*b*) Transformation
(*c*) Plant breeding (*d*) DNA replication

283. The new strain of bacteria produced by biotechnology in alcohol industry is :
(*a*) *Escherichia coli*
(*b*) *Saccharomcyces cerevisiae*
(*c*) *Bacillus subtilis*
(*d*) *Pseudomonas putida*

284. The basis of DNA finger printing is :
(*a*) Availability of cloned DNA
(*b*) Knowledge of human karyotype
(*c*) Occurrence of restriction fragment length polymorphism (RELP)
(*d*) Phenotypic differences between individuals

285. Genetically engineered bacteria have been used in commercial production of :
(*a*) Thyroxine (*b*) Testosterone
(*c*) Human insulin (*d*) Melatonin

286. Which of the following correctly defines a transgenic animal?
(*a*) An animal which has foreign DNA in all its cells becuase of an injection of DNA into the nuclei of the zygote from which it is developed
(*b*) An animal which has foreign DNA in all its cells because of an injection of DNA into the nuceli of some of the cells in adulthood
(*c*) An animal which has foreign DNA and RNA in some of its cells because of an injection of DNA and RNA into the nucleus of the zygote from which it is developed
(*d*) An animal which has foreign DNA in some of its cells becaue of an injection of DNA, into the nuclei of some of the cells of the blastocyst

287. Which one of the following is not true about antibiotics ?
(*a*) First antibiotic was discovered by Alexander Fleming
(*b*) The term 'antibiotic' was coined by Selman Waksman in 1942
(*c*) Some persons can be allergic to a particular antibiotic
(*d*) Each antibiotic is effective only against one particular kind of germ

288. Rennin used in cheese industry is :
(*a*) Antibiotic (*b*) Alkaloid
(*c*) Enzyme (*d*) Inhibitor

289. The organism used for alcoholic fermentation is :
(*a*) Saccharomyces (*b*) Aspergillus
(*c*) Pseudomonas (*d*) Pencillium

290. A cell coded protein that is formed in response to infection with most animal viruses is called :
(*a*) histone (*b*) vaccine
(*c*) antibody (*d*) interferon

291. Which of the following organelles is related with genetic engineering?
(*a*) Mitochondria (*b*) Golgi apparatus
(*c*) Plasmids (*d*) Lysosomes

292. A chemical substance derived from a living source that has the capacity to inhibit growth or to destroy microbes is called
(*a*) Vaccine (*b*) Toxoid
(*c*) Toxin (*d*) Antibiotic

293. The Central Drug Research Institute (CDRI) is situated in :
(*a*) New Delhi (*b*) Allahabad
(*c*) Lucknow (*d*) Kanpur

294. Wine and Beer are produced directly by fermentation. Brandy and Whisky require both fermentation. Brandy and Whisky require both fermentation and distillation because :
(*a*) fermentation is inhibited at an alcoholic level of 10-18%
(*b*) distillation prolongs storage
(*c*) distillation improves quality
(*d*) distillation purifies the beverage

295. The antibiotics obtained from *Streptomyces* are :
(*a*) Chloramphenicol, Erythromycin
(*b*) Leucomycin, Neomycin
(*c*) Novobiocin, Spiramycin
(*d*) All of these

296. Human insulin has 51 amino acids in two chains. Mark the correct statement
(*a*) A chain with 21 and B chain with 30 amino acids
(*b*) A chain with 20 and B chain with 31 amino acids
(*c*) A chain has 31 has B has 20 amino acids
(*d*) A chain has 30 and B has 21 amino acids

297. Lymphocytes that inhibit the development and proliferation of T and B cell are :
(*a*) suppressor B cells
(*b*) suppressor T cells
(*c*) macrophages
(*d*) neutrophils

298. Which one of the following is a viral disease?
(*a*) AIDS (*b*) Tetanus
(*c*) Whooping cough (*d*) Cholera

299. When body starts rejecting its own cells, it is called :
(*a*) Immunodeficiency
(*b*) Immunosuppression
(*c*) Autografting
(*d*) Autoimmunity

300. For a T cell to recognize an antigen, it must interact with :
(*a*) Complement (*b*) A macrophage
(*c*) A B cells (*d*) All of the above

301. Antibodies combine with antigens :
(*a*) At variable regions
(*b*) At constant regions
(*c*) Only if macrophages are present
(*d*) Both (*a*) and (*c*) are correct

302. Which one of these is mismatched :
(*a*) Helper T cells – Help complement react
(*b*) Cytotoxic T cells – Active in tissue rejection
(*c*) Suppressor T cells – Shut down the immune response
(*d*) Memory T cells – Long-living line of T cells

303. Vaccines are :
(*a*) The same as monoclonal antibodies
(*b*) Treated bacteria or viruses or one of their proteins
(*c*) MHC proteins
(*d*) All of the above

304. Endogenous pyrogen causes :
(*a*) Higher body temperature
(*b*) Production of antibodies
(*c*) Both (*a*) and (*b*)
(*d*) None of the above

305. An allergic reaction is initiated by antibodies of the :
(*a*) IgG group (*b*) IgM group
(*c*) IgA group (*d*) IgE group

306. The symptoms of an allergic reaction develop in response to :
(*a*) interferons (*b*) interleukins
(*c*) histamines (*d*) complement

307. Someone with severe combined immunodeficiency has no :
(*a*) interferons
(*b*) macrophages
(*c*) T or B cells
(*d*) functioning lymph nodes

308. Untreated victims of severe combined immunodeficiency usually die from :
(*a*) infections that in other people are minor
(*b*) anaphylactic shock
(*c*) congested lungs
(*d*) unusually high fever

309. The virus that causes acquired immune deficiency syndrome (AIDS) parasitizes :
(*a*) B cells
(*b*) cytotoxic T cells
(*c*) helper T cells
(*d*) the membranes of lymph nodes

310. Interferons inhibit the infection of :
(*a*) Bacteria (*b*) Viruses
(*c*) Protozoans (*d*) Helminth

311. Chances of developing a disease are increased due to :
(*a*) Infective dose (*b*) Invasiveness
(*c*) Toxigenicity (*d*) All the of above

312. Fever causing substance is called :
(*a*) Pathogen (*b*) Pyrogen
(*c*) Interferon (*d*) Antigen

313. The theory behind the use of lymphokines in cancer therapy is that :
(*a*) If cancer develops, the immune system has been ineffective
(*b*) lymphokines stimulate the immune system
(*c*) Cancer cells bear antigens that should be recognizable by cytotoxic T cells
(*d*) All of the above

314. Bradykinin is related with :
(*a*) Inflammation (*b*) Sensation of Pain
(*c*) Histamine release (*d*) All of the above

315. The major histocompatibility complex is a :
(*a*) series of complement-enhanced reactions to antigens
(*b*) group of antigens, coded by a family of genes on the surface of body cells
(*c*) form of autoimmunity
(*d*) the major cause of cancer

316. Which of the following blood groups enables a person to give blood to any other person?
(*a*) A (*b*) B
(*c*) AB (*d*) O

317. What happens to a person who receives the wrong type of blood?
(*a*) All the arteries dilate
(*b*) All the arteries constrict
(*c*) The red blood cells agglutinate
(*d*) The spleen and lymph nodes deteriorate

318. An example of an autoimmune disease it :
(*a*) asthma
(*b*) cancer
(*c*) systemic lupus erythematosus
(*d*) erythroblastosis foetalis

319. Which of the following disease is common among individuals with deficient immune systems?
(*a*) Asthma
(*b*) Cancer
(*c*) Systemic lupus erythematosus
(*d*) Erythroblastosis foetalis

320. Allergic reactions are related with :
(*a*) IgE (*b*) IgD
(*c*) IgG (*d*) IgM

321. Which of these pertain, (s) to T cells
(*a*) They have specific receptors
(*b*) They have cell-mediated immunity
(*c*) They stimulate antibody production by B cells
(*d*) All of the above

322. Which of the following does not pertain to B cells :
(*a*) Have passed through the thymus
(*b*) Specfic receptors
(*c*) Antibody-mediated immunity
(*d*) Synthesize and liberate antibodies

323. The term *humor* refers to :
(*a*) bone marrow
(*b*) plasma and lymph
(*c*) all internal tissues
(*d*) all subcutaneous tissues

324. The humoral immune system defends mostly against bacteria and viruses in the :
(*a*) body fluids
(*b*) digestive tract
(*c*) internal organs
(*d*) regions beneath the skin

325. The term *immunity* refers to :
(*a*) the combined actions of all white blood cells
(*b*) events that occur within the lymphatic system
(*c*) general defence against all microorganisms
(*d*) specifric defence against microbes encountered during an earlier exposure.

326. Artificial immunity can be acquired from a :
(*a*) serious illness
(*b*) vaccination
(*c*) repeated exposure to the same microbe
(*d*) treatment with penicillin

327. Antibiodies are synthesized by :
(*a*) B lymphocytes
(*b*) phagocytes
(*c*) helper T lymphocytes
(*d*) killer T lymphocytes

328. The regions of regions of an antibody that make it distinct from all other kinds of antibodies are its :
(*a*) variable (V) regions
(*b*) constant (C) regions
(*c*) mutated (M) regions
(*d*) bifurcated (B) regions

329. The regions of an antibody that determine its general role or effector function are its :
(*a*) variable (V) regions
(*b*) constant (C) resions
(*c*) mutated (M) regions
(*d*) bifurcated (B) regions

330. Antigenic determinant sites bind to which positions of an antibody molecule :
(*a*) Heavy chains (*b*) Light chains
(*c*) Both (*a*) and (*b*) (*d*) None of these

331. A person without thymus would not be able to :
(*a*) produce antibodies
(*b*) reject an tissue transplant
(*c*) develop an inflammatory response
(*d*) All of the above

332. The cells which actually release the antibodies are :
(*a*) Helper T-cells
(*b*) Cytotoxic T-cells
(*c*) Supperssor T-cells
(*d*) Plasma cells

333. The clonal selection theory says that :
(*a*) An antigen selects certain B cells an suppresses them
(*b*) An antigen strimulates the multiplication of B cells that produce antibodies against it
(*c*) T cells select those B cells that should produce antibodies, regardless of antigens
(*d*) T cells suppress all B cells except the ones that should multiply and divide

334. Plasma cells are :
(*a*) The same as memory cells
(*b*) Formed from blood plasma
(*c*) B cells that are actively secreting antibody
(*d*) Inactive T cells carried in the plasma

335. Tissue rejection is related with :
(*a*) Helper T cells
(*b*) Cytoxic T cells
(*c*) Supperssor T cells
(*d*) All of the above

336. T cell of the cell-mediated immune system make specific proteins, similar to antibodies, that become :
(*a*) embedded within membranes of lymph nodes
(*b*) receptors on the plasma membrane of the T cell
(*c*) embedded in interstitial fluid
(*d*) linked to antibodies by disulphide bridges

337. When a T cell recognizes an antigen it :
(*a*) multiplies
(*b*) moves from the thymus to the spleen
(*c*) releases interferons
(*d*) releases antibodies

338. Messenger molecules, secreted by helper T cells, that recruit other white blood cells are called :
(*a*) interferons (*b*) antibiotics
(*c*) cytotoxins (*d*) lymphokines

339. Messenger molecules, released by virus, infected cells that bind to the surfaces of healthy cells and stimulate them to synthesize proteins that prevent viral reproduction are called :
(*a*) interferons (*b*) antibiotics
(*c*) cytotoxins (*d*) lymphokines

340. Lymphocytes that cause the formation of holes in plasma membranes are :
(*a*) B cells
(*b*) killer (or cytotoxic)
(*c*) suppressor T cells
(*d*) helper T cells

341. Vaccination with anitbody (Immunoglobulin) causes :
(*a*) Active immunity
(*b*) Passive immunity
(*c*) Humoral immunity
(*d*) All of the above

342. Who devised monoclonal antibody technology :
(*a*) Cesar Milstein
(*b*) Georges Kohler
(*c*) Both of the above
(*d*) None of the above

343. Lymphocytes that activate B cells and T cells are :
(*a*) activator B cells (*b*) cytotoxic cells
(*c*) macrophages (*d*) helper T cells

344. It is now possible to breed plants and animals with desired characters through :
(*a*) Ikebana technique
(*b*) Tissue culture
(*c*) Genetic engineering
(*d*) Chromosome engineering

345. Arhenotoky is a type of :
(*a*) Parthenogenesis found in honey bees, wasp and ants
(*b*) Parthenogenesis found in every insect
(*c*) Parthenogenesis found in mosquito
(*d*) Parthenogenesis found in butterflies

346. A strain of "golden" rice contains high contents of :
(*a*) Vitamin A (*b*) Vitamin K
(*c*) Vitamin E (*d*) Vitamin C

347. Biofertilizers increase the availability of nutrients like :
(*a*) Nitrogen (*b*) Phosphorus
(*c*) Calcium (*d*) Both (*a*) and (*c*)

348. Which bacterium was the first biopesticide to be used on a commercial scale in the world?
(*a*) *Bacillus thuringiensis*
(*b*) *Bacillus polymyxa*
(*c*) *Bacillus breuis*
(*d*) *Bacillus licheniformis*

349. Biological weapons :
(*a*) are low cost weapons
(*b*) cause far more casualities than chemical or conventional weapons
(*c*) are invisible, odourless and tasteless
(*d*) all of the these

350. Biopiracy is related to which of the following?
(*a*) Traditional knowledge
(*b*) Biomolecules and regarding bioresources genes isolated from bioresources
(*c*) Bioresources
(*d*) All of the above

351. Solution of polyethylene glycol (PEG) or a very brief high voltage electric current is used in fusion of :
(*a*) Germinal cells (*b*) Protoplasm
(*c*) Somatic cells (*d*) None of these

352. BGA is chiefly used as fertilizers in :
(*a*) wheat (*b*) paddy
(*c*) mustard (*d*) gram

353. A biofertilizer is :
(*a*) farmyard manure consisting of mixture of cattle dung and crop residues
(*b*) green manure in which a quick growing crop is cultivated and ploughted under the soil
(*c*) a cyanobacterium like *Anabaena sp.* living in cavities of Azolla leaves
(*d*) symbiotic bacteria like *Azotobacter* which fix atmospheric nitrogen

354. Gottlieb Haberlandt started the technique of plant tissue culture in :
(*a*) 1900 (*b*) 1901
(*c*) 1902 (*d*) 1903

355. The technique for another culture was first used in India to produce haploids of :
(*a*) wheat (*b*) rice
(*c*) datura (*d*) brassica

356. Single cell protein (SCP) is obtained from :
(*a*) Unicellular micro-organisms
(*b*) Multicellular micro-organisms

(*c*) Both (*a*) and (*b*)
(*d*) Bacteria only

357. SCP is rich in high quality protein and :
(*a*) high quality of fat
(*b*) high quality of carbohydrates
(*c*) high quality of minerals
(*d*) poor in fats

358. Biopiracy is :
(*a*) formation of transgenic plants
(*b*) another name of biopatents
(*c*) legal removal of biological material
(*d*) illegal removal of biological material

359. *Pentadiplandra brazzeana produces* a protein called brazzein which is about 2,000 times as sweet as sugar. This plant belongs to :
(*a*) Australia (*b*) Africa
(*c*) South America (*d*) Canada

360. Utilization of living organisms/systems processes for producing materials useful to human society is known as :
(*a*) applied biology
(*b*) technology
(*c*) biotechnology
(*d*) biomedical engineering

361. Biotechnology utilizes new organisms developed present orgaisms utilizing
(*a*) mutations
(*b*) recombinant DNA technology
(*c*) both are correct
(*d*) None of these

362. Which of the following is not concerned with biotechnology?
(*a*) Biogas production
(*b*) Sewage treatment
(*c*) Biofertilizers
(*d*) Wood seasoning

363. The first product of ancient biotechnology was :
(*a*) Alcohol (*b*) Lactic acid
(*c*) Insulin (*d*) Steroid

364. Which of these would you expect to be a product of biotechnology?
(*a*) Modified enzyme (*b*) DNA probe
(*c*) Protein hormone (*d*) Steroid hormone

365. Yeasts are single celled fungi. The most common yeast is :
(*a*) *Saccharomyces sake*
(*b*) *Saccharomyces cerevisiae*
(*c*) *Sacchromyces ellipsoides*
(*d*) *Saccharomyces pireformis*

366. Yeasts are of immense use because :
(*a*) they cause diseases
(*b*) they are used in curing of tea and tobacco leaves
(*c*) they are used in breweries and bakeries
(*d*) All of the above

367. Vaccination protects the body against catching a disease because :
(*a*) in provides antibodies synthesized by another animal
(*b*) it makes the diseased organism compatible with the body
(*c*) it produces an enlarged clone of memory cells against that disease
(*d*) it releases large amount of unspecific defensive secretions

368. Bubonic plague is transmitted through the bite of :
(*a*) *Xenopsylla cheopis*
(*b*) *Pediculus humanus*
(*c*) *Glossina palpalis*
(*d*) *Aedes aegypti*

369. Just as culex is to elephantiasis (filariasis), so is :
(*a*) Pork to tapeworm
(*b*) Sand fly to sleeping sickness
(*c*) Entamoeba to amoebic dysentery
(*d*) Rat flea to plague

370. Disease spread by bed bug is :
(*a*) Typhoid
(*b*) Trench ferer
(*c*) Yellow fever
(*d*) Typhus relapsing fever

371. Pus is a collection of :
(*a*) dead cells
(*b*) body fluids

(c) dead cells, body fluids and water
(d) dead cells and body fluids only

372. Many allergic disorders are cured by giving :
(a) Insulin (b) Tolbutamide
(c) Antihistamines (d) Antigens

373. A recombinant vaccine against hepatitis virus has been produced which causes :
(a) Jaundice
(b) Cancer
(c) Jaundice and lever cancer
(d) Jaundice and diabetes

374. B-cells and T-cells are produced in the :
(a) thymus gland (b) spleen
(c) bone marrow (d) liver

375. T-cells respond to the pathogens by producing :
(a) Killer T-cells
(b) Helper T-cells
(c) Suppressor T-cells and memory cells
(d) Killer T-cells, helper T-cell and suppressor T-cells

376. Whenever you have deep wound burns, it is advised to take :
(a) Anti-tetanus serum
(b) Anti-wound serum
(c) DPT vaccine
(d) BGC vaccine

377. Gout results from accumulation of :
(a) urease in the synovial joints
(b) uric acid in the synovial joints
(c) calcium oxalate in the synovial joint
(d) uric acid and calcium oxalate in synovial joints

378. A disorder in which there is complete absence of eyes is known as :
(a) Anophthalmia
(b) Trachoma
(c) Retinophobia
(d) Tay-Sach's disorder

379. Enterobiasis is a disease caused by :
(a) Helminthes (b) Bacteria
(c) Viruses (d) Protozoans

380. Which one of the following has intermediate host?
(a) Tapeworm (b) Liverfluke
(c) Roundworm (d) Plasmodium

381. Rheumatoid arthritis first attacks :
(a) cartilage
(b) bone
(c) synovial membrane
(d) ligaments

382. Which of the following pairs is not correctly matched?
(a) Dengue fever-*Arbovirus*
(b) Plague-*Yersinia pestis*
(c) Syphilis-*Trichuris trichiura*
(d) Sleeping sickness-*Trypanosoma gambiensis*

383. Antigens are present :
(a) inside nucleus
(b) on cell surface
(c) inside cytoplasm
(d) no nuclear membrane

384. Blood cancer is known as :
(a) Leukaemia
(b) Thrombosis
(c) Haemolysis
(d) Haemophilia

385. Perspiration saliva and tears contain an enzyme, lysozyme, that kills :
(a) virus, infected cells
(b) protozoa
(c) bacteria
(d) viruses

386. Lysozyme kills by destroying :
(a) cell walls
(b) mitochondrial enzymes
(c) lipid bilayer
(d) the machinery for DNA replication

387. Most bacteria ingested with food are killed by :
(a) cilia and mucus on the linings of the tract
(b) stomach acids
(c) the intrinsic factor in the stomach
(d) bile in the small intestine

388. White blood cells that are non-specific killers of microbes are :
(*a*) B-cells (*b*) phagocytes
(*c*) killer T-cells (*d*) helper T-cells

389. Blood vessels near a wound dilate and become more permeable in response to which material released from damaged cells?
(*a*) Pyrogens (*b*) Antibodies
(*c*) Histamine (*d*) Interferons

390. Who is called Father of Immunology?
(*a*) Louis Pasteur (*b*) Robert Koch
(*c*) Edward Jenner (*d*) Iwanovsky

391. B-cells are stimulated to produce antibodies by :
(*a*) Helper T-cells (*b*) Killer T-cells
(*c*) Suppressor T-cells (*d*) Plasma cells

392. Complement :
(*a*) is a general defence mechanism
(*b*) is a series of proteins present in the plasma
(*c*) plays a role in destroying bacteria
(*d*) All of the above

393. Which of the following has been recently used for increasing productivity of super milk cows :
(*a*) Artificial insemination by pedigree bull only
(*b*) Super ovulation of high production cow only
(*c*) Embryo transplantation only
(*d*) A combination of super ovulation, artificial insemination and embryo transplantation into a carries cow (Surrogate Mother)

ANSWERS

1	**2**	**3**	**4**	**5**	**6**	**7**	**8**	**9**	**10**
(*b*)	(*b*)	(*a*)	(*b*)	(*b*)	(*a*)	(*d*)	(*c*)	(*d*)	(*b*)
11	**12**	**13**	**14**	**15**	**16**	**17**	**18**	**19**	**20**
(*a*)	(*b*)	(*c*)	(*a*)	(*a*)	(*b*)	(*d*)	(*c*)	(*a*)	(*a*)
21	**22**	**23**	**24**	**25**	**26**	**27**	**28**	**29**	**30**
(*a*)	(*c*)	(*d*)	(*d*)	(*c*)	(*b*)	(*d*)	(*d*)	(*c*)	(*b*)
31	**32**	**33**	**34**	**35**	**36**	**37**	**38**	**39**	**40**
(*d*)	(*c*)	(*d*)	(*d*)	(*b*)	(*b*)	(*b*)	(*c*)	(*a*)	(*b*)
41	**42**	**43**	**44**	**45**	**46**	**47**	**48**	**49**	**50**
(*c*)	(*d*)	(*b*)	(*a*)	(*d*)	(*a*)	(*c*)	(*a*)	(*b*)	(*d*)
51	**52**	**53**	**54**	**55**	**56**	**57**	**58**	**59**	**60**
(*a*)	(*a*)	(*b*)	(*d*)	(*b*)	(*b*)	(*c*)	(*d*)	(*d*)	(*d*)
61	**62**	**63**	**64**	**65**	**66**	**67**	**68**	**69**	**70**
(*d*)	(*d*)	(*b*)	(*d*)	(*c*)	(*a*)	(*b*)	(*c*)	(*a*)	(*a*)
71	**72**	**73**	**74**	**75**	**76**	**77**	**78**	**79**	**80**
(*a*)	(*c*)	(*a*)	(*a*)	(*c*)	(*b*)	(*b*)	(*b*)	(*d*)	(*d*)
81	**82**	**83**	**84**	**85**	**86**	**87**	**88**	**89**	**90**
(*a*)	(*d*)	(*c*)	(*a*)	(*d*)	(*b*)	(*d*)	(*d*)	(*b*)	(*d*)
91	**92**	**93**	**94**	**95**	**96**	**97**	**98**	**99**	**100**
(*c*)	(*d*)	(*c*)	(*b*)	(*d*)	(*c*)	(*d*)	(*b*)	(*b*)	(*a*)
101	**102**	**103**	**104**	**105**	**106**	**107**	**108**	**109**	**110**
(*b*)	(*c*)	(*c*)	(*c*)	(*b*)	(*c*)	(*d*)	(*c*)	(*b*)	(*a*)

111	**112**	**113**	**114**	**115**	**116**	**117**	**118**	**119**	**120**
(*c*)	(*b*)	(*c*)	(*d*)	(*d*)	(*c*)	(*a*)	(*b*)	(*b*)	(*a*)
121	**122**	**123**	**124**	**125**	**126**	**127**	**128**	**129**	**130**
(*b*)	(*c*)	(*b*)	(*d*)	(*d*)	(*b*)	(*b*)	(*a*)	(*a*)	(*a*)
131	**132**	**133**	**134**	**135**	**136**	**137**	**138**	**139**	**140**
(*a*)	(*b*)	(*d*)	(*b*)	(*d*)	(*c*)	(*d*)	(*b*)	(*d*)	(*a*)
141	**142**	**143**	**144**	**145**	**146**	**147**	**148**	**149**	**150**
(*b*)	(*c*)	(*d*)	(*c*)	(*d*)	(*a*)	(*b*)	(*a*)	(*d*)	(*a*)
151	**152**	**153**	**154**	**155**	**156**	**157**	**158**	**159**	**160**
(*b*)	(*a*)	(*c*)	(*b*)	(*d*)	(*c*)	(*b*)	(*a*)	(*b*)	(*b*)
161	**162**	**163**	**164**	**165**	**166**	**167**	**168**	**169**	**170**
(*a*)	(*c*)	(*a*)	(*a*)	(*a*)	(*a*)	(*a*)	(*c*)	(*d*)	(*d*)
171	**172**	**173**	**174**	**175**	**176**	**177**	**178**	**179**	**180**
(*a*)	(*a*)	(*d*)	(*d*)	(*a*)	(*a*)	(*a*)	(*b*)	(*c*)	(*c*)
181	**182**	**183**	**184**	**185**	**186**	**187**	**188**	**189**	**190**
(*d*)	(*c*)	(*c*)	(*c*)	(*a*)	(*a*)	(*a*)	(*d*)	(*a*)	(*c*)
191	**192**	**193**	**194**	**195**	**196**	**197**	**198**	**199**	**200**
(*a*)	(*c*)	(*b*)	(*b*)	(*c*)	(*d*)	(*d*)	(*d*)	(*a*)	(*a*)
201	**202**	**203**	**204**	**205**	**206**	**207**	**208**	**209**	**210**
(*b*)	(*b*)	(*c*)	(*d*)	(*a*)	(*d*)	(*c*)	(*a*)	(*b*)	(*b*)
211	**212**	**213**	**214**	**215**	**216**	**217**	**218**	**219**	**220**
(*a*)	(*c*)	(*a*)	(*b*)	(*d*)	(*d*)	(*d*)	(*b*)	(*c*)	(*a*)
221	**222**	**223**	**224**	**225**	**226**	**227**	**228**	**229**	**230**
(*d*)	(*c*)	(*a*)	(*d*)	(*a*)	(*c*)	(*a*)	(*d*)	(*c*)	(*b*)
231	**232**	**233**	**234**	**235**	**236**	**237**	**238**	**239**	**240**
(*a*)	(*b*)	(*d*)	(*a*)	(*a*)	(*c*)	(*b*)	(*c*)	(*c*)	(*d*)
241	**242**	**243**	**244**	**245**	**246**	**247**	**248**	**249**	**250**
(*b*)	(*b*)	(*b*)	(*c*)	(*a*)	(*a*)	(*a*)	(*d*)	(*a*)	(*a*)
251	**252**	**253**	**254**	**255**	**256**	**257**	**258**	**259**	**260**
(*c*)	(*d*)	(*a*)	(*a*)	(*c*)	(*c*)	(*b*)	(*c*)	(*b*)	(*a*)
261	**262**	**263**	**264**	**265**	**266**	**267**	**268**	**269**	**270**
(*b*)	(*b*)	(*a*)	(*c*)	(*a*)	(*b*)	(*d*)	(*b*)	(*a*)	(*d*)
271	**272**	**273**	**274**	**275**	**276**	**277**	**278**	**279**	**280**
(*d*)	(*c*)	(*c*)	(*b*)	(*b*)	(*c*)	(*b*)	(*b*)	(*b*)	(*c*)
281	**282**	**283**	**284**	**285**	**286**	**287**	**288**	**289**	**290**
(*a*)	(*a*)	(*d*)	(*c*)	(*c*)	(*a*)	(*d*)	(*c*)	(*a*)	(*d*)
291	**292**	**293**	**294**	**295**	**296**	**297**	**298**	**299**	**300**
(*c*)	(*d*)	(*c*)	(*a*)	(*d*)	(*a*)	(*b*)	(*a*)	(*b*)	(*b*)
301	**302**	**303**	**304**	**305**	**306**	**307**	**308**	**309**	**310**
(*a*)	(*a*)	(*b*)	(*a*)	(*d*)	(*c*)	(*c*)	(*a*)	(*c*)	(*b*)

311	312	313	314	315	316	317	318	319	320
(*d*)	(*b*)	(*d*)	(*d*)	(*a*)	(*d*)	(*c*)	(*c*)	(*b*)	(*a*)
321	**322**	**323**	**324**	**325**	**326**	**327**	**328**	**329**	**330**
(*d*)	(*a*)	(*b*)	(*a*)	(*d*)	(*b*)	(*a*)	(*a*)	(*b*)	(*c*)
331	**332**	**333**	**334**	**335**	**336**	**337**	**338**	**339**	**340**
(*b*)	(*d*)	(*b*)	(*c*)	(*b*)	(*b*)	(*a*)	(*d*)	(*a*)	(*b*)
341	**342**	**343**	**344**	**345**	**346**	**347**	**348**	**349**	**350**
(*b*)	(*c*)	(*d*)	(*c*)	(*a*)	(*a*)	(*a*)	(*a*)	(*d*)	(*c*)
351	**352**	**353**	**354**	**355**	**356**	**357**	**358**	**359**	**360**
(*b*)	(*b*)	(*c*)	(*d*)	(*c*)	(*c*)	(*d*)	(*d*)	(*b*)	(*c*)
361	**362**	**363**	**364**	**365**	**366**	**367**	**368**	**369**	**370**
(*c*)	(*d*)	(*b*)	(*d*)	(*b*)	(*c*)	(*c*)	(*a*)	(*d*)	(*d*)
371	**372**	**373**	**374**	**375**	**376**	**377**	**378**	**379**	**380**
(*d*)	(*c*)	(*c*)	(*c*)	(*d*)	(*a*)	(*b*)	(*a*)	(*a*)	(*c*)
381	**382**	**383**	**384**	**385**	**386**	**387**	**388**	**389**	**390**
(*c*)	(*c*)	(*b*)	(*a*)	(*c*)	(*a*)	(*b*)	(*b*)	(*c*)	(*c*)
391	**392**	**393**							
(*a*)	(*d*)	(*d*)							

18

ENVIRONMENTAL IMPACT ASSESSMENT, ENVIRONMENTAL AUDITING AND STATISTICS

1. Environmental Impact Assessment is :
   (*a*) the study of impact of environment of proposed action like policy plan or project
   (*b*) a process of anticipating or establishing the changes in physical ecological and socio-economic component of the environment
   (*c*) both of the above
   (*d*) None of the above

2. The stage/s of EIA precede every decision making step of the project is/are :
   (*a*) rapid assessment
   (*b*) comprehensive assessment
   (*c*) initial scrutiny
   (*d*) All of these

3. Match the following :

A. Initial scrutiny	1. To clear the type of project
B. Rapid assessment	2. Cost benefit analysis, listing of issues
C. Comprehensive assessment	3. Impact identification, impact prediction etc.

Codes :

	A	B	C
(*a*)	1	2	3
(*b*)	2	3	1
(*c*)	1	3	2
(*d*)	2	1	3

4. The developmental activities requiring environmental impact assessment are :
   (*a*) Construction activities and manufacturing industries
   (*b*) Mining and power generation projects
   (*c*) Both of these
   (*d*) None of these

5. In a geographic region the rainfall is low, temperature is high, the soil is loose and sandy with low water table. It is reasonable to expect there :
   (*a*) a grassy land
   (*b*) screw pine forest
   (*c*) a xerophytic vegetation
   (*d*) None of these

6. The result of integrated environmental, economic and social needs to achieve both an increased standard of living in the short term, and a net gain or equilibrium among huma, natural and economic resources to support future generations, is :
   (*a*) Environmental Impact Assessment
   (*b*) Sustainable development
   (*c*) Biological magnification
   (*d*) Environmental analysis

7. The responsible people in EIA are :
   (*a*) Decision makers and Assessor
   (*b*) Reviewer and advisor
   (*c*) Proponent and International bodies
   (*d*) All of the above

8. In Ballette environmental evaluation system the human concerns are separated into :
(*a*) ecological factors
(*b*) physical and chemical factors
(*c*) asthetics factor
(*d*) All of the above

9. Which of the following is **not** require clearance from Ministry of Environment and Forests?
(*a*) Chemical Industries
(*b*) Power and Refineries
(*c*) Textile and Rubber Industries
(*d*) Hotel Industries

10. The environmental auditing is :
(*a*) The basic management tool which consists of a systematic, documented, periodic and objective evaluation of, how well organis-ation management systems and equipment are performing
(*b*) The study of impact of environment of proposed action like policy, plan or project
(*c*) Both of the above
(*d*) None of the above

11. The precipitation reaching the ground distribute in different ways as :
1. evaporate and reach the atmosphere
2. infiltrate the soil
3. detained in catchment area
4. become a form of run-off

Select the correct answer from the codes :
(*a*) 1, 2 and 3
(*b*) 2, 3 and 4
(*c*) 1, 3 and 4
(*d*) All of these

12. Match the following :

Column A	Column B
A. Cold weather season	1. Atmospheric temperature goes very down
B. Hot weather season	2. Temperature rises and humidity dec-decreases
C. Rainy season	3. Sets in middle of June and upto to begining of July

Codes :

	A	B	C
(*a*)	1	2	3
(*b*)	2	3	1
(*c*)	3	1	2
(*d*)	1	3	2

13. The great ocean currents are set in motion by:
(*a*) rotation of moon
(*b*) rotation of sun
(*c*) dragging of wind over vast areas of sea surface
(*d*) rise and cooling of air

14. Most of the clouds and the weather systems occurred in :
(*a*) Mesosphere (*b*) Troposphere
(*c*) Ionosphere (*d*) None of these

15. With an increase in altitude, the temperature gradually :
(*a*) increase (*b*) decrease
(*c*) both (*a*) and (*b*) (*d*) None of these

16. The projects of which of the following are being assessed for Environmental Impact?
(*a*) Irrigation and power
(*b*) Administration
(*c*) Public investment
(*d*) All of these

17. Parameter Importance Unit is :
(*a*) a subjective process
(*b*) a weightage given to parameters
(*c*) a technique to select parameters
(*d*) None of the above

18. Which is **not** an objective of EIA?
(*a*) Recycling and reduction of waste
(*b*) Risk analysis and disaster management
(*c*) Assessment of international funding
(*d*) All of the above

19. The term which shows relationship existing between parts of measures is :
(*a*) range
(*b*) correlation
(*c*) standard deviation
(*d*) regression

20. Hypothesis is :
(*a*) guess of scholar
(*b*) hunch of scholar
(*c*) tentative conclusion
(*d*) All of these

21. In an unbalanced, skewed, distribution which measure of central tendency is least biased?
(*a*) mode (*b*) median
(*c*) mean (*d*) range

22. Data deals with *datum* and also with :
(*a*) Scientific study
(*b*) Numericals
(*c*) Only (*b*) and (*d*)
(*d*) Quantities of information

23. The symptoms of a goitre include :
(*a*) enlargement of the throat
(*b*) swelling problems in oesophagus also
(*c*) breathing problems
(*d*) All of the above

24. The radius of tropical cyclones is about
(*a*) 100 miles (*b*) 50 miles
(*c*) 20 miles (*d*) All of these

25. Which pair is **incorrect**?
(*a*) Summer solistice → Sept. 22
(*b*) Vernal equinox → March 20
(*c*) Autumn equinox → Dec. 22
(*d*) Winter solistice → June 21

26. The average occupancy per passenger vehicle in India is :
(*a*) 2 (*b*) 1.2
(*c*) 2.5 (*d*) 5

27. The important sector/s that feed the mankind is/are :
(*a*) agriculture sector
(*b*) forest and wildlife
(*c*) livestock and fisheries
(*d*) All of these

28. A simple matrix is applied by :
(*a*) value of parameters on Y-axis
(*b*) value of parameters on X-axis
(*c*) use of corresponding functional relationship
(*d*) All of the above

29. The mathematical models for prediction of environmental impact attempt to :
(*a*) quantitatively describe the cause and effect relationship between the various system variables
(*b*) qualitatively describe the cause and effect relationship between the various system variables
(*c*) both of the above
(*d*) None of the above

30. The technique used to monitor SO_2 in air is :
(*a*) H_2O_2 acidometry
(*b*) Polyurethane filter
(*c*) Chromatography
(*d*) None of these

31. The technique used to assign parameter importance unit (PIU) is :
(*a*) Chromatography (*b*) Delphi technique
(*c*) Baseline process (*d*) None of these

32. The importance step/s in evaluating the project is/are :
(*a*) a list of parameters defining ecology
(*b*) a list of relevant parameters
(*c*) an inventory of existing environment in the influence zone
(*d*) All of the above

33. How many projects in the list of Schedule I of Environmental Impact Assessment guidelines require environmental clearance from Ministry of Environment and Forests?
(*a*) 17 (*b*) 21
(*c*) 23 (*d*) 25

34. The statement/s that is/are **correct** regarding Environmental Impact Assessment (EIA), 1994
(*a*) Responsibility for implementation of EIA notification lies with Ministry of Environment and Forests
(*b*) EIA notification is applicable to all States or Union territories

(*c*) Schedule I of the guidelines list the projects requiring environmental clearance
(*d*) All of the above

35. The **correct** pair is :
(*a*) The Institute of Remote Sensing → Anna University
(*b*) Institute of Remote Sensing (CSIR) → Delhi
(*c*) The Institute of Remote Sensing → India Science Centre
(*d*) Institute of Public Administration → Dehradun

36. Match the following :

Column A (Contamination of H_2O)	Column B (Impact)
A. Pathogens	1. transmission of communicable diseases
B. Trace elements	2. initiates carcinogenic characters
C. Nutrients	3. lead to growth of undesirable growth life

Codes :

	A	B	C
(*a*)	2	3	1
(*b*)	3	1	2
(*c*)	1	2	3
(*d*)	2	1	3

37. The important air contaminant is :
(*a*) carbon monoxide
(*b*) pathogens
(*c*) heavy metals
(*d*) trace elements

38. An important water contaminant is
(*a*) Heavy metals (*b*) Nitrogen oxides
(*c*) Carbon monoxide (*d*) NO_2 and SO_2

39. Which of the following pair is **incorrectly** matched w.r. to the air quality standard in industrial and mixed use?
(*a*) CO → 5000 μg/m^2
(*b*) SO_2 → 120 μg/m^2
(*c*) NO_x → 80 μg/m^2
(*d*) None of the above

40. Environmental auditing helps in pollution control, improves production, safety and health and conservation of natural resources by way of :
(*a*) ensuring waste prevention and reduction
(*b*) assessing compliance with regulatory environment.
(*c*) placing environmental information to the public
(*d*) All of the above

41. Which is not correctly matched?
(*a*) ISO → International Organisation of Standards
(*b*) EMC → Environmental Management System
(*c*) EIA → Environmental Impact Assessment
(*d*) WTO → Whole Trade Output

42. The agency which is **not** certifying the ISO is :
(*a*) Bureau of Indian Standards (BIS) Delhi
(*b*) Quality Assurance Services (QAS)
(*c*) Central Pollution Control Board (CPCB), Delhi
(*d*) All India Instt. of Local Self Government, Mumbai

43. Which of the following is an impact of SPM and RPM?
(*a*) obscures vision
(*b*) causes cancer
(*c*) corrodes metals
(*d*) initiates soil pollution

44. Population of India is growing at the rate of :
(*a*) 1.23% per year (*b*) 2.12% per year
(*c*) 3% per year (*d*) 5% per year

45. The **false** statement regarding the environmental impact assessment is :
(*a*) Schedule I → Lists of projects
(*b*) Schedule II → Application forms
(*c*) Schedule III → Details of EAC
(*d*) All of the above

46. The important step/s in the prediction of impacts is/are :

(*a*) Carrying out the evaluation of impacts
(*b*) Study of EIA
(*c*) Preparation of environmental management plan
(*d*) All of the above

47. All the cases of diversion of forests land should be approved by :
(*a*) Central Government
(*b*) Conservation of Forests
(*c*) State Land Use Board
(*d*) Ministry of Environment and Forests

48. Land degradation is a great challenge for India because of
(*a*) the 83 mha forest land, over half is used to various degrees
(*b*) only 250 mha land of 330 mha posses any potential for production
(*c*) 406 million of livestock have to supported on 13 mha land
(*d*) All of the above

49. The approximate population of Urban India is :
(*a*) 5.5 million
(*b*) 25.7% of total population
(*c*) 32% of total population
(*d*) 1.5 billion

50. The environmental planning is :
(*a*) the analysis of how we can prevent the poaching of environment
(*b*) the analysis of how people impact natural resources
(*c*) the analysis of how we can preserve our biodiversity
(*d*) the supply of management tool to conserve our environment

51. The **correct** pair regarding the air quality monitoring technique is :
(*a*) $O_3 \rightarrow$ Ultraviolet Photometry
(*b*) $SO_2 \rightarrow$ Diffusion Tube
(*c*) $NO_2 \rightarrow$ Infrared absorption
(*d*) C N P → Polyurethrane filter

52. An environment audit helps in achieving the :
(*a*) resource optimisation
(*b*) waste minimization
(*c*) public awareness
(*d*) All of these

53. Match the following :

Column A	Column B
A. Sulphur oxides	1. Corrodes metals causes acute and chronic leaf injury
B. Carbon monoxide	2. causes headaches, dizziness and nausea, reduces O_2 level in blood
C. Hydrocarbons	3. irritate eyes and nose

Codes :

	A	B	C
(*a*)	3	1	2
(*b*)	1	2	3
(*c*)	2	3	1
(*d*)	1	3	2

54. The maximum tidal energy potential in India is
(*a*) in Gulf of Khambhat
(*b*) in Gangetic delta in Sundarbans
(*c*) along the coast of Odisha
(*d*) along the coast of Chennai

55. The impacts caused by construction of dams and reservoirs include :
(*a*) soil erosion
(*b*) loss of vegetation cover
(*c*) changes in microclimate
(*d*) All of the above

56. All major project plans should be examined to ensure :
(*a*) quality of environment
(*b*) public health and safety
(*c*) both of these
(*d*) None of these

57. The areas upto the 100 meters around the premises such as hospitals, educational institutions and courts are :
(*a*) Silence Zones (*b*) Eutrophic Zones
(*c*) EMP Zones (*d*) Irrigation Zones

58. Match the following :

Column A (Decibles)	Column A (Vehicles)
A. 80	1. Motorcycle scooter and 3-wheeler
B. 85	2. Commercial vehicles upto 4 MT
C. 90	3. Commercial vehicles upto 12 MT

Codes :

	A	B	C
(*a*)	2	3	1
(*b*)	3	1	2
(*c*)	1	2	3
(*d*)	1	3	2

59. The agency that has laid down the standards for the control of pollution of air, water and noise is :
(*a*) Central Polluton Control Tribunal
(*b*) Central Pollution Control Agency
(*c*) Ministry of Home Affairs
(*d*) Central Pollution Control Board

60. The Government of India approved the EIA clearance on :
(*a*) Jan. 26; 1996
(*b*) April. 03; 1998
(*c*) Jan. 27; 1994
(*d*) March. 31; 1998

61. The comprehensive legislation that is truly a milestone in the field of environmental protection was enacted in
(*a*) 1985 (*b*) 1987
(*c*) 1991 (*d*) 1994

62. The legislation that provides legal framework for the improvement of environment is :
(*a*) Water (Prevention and Control of Pollution Act), 1986
(*b*) Water (Prevention and Control of Pollution Act), 1989
(*c*) Water Crisis and Pollution Act, 1994
(*d*) Legislation yet to be declared

63. The environmental impact assessment of development projects has so been done on the basis of :
(*a*) the provisions of the Environment Protection Act, 1986
(*b*) the provisions of the Municipalities Act, 1986
(*c*) executive order of the President
(*d*) All of the above

64. The applications of statistical methods to the solution of biological problems is :
(*a*) Biostatistics (*b*) Data
(*c*) Numeratics (*d*) Scientific study

65. The scientific study of numerical data based on natural phenomena is :
(*a*) Biostatistics
(*b*) Statistics
(*c*) Data
(*d*) Inductive inference

66. The basic understanding of **biometry** is necessary for the students of Biology, Agriculture and Ecology because it :
(*a*) helps the potential ecologist to understand the nature of variability
(*b*) helps us in driving general laws from small samples
(*c*) both of the above
(*d*) None of the bove

67. The process of summing all the individual abbrevations or items of a sample and dividing this sum by the number of items in the sample is :
(*a*) mean (*b*) arithmetic mean
(*c*) average (*d*) All of these

68. The formula for geometric mean is :

(*a*) $\frac{1}{H_4} = \frac{1}{n} \Sigma \frac{1}{Y}$

(*b*) $(Y) = \text{antilog } \frac{1}{n} \log Y$

(*c*) $\frac{1}{H_x} = \Sigma \frac{1}{Y}$

(*d*) $(Y) = \log \frac{1}{n} \Sigma f$

69. The most commonly used measure of spread in biological statistics is :
(*a*) Standard deviation
(*b*) Geometric mean
(*c*) Harmonic mean
(*d*) All of these

70. The measure of the relative chance of the occurrence of an event from among a set of alternatives is :
(*a*) standard mean
(*b*) probability
(*c*) bionomical expression
(*d*) harmonic mean

71. "The chance probability of the simultaneous occurrence of two or more independent event equal to the product of the probability that each will occur separately" is the law of :
(*a*) bionomical expression
(*b*) harmonic mean
(*c*) probability
(*d*) median

72. Test of significance is done by :
(*a*) *Chi*-square test
(*b*) *f*-test
(*c*) probabilitry
(*d*) null hypothesis

73. Economics is concerned with environmental issues in :
(*a*) resource scarcity
(*b*) outputs or pollution
(*c*) environmental degradation
(*d*) All of the above

74. Which of the following statements is NOT correct?
Fischer's index :
(*a*) lies between Laspeyres's index (L) and Paasche's index (P)
(*b*) is the arithmetic mean of L and P
(*c*) is the geometric mean of L and P
(*d*) is equal to L or if L = P

75. Consider the following statements :
1. Quartile deviation is more instructive range as it discards the dispersion of extreme items
2. Coefficient of quartile deviation can not be used to compare the degree of variations in different distributions
3. There are 10 deciles for a series

Which of the above statements is/are correct?
(*a*) 1 alone (*b*) 2 alone
(*c*) 3 alone (*d*) All of these

76. Which one of the following indices satisfies both time reversal and factor reversal tests?
(*a*) Laspeyre's index
(*b*) Fischer's index
(*c*) Passche's index
(*d*) Keely's index

77. Consider the following statements :
1. Correlation analysis helps in determining the relationship between two or more variables, it does not tell us anything about the cause and effect relationship
2. The ratio is explained variation to the total variation is called the coefficient of correlation
3. Pearsonian coefficient always assumes linear relationship and is unduly effected by the extreme items.

Which of the a bove statements is/are correct?
(*a*) 2 alone (*b*) 1 and 2
(*c*) 1 and 3 (*d*) 2 and 3

78. The Fischer index number is :
(*a*) GM of Laspeyres and Passche index numbers
(*b*) AM of Laspeyres and Passche index numbers
(*c*) HM of Laspeyres and Passche index numbers
(*d*) GM of Laspeyres and Marshall-Edge worth index numbers

79. The significance of the difference between the two means of populations, when σ^2 values are known and equal, is tested by :
(*a*) z-test (*b*) t-test
(*c*) f-test (*d*) x^2-test

80. The sum of squared deviation is the least when taken from :

(*a*) mode (*b*) median
(*c*) arithmetic mean (*d*) geometric mean

81. Which one of the following statistical measures is NOT affected by extremely large or small values?

(*a*) Median
(*b*) Harmonic mean
(*c*) Standard deviation
(*d*) Coefficient of variation

82. Given is the following distribution of two variables x and y :

x :	1	2	3	4	5
y :	3	4	5	6	7

The standard deviation of y is :

(*a*) same as standard deviation of x
(*b*) (the standard deviation of x) × 2
(*c*) (the standard deviation of y) + 2
(*d*) (the standard deviation of x) – 2

83. Quartile deviation is :

(*a*) $\frac{4}{5}\sigma$ (*b*) $\frac{3}{2}\sigma$

(*c*) $\frac{2}{3}\sigma$ (*d*) $\frac{5}{4}\sigma$

84. If for a sample data :

Mean < Median < Mode, then the distribution is :

(*a*) skewed to the right
(*b*) symmetric
(*c*) skewed to the left
(*d*) None of these

85. Match the following :

Column A	Column B
A. The study of how individuals and groups make economic decisions about how to meet their needs and wants	1. Economics
B. Any economic good that can be owned and enjoyed on a private or exclusive	2. Private good
C. OPEC	3. Cartel

Codes :

	A	B	C
(*a*)	2	3	1
(*b*)	1	3	2
(*c*)	1	2	3
(*d*)	2	1	3

86. Economic resources are divided into :

(*a*) natural resources (*b*) capital
(*c*) labour (*d*) All of these

87. Stratified sampling is a combination of :

(*a*) Random and Purposive
(*b*) Quota and Random
(*c*) Quota and Cluster
(*d*) Purposive and Quota

88. What does hypothesis become after verification?

(*a*) Formulation
(*b*) Theory principles
(*c*) Reserch problem
(*d*) Solution of problem

89. The hypothesis is verified by :

(*a*) observation (*b*) experiments
(*c*) solution (*d*) analysis

90. The occasionally used research hypothesis is :

(*a*) observational (*b*) applied
(*c*) historical (*d*) experimental

91. If the size of the sample is very small which method of sampling give better results?

(*a*) Census (*b*) Random
(*c*) Stratified (*d*) Purposive

92. The hypothesis is :

(*a*) solution to a problem
(*b*) tentative solution to a problem
(*c*) blueprint of a research project
(*d*) providing mean of data

93. The most useful criteria for hypothesis is/are :

(*a*) it must tally with experiments and observations
(*b*) it must be established

(*c*) it must be the same
(*d*) it must be a blueprint of a research

94. The *nth*-test of the product of *n*-terms or values is :
(*a*) geometric mean
(*b*) harmonic mean
(*c*) arithmetic mean
(*d*) median

95. The coincide of median, mean and mode occur in :
(*a*) symmetrical distribution
(*b*) normal distribution
(*c*) dispersion distribution
(*d*) None of the above

96. The difference between the value of the smallest item and the value of the largest item included in distribution is :
(*a*) standard deviation
(*b*) range
(*c*) mean diviation
(*d*) inter-range

97. The measure of the variation of the items in a distribution is :
(*a*) mode (*b*) dispersion
(*c*) mean (*d*) median

98. The reciprocal of arithmetic mean of the reciprocal of the individual observation is :
(*a*) mode (*b*) geometric mean
(*c*) harmonic mean (*d*) arithmetic ratio

99. The arithmetic mean of a continuous series is given by :
(*a*) $\bar{X} = \frac{\Sigma x}{N}$ (*b*) $\bar{X} = \frac{\Sigma fx}{N}$
(*c*) $\bar{X} = A + \frac{\Sigma dx_i}{N}$ (*d*) $\bar{X} = A + \frac{\Sigma fx}{\Sigma f}$

100. From the cumulative frequency diagram which one of the following types of average can be estimated?
(*a*) Geometric mean (*b*) Harmonic mean
(*c*) Median (*d*) Mode

101. The following equation indicates the relationship among average median and mode :
(*a*) Mode = 3 Median – 2 Mean
(*b*) Mean = 2 Mode – 3 Median
(*c*) Median = 3 Mean – 2 Mode
(*d*) None of these

102. In a moderately asymmetrical distribution :
(*a*) A. M. < G. M. > H. M
(*b*) A. M. < G. M. < H. M
(*c*) A. M. > G. M. > H. M
(*d*) None of these

103. Histogram is useful to determine graphically the value of :
(*a*) arithmetic mean (*b*) median
(*c*) mode (*d*) None of these

104. In s series of values if one value is zero, G.M. is :
(*a*) positive (*b*) zero
(*c*) indeterminate (*d*) negative

105. The sum of squared deviations is mininium when taken from :
(*a*) mean (*b*) median
(*c*) mode (*d*) None of these

106. Coefficient of quartile diviation is calcluted by the formula :
(*a*) $\frac{Q_3 + Q_1}{4}$ (*b*) $\frac{Q_3 + Q_1}{2}$
(*c*) $\frac{Q_3 - Q_1}{Q_3 + Q_1}$ (*d*) $\frac{Q_3 + Q_1}{Q_3 - Q_1}$

107. Coefficient of variation is calculated by the formula :
(*a*) $\frac{\bar{x}}{\sigma} \times 100$ (*b*) $\frac{\sigma}{\bar{x}} \times 100$
(*c*) $\frac{\bar{x}}{\sigma}$ (*d*) $\frac{\sigma}{\bar{x}}$

108. Sampling in which elements are grouped together because they share certain features :
(*a*) stratified sampling
(*b*) cluster sampling

(*c*) systematic sampling
(*d*) random sampling

109. Product moment coefficient of correlation measures which particular type of relationship between two variables?
(*a*) Circular (*b*) Linear
(*c*) Parabolic (*d*) Hyperbola

110. The term which shows relationship existing between parts of measures is :
(*a*) range
(*b*) correlation
(*c*) standard deviation
(*d*) regression

111. The first step in the process of Environmental Impact Assessment is :
(*a*) Rapid assessment
(*b*) Comprehensive assessment
(*c*) Initial screening
(*d*) None of these

112. E.I.A. System have been adopted independently by both industrialized as well as under dveloped countries world wide since :
(*a*) 1975 (*b*) 1970
(*c*) 1960 (*d*) None of these

113. E.I.A. in its present form was introduced with the 'action of forcing provisions' of :
(*a*) U.S. National Environmental Act of 1969
(*b*) Environment Protection Act of 1986
(*c*) both (*a*) and (*b*)
(*d*) None of these

114. Mode distributions having two peaks (equal or unequal in height) are called :
(*a*) variance (*b*) bimodal
(*c*) antimode (*d*) correlation

115. In U-shaped mode distribution, the low point at the middle of the distribution is known as :
(*a*) antimode (*b*) bimodal
(*c*) multimodal (*d*) regression

116. Sex determination is suggested by :
(*a*) probability
(*b*) standard deviation
(*c*) bionomial expression
(*d*) None of these

117. Normal probability distribution was rediscovered and developed by :
(*a*) Gauss and Laplace
(*b*) Watson and Crick
(*c*) De Moirre
(*d*) Boyle

118. The economic goods that cannot be divided and sold in units and can be enjoyed by anybody, is :
(*a*) private goods (*b*) public goods
(*c*) natural resources (*d*) All of the above

119. The things used in an economy to produce material goods and services are :
(*a*) economic resources
(*b*) factors of production
(*c*) both of these
(*d*) None of these

120. Match the following :

Column A	**Column B**
A. Labour	1. physical and mental talents of people
B. Natural resources	2. plants, animals, water, air, nutrients, etc.
C. Intermediate goods	3. tools, machinery, factory, buildings etc.

Codes :

	A	B	C
(*a*)	1	2	3
(*b*)	3	2	1
(*c*)	2	3	1
(*d*)	2	1	3

121. The market value in current rupees or dollars of all goods and services, for final use, produced by an economy during a year is :
(*a*) Economic Growth (EG)
(*b*) Gross National Product (GNP)
(*c*) Gross State Economy (GSE)
(*d*) None of the above

122. The Earth capital is/are :
(*a*) Air, water and soil
(*b*) Wildlife, raw materials and minerals
(*c*) Energy resources and degradation
(*d*) All of the above

123. The measure variation that is least effected by extreme observations is :
(*a*) Range
(*b*) Mean deviation
(*c*) Standard deviation
(*d*) Quartile deviation

124. When coefficient of skewness is zero the distribution is :
(*a*) J-shaped (*b*) U-shaped
(*c*) Symmetrical (*d*) L-shaped

125. In negatively skewed distribution :
(*a*) Mode > Median > Mean
(*b*) Median > Mode > Mean
(*c*) Mode > Median > Mean
(*d*) None of these

126. Karl Pearson's coefficient of skewness is .... Bowley's coefficient of skewness for any skewed distribution.
(*a*) equal to (*b*) less than
(*c*) greater than (*d*) not related to

127. If a frequency distribution is positively skewed, the mean of the distribution is :
(*a*) greater than mode
(*b*) less than the mode
(*c*) equal to the mode
(*d*) None of these

128. The coefficient of correlation :
(*a*) has no limits
(*b*) can be less than one
(*c*) can be more than one
(*d*) varies between ± 1

129. If both the regression coefficients are negative, the correlation coefficient would be :
(*a*) negative (*b*) positive
(*c*) zero (*d*) none ot these

130. The under root of two...... coefficients gives us the value of correlation coefficient.
(*a*) regression (*b*) S.E.
(*c*) S.D. (*d*) None of these

131. Both the regression coefficients cannot be :
(*a*) less than one (*b*) greater than one
(*c*) equal to one (*d*) None of these

132. The regression lines cut each other at the point of :
(*a*) average of *x* and *y*
(*b*) average of *x* only
(*c*) average of *y* only
(*d*) None of these

133. Regression coefficient is independent of change of :
(*a*) origin but not of scale
(*b*) both origin and scale
(*c*) scale but not of origin
(*d*) None of these

134. When one regression coefficient is negative the other would be :
(*a*) negative (*b*) positive
(*c*) zero (*d*) None of these

135. Laspeyre index is based on :
(*a*) base year quantities
(*b*) current year quantities
(*c*) average of current and base year
(*d*) None of these

136. A good number is one that satisfies :
(*a*) Unit test
(*b*) Time test
(*c*) Time Reversal Test and Factor Reversal Test
(*d*) None of these

137. Theoretically the best average in the construction of index numbers :
(*a*) median (*b*) geometric mean
(*c*) mode (*d*) arithmetic mean

138. .... is known as ideal formula for constructing index numbers.
(*a*) Fisher's Ideal Index
(*b*) Laspeyre's Index
(*c*) Passche's Index
(*d*) None of these

139. The most important factors causing seasonal variations are :
(*a*) growth of population
(*b*) technological improvements
(*c*) weather and social customs
(*d*) change is fashions

140. The most widely used method of measuring seasional variation is :
(*a*) Ratio-to-moving average method
(*b*) Ratio-to-trend method
(*c*) Like relative method
(*d*) None of these

141. Cyclical fluctuations are caused by :
(*a*) wars (*b*) earth quakes
(*c*) floods (*d*) None of these

142. The standard deviation of Binomial distribution is :
(*a*) $\sqrt{npq}$ (*b*) npq
(*c*) $n^2p^2q^2$ (*d*) np

143. The standard deviation of poisson distribution is : (m = mean)
(*a*) m (*b*) $\sqrt{m}$
(*c*) m^2 (*d*) $1/\sqrt{m}$

144. The normal distribution is an approximation to :
(*a*) Binomial distribution
(*b*) Poisson distribution
(*c*) Both (*a*) and (*b*)
(*d*) None of these

145. .... asserts that there is no true difference in the sample and the population in the particular matter under consideration.
(*a*) Null hypothesis
(*b*) Alternate hypothesis
(*c*) Both (*a*) and (*b*)
(*d*) None of these

146. Large sample theory is applicable when :
(*a*) N is > 30 (*b*) N is < 30
(*c*) N = 30 (*d*) None of these

147. Student's '*t*' distribution was discovered by :
(*a*) Karl Pearson (*b*) Laplace
(*c*) Fisher (*d*) Gosset

148. Which one of the following average can be computed from a cumulative frequency curve?
(*a*) Geometric mean (*b*) Harmonic mean
(*c*) Mode (*d*) Median

149. Which one of the following statistical measures is based on all observation?
(*a*) Quartile Deviation
(*b*) Harmonic Mean
(*c*) Range
(*d*) Mode

150. Consider the following measures :
A. Correlation coefficient
B. Covariance
C. Coefficient of variation
D. Index number
Which of these are unit-free?
(*a*) A and B (*b*) A and C
(*c*) B and D (*d*) A, C and D

ANSWERS

1	2	3	4	5	6	7	8	9	10
(*c*)	(*d*)	(*a*)	(*c*)	(*c*)	(*b*)	(*d*)	(*d*)	(*d*)	(*a*)
11	**12**	**13**	**14**	**15**	**16**	**17**	**18**	**19**	**20**
(*d*)	(*a*)	(*c*)	(*a*)	(*c*)	(*a*)	(*b*)	(*c*)	(*b*)	(*b*)
21	**22**	**23**	**24**	**25**	**26**	**27**	**28**	**29**	**30**
(*d*)	(*c*)	(*d*)	(*a*)	(*b*)	(*b*)	(*d*)	(*c*)	(*c*)	(*a*)
31	**32**	**33**	**34**	**35**	**36**	**37**	**38**	**39**	**40**
(*b*)	(*c*)	(*a*)	(*d*)	(*a*)	(*c*)	(*a*)	(*a*)	(*a*)	(*d*)

41	**42**	**43**	**44**	**45**	**46**	**47**	**48**	**49**	**50**
(*d*)	(*d*)	(*a*)	(*a*)	(*a*)	(*d*)	(*c*)	(*d*)	(*a*)	(*b*)
51	**52**	**53**	**54**	**55**	**56**	**57**	**58**	**59**	**60**
(*a*)	(*d*)	(*b*)	(*a*)	(*d*)	(*c*)	(*a*)	(*c*)	(*d*)	(*b*)
61	**62**	**63**	**64**	**65**	**66**	**67**	**68**	**69**	**70**
(*a*)	(*a*)	(*a*)	(*a*)	(*b*)	(*c*)	(*d*)	(*b*)	(*a*)	(*b*)
71	**72**	**73**	**74**	**75**	**76**	**77**	**78**	**79**	**80**
(*c*)	(*d*)	(*d*)	(*b*)	(*c*)	(*a*)	(*c*)	(*a*)	(*d*)	(*c*)
81	**82**	**83**	**84**	**85**	**86**	**87**	**88**	**89**	**90**
(*a*)	(*a*)	(*c*)	(*c*)	(*c*)	(*d*)	(*b*)	(*b*)	(*b*)	(*c*)
91	**92**	**93**	**94**	**95**	**96**	**97**	**98**	**99**	**100**
(*d*)	(*b*)	(*a*)	(*a*)	(*a*)	(*b*)	(*b*)	(*c*)	(*d*)	(*c*)
101	**102**	**103**	**104**	**105**	**106**	**107**	**108**	**109**	**110**
(*a*)	(*c*)	(*c*)	(*b*)	(*a*)	(*c*)	(*b*)	(*a*)	(*b*)	(*b*)
111	**112**	**113**	**114**	**115**	**116**	**117**	**118**	**119**	**120**
(*c*)	(*b*)	(*a*)	(*b*)	(*a*)	(*a*)	(*a*)	(*b*)	(*c*)	(*a*)
121	**122**	**123**	**124**	**125**	**126**	**127**	**128**	**129**	**130**
(*b*)	(*d*)	(*b*)	(*c*)	(*a*)	(*d*)	(*a*)	(*d*)	(*a*)	(*a*)
131	**132**	**133**	**134**	**135**	**136**	**137**	**138**	**139**	**140**
(*b*)	(*a*)	(*a*)	(*a*)	(*a*)	(*c*)	(*b*)	(*a*)	(*c*)	(*a*)
141	**142**	**143**	**144**	**145**	**146**	**147**	**148**	**149**	**150**
(*d*)	(*a*)	(*b*)	(*a*)	(*a*)	(*a*)	(*d*)	(*d*)	(*b*)	(*d*)

19

Environmental Legislation

1. World Wildlife Fund was established in the year :
(a) 1971 (b) 1961
(c) 1981 (d) 1951

2. The Indian Forests Act, 1927 contains provisions for prevention of :
(a) Water pollution by deforestation
(b) Air pollution by deforestation
(c) Land pollution by deforestation
(d) None of these

3. The purpose of Public Insurance Act, 1991 is :
(a) to reduce hazard from the handling and accidents related with hazardous chemicals
(b) to providing immediate relief to the persons affected by accidents occurring
(c) to hear appeals with respect to restrictions of areas in which any industries, operations or process or class of industries operation a process shall not be carried out
(d) None of these

4. International Union for Conservation of Nature and Natural Resources (IUCN) was established in :
(a) 1950 (b) 1948
(c) 1970 (d) 1956

5. The Air (Prevention and Control of Pollution) Act, 1981, Amended in :
(a) 1982 (b) 1984
(c) 1986 (d) 1988

6. International Environmental Law Commission in 1947 established by :
(a) 'United Nations' General Assembly
(b) International Council of Scientific Unions (ICSU)
(c) International Union for Conservation of Nature and Natural Resources (IUCN)
(d) None of these

7. Motor Vehicle Act, 1938, Amended in :
(a) 1978 (b) 1981
(c) 1988 (d) None of these

8. The Headquarters of "International Union for Conservation of Nature and Natural Resources (IUCN) are situated in :
(a) Australia
(b) Brazil (South America)
(c) India
(d) Gland, Switzerland

9. Forest Conservation Act, 1980, amended in :
(a) 1988 (b) 1990
(c) 1995 (d) None of these

10. Salim Ali Centre for Ornithology and Natural History (Centre of Excellence) is situated in :
(a) Dhanbad (b) Chennai
(c) Coimbatore (d) New Delhi

11. The first meeting of the National Tiger Conservation Authority was held on :
(a) Nov. 6, 2007 (b) Nov. 6, 2006
(c) Nov. 5, 2004 (d) June 5, 2003

12. The Wildlife (Protection) Act, 1972 was amended in 2006 to incorporate the creation of the National Tiger Conservation Authority. The amendment was notified on :
(a) November 6, 2006
(b) September 4, 2007
(c) September 4, 2006
(d) None of these

13. The First National Wildlife Action Plan (NWAP) of 1983 has been revised and the new

Wildlife Action Plan has been adopted for the period :

(*a*) 2002 – 2016 (*b*) 2003 – 2017
(*c*) 2004 – 2018 (*d*) 2005 – 2019

14. The Indian Board of Wildlife, headed by the :
(*a*) President
(*b*) Prime Minister
(*c*) Minister of Environment and Forests
(*d*) None of these

15. Indian Wild-Life (Protection) Act framed in :
(*a*) 1970 (*b*) 1972
(*c*) 1971 (*d*) None of these

16. Project Tiger was launched in 1973, this has now been renamed as :
(*a*) National Tiger Conservation Authority
(*b*) National Project Tiger
(*c*) Project Tiger Authority
(*d*) None of these

17. Central Pollution Control Board was setup in September, 1974 under the provisions of the :
(*a*) The Indian Forests Act, 1927
(*b*) Water (Prevention and Control of Pollution) Act, 1974
(*c*) Indian Wildlife Protection Act, 1954
(*d*) None of these

18. Recycled Plastic Manufacture and Usage Rules 1999, amended in :
(*a*) 2003 (*b*) 2002
(*c*) 2000 (*d*) 2004

19. The Batteries (Management and Handling) Rules, 2001 were notified in :
(*a*) May 2002 (*b*) June 2003
(*c*) May 2001 (*d*) None of these

20. Legislation passed in the wake of Bhopal tragedy, in order to cover the areas not covered by other laws regarding :
(*a*) The Air (Prevention and Control of Pollution) Act 1981
(*b*) The Indian Forests Act, 1927
(*c*) The Environmental (Protection) Act, 1986
(*d*) None of these

21. The Scientific Committee on Problems of Environment (SCOPE) established in :
(*a*) 1969 (*b*) 1971
(*c*) 1984 (*d*) 1990

22. SCOPE Committee is established by :
(*a*) IUCN (*b*) ICSU
(*c*) UNEP (*d*) None of these

23. The Water (Prevention and Controls of Pollution) Act, 1974, Amended in the year :
(*a*) 1976 (*b*) 1977
(*c*) 1980 (*d*) 1988

24. In India, the Wildlife Protection Act of 1972 was amended thrice :
(*a*) in 1973, 1984 and 1986
(*b*) in 1975, 1981 and 1990
(*c*) in 1983, 1986 and 1991
(*d*) None of these

25. The objective of the National Forestry Action Programme (NFAP) is to bring :
(*a*) two-third of the area of the country under tree/forest cover and to arrest deforestation
(*b*) one-fourth of the area of the country under tree/forest cover and to arrest deforestation
(*c*) one-third of the area of the country under tree/forest cover and to arrest deforestation
(*d*) None of these

26. If we have problems in Environmental Law, then which disciple solve the problems in Environmental Science?
(*a*) Global environmental problems
(*b*) Medical Science
(*c*) Deforestation
(*d*) Any of the above

27. According to Wildlife Protection Act 1972, the animal article means :
(*a*) object made from any captive animal or wild animals, other than vermin and any part of such animal.
(*b*) the things made of animal products
(*c*) the things made up of body parts of wild animals.
(*d*) all of the above.

28. Stray animals shall not be allowed to move around waste storage facilities or at any other place in city is a provision of :

(*a*) Municipal Corporation Act, 1957
(*b*) Central Government Act, 1984
(*c*) Central Pollution Act, 1994
(*d*) Data insufficient

29. Which of the following Act is the first legislation in Post-independence India which deals with environmental pollution caused by Municipal Solid Wastes?
(*a*) Delhi Municipal Corporation Act, 1957
(*b*) Municipal Solid Wastes Rules, 2000
(*c*) Delhi Government Pollution Act, 1984
(*d*) All of the above

30. The maximum theoretical efficiency of a silicon solar cell can be
(*a*) 45%
(*b*) 30%
(*c*) 12%
(*d*) 50%

ANSWERS

1	2	3	4	5	6	7	8	9	10
(*b*)	(*c*)	(*b*)	(*b*)	(*d*)	(*a*)	(*c*)	(*d*)	(*a*)	(*c*)
11	**12**	**13**	**14**	**15**	**16**	**17**	**18**	**19**	**20**
(*b*)	(*c*)	(*a*)	(*b*)	(*b*)	(*a*)	(*b*)	(*a*)	(*c*)	(*c*)
21	**22**	**23**	**24**	**25**	**26**	**27**	**28**	**29**	**30**
(*a*)	(*b*)	(*d*)	(*c*)	(*c*)	(*a*)	(*c*)	(*a*)	(a)	(*a*)

YOUR SPACE

YOUR SPACE